Mac OS X (Little) Black B
Quick Reference

D1046363

Mac OS X System Requirements

- Apple desktop or laptop that shipped with a G3 or G4 processor (except for first generation PowerBook G3.
- 128MB of RAM (64MB with Classic O.S). Older Macs upgraded with processor cards are not officially supported.
- 1.5GB free disk storage space.

Preparing for Mac OS X

- Check your hard drive with Disk First Aid or a commercial hard drive diagnostic program.
- Back up your files, in case something goes wrong during the installation.
- Double-check compatibility of your Mac peripherals and graphic cards.
- Copy Internet and Network settings.
- Make sure you have an installed copy of Mac OS 9.1 to use Classic compatibility environment. A 9.1 CD is provided with Mac OS X.

Installing Mac OS X

1. Insert the Mac OS X CD into your Mac's drive.
2. Restart your Mac, holding down the Shift key, so that it boots from the CD.
3. Choose the language option, and continue to proceed.
4. Double-check Important Information screen to make sure there are no problems that would prevent a satisfactory installation.
5. Read and OK the Software License Agreement. You must agree for installation to continue.
6. Choose the destination drive. If you want to erase the drive first, choose the Erase Destination And Format As checkbox (this wipes out all of your data). Keep the default file system, Mac OS Extended, if you're also using Mac OS 9.1 on the same drive partition.
7. Choose Easy Install on the next screen for the most efficient installation process.
8. At the completion of the installation process, click the Restart button to move on to the Setup Assistant (it'll automatically restart after 30 seconds otherwise).

Running the Setup Assistant

1. When you see the Welcome screen, choose a keyboard layout from the choices listed, then click the right arrow (labeled Continue) to proceed.

2. Enter your user registration information (which will be sent via the Internet to Apple).
3. To create your main user account, enter the name of the person who will be the administrator for this Mac.
4. Give yourself a nickname; it can contain up to 8 characters.
5. Choose a password of up to 8 characters, consisting of random upper and lower case letters and numbers to make it difficult to guess. If you want, also write a hint, a phrase or word that'll remind you of the password if you forget it.
6. Choose your Internet access option. If you pick Telephone Modem, you'll need to run the Internet Connect application after installation to finish the setup. Otherwise, choose your net access options from the choices shown.
7. Enter your TCP/IP settings information for Internet access via cable modem or DSL or local area network.
8. If you want to set up an iTools account, enter the setup information where requested, then click Continue to send your registration to Apple and move on to the next step of setup process.
9. Enter your email settings, including your email address, and the incoming and outgoing email servers required by your ISP.
10. Select your proper geographic location, so the time display of the menu bar clock is accurate.
11. Review you settings. You can click the back arrow to redo an earlier setting.
12. Once your settings are finished, click the Go Ahead button to restart your Mac under Mac OS X.

How to Make System Settings

Use the System Preferences application, and select a settings panel from the icon list. Some settings may require that the administrator for the Mac login if another user accesses your Mac.

Key System Settings described:

- *Classic Preferences:* The Classic Preferences panel lets you specify the startup volume for the Classic operating system. The Advanced preference panel is used to configure additional options, such as whether or not to rebuild the Mac OS 9.1 system's desktop or restart with extensions off or to bring Extensions Manager up when Classic opens.
- *ColorSync Preferences:* Apple's ColorSync technology is tightly integrated into Mac OS X. You can

use this settings panel to choose a ColorSync profile for input devices, such as a scanner, your Mac's display, output devices (a printer), or a proofing device.

- *Date & Time Preferences:* These settings mirror the ones you've already done in the SetupAssistant. There is, however, a new wrinkle to these settings. At the bottom left of the settings screen, you'll notice a button labeled Click The Lock To Prevent Further Changes. This means you can protect this panel and any other panel with a padlock icon so that only users with administrator's access.

- *Display Preferences:* This settings panel is used to configure the size (resolution) of the images on your Mac's display and the color depth setting. If you wish to change color depth, click on the Colors pop-up menu. Click the Color tab if you want to adjust the color balance or calibration of your display.

- *Dock Preferences:* Apple's famous Mac OS X taskbar can be configured in a several ways to adjust display. The settings include Dock size, magnification and whether the Dock will be hidden unless you move the mouse cursor to the bottom of the screen.

- *Energy Saver Preferences:* These settings perform such functions is putting the system into sleep mode after a preset period of time. There are also separate settings for display and hard drive sleep modes. iBook and PowerBook users get additional power management features to get more battery life.

- *General Preferences:* In part, Aqua equivalent of the Appearance control panel, which lets you choose from Aqua or Graphite color themes and highlight color. You can also select whether to display the name or an icon in the application menu.

- *International Preferences:* Select the preferred keyboard layout from the list, and then choose how date, time, and numbers will appear. The Keyboard Menu feature puts up a menu bar icon to allow for fast keyboard layout switches.

- *Internet Preferences:* Mirrors the Internet Control Panel of earlier Mac OS versions. Set up your iTools user account and then configure your regular email, Web and newsgroup access and the applications you want to use.

- *Keyboard Preferences:* These settings affect your Mac keyboard's Automatic Repeat modes.

- *Login Preferences:* This setting works the same as the Startup Items folder under previous versions of the Mac OS. The programs that appear in this window launch when you log in. Click on the Add button to locate and select startup applications that will open when you boot or login to your

Mac, and click on the Remove button to delete a selected items.

- *Mouse Preferences:* Move the Mouse Speed slider to adjust the tracking speed. The Double-Click Delay setting is used to configure the ideal interval for a double-click to activate a Mac OS function. If you have an iBook or PowerBook there will be a separate Trackpad tab for additional settings.

- *Network Preferences:* This configuration screen is used for setting up Internet access and LAN hookups. Settings include network type, PPoE for DSL hookups, AppleTalk, plus configuring your modem for dial-up access. It combines the functions of Mac OS 9.1's Modem, Remote Access and TCP/IP Control Panels.

- *QuickTime Preferences:* This settings panel is used to set how QuickTime works on your Mac. You can choose connection speed to optimize performance, depending on your Internet connection, and automatically update QuickTime software.

- *Screen Saver:* Apple's built-in screen saver offers cool, liquid images of icons, beaches, the cosmos, forests, and more.

- *Sharing Preferences:* Peer-to-peer file sharing is one of the delights of the Mac OS. Open this panel (and click on the Start button for file sharing and the Start button for Web sharing (which uses the Apache Web Server software to let you host a site). You also have the option to allow remote login (Telnet) or FTP access to your Mac.

NOTE: *File sharing under Mac OS X is done via TCP/IP. If you have an older Mac, running versions of the Mac OS prior to 8.5, the older systems may see the Mac OS X computer, but not the other way around.*

- *Software Update Preferences:* Regular updates will be available to make Mac OS X run better, and to add new features. You can update your software manually, whenever you want or click the Automatically button to have Apple's Web site checked on a Daily, Weekly or Monthly basis for needed updates. The status display will show the last time you attempted the update. Click Update Now whenever you want to recheck for updates.

- *Sound Preferences:* The Sound settings control overall system volume, alert volume and you also have the option to pick from a selection of alert sounds. Some computer speakers or multimedia hardware may place additional settings on this panel.

- *Speech Preferences:* Some Mac programs support Mac OS X's Speech Manager, which allows you to activate Mac functions via spoken commands and have text to be read back to you. In this settings pane, you can decide whether to activate the speech recognition feature. Click On and then click Listening to specify whether you can speak a command with or without a listening key (a keyboard shortcut that precedes the speech command. The Text-to-Speech tab brings up a screen you can choose a voice from the list, then specify the rate at which the voice is played back.

• *Startup Disk Preferences:* This setting lets you switch startup disks, if you have additional volumes with system software on them on your Mac. The change is usually made will be made to switch from Mac OS X back to Mac OS 9.1.

• *User Preferences:* Bring up this screen if you want to change your login password or add additional users to your Mac, to take advantage of its multiple users features. To make the change, click on your user name, then click the Edit User button and enter the new password twice in the appropriate text fields and then the appropriate hint, if you want a reminder. Once you click the OK button, your new password goes into effect. The Cancel button undoes the changes you've made.

Setting Up Printers Under Mac OS X

Use the Print Center application to add and configure the printers connected to your Mac or to your network. When printing, the Print Center application will automatically appear in the Dock, and you can launch it to check the progress of the print queue.

To add a printer:

1. Go to the Utilities folder and locate and double-click on the Print Center application icon to launch it.

2. If you have no printers selected, you'll see a dialog box asking if you wish to add a printer. Click on the Add button. If you already have printers selected, click on the Add Printer button in the Printers window. If your printer uses AppleTalk, make sure the feature is turned on in the Network panel of System Preferences.

3. On the next screen, click on the Connection pop-up menu and select the network or peripheral connection on which you want to check for printers. Depending on the kind of Mac you have, you can choose from AppleTalk, LPR Printers Using IP, or USB. The Directory Services option can locate an enterprise printer located on your network.

NOTE: *Mac OS X ships with a number of standard printer drivers, and some printers will be located and recognized by default. The best way to use a networked laser printer is via the LPR Printers Using IP mode, but you need to retrieve the IP number for your printer to access this mode.*

---

4. If your printer is located in another network zone, click on the second pop-up menu to pick that zone.

5. Continue browsing for printers until they are all displayed.

6. Click on the red button to close the window. At this point, all of your available printers should appear in the main Printer window.

7. To select a default printer, the one normally selected when you wish to print a document, click on the name of the printer to select it, then choose Make Default from the Printers menu (or just press Command+D).

8. If you want to change your printer's custom settings, choose Setup from the Printers menu, and then select your printer's features from the dialog box. Depending on the kind of printer you have, you can configure extra paper trays, different printer resolutions, or perhaps the ability to print on both sides of the paper (also known as duplexing).

9. Once you've completed setting your preferences, click on the close box or choose Quit from the application menu to close the program.

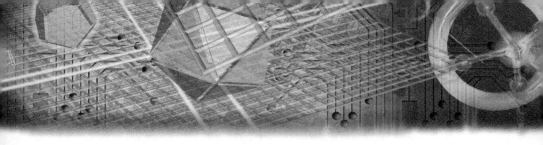

Mac® OS X
Little Black Book

Gene Steinberg

President and CEO
Keith Weiskamp

Publisher
Steve Sayre

Acquisitions Editor
Charlotte Carpentier

Development Editor
Michelle Stroup

Product Marketing Manager
Tracy Rooney

Project Editor
Stephanie Palenque

Technical Reviewer
Pieter Paulson

Production Coordinator
Todd Halvorsen

Cover Designer
April Nielsen

Layout Designer
April Nielsen

Mac OS X Little Black Book

Limits of Liability and Disclaimer of Warranty

The author and publisher of this book have used their best efforts in preparing the book and the programs contained in it. These efforts include the development, research, and testing of the theories and programs to determine their effectiveness. The author and publisher make no warranty of any kind, expressed or implied, with regard to these programs or the documentation contained in this book.

The author and publisher shall not be liable in the event of incidental or consequential damages in connection with, or arising out of, the furnishing, performance, or use of the programs, associated instructions, and/or claims of productivity gains.

Trademarks

Trademarked names appear throughout this book. Rather than list the names and entities that own the trademarks or insert a trademark symbol with each mention of the trademarked name, the publisher states that it is using the names for editorial purposes only and to the benefit of the trademark owner, with no intention of infringing upon that trademark.

The Coriolis Group, LLC
14455 North Hayden Road
Suite 220
Scottsdale, Arizona 85260

(480) 483-0192
FAX (480) 483-0193
www.coriolis.com

Library of Congress Cataloging-in-Publication Data
Steinberg, Gene.
    Mac OS X little black book / by Gene Steinberg.
        p.   cm.
    Includes index.
    ISBN 1-57610-701-9
    1. Mac OS.   2. Macintosh (Computer)   3. Operating systems
(Computers)   I. Title.
QA76.76.063   S73678   2001
005.4'469–dc21   00-069424
                                                                                        CIP

Printed in the United States of America
10 9 8 7 6 5 4 3 2 1

The Coriolis Group, LLC • 14455 North Hayden Road, Suite 220 • Scottsdale, Arizona 85260

Dear Reader:

Coriolis Technology Press was founded to create a very elite group of books: the ones you keep closest to your machine. Sure, everyone would like to have the Library of Congress at arm's reach, but in the real world, you have to choose the books you rely on every day *very* carefully.

To win a place for our books on that coveted shelf beside your computer, we guarantee several important qualities in every book we publish. These qualities are:

- *Technical accuracy*—It's no good if it doesn't work. Every Coriolis Technology Press book is reviewed by technical experts in the topic field, and is sent through several editing and proofreading passes in order to create the piece of work you now hold in your hands.

- *Innovative editorial design*—We've put years of research and refinement into the ways we present information in our books. Our books' editorial approach is uniquely designed to reflect the way people learn new technologies and search for solutions to technology problems.

- *Practical focus*—We put only pertinent information into our books and avoid any fluff. Every fact included between these two covers must serve the mission of the book as a whole.

- *Accessibility*—The information in a book is worthless unless you can find it quickly when you need it. We put a lot of effort into our indexes, and heavily cross-reference our chapters, to make it easy for you to move right to the information you need.

Here at The Coriolis Group we have been publishing and packaging books, technical journals, and training materials since 1989. We're programmers and authors ourselves, and we take an ongoing active role in defining what we publish and how we publish it. We have put a lot of thought into our books; please write to us at **ctp@coriolis.com** and let us know what you think. We hope that you're happy with the book in your hands, and that in the future, when you reach for software development and networking information, you'll turn to one of our books first.

Keith Weiskamp
President and CEO

Jeff Duntemann
VP and Editorial Director

*I wish to pay special thanks to my "muse" (she knows who she is)
for always helping me to find the right things to say
and the means to say it.*

❧

About the Author

Gene Steinberg is a full-time writer, and computer software and systems consultant. He is the author of more than 20 books on computing, the Internet, and telecommunications and he has written articles for such diverse sources as CNET, *MacAddict, MacHome,* and *Macworld.* His weekly column, "Mac Reality Check," is carried by *The Arizona Republic*/azcentral.com and his Mac support site, The Mac Night Owl (**www.macnightowl.com**) is regularly visited by thousands of Mac users each day. In his spare time, Gene and his teenaged son, Grayson, are developing a science fiction adventure series, *Attack of the Rockoids.*

Acknowledgments

Books are never produced in a vacuum, and this work is no exception. During the course of researching and writing this book, I've been pleased to receive the help of a number of folks who have made this daunting task far more pleasant.

First of all, I want to thank the folks at Apple's corporate communications department for letting me see the future of the Mac OS and answering all my questions, whether simple, complex, or just downright silly. I'm particularly grateful to Matt Hutchison (who has since joined the corporate communications department at Sony), and Alicia Awbrey for their able assistance. Apple's Director of OS Technologies, Worldwide Product Marketing, Ken Bereskin, was especially helpful in delineating the key aspects of Mac OS X for both this book and my ongoing online articles on the subject.

This book would not have been possible were it not for my friend, Pieter Paulson, who took on the task as Technical Editor to make sure every single fact in this book was as accurate as possible. In addition, an author cannot work without a publisher and editors, and the terrific folks at The Coriolis Group were especially helpful in putting up with my quirks and demands without protest. I'm particularly thankful to Charlotte Carpentier, acquisitions editor; Stephanie Palenque, project editor; Todd Halvorsen, production coordinator; and April Nielsen, cover and layout designer, for ensuring that the words I wrote were understandable to all of our readers, and for making this book look good.

Finally, I am especially thankful for the help and support from my little family, my beautiful wife, Barbara, and my brilliant son, Grayson, for putting up with the long hours I spent at the keyboard in order to deliver the manuscript for this book on schedule.
—*Gene Steinberg*

Contents at a Glance

Part I   **Mac OS X Arrives**

Chapter 1   Mac OS X: New Features from A to Z   3

Chapter 2   Upgrading to Mac OS X   19

Chapter 3   Mac OS X User Preferences   31

Chapter 4   Introducing the Mac OS X Finder   69

Chapter 5   Mac OS X Desktop Management   89

Chapter 6   Setting Up Mac OS X for Multiple Users   103

Chapter 7   Mac OS X's Search Feature   119

Chapter 8   The Networking Overview   141

Chapter 9   The New AppleScript   165

Chapter 10   Installing Programs Under Mac OS X   177

Part II   **Mac OS X and Hardware**

Chapter 11   Hardware Management   195

Chapter 12   Hooking Up Accessories   209

Chapter 13   Taking Mac OS X on the Road   223

Part III   **The Software Review**

Chapter 14   Mac OS X-Savvy Applications   239

Chapter 15   Using Older Programs with Mac OS X   257

Chapter 16   Mac OS X Font Management   273

Chapter 17   Performing Backups   289

Chapter 18   Computer Viruses and Mac OS X   309

Chapter 19   Troubleshooting Mac OS X   325

Part IV   **Taking Mac OS X Online**

Chapter 20   Surfing the Net   347

Chapter 21   Email Options Explored   367

Chapter 22   Apple's iTools Explored   395

Table of Contents

Introduction xxiii

Part I   Mac OS X Arrives

Chapter 1
Mac OS X: New Features from A to Z 3
In Brief
  Apple Goes Operating System Shopping   4
  A Brief Look at the New Features   5
    Darwin   6
    Quartz   8
    Cocoa   8
    Carbon   9
    Classic   9
    Aqua   10
    The Mac OS X Finder   12
    The Dock   14
    Desktop   15
Immediate Solutions
  Installing Mac OS X   16

Chapter 2
Upgrading to Mac OS X 19
In Brief
  Preparing for Mac OS X   20
    Make Sure You Have Mac OS 9.1 for Classic Applications   20
    Check Your Hard Drive   21
    Back Up Your Data   25
    Mac OS X: Hardware-Related Issues   25

Immediate Solutions
　Preparing for Mac OS X　27
　Installing Mac OS X　28

Chapter 3
Mac OS X User Preferences **31**
　In Brief
　　Control Panel Settings: A Mixture of the Old and New　32
　　Selecting Printers without a Chooser　34
　Immediate Solutions
　　Configuring the SetupAssistant　35
　　Setting System Preferences under Mac OS X　39
　　　Setting Classic Preferences　41
　　　Setting ColorSync Preferences　42
　　　Setting Date & Time Preferences　43
　　　Setting Displays Preferences　44
　　　Setting Dock Preferences　50
　　　Setting Energy Saver Preferences　51
　　　Setting General Preferences　52
　　　Setting International Preferences　53
　　　Setting Internet Preferences　54
　　　Setting Keyboard Preferences　55
　　　Setting Login Preferences　56
　　　Setting Mouse Preferences　56
　　　Setting Network Preferences　57
　　　Setting QuickTime Preferences　59
　　　Setting Screen Saver Preferences　60
　　　Setting Sharing Preferences　61
　　　Setting Software Update Preferences　61
　　　Setting Sound Preferences　62
　　　Setting Speech Preferences　63
　　　Setting Startup Disk Preferences　64
　　　Setting Users Preferences　65
　　Configuring a Printer　65

Chapter 4
Introducing the Mac OS X Finder **69**
　In Brief
　　More Finder Navigation Features　73
　　Visiting the Finder's Toolbar　73
　　The New Finder Menus　75

Immediate Solutions
Setting Finder Preferences   81
  Keeping Folder Views Consistent   81
  Setting Viewing Preferences   82
  Changing Finder List View Columns   84
  Customizing the Finder's Toolbar   85
Using the New Finder on a Day-to-Day Basis   86
  Moving a File   86
  Copying a File   86
  Making an Alias   87
  Creating Favorites   87
  Accessing Contextual Menus   87
  Ejecting a Disk   87
  Using the Show Info Window   88

Chapter 5
Mac OS X Desktop Management **89**
In Brief
The Dock Dissected   90
Immediate Solutions
Setting Dock & Desktop Preferences   96
Using the Dock   100
  Dock Scripts   101
  Making Your Mac OS X Desktop as Cluttered as Ever   101

Chapter 6
Setting Up Mac OS X for Multiple Users **103**
In Brief
Mac OS X Multiple Users Features   104
Using Strong Passwords   107
Immediate Solutions
Setting Up Multiple-User Access   108
Editing a User Account   110
Setting Up Keychain Access   111
Checking and Using Your Keychain   113
Changing Keychain Settings   113
Running a Keychain on Another Mac   114
Coping with Problems Involving Keychains and Multiple Users   115
Suggestions for Setting up Multiple Users for Use with Children   116

Chapter 7
Mac OS X's Search Feature **119**
  In Brief
    Sherlock Searches Locally and Internationally   121
  Immediate Solutions
    Searching for Files   124
    Searching Files for Content   125
      Indexing a Drive   126
      Setting Sherlock Preferences   127
    Searching the Internet   128
    Finding People on the Internet   131
      Customizing Your Information Request   132
    Saving Your Custom Searches   135
    Searching for Files in a Single Folder   136
    Making Your Own Sherlock Channel   137
    Installing Additional Search Modules   138

Chapter 8
The Networking Overview **141**
  In Brief
    Accessing Networked Macs from Mac OS X   143
      A Different Way to Share Files   144
      A Look at Mac OS X's Networking Components   145
  Immediate Solutions
    Sharing Files with Mac OS X   147
    Connecting to Shared Macs Under Mac OS X   152
    Using Internet Connect for Dial-Up Networking   155
    Verifying Connectivity   159
    Using Apple's Location Manager to Create Custom Setups   160
    Accessing a Drop Box   161
    Correcting Network Access Problems   162
    Protecting Your Network from the Internet   163

Chapter 9
The New AppleScript **165**
  In Brief
    What AppleScript Can Do   167
    What Doesn't Work in Mac OS X   168
    Mac OS X Script Features   169
    The Tools for Using Scripts in Mac OS X   169
    AppleScript: The Future   170

Immediate Solutions
Locating Mac OS X's AppleScript Collection   171
Choosing Mac OS X's Sample Scripts   171
Using Script Runner   173
Making or Editing Your First AppleScript   173
Running a Script from the Unix Command Line   176

Chapter 10
Installing Programs Under Mac OS X **177**
In Brief
Introducing the Package   178
The Microsoft Way   179
Exploring New Application Features   179
Immediate Solutions
Handling Complex Application Installations   182
   Using an Installer   182
   Using a Disk Image   182
   Making a Startup Application   184
Using the New Open Dialog Box   185
Using the New Save Dialog Box   187
Using the Services Menu   189
Troubleshooting Software Installation Problems   191

Part II   Mac OS X and Hardware

Chapter 11
Hardware Management **195**
In Brief
A Look at Two of Mac OS X's Special Hardware Features   196
Immediate Solutions
Installing New Hardware   199
Maintaining Your Mac on a Daily Basis   200
Buying a New Mac   202
Looking at Extended Warranties   204
Solving Hardware and Software Problems   205

Chapter 12

Hooking Up Accessories **209**

In Brief

A Review of Mac Peripheral Ports   210

Adding a Missing Port   212

Peripherals Available for Macs   214

Immediate Solutions

Installing a New Scanner   218

Installing New Storage Devices   219

Installing Digital Cameras, eBook Readers, Palm OS Handhelds, and Other Products   220

Determining What to Do If It Doesn't Work   221

Chapter 13

Taking Mac OS X on the Road **223**

In Brief

Exploring Mac OS X Tools for Laptops   224

Superior Power Management   224

Integrated Mouse Control Panel   224

Superfast Sleep and Awake Features   225

Editing Vacation Videos on the Road   225

Immediate Solutions

Computing on the Road   227

Using the Battery Monitor   227

Getting the Maximum Amount of Battery Life   228

Using an Apple Laptop Travel Kit   230

Getting the Most Efficient Online Performance   234

Missing Laptop Features from Mac OS X   235

Part III   The Software Review

Chapter 14

Mac OS X-Savvy Applications **239**

In Brief

The Two Forms of Mac OS X Applications   240

Key Mac OS X Software Profiled and Previewed   241

Microsoft   241

Apple Computer   242

FileMaker   247

Adobe Systems   247

Alias|Wavefront   248

Macromedia   249
Quark, Inc.   249
Stone Design   249
AOL   249
Immediate Solutions
Introducing AppleWorks for Mac OS X   251
Using AppleWorks Starting Points   251
Using Tables in AppleWorks   252
Introducing Create for Mac OS X   254
Using the Inspector   254
Starting a Web Page in Create   255

Chapter 15
Using Older Programs with Mac OS X 257
In Brief
Introducing the Classic Environment   258
Classic Environment Limitations   259
Immediate Solutions
Launching Older Mac Programs   263
Running Classic as a Startup Application   264
Getting Reliable Performance from Classic Applications   266
Keeping Your Mac OS 9.1 System Folder Safe and Sound   269
Solving Classic Environment Problems   270
Returning to Mac OS 9.1   271

Chapter 16
Mac OS X Font Management 273
In Brief
There Are Fonts and There Are Fonts   274
Font Formats Defined   274
Font Organization under the Mac OS   275
Mac OS X's New Font-Handling Scheme   277
Introducing the Font Panel   278
Special Font Features of Mac OS X   279
Immediate Solutions
Installing Fonts under Mac OS X   281
Using the Font Panel   281
Adding Font Favorites   283
Using Favorites   283
Creating a Font Collection   284
Choosing Custom Font Sizes   285

Checking the Characters in a Font 286
Avoiding Too-Small Fonts in TextEdit 287
Handling Mac OS X Font Problems 288

Chapter 17
Performing Backups 289
In Brief
A Survey of Backup Software 290
An Overview of Retrospect 291
An Overview of ASD Personal Backup 293
Other Backup Programs 295
An Overview of Internet Backups 296
An Overview of Backup Media 298
Immediate Solutions
The No-Frills Daily Backup Plan 302
What You Need 302
Performing No-Frills Backups 303
The Special Software Backup Plan 303
What You Need 304
Performing Your Regular Backup Routine 304
Tips and Tricks for Robust Backups 305

Chapter 18
Computer Viruses and Mac OS X 309
In Brief
An Overview of Mac Viruses 311
Types of Computer Viruses 311
Viruses and Mac OS X 311
Broadband Internet and Invaders from the Outside 312
Immediate Solutions
Choosing a Mac Virus Program 314
Micromat's TechTool Pro 314
Intego's VirusBarrier 315
Network Associates' Virex 317
Symantec's Norton AntiVirus 318
Choosing Personal Firewall Software 320
Open Door Networks' DoorStop Personal Firewall 321
Intego's NetBarrier 321
Intego's ContentBarrier 322
Hardware Firewalls 322

Chapter 19
Troubleshooting Mac OS X **325**

In Brief

Mac OS X's Crash-Resistant Features   326

The Software Update Application   328

Immediate Solutions

Solving Installation Failures   329

Solving System Crashes and Freezes   331

The Application Won't Quit   331

Applications Refuse to Launch   332

The Classic Environment Fails to Run   333

Solving Network Access Failure   333

Solving Shaking of Login Window   334

Desktop Folder Contents Not Visible under Mac OS 9   335

Mac OS X Can't Boot after You Deleted a File by Mistake   335

Performing a Clean Installation of Mac OS X without Reformatting   336

Solving Other Common Mac OS X Problems   338

Performing System-Level Disk Diagnostics   340

Setting Root Access   342

Monitoring System Use to Check for Conflicts   343

Part IV   Taking Mac OS X Online

Chapter 20
Surfing the Net **347**

In Brief

The Coming of Broadband Access   348

Mac OS X Web Browsers Profiled   350

Microsoft Internet Explorer   351

iCab   353

OmniWeb   354

Immediate Solutions

Deleting Browser Caches   358

Killing the Cache in Internet Explorer   358

Killing the Cache in iCab   359

Configuring the Cache in OmniWeb   360

Determining Whether a Larger Cache Is Necessary   361

Using Bookmarks to Get There Faster   362

Solving Internet Connection Problems   362

Chapter 21
Email Options Explored **367**

In Brief

Introducing Mail   369

How Does Mail Rate?   370

Immediate Solutions

Setting Up Your User Account   373

Importing Your Email Messages   376

Customizing Mail's Toolbar   378

Composing a New Message   379

Responding to a Message   380

Quoting Messages   381

Spellchecking Your Messages   382

Sending Email Attachments   383

Forwarding Email   385

Adding Email Signatures   385

Formatting Email   386

Setting Mail Rules   386

Getting Your Email Automatically   388

Using the Address Book   389

Importing an Address Book   391

Finding a Message   392

Why Can't I Send My Email?   393

Why Are Messages Scrambled?   394

Why Doesn't Mail Check All My Accounts?   394

Chapter 22
Apple's iTools Explored **395**

In Brief

Reviewing iTools Features   396

Immediate Solutions

Installing iTools   402

Configuring Email Software to Access Your Mac.com
Email Address   404

Forwarding Mac.com Email   406

Telling Your Friends about Your New Address   408

Sending Vacation Notices   409

Configuring KidSafe   410

Using the iDisk Feature   411

Creating a Web Site with HomePage   413
   Editing or Updating Your Web Page   416
   Removing a Web Page   416
Solving HomePage Problems   417

Glossary **419**
Index **443**

Introduction

If someone told you for nearly a decade that they were going to do something in the very near future, and it never seemed to happen, would you believe them the next time they delivered the promise? This is the dilemma Apple faced when they first announced plans for Mac OS X.

Apple's road for producing a modern operating system to replace the Mac OS has been littered with failed projects, wrong turns, and missed deadlines. So it almost came as a relief when I attended a press briefing on Mac OS X Public Beta at the San Francisco headquarters of CNET, the online and broadcast technology news service, in September of 2000.

Within a few hours I was back at my home office, installing the future of the Mac OS on my computer. I examined the documentation, and checked my notes as the installation proceeded. Within less than fifteen minutes, my Mac restarted. A short trip to the Setup Assistant, and a second restart, and I was a believer!

Mac OS X was at last a reality, not vaporware to be touted strictly for public demonstrations.

However, that was only the beginning. By January, 2001, Apple had poured through tens of thousands of feedback messages from devoted Mac users. In the Macworld Expo keynote, CEO Steve Jobs announced some important changes to the user interface to satisfy the clamoring of thousands to restore the Apple menu, restore disk icons to the desktop, bring back the menu bar clock and, if need be, allow the Finder to work just as the old "Classic" version did.

The Bill of Fare

Since this book is part of The Coriolis Group's Little Black Book series, it covers the essential information you need to install, configure and use Mac OS X. There are no frills and no fluff. Useless tips and tricks that will satisfy one's intellectual curiosity or perhaps trigger a chuckle, but not enhance your productivity, aren't included.

The 22 chapters here are divided into four parts, each covering a particular area of your Mac user experience.

In "Part I: Mac OS X Arrives," I run through the important new features, and then help you plot installation strategies. You are then taken step-by-step through the actual installation and configuration. From here you'll be introduced to the new Mac OS X Finder, the Dock, multiple user features, search features, plus the big changes in the networking architecture. This part closes with information about AppleScript and how to install and use your programs. There's even a section covering the new Open and Save dialog boxes, which are sure to simplify file management.

Next there's "Part II: Mac OS X and Hardware." Are you planning to install Mac OS X on a new Mac, or just one you've upgraded with extra memory, drive space and other additions? These critical subjects are dealt with here. You'll also learn how to add peripherals, such as printers, scanners and removable drives, on your Mac. Finally, there's a section on using Mac OS X with one of Apple's iBooks or PowerBooks.

Moving on to "Part III: The Software Review," you'll discover some of the new Mac OS X applications, how to run older "Classic" software on your Mac and how to handle fonts, perform backups, and check for computer viruses. Finally, there's a comprehensive section on troubleshooting, that includes a visit to the Unix command line of the new operating system to perform a hard drive diagnostic if all else fails.

The last part of this book, "Part IV: Taking Mac OS X Online," covers Internet access from stem to stern. You'll have a birds-eye view of the newest Web browsers, Apple's Mail application and their iTools feature.

How to Use This Book

The *Mac OS X Little Black Book* isn't designed to be read from cover to cover as you might read a novel, though I don't particularly mind it if you do it all in a single sitting. You'll probably just want to read the chapters that answer your questions about the new Mac OS.

As part of the Little Black Book series, each chapter is divided into two sections. The first, *In Brief*, gives you the basics and theories about the subject. The second, *Immediate Solutions*, offers step-by-step instructions on how to accomplish tasks, along with guides on what to do if something goes wrong.

Although the Mac OS X user interface is ultra simple and smooth, it's a highly complex operating system, one that will be updated regularly as time goes by. A book of this sort is also a developing process, and future editions will reflect those changes, plus what I've learned as I continue to use Mac OS X.

I also welcome your comments, questions, and suggestions for future editions. If you have a problem with the new operating system, or discover something totally unique and utterly cool, let me know. You can either email The Coriolis Group directly at **ctp@coriolis.com** or email me directly at the address below. Erratas, updates, and more are available at **www.coriolis.com**.

Gene Steinberg
Scottsdale, AZ
Email: **gene@macnightowl.com**
www.macnightowl.com

Part I

Mac OS X Arrives

Chapter 1

Mac OS X:
New Features from A to Z

If you need an immediate solution to:	*See page:*
Installing Mac OS X	16

In Brief

There's little doubt that a major upgrade to the aging Mac operating system is one of the momentous developments in the personal computing industry. For years, Apple has tried and failed to provide a completely stable, robust operating system of a sort that would appeal to both newcomers and power users alike.

Apple's previous efforts have been doomed to failure. In the most notable (and perhaps notorious) example, Apple spent tens of millions of dollars, thousands and thousands of man (and woman) hours, and several frustrating years developing an operating system, code-named Copland, which was designed to offer all the industrial-strength features needed to bring the Macintosh user experience into the twenty-first century. The project, though laudable in its intentions, fell apart when serious problems were encountered in such areas as offering backward-compatibility with older Mac software.

Eventually, the original expected shipping name for Copland, Mac OS 8, was used for a modest system upgrade that offered interface improvements but none of the under-the-hood features expected of a modern operating system. The upgrade and subsequent system versions used some of the appearance features left over from Copland, but with only minor improvements in overall system reliability.

Apple Goes Operating System Shopping

When its own in-house talent was unable to finish the job, Apple went operating system shopping in 1996. According to published reports at the time, Apple flirted with acquiring a fledgling operating system, called BeOS, from a company run by a former Apple executive, Jean-Louis Gassée. The BeOS was briefly offered in a series of twin-processor computers, but the company soon abandoned the hardware and concentrated on the software.

Although the BeOS still works on the older PowerPC Macs, Apple would not deliver support for the G3 or G4 CPUs, and thus the company went to the Intel world in search of more enthusiastic support. However, the BeOS may gain its greatest market penetration with dedicated Internet or multimedia appliances.

Apple finally took what has become the action that saved its neck. It agreed to spend some $400 million to acquire NeXT Inc., which had been established by Apple cofounder Steve Jobs after he was ousted from the company he helped create back in 1985, nine years after he and Steve Wozniak founded the company. The company's product, NeXTSTEP, is a Unix-based operating system that provides the basic underpinnings and technology Apple needed to develop its next-generation Mac OS. As soon as the former NeXT folks were onboard, Apple went ahead to develop a new operating system that would, in effect, merge NeXTSTEP with the Mac OS, bearing the code name Rhapsody. In short order, Steve Jobs was back at the helm of Apple, where he diced and sliced and brought the company into sharp focus with a new line of striking consumer-oriented products.

Although Rhapsody's focus, direction, and release dates changed, the first realization of the technology was delivered with the arrival of Mac OS X Server in 1999. It was a mixture of the old and the new, combining a large portion of NeXT Inc. core technology with elements of the traditional Mac user interface.

Once the server version was released, it was time to focus on a consumer version. The end result, the subject of this book, is Mac OS X.

A Brief Look at the New Features

The striking new look of the Mac OS X interface, called Aqua, is just a small part of the changes wrought by the new Mac operating system. Under the surface, there are a tremendous number of changes designed to provide improved support and make the Mac run more reliably than ever. Before we look at the new, however, it is fitting to examine where we've come from. For example, when the Macintosh first shipped in 1984, its graphical interface was unique (see Figure 1.1). Instead of typing commands to make your computer perform a given function, you used a pointing device—a mouse—and you clicked on icons and command menus representing common functions, such as files, folders, and disks.

Over the years, a number of changes have been made to the Mac. However, even the user interface of Mac OS 9, the last "classic" or traditional Mac operating system version, bears a striking resemblance to the original, despite its more colorful, more delicately constructed desktop and icons (see Figure 1.2).

Now that you've seen a before and after look at the evolution of the Mac OS, the following sections detail what Mac OS X brings to the table.

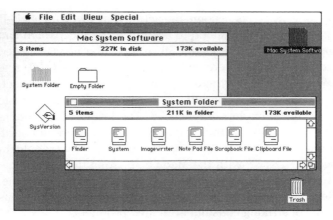

Figure 1.1   This is the Macintosh desktop that was introduced with
the very first models.

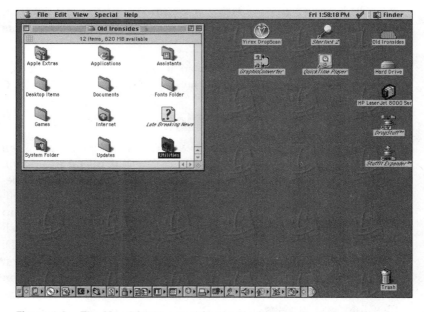

Figure 1.2   The Mac OS has grown in complexity and size, yet retains many
of the core visual elements of previous versions.

Darwin

The open source core of Mac OS X is based on a Unix microkernel,
consisting of the Mach 3 microkernel and FreeBSD 3.2. The Apache
Web server, which powers a majority of Web sites, has been tamed and
forms the basis of the new operating system's file sharing capabilities.

NOTE: *Apple's open source project, called Darwin, allows the core components of the operating system to be made available, free, to software developers, with Apple retaining full rights to the code. These developers can test and debug the software, then make available bug fixes and enhancements to the entire developer community. For more information about this feature, feel free to visit Apple's Darwin Web site,* ***www.apple.com/darwin***.

Although its Unix underpinnings are well hidden beneath Aqua's striking user interface, they are not invisible. Power users can easily pour beneath the surface, bypassing the graphical user interface, and run regular Unix-based applications under Mac OS X. Apple has even provided a Terminal application in the Utilities folder, so power users can visit the command line and access the core Unix functions.

In addition, the new Mac operating system offers the very same industrial-strength features that are the hallmark of Unix. These include the following:

- *Protected memory*—Each program you run resides in its own address space, walled off from other programs. If a single program crashes, that application is shut down, along with the memory address space it occupies. You can continue to run your Mac without the need to restart. This will help to sharply reduce the Mac OS's tendency to crash at the least sign of a software conflict.

- *Preemptive multitasking*—Apple's previous multitasking method was cooperative, meaning that each application would, in effect, have to share CPU time with other programs. This meant that if you were working in a program, such as typing in a word processing document, background tasks, such as printing or downloading a file, could come almost to a screeching halt, particularly if a program hogs processor time unnecessarily. With Mac OS X, the operating system serves as the traffic cop, performing the task management. This allows programs to run more efficiently, and with fewer slowdowns when multiple processes are running.

- *Advanced virtual memory*—With previous versions of the Mac operating system, virtual memory meant slower performance, poor performance with multimedia programs, stuttering sounds, and other shortcomings. Under Mac OS X, virtual memory management is dynamic. Programs are automatically given the amount of memory they require, whether available via RAM or virtual memory disk swapping. Performance is optimized, so you get the maximum-possible performance from your programs.

NOTE: Virtual memory in Mac OS X is super-efficient, but it can't do miracles. There is no substitute for having sufficient RAM to run your high-energy programs, such as Adobe Photoshop or Apple's Final Cut Pro, to get the best possible performance. But you will no longer have to visit the Get Info window to keep changing a program's memory allocation to meet your needs.

Quartz

In previous versions of the Mac OS, Apple used an imaging model called QuickDraw to generate pixels on your display. For Mac OS X, Apple has given up this technology, moving instead to Adobe's Portable Document Format (PDF). As you probably know, most electronic documents are available in PDF trim, which retains the exact formatting, fonts, pictures, and colors of the original.

There is full system-wide support for the major font formats—PostScript, TrueType, and the new OpenType format. That means that Adobe Type Manager (ATM) is no longer needed to render fonts crisply on the screen, although font management is not quite as extensive as the Deluxe version of ATM.

The Quartz 2D graphics system is extremely powerful, with speedy rendering of images and anti-aliasing, providing sharp screen display. You'll see some of this elegance in the illustrations provided in this book, but you have to see the real thing to get the flavor of the effects of this unique technology.

There's also system-level support for PDF, which makes it easy for Mac software developers to provide built-in support to save documents in this format. In addition to PDF, Apple includes support for ColorSync to ease color management from input to display to output; the industry-standard OpenGL, which provides superlative performance for many 3D games; and Apple's famous QuickTime, used worldwide for generating multimedia content.

Cocoa

One of the technologies inherited from NeXTSTEP, which forms the basis for a large part of Mac OS X's capabilities, is Cocoa. This is the new name for an advanced object-oriented programming environment that's supposed to allow programmers to develop new applications much more quickly than with other programming tools. In one spectacular example, Stone Software's integrated illustration program, Create, which features drawing, HTML, and page layout capabilities, is largely the work of one programmer. With traditional programming tools, a large, highly skilled team would be required to perform the same work.

NOTE: *If there's a downside to all this flexibility, it's that programs created in this fashion cannot run on older Macs. However, that situation may be of less significance as more and more Macs are shipped or upgraded to Mac OS X in the years ahead.*

Carbon

Once referred to by Apple CEO Steve Jobs as the "basis for all life forms," Carbon is, in fact, a new set of application programming interfaces. These interfaces are designed to offer software publishers a relatively easy upgrade path to deliver Mac OS X-savvy applications. At this writing, over 200 Mac developers, including such heavyweights as Adobe, Macromedia, Microsoft, and Quark, have committed themselves to providing Carbon updates to their programs. In fact, to emphasize its commitment, Microsoft included a beta copy of the Carbon version of its Internet Explorer Web browser with the Public Beta release of Mac OS X. As this book went to press, Microsoft was hard at work porting the newly released Office 2001 for the Macintosh to Mac OS X.

NOTE: *Even though Carbon greatly simplifies conversion of software to Mac OS X, it's not a cakewalk. Office 2001, for example, consists of millions of lines of computer code. Microsoft has the largest Mac programming team outside of Apple Computer, and yet they didn't expect to complete their work until the fall of 2001.*

The main advantage of an application that is "Carbonized" is that it supports the major features of Mac OS X, such as preemptive multitasking, protected memory, and advanced virtual memory, plus the eye-catching Aqua interface. In addition, when Apple's CarbonLib extension (which first appeared as part of Mac OS 9) is installed, the very same program can run on older Mac operating system versions, though, of course, without the advanced features of Mac OS X.

Classic

Although a reasonably useful number of Mac OS X-savvy programs are shipping with the release of the new operating system, there will still be thousands of older programs you will want to use. Fortunately, that's possible by virtue of the Classic feature.

Classic is, in effect, Mac OS 9.1 running as a separate application under Mac OS X. You can think of it as being somewhat similar to running Connectix Virtual PC or FWB's SoftWindows to emulate the Windows environment on a Mac. But it goes further than that. Apple's Classic feature runs transparently under Mac OS X. The feature lets you run most of your older applications with good performance and a high level of compatibility, but without taking advantage of the Aqua user interface or the robust underpinnings of the new operating system. This is designed to ease the transition to the new Mac computing paradigm.

NOTE: *The Classic environment is not a panacea. Some cherished system extensions, particularly those that modify Finder functions and hardware drivers for such peripherals as ink jets, scanners, and CD writers, won't run. You'll need to get Mac OS X-compatible drivers for all these products.*

Aqua

The Macintosh user interface is reborn with Aqua (see Figure 1.3). Although at first glance, Aqua clearly comes across as eye candy, a software interface that is consistent with the striking industrial designs for Apple's latest computers, there is much more involved here.

Aqua's translucent, shimmering, ocean-blue-inspired look is designed to address many of the usability problems with older graphical user interfaces (both Mac- and Windows-based). It is designed to be relatively easy to master by novice computer users, who amount to a

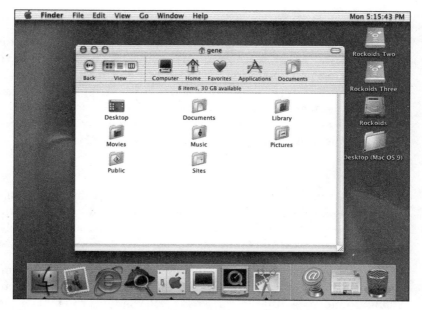

Figure 1.3   After you boot a Mac with OS X installed, you will witness a brand-new, eye-catching user interface.

large percentage of purchasers of Apple's consumer-level products: the iBook and the iMac. But it's also intended to provide the power that will appeal to the sophisticated computer professional.

NOTE: *Apple is also offering a slightly more subdued graphite version of its user interface as an appearance option, paying attention to professional users who might consider Aqua just a bit too imposing for an office environment. You'll learn more about setting this option in Chapter 3.*

From large, photo-quality icons to translucent menus, drop shadows, and realtime object dragging (without a performance penalty), Aqua is designed to provide Mac users new and old with a convenient, easy-to-manage user experience. The standard single-window mode, for example, which automatically hides all windows but the active one, helps reduce the clutter and confusion of previous operating system versions. However, the new Mac OS X Finder has many options for adjustment, so you can easily configure it to spawn additional Finder windows when you open a folder, just like the Classic Mac OS.

NOTE: *In prior versions of the Mac operating system, when you moved an object about the screen, you'd see its outline or bounding box rather than the object's contents. With Mac OS X, the power of the Quartz graphic layer allows you to see the actual object while it's moved. Although some third-party programs, such as Power Windows (a shareware utility), allow you to do this under prior Mac operating system versions, it requires a powerful Mac to avoid a serious performance penalty.*

One common interface problem addressed with the new operating system is the Save dialog box. Even experienced Mac users have, at times, had trouble navigating through complex folder hierarchies. Under Mac OS X, however, when you're ready to save an open document for the first time, the Save As dialog box opens as a sheet of paper right below the title bar of the document in question (see Figure 1.4). Unlike the present Mac operating system, you aren't prevented from doing something else while the dialog box is open. You can simply

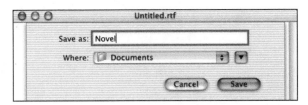

Figure 1.4   The new translucent Save As dialog box stays hooked to the document window you're going to save.

switch to another document window, and the Save As dialog box remains anchored to the document you want to save. Then, you just return to it when you're ready to save it.

The Mac OS X Finder

The core of the Mac user experience is the Finder, an application that runs full-time on a Mac, providing the desktop appearance as well as file and disk management chores. For Mac OS X, the venerable Finder has undergone a complete redesign (see Figure 1.5), ending up as a composite of technologies from the original Finder and from the NeXTSTEP file viewer. The combination is designed to make it possible to access your applications, files, and disks easily, without having to dig deep into numerous nested folders and numerous scattered icons and directory windows.

At the top of the Mac OS X Finder are large, clearly labeled toolbar buttons that take you directly to the most frequently accessed areas on your Mac. The Computer button, for example, displays your mounted disks, those available for file access, and network connections. The Home button takes you to your main Users directory or folder, regardless of whether it's on your Mac's hard drive or on a local or Internet-based network. There are also standard buttons for your favorites (files, folders, disks, and sites) and documents. However, that is just the beginning. The toolbar can be customized with a

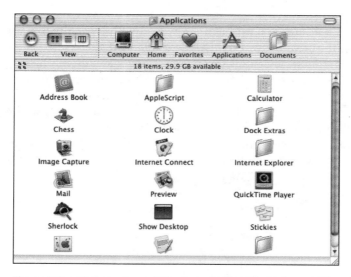

Figure 1.5   The new face of the famous Mac Finder has striking differences, yet retains some familiar elements.

Figure 1.6 There is a wide range of possibilities inherent in the new Finder toolbar setup window.

variety of icons (see Figure 1.6), which can, additionally, be sized to your taste. You can even hide the toolbar altogether and have the Finder behave very much like the old Mac OS, despite the daringly different look.

TIP: *Combining local, network, and Internet access in a single interface is part of Apple's Internet integration efforts. These also include the iTools feature at Apple's Web site, which provides a set of Web-based enhancements that only work with Macs fitted with Mac OS 9 and Mac OS X. I cover the subject in more detail in Chapter 22.*

The Finder offers not only new, more colorful variations of the list and icon views that exist on the original Finder, it also offers a new column view that makes locating deeply nested items easier (see Figure 1.7). It's all accomplished with a single click on a folder or disk, which quickly displays the contents in the window at the right. Reminiscent of Greg's Browser, a popular Mac shareware program, this file viewing feature allows you to easily access anything from a file to a networked drive with equal ease.

Figure 1.7   The Finder's column view option speeds navigation through even complex file directories.

The Dock

The Apple menu was once the principal repository on the Mac for your frequently accessed files, folders, and disks. Apple's Control Strip was a floating palette of control panels and other programs, offering one-click access. The latter is history, replaced by the Dock (see Figure 1.8). This new feature puts a set of colorful, almost cartoonish icons at the bottom of your Mac's display, containing files, folders, disks, programs—whatever you choose to store there. The icons are designed to easily reflect the contents. For example, a picture file contains a preview of the image, so you can recognize it immediately. If you prefer to view titles, you'll be pleased to see the title of an item displayed as soon as the mouse passes over it.

To access an item on the Dock, just click once on it, and it will open in a new window. When you minimize a window, in a flashy motion that looks like a sheet of paper being folded, it transfers to the Dock (in a sense, the end result is similar to the way a minimized window is moved to the Microsoft Windows taskbar). The motion is sometimes known as the "Genie Effect." With the standard single-window mode,

Figure 1.8   The Dock automatically resizes to accommodate additional items.

you'll find that your previous open window is closed and moved to the Dock. You can also use the Mac's drag-and-drop feature to add items to the Dock.

Even the venerable Mac trashcan is now part of the Dock, though it performs precisely the same functions as in previous Mac operating system versions.

Desktop

The famous Apple desktop isn't left untouched by Mac OS X either. Although on the surface it looks very different (again, see Figure 1.3), looks can be deceiving. The versions of Aqua that were first displayed showed a clear desktop, without even a disk icon to clutter the landscape. Apple answered the call of devoted Mac users and has restored much of the desktop behavior of previous versions of the Mac OS.

Immediate Solutions

Installing Mac OS X

If you're ready to take the plunge into a whole new world of ultrareliable and speedy Macintosh computing, you should make sure that your Mac is ready for the upgrade.

Here are some points to consider when moving to Mac OS X:

- *System requirements*—Mac OS X will work on almost any Apple Macintosh computer that shipped with a PowerPC G3 or G4 CPU. This includes even the original Bondi Blue iMac. There is, however, one important exception—the first generation PowerBook G3, which was built on the original PowerBook 3400 chassis. In addition, Apple specifies a minimum of 128MB of RAM. If you don't plan on using Classic programs, you'll probably get away with 64MB of RAM, but it's highly unlikely you'll be able to avoid using such software, because it will take a while for most of the major programs to show up in Mac OS X trim. You'll also want to allow 1.5GB of disk storage space for the installation. Apple includes Mac OS 9.1 in the package, so you won't have to buy a separate copy to use Classic.

TIP: If you have a very large hard drive, you might want to consider making a separate partition for Mac OS X but keep your older Mac OS version on the first partition. That way, if you run into a compatibility issue, you can restart with the older OS and continue to be productive until the conflicts are resolved.

- *Peripheral compatibility*—If your Mac has a non-Apple expansion card of any sort, such as a graphic card, SCSI accelerator card, or video capture card, contact the manufacturer about driver software that might be required for full compatibility with Mac OS X. Although the Classic feature lets you run older Mac software, it doesn't provide the deep-level support you need for unsupported hardware.

- *Software compatibility*—Most older programs ought to run fine in the Classic mode under Mac OS X. You should contact the publishers directly, however, to be sure that the programs will run without a hitch. System extensions, for example, are not part of the Mac OS X architecture but might, within limits, work under

Classic. However, programs that directly access the hardware, such as a CD writing program or hard disk formatter, will need an update to work properly—more than likely a Carbon version that's tuned to recognize Apple's updated hardware driver model.

• *Printer and serial devices*—Regular PostScript laser printers should work reasonably well under Mac OS X. Other printers, especially ink jets, will need driver updates to function with the new OS. However, Mac OS X printer drivers from such major companies as Canon, Epson, HP, and Lexmark are expected to be available with the final release; a small number of these printer drivers are included as part of the easy install. As far as other peripherals are concerned, in each case, you'll need to check with the manufacturer about compatibility. Apple Computer has provided tools to help developers make its products Mac OS X-aware, but how quickly this is done depends on each particular company, its priorities, and the amount of work required.

WARNING! *Apple Computer doesn't officially support Macs or Mac OS clones upgraded from older PowerPC CPUs to G3s or G4s. If you decide to take the risk anyway and attempt to install Mac OS X on one of these unsupported models, you cannot depend on Apple for support. Be prepared to have a full backup of your data, in case you run into a disk-related problem or want to return to your previous Mac OS version. Some of the companies who make G3 and G4 upgrades were promising to deliver Mac OS X support, but it won't come with Apple's blessings, and you will have to depend on those companies to provide help if something goes wrong with the use of the products.*

Chapter 2

Upgrading to Mac OS X

If you need an immediate solution to:	See page:
Preparing for Mac OS X	27
Installing Mac OS X	28

In Brief

Are you ready to install your new operating system? Mac OS X is a huge leap over previous versions of the Mac OS. As explained in Chapter 1, there is really no comparison under the hood. Many of the familiar elements aren't there anymore. If anything, the new operating system, because it is Unix-based, has more in common with high-end workstations that are used to power Web and network servers around the world.

Despite the complexity of the software under the hood, Apple has gone the extra mile to simplify installation. However, don't be lulled into a sense of complacency by the ease of the process. A lot of complicated things are happening very, very fast to install the new operating system as quickly as possible without undue delay. During that time, literally thousands of new files will be copied to your Macintosh. It's not something to take lightly, and you should take a few precautions to make the process as seamless as possible.

Preparing for Mac OS X

Before you attempt to install Mac OS X, you should make sure that your Mac has been prepared for the installation. First, you should review Chapter 1 to see if your Mac can run the new operating system. Take the warnings about attempting an installation on unsupported hardware very seriously. Although it's possible some Mac peripheral manufacturers will devise a way around this, you should be guided by their recommendations and cautions.

Don't say I didn't warn you.

In the following pages, I cover the basics of getting ready for the installation. Once you're prepared, proceed to the "Immediate Solutions" section for step-by-step instructions of the entire installation process and what you should expect along the way.

Make Sure You Have Mac OS 9.1 for Classic Applications

Because the vast majority of Mac OS programs you'll be running are of the older "Classic" variety, you'll need an installed copy of Mac OS 9 on your Mac. Fortunately, Apple included the Mac OS 9.1 installation CD as part of the Mac OS X package. Feel confident that you can install it if necessary to use your older applications. You can place Mac OS 9.1 on the same disk volume as Mac OS X. If you choose to install it on a separate partition, make sure it's the first partition.

NOTE: *Mac OS X requires 9.1 (or later) for the Classic environment, so you need to install that operating system if you have an older one on your Mac now. While the Pubic Beta did work with earlier Mac OS 9 releases, that changed with the final release.*

Check Your Hard Drive

During the installation process, the Mac OS X Installer has a lot of work to do. Whereas older versions of the Mac operating system generally consisted of hundreds of files, literally thousands of files (taking up nearly one gigabyte of storage space) are part of the agenda this time. All that work is done behind the scenes in minutes, which means your Mac and its disk storage system is going to be taxed to the limit to keep up.

As a result, you should make sure that the target drive for Mac OS X is working properly. Fortunately, this isn't hard to accomplish. Apple provides a free hard drive diagnostic and repair utility—Disk First Aid (see Figure 2.1)—in the Utilities folder of every Mac. This program, although not as full-featured as the commercial alternatives, should be able to do the job. While it is true the Mac OS X Installer will also check the drive during the setup process, it doesn't hurt to run an extra check.

NOTE: *One of the great features of Disk First Aid is the ability to repair directory damage to a startup drive without having to boot from a separate volume or system CD.*

If you want to make doubly sure that your drive is in tip-top shape, however, you may want to look at one of these three commercial alternatives:

- *Norton Utilities*—This is the oldest existing hard drive utility package. The latest versions of the Disk Doctor application (see Figure 2.2) are, like Disk First Aid, capable of repairing drive directory problems on a startup disk. This saves trips to the program CD except where the startup drive won't boot or when you wish to optimize it.

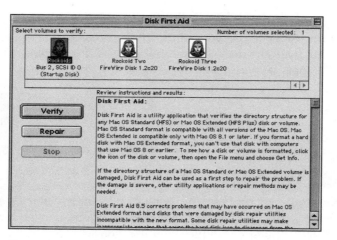

Figure 2.1   The best part of Disk First Aid is that it's free with every new Mac and included with every Mac OS installation.

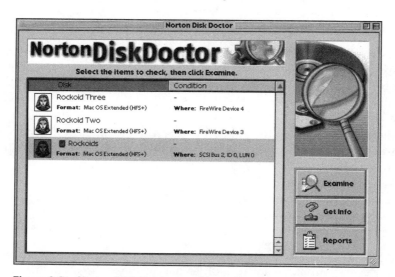

Figure 2.2   Norton Disk Doctor provides a far more comprehensive level of disk repairs than Disk First Aid.

NOTE: *At the time this book went to press, Symantec was in the process of developing a version of Norton Utilities that would run from the Mac OS X environment, so check their Web site for updates. However, Norton Utilities 6 was designed to examine problems with a drive running Mac OS X.*

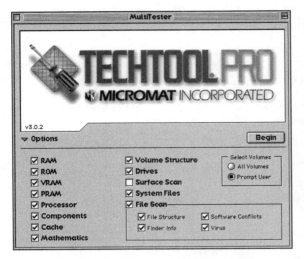

Figure 2.3   TechTool Pro 3 checks can be used to check a hard drive for directory damage prior to the Mac OS X installation.

- *TechTool Pro*—MicroMat's upstart utility application (see Figure 2.3) performs many of the same tasks as Norton Utilities, plus the application can run an extensive set of hardware checks on your Macintosh, including several levels of RAM tests. In addition, beginning with version 3, virus protection capability is part of the package. A Mac OS X derivative of TechTool Pro, called Drive X (see Figure 2.4), due for release sometime after Mac OS X was shipped.

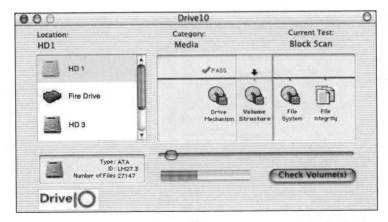

Figure 2.4   This is an early mockup of Drive 10 in action, courtesy of MicroMat.

NOTE: *A limited feature version of this application—TechTool Deluxe—is provided under Apple's AppleCare extended service policy. That particular version of the program, however, doesn't offer disk drive maintenance, nor does it offer virus protection.*

WARNING! TechTool Pro is only supported under "Classic" Mac OS versions; it cannot repair directory problems on the startup drive, so you have to boot from the program's CD or another startup volume to handle those problems.

- *DiskWarrior*—Reviewers call Alsoft's DiskWarrior (see Figure 2.5) a "one-trick pony" because it's limited to checking and replacing hard drive directories. However, it does that task extraordinarily well. Rather than just fixing damage found in a hard drive's directory, it prepares a new, optimized directory, delivering the promise of speedier performance. If it lacks anything, as with TechTool Pro, you cannot run the program on the startup drive, and you need to boot from the CD or another volume.

WARNING! You should try to restrict installation of Mac OS X to a hard drive formatted with Apple's Drive Setup. There are major changes to the file structure, and although third-party disk formatting tools might be just fine, the safest course is to stick with the tried-and-true. If Apple's disk formatter won't work with your drive (and it doesn't support many third-party SCSI devices), you should check with the manufacturer of the formatting utility you're using for compatibility information. At the time this book was written, the folks at FWB, publishers of Hard Disk ToolKit, said it would take a while for them to deliver a compatible version of their hard drive formatting application.

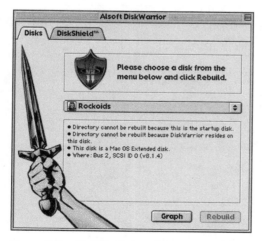

Figure 2.5   DiskWarrior performs its lone function so well that it merits a place in any Mac user's software library.

Back Up Your Data

Back up chores tend to get put off until the next day, but it is supercritical for any operating system installation, whether it's a Public Beta or release. The most effective backup is the one that's complete, covering all your data. If you have backups of all of your applications (such as the original CDs) and your original System Install or System Restore disks for your Mac, you can, as a time-saver, restrict the backup to the documents you've created with your software, along with critical program preferences, such as your Internet preferences.

However, having your entire drive backed up on a single set of disks is far more convenient, and it makes the process of restoring your files much easier. I cover the subject of backups in more detail in Chapter 17.

Mac OS X: Hardware-Related Issues

If you're ready to go ahead with the installation, there are some hardware issues and strategy suggestions you'll want to consider before proceeding with the installation. This will avoid problems and confusing performance later on.

Here's a list of primary concerns:

- *Firmware*—You should make sure firmware is current. Many Macs produced since the summer of 1998 have firmware (a boot ROM) that can be upgraded by software. You'll want to check Apple's support Web site (**http://asu.info.apple.com**) to be sure that the firmware on your computer is up-to-date.

- *Beige PowerMac G3, PowerBook G3 (non-USB versions), and Rev A through D iMac (those with pop-up CD trays)*—For these models, if you choose to divide your hard drive into multiple partitions or volumes, make sure that the Mac OS X installation is performed on the first 8GB of the drive.

NOTE: *It is perfectly possible to install Mac OS X on a drive with a single partition and have it coexist with Mac OS 9.1. With this installation scheme, the existing contents of your Mac's drive will be placed in a folder labeled Mac OS 9.1. Partitioning a drive can be done for protection, as a way to start your Mac, if the other partition goes down, or for organization. However, it's not required.*

- *FireWire and USB drives*—Sorry, such an installation isn't supported. Although some FireWire drives—notably those from LaCie and VST Technologies—will work just fine under Mac OS X, don't think of attempting to use them for the new operating system. Apple says they won't support such an installation, which means if something goes wrong, it is up to you to sort it out.

- *Third-party SCSI cards*—If you can't boot your Mac after Mac OS X is installed, place a drive or terminator on one of the ports of your third-party SCSI card.

- *AirPort*—Apple's fancy wireless networking hardware works fine under Mac OS X, but you need to return to Mac OS 9.1 to set up the network or to reconfigure the base station.

- *Third-party graphics cards*—Most third-party graphics cards aren't supported. Mac OS X was, at release, only compatible with graphic chips and cards from ATI, IX Micro, and NVIDIA, all of whom have supplied products for a number of Macs over the years. It's up to such manufacturers of graphic cards as Formac and any other entrants into this arena to supply Mac OS X-compatible drivers for their own products. With the departure of 3dfx Interactive from the scene in late 2000, it's not at all certain when, if ever, their products will become compatible.

- *Processor upgrade cards*—Again, it's the responsibility of the manufacturers of these products to make a processor card function. Some of these products use special software to activate a G3's or G4's backside cache. Even if they worked otherwise, there might be a severe performance penalty. However, most existing makers of such products did promise to deliver Mac OS X compatible versions, so there is hope for most users, except for those who bought cards made by Newer Technology. The failure of that company put into doubt the possibility that such updates would happen, although some Newer engineers did join some of the other companies out there, so I'll never say never.

NOTE: *This might sound like a bleak picture, but we're talking totally new operating system here. Most third-party companies offer updates to their products over time, particularly as Apple provides more and more development assistance, and the use of Mac OS X spreads. You'll want to check with these companies for their Mac OS X upgrade policies before you decide whether to deploy Mac OS X in your environment.*

Immediate Solutions

Preparing for Mac OS X

Before you install Mac OS X, you'll need to make a few decisions on how to proceed:

- *Determine where to install*—You can install Mac OS X on the same drive partition as Mac OS 9 or a separate partition. Apple includes a special utility—System Disk—with Mac OS X that allows for switch booting from Mac OS 9. The Startup Disk control panel will only function if you install Mac OS 9.1, but because you need this to run in Classic mode, you might have already dealt with this issue. You can return from the new operating system to the old via the System Preferences application that's part of Mac OS X. Chapter 3 covers the subject in detail.

- *Install Mac OS 9.1*—If you need to run Classic applications, you must install Mac OS 9 first before proceeding with Mac OS X. A copy of the installation CD comes with Mac OS X at no charge with the shipping package.

- *Copy Internet and networking setups*—During the installation of the Mac OS X, you'll need to enter information manually to get access to a local network or the Internet. You'll then need to copy these settings from the Modem, Internet (see Figure 2.6), Remote Access, and TCP/IP control panels.

TIP: You might be able to access information about a network configuration if you select the BOOTP network setting. If it works, you'll get a message asking if you want to use the network configuration BOOTP has provided.

TIP: A quick way to capture these settings is with a screenshot. To take a picture of just the Control Panel window (rather than the entire screen), press Command+Shift+4+Caps Lock. Then, click on the window that you want to capture to complete the action. You'll hear the sound of a shutter clicking in confirmation. Each file will be identified by the name "Picture" plus the number (1, 2, and so on). You can then open these files in SimpleText and print them, so you'll have a copy to refer to when needed for Mac OS X's Setup Assistant.

---

2. Upgrading
to Mac OS X

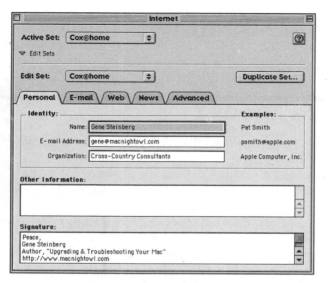

Figure 2.6   **The Internet control panel has several tabs you need to check to pick up all of your configuration information.**

Installing Mac OS X

Now that you're ready to proceed, these instructions will take you through the entire installation process through the actual restart:

1. Insert the Mac OS X CD into your Mac's drive.

2. Restart your Mac, holding down the Shift key, so that it boots from the CD. After restarting, it'll take several minutes for the Installer to begin, so be patient. During each step of the process, you'll have to click on a button or click on a checkbox or pop-up menu to make a choice before proceeding. Therefore, read the onscreen instructions carefully, in case they've changed from those present when this book was written.

NOTE: If you just double-click on the Installer from Mac OS 9.1, it'll put up a screen explaining that it will proceed to restart your Mac for the Mac OS X installation when you press the Continue button. There's no way to do the installation otherwise.

3. The first screen to appear allows you to select the language kit used for the installation. You're not restricted to English. After you've made your selection, click on Continue to proceed.

---

4. Next, the Welcome screen appears. This is just a message to get ready for the main event. Click on the Continue button to move on to the next step in the process.

5. The Important Information screen appears next. You should consult this ReadMe file to see if there are any factors you have to consider before proceeding with the installation. Spend a few moments reading this document. You'll see for the first time the ultra-clear text display afforded by Mac OS X. After you're finished reading the document, click on Continue to proceed, or click on Go Back to review the previous screen.

6. The next screen shows the Software License Agreement. This is a fairly standard license agreement covering Mac OS X. Click on Continue after reviewing the information. You'll see a dialog box where you must press the Agree button and accept the agreement to continue with the installation. If you click on Disagree, you'll end the process then and there. There are only two alternatives here. Click on agree to continue.

7. Next, the Select a Destination screen appears, showing the available drive volumes. Click on the icon representing the drive on which you want to place Mac OS X. Even FireWire drives will be shown by distinctive FireWire icons, but you cannot, of course, install Mac OS X on those. There is yet another option. If the volume has no other data on it, or data you no longer need, you can click on the Erase Destination And Format As checkbox to format the drive and then select the file format from the pop-up window. Should you take this route, keep the default file system—Mac OS Extended (also known as HFS+)—because it will provide maximum compatibility with Mac OS 9.1. Click on Continue after your destination and disk formatting options are selected.

WARNING! *Formatting a hard drive can be a destructive process. If you select that option, all the data on the selected volume will be wiped out with little or no chance of recovery. So be certain that's the decision you want to make. There's no going back.*

NOTE: *If you cannot locate the right startup volume on the Select a Destination screen, you should go to the Installer application window and quit the Installer so you can cancel the process and reboot your Mac. You should then verify that the drive on which you wanted to install Mac OS X is indeed available. After everything has been rechecked, you can attempt installation again by restarting from the CD.*

8. The Easy Install screen appears next. There are actually four elements of Mac OS X that are included in this package: Base System, Essential System Software, BSD Subsystem, and Additional Printer Drivers. However, the distinction is academic, because you need all four for a successful installation of Mac OS X and support for some popular printers. So forget the Customize button, and click on Install to proceed.

NOTE: *If you add up the four components of Mac OS X's installation, you come up with close to one gigabyte. So where does Apple get the 1.5GB figure? Simple. There has to be elbow room for movement and copying files and for virtual memory storage space. Mac OS X uses a large virtual memory file to provide its extraordinary memory management.*

After the installation process begins, the hard drive on which Mac OS X is to be installed is examined for drive directory issues, and minor problems are repaired. If everything is all right, the installation proceeds with several status messages and a progress bar estimating the amount of time left. You should expect installation to take anywhere from 15 minutes to a half hour, depending on the speed of your Mac's processor, the speed of your CD (or DVD) drive, and the speed of your hard drive. When the installation is complete, your Mac will restart under its new operating system version. Then, you'll experience a brief multimedia presentation, and you'll be guided through the Setup Assistant, where you'll be asked to make some very basic system settings to get Mac OS X up and running to your satisfaction. These include registration of your copy of Mac OS X, optional registration for Apple's iTools feature, plus setting up your Mac for Internet access. I cover these and other settings in Chapter 3.

Chapter 3

Mac OS X User Preferences

If you need an immediate solution to:	See page:
Configuring the SetupAssistant	35
Setting System Preferences under Mac OS X	39
Setting Classic Preferences	41
Setting ColorSync Preferences	42
Setting Date & Time Preferences	43
Setting Displays Preferences	44
Setting Dock Preferences	50
Setting Energy Saver Preferences	51
Setting General Preferences	52
Setting International Preferences	53
Setting Internet Preferences	54
Setting Keyboard Preferences	55
Setting Login Preferences	56
Setting Mouse Preferences	56
Setting Network Preferences	57
Setting QuickTime Preferences	59
Setting Screen Saver Preferences	60
Setting Sharing Preferences	61
Setting Software Update Preferences	61
Setting Sound Preferences	62
Setting Speech Preferences	63
Setting Startup Disk Preferences	64
Setting Users Preferences	65
Configuring a Printer	65

In Brief

When the installation of Mac OS X is complete, your Mac will restart, and, as soon as the new Mac desktop appears, you'll be introduced to a pleasant multimedia presentation, providing a musical introduction to the new operating system, followed by the appearance of Apple's SetupAssistant. The SetupAssistant is used to register Mac OS X with Apple, then configure a basic set of user and networking settings for Mac OS X. Typical of a Unix-based operating system, Mac OS X is designed for multiple users, allowing each person who works on the Mac to have a different level of access. If you're upgrading from Mac OS 9.1, you'll find this concept is nothing new. In almost every installation, more than one person is using a Mac. Even in a home setup, the family computer may be used by parents and children, each of whom may have a different set of requirements—and an equally diverse need to restrict certain elements of user access. (I cover the subject of configuring your Mac to work in such an environment in much more detail in Chapter 6.)

This chapter first covers the various preference settings you'll make right after installing Mac OS X using the SetupAssistant. These settings, in large part, cover access to your Mac by you as administrator of the system and by other users to whom you will grant access. You'll also make basic network setups, including your Mac's network name and various types of Internet access. In addition, there will be time zone adjustments so your Mac will put the correct time on your documents and email messages.

Control Panel Settings: A Mixture of the Old and New

After you've completed the basic setups, you can use your Mac and your favorite programs without altering anything further. However, to get the optimum performance from your computer, you'll also want to tackle the preference panels. For Mac OS X, rather than offer each item as a separate control panel, they are all merged into a single System Preferences application. This greatly simplifies the setup process, because you don't have to hunt down multiple applications from the Control Panel's submenu in the Apple menu or directly from that folder to enter the settings you want.

NOTE: *The Apple menu, although still present, is rather a different breed from the one with which you're familiar from the "Classic" Mac OS. For one thing, it replaces the functions of the Finder's Special menu, and that adds a few elements from the original version. I cover that subject in more detail in Chapter 4.*

In some ways, the new design is a throwback to the way system set-ups existed under older versions of the Mac operating system prior to System 7. Even though control panels were separate items then, they would all display in a single window. Apple has apparently taken the simplicity of this design to heart, except for making the icons a horizontal Finder-like display, rather than the vertical array of icons you needed to click to get to a particular setting.

Click on an icon to bring up the labeled function, which will launch essentially as a separate application within the Preferences window. You'll see how it's set up in the "Immediate Solutions" section of this chapter.

Before I discuss the various preference settings, let's look at some new Finder-level features of Mac OS X. The rest are explained in Chapter 4. Unlike previous Mac OS versions, you don't have square boxes representing closing, minimizing, or maximizing Finder windows. Instead, three separate traffic-light-colored buttons mounted at the left provide these functions:

- *Red ("X" Symbol)*—Close the window. This may or may not quit the application (in most cases, it won't).

- *Yellow ("–" Symbol)*—Minimize the window. When you click on this button, the window is collapsed and appears as an icon on the Dock.

- *Green ("+" Symbol)*—Maximize the window. This command expands the window to the largest size necessary to encompass its contents, limited only by the size of your Mac's display.

NOTE: *When you pass your mouse over any of these buttons, you'll see a symbol inside representing its function. If you choose the Graphite interface as a General preference as described in the section on using the System Preferences application later in this book, the button colors will all switch to the same color, graphite, but the symbols will still appear whenever the mouse is brought to the vicinity of these buttons.*

Additionally, you no longer quit a Mac OS X application from the File menu. Apple Computer decided to move that function to the Application menu (the one in bold at the left end of the menu bar, right next to the Apple menu).

3. Mac OS X User Preferences

Selecting Printers without a Chooser

In every version of the Mac operating system prior to Mac OS X, a somewhat clumsy little application—the Chooser (see Figure 3.1)—was used for both selecting a printer and connecting to a Mac or PC with the proper networking software installed across a network.

TIP: *If you want to know more about networking Macs and Windows-based PCs, check out another book that I wrote with networking guru Pieter Paulson,* The Windows 2000 Mac Support Little Black Book. *This fairly technical instruction book covers networking Macs with Windows NT servers and Windows 2000 servers.*

For Mac OS X, Apple has moved to a more conventional solution, called Print Center. As you will learn later in this chapter, this application can be used to ferret out the printers on your network or direct connection. You can then select the ones you want to use, configure custom features, and monitor and adjust your print queue while printing is in progress (same as the Desktop or regular PrintMonitor applications).

One big advantage over the older Chooser is that it can actually search for any available printer, even if it's on a serial or USB port or accessible via TCP/IP across the Internet without having to fiddle with multiple network adjustments other than turning to AppleTalk. After you've set up your printers, the regular Page Setup and Print dialog boxes can be used to switch among the available printers.

No more awkward visits to the Chooser.

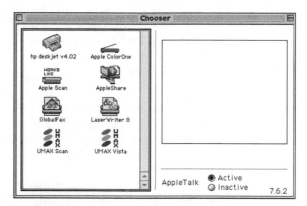

Figure 3.1   The venerable (and clunky) Apple Chooser is now history.

Immediate Solutions

Configuring the SetupAssistant

As you go through the setup screens, check the instructions carefully. They will change from time to time as Apple updates Mac OS X. As you progress through the setup process, click on the right arrow at the lower right to move to the next setup screen, and click on the back or left arrow to review or change a previous setting. At the top left of the screen, you'll see the title of the setup category you've entered.

WARNING! After the SetupAssistant is run during the initial setup process, it is no longer functional. Even though you can launch it again (you'll find it inside the Utilities folder), all you will see is a prompt that Apple's System Preferences application can be launched to make your system settings.

The introduction will consist of a short multimedia presentation, punctuated by music, but you don't need to dismiss it. Soon, you'll see the message, "We'll have you up and running in no time."

NOTE: Aside from the initial registration of Mac OS X, all user settings you make now can be changed in the System Preferences application as needed. Nothing is set in stone.

1. *Welcome*—When you see the Welcome screen, select the country from the list. Click on Show All to see more options. After you've checked the appropriate country, click on Continue.

2. *Registration Information*—There are several screens where you will enter the information needed to register your product with Apple Computer. The first screen asks for your name, address, phone number, email address, and so forth. The next screen will inquire about some simple marketing information (you don't have to answer). Then, you click on Continue to receive an acknowledgement that your registration information has been recorded and will be sent to Apple when you have connected to the Internet.

NOTE: You won't have to toil through the registration process if you have to reinstall Mac OS X, unless you've removed the original installed files.

3. *Create Your Account*—Now, you need to enter your username as owner or administrator of the Mac. For convenience, click on the Tab key to move to the next text field. Press Shift+Tab to return. You will also be asked to enter a short name or nickname for yourself containing eight lowercase characters; when you enter that text field, Mac OS X's SetupAssistant will enter a shortened version of your name by default, but feel free to change it. The next three text fields are for you to enter a password, reconfirm your password, and enter a password hint—a word or phrase that will remind you of the password in case you forget.

NOTE: *If you are using your Mac in a home or small office, a secure password probably doesn't matter. However, if you want the utmost in security, try to use what is considered a "strong password." That's a password that consists of random numbers and mixed upper- and lowercase letters so it cannot easily be guessed by anyone who might try to break into your computer. An example is "OBfusc8." You'll want to pick a password, however, that is easy for you to remember (or at least write it down and put it in a safe place).*

4. *Get Internet Ready*—After you've created a username and password, you'll move on to a setup screen where you can configure your Mac for Internet access. Just click the button to indicate whether you already have an ISP or want Apple to set you up with one (and that'll be EarthLink, their default provider). Assuming you are already connected and select the option to add your existing settings, you'll have the following options:

   • *Telephone Modem*—This is for a standard, garden-variety, dial-up connection to an ISP. When you check this option and click Continue, you'll be greeted with a Your Internet Connection screen where you'll enter the basic login information required to connect to your ISP.

NOTE: *The SetupAssistant will not work with AOL or CompuServe 2000 because their client software has to be separately configured to access these services. In order for you to use their software, you'll have to get a Mac OS X-savvy version, which was in development at the time this book was written.*

   • *Local Area Network*—If you log onto the Internet via your local area network (perhaps using a server for the connection), choose this option. The next screen you see will be used to enter your network setup information.

- *Cable Modem*—This is used for high-speed Internet provided by a cable service. Click on Continue to see a setup screen where you enter your setup information. You might have to put in a DHCP client ID number to allow your cable modem to connect, or PPPoE (PPP over Ethernet) settings, as required.

- *DSL Modem*—Another connection option for high-speed Internet service is accessing the Digital Subscriber Line broadband option. Again, if you click on Continue after selecting this option, a setup screen will appear for you to enter the required information.

- *AirPort*—When you use Apple's AirPort wireless networking system, click on this option to access the network.

NOTE: *The first release of Mac OS X doesn't let you configure your AirPort base station or other networking configuration choices. For that, you need to return to Mac OS 9.1, using the Startup Disk preferences pane, and then make the adjustments as required in your AirPort user documentation.*

5. *Get iTools*—One of Apple's better ideas to move the platform beyond the box is iTools, a set of special features at the Apple Web site that enhance the user experience. In this settings screen, you'll be asked to choose whether you want to create an iTools account or use the one you already have, by entering the appropriate information.

NOTE: *If you need to set up a new iTools account, be sure your Mac has been set up for your ISP, so Apple's Web site can be checked to establish your account and make sure your username hasn't already been taken (in which case, you'll be given a chance to try a different one).*

6. *Now You're Ready to Connect*—Click on Continue to send your registration to Apple via your ISP and do the first stage of setups for your Mac. You'll see a progress screen indicating that you're connecting to Apple. Once you're done, continue on to the next screen to perform the last setups.

7. *Set Up Mail*—Mac OS X includes a brand new email application, called Mail, that provides speed and powerful mail-handling features. You'll be asked here to indicate whether you want to use your iTools account or choose the option to "Add My Existing E-mail Account." The setup screen will ask for your email address, incoming mail server, account type (POP or IMAP), user account ID, password, and outgoing mail server. These settings are the same ones you've always used for your email.

3. Mac OS X User Preferences

8. *Select Time Zone*—In order for such things as your email and documents to display the proper time, you first need to click and move the slider in the map until it points to the correct time zone. Then, choose the time zone or city nearest you from the pop-up menu.

9. *Thank You*—This final setup screen gives you one last chance to recheck all the entries you've made before they are stored in Mac OS X. You can use the back arrow to return to any setting and change it now. If you accept the setup, click on the Go button to move on.

NOTE: *Once again, your setups aren't set in stone. Feel free at any time to change everything from networking to passwords in the System Preferences application. I explain how later in this chapter.*

---

10. *Restart*—Once you're done, your Mac will restart and you will go through the full restart process. When you first see the Mac OS X desktop (see Figure 3.2), you'll feel, for a moment, as if you've visited an alien environment. The new Aqua interface has familiar elements, but there are unfamiliar elements as well. In the next few chapters, I cover every aspect of the revised look of the Mac OS. For now, get comfortable, and get ready to explore the system setup and printer setup options.

NOTE: *This is the last time you'll see the SetupAssistant under Mac OS X, unless you want to reinstall the operating system on a different volume. If you launch the application yet again, you'll be reminded that settings are made in the System Preferences application. In addition, if you've used the Mac OS X Public Beta, you might have seen that there was no login panel. This is now an option, which you can activate for increased security or in the event you have to add extra users to your system.*

Related solution:	Found on page:
Setting Up Multiple-User Access	108

Figure 3.2 Your first exposure to Mac OS X, already configured with your username.

Setting System Preferences under Mac OS X

After you've configured your basic Mac settings with the SetupAssistant, you can go ahead and compute without having to change any other settings. However, if you want to make adjustments to the look and feel of your Mac, you'll want to use the System Preferences application (see Figure 3.3).

You'll find the System Preferences application on the Dock when you've done a normal installation of Mac OS X. If for some reason the program isn't where you expect it to be, click on the Applications button on the Finder's Toolbar (or use the same command in the Apple menu) to launch the application.

TIP: If a program isn't already on the Dock, drag its icon there, and the Dock will expand to accommodate it and icon size will be reduced as needed. Applications go on the left, and documents appear at the right, separated by a white vertical line. Don't worry if you miss the separator line. Sometimes, you have to glance twice to notice it.

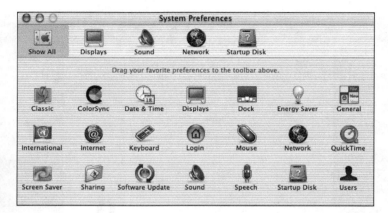

Figure 3.3   Click on an icon to access a specific system setting.

To switch from one program setting pane to the next, click on the icon you want. After settings are made, click on the red close button, or press Command+Q to quit the program. Depending on the settings you make, there might be an additional confirmation dialog box you have to click to store your settings. Some system-critical functions can be secured by clicking on the padlock, in which case only users granted "administrator" status will be able to change those settings after entering the correct username and password.

NOTE: *If you've used previous versions of the Mac operating system, you'll find some of these preferences are quite familiar. Aside from the distinctive Aqua interface, they actually work pretty much the same as in the previous versions.*

You do not have to set all the settings in the Preferences application right now. You can try each one for size or just experiment with one particular setting without changing any of the others. If the setting isn't what you like, you can quickly restore it to the previous one. In addition, depending on your specific Mac setup, you may find additional preference components to adjust.

The following sections detail, from left to right, top to bottom, the settings you can make in the System Preferences application.

TIP: *A fast way to bring up the settings pane you want is to click on Pane from the menu bar and choose the one you want from the pop-up menu.*

Setting Classic Preferences

The Classic mode lets you use Mac OS 9.1 applications by opening the older version of the operating system within Mac OS X. In a sense, it's somewhat similar to running Windows applications on a Mac using Connectix Virtual PC. The major difference is that the Classic mode runs applications transparently, without inheriting the Aqua interface, using the Mac OS X Finder. What's more, performance is better than any of those emulation programs, because you're not emulating a foreign processor.

NOTE: A Mac OS 9.1 CD-ROM comes with your Mac OS X package. In order for you to use the Classic environment, you need to install 9.1, if you're not already using it. Earlier versions of Mac OS 9 or previous Mac OS versions will not work (except for rebooting into the old environment after changing your Startup Disk settings).

The Classic Preferences panel (see Figure 3.4) lets you specify the startup volume for the Classic operating system, which is especially important if you have more that one volume with a System Folder installed. If your Mac has Mac OS 9.1 on another hard disk (or partition), you'll see the drive's name displayed in the list (drives without a 9.1 partition will be grayed out). You can click on the disk from which you want to run the Mac in Classic mode, then specify whether you want to have the Classic environment automatically start when you boot (log in to) your Mac. This is not an essential selection unless

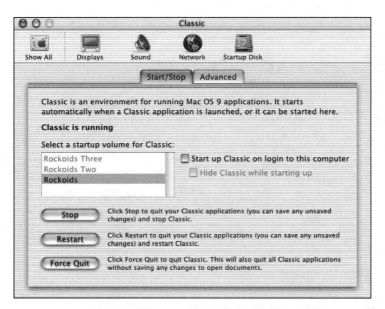

Figure 3.4   Choose your startup disk for Classic mode on this screen.

you want to begin using Classic applications without having to wait for Classic to boot. You can also Restart or Force Quit Classic. The Advanced preference panel is used to configure additional options, such as whether to rebuild the Mac OS 9.1 system's desktop or restart with Extensions off or to bring Extensions Manager up when Classic opens. I cover the subject in more detail in Chapter 15.

TIP: *If a preference panel is already open, you can access another panel by its icon on the top of the screen; if that icon isn't there, click on the Show All button to see the rest of the list.*

**3. Mac OS X
User Preferences**

Setting ColorSync Preferences

Apple's ColorSync technology is tightly integrated into Mac OS X. You can use this settings pane (see Figure 3.5) to choose a ColorSync profile for input devices, such as a scanner, your Mac's display, output devices (a printer), or a proofing device. Click on the pop-up menu to select the profile you want. To choose the color management method, or CMM, click on that tab in the ColorSync pane. The final tab is designed strictly for custom color workflow settings that may be required when you are working in an art department or prepress establishment.

NOTE: *Many manufacturers of input and output peripherals provide their own ColorSync profiles. If one didn't come with a particular device, ask the manufacturer how one might be obtained or whether an existing ColorSync profile will do.*

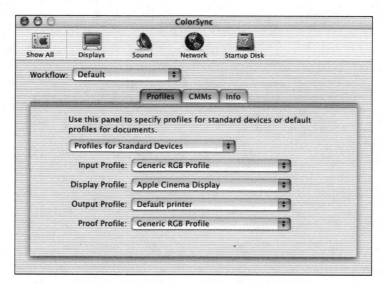

Figure 3.5   Select a ColorSync profile in this pane.

Setting Date & Time Preferences

In effect, the settings you create here (see Figure 3.6) mirror the ones you've already configured in the SetupAssistant. There is, however, a new wrinkle to these settings. At the bottom left of the settings screen, you'll notice a button labeled Click The Lock To Prevent Further Changes. This means you can protect this panel and any other panel with a padlock icon so that only users with administrator's permissions can access them.

TIP: If you plan to access a particular preference panel often, drag its icon to the top of the System Preferences window.

You can access any of the four settings categories by clicking on the appropriate tab:

- The first tab—Date & Time—and the second—Time Zone—are identical to those you've already configured in the SetupAssistant. You can leave them alone or make further adjustments now.

- The third tab—Network Time (see Figure 3.7)—allows you to have your Mac's clock synchronized to another computer on your network or to an Internet-based time server (such as Apple's, which is the one I copied from Mac OS 9.1's Date & Time Control

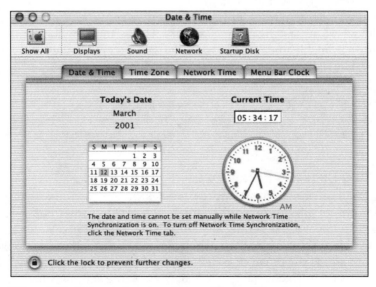

Figure 3.6   Make your various time-related settings here.

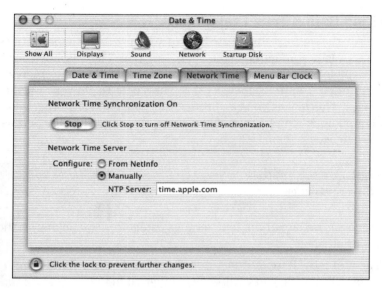

Figure 3.7   You can synchronize your Mac's clock via a network server.

Panel). The latter setting requires that you connect to the Internet to adjust the time, but when it's done, both the date and time will be configured automatically as needed.

- The final tab—Menu Bar Clock—allows you to specify whether you want to show the clock in the menu bar (it's on by default) and whether you want it to display seconds, AM/PM, the date of the week, or flashing time separators. The settings are identical to those available under the Classic Mac OS, except for the inability to change the font and size of the menu bar clock's display.

TIP: If you're not happy with the limitations of Apple's menu bar clock, check for a shareware alternative. One resource for information about them is VersionTracker.com, a popular Web site that includes information about software, plus links to actual download sites.

Setting Displays Preferences

The Displays screen (see Figure 3.8) is used to configure the size (resolution) of the images on your Mac's display and the color depth setting. The Resolutions setting specifies the number of pixels that are shown on your Mac's display. When you make this adjustment, you want to weigh the range of your Mac's desktop against the clarity of the items on it. To change resolution, click on the setting you want.

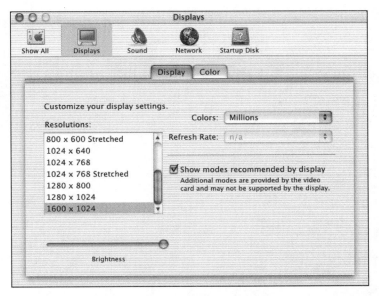

Figure 3.8   Choose your Mac's display preferences on this setup screen.

NOTE: *On some Macs, you can configure contrast and brightness settings from the Displays pane; on others, the settings will be grayed out. On iMacs and some models equipped with an Apple display, you can also set screen geometry, so you can make sure your display's image is as wide as possible and that the shapes are straight and true.*

If you want to change color depth, click on the Colors pop-up menu. For most purposes, the differences between thousands and millions is slight. But if you do graphics work, configure your Mac for the latter.

The Show Modes Recommended By Display checkbox restricts settings to those that are supported by your monitor. But if you uncheck it, you might gain additional choices, with which you can experiment (don't be concerned—if you pick one that can't be used, your Mac will revert, within a few seconds, to the previous setting).

Click on the Color tab (see Figure 3.9) if you want to adjust the color balance or calibration of your display. These settings take advantage of Apple's ColorSync technology so that your display more nearly matches the color balance of your printer or other output device.

NOTE: *In some older Macs, setting a lower color depth will deliver a slightly speedier graphics display. But for any of the Macs with 128-bit or AGP-based graphics capability, the performance difference will be difficult, if not impossible, to notice unless you sit down with a stopwatch to compare program scrolling and other functions.*

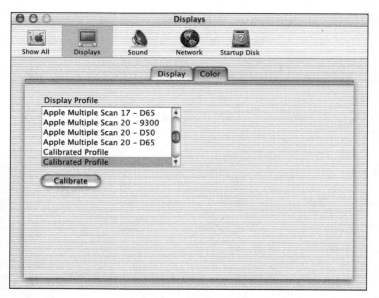

Figure 3.9   You can create a calibrated color profile to give your Mac a more accurate color balance.

The settings on the Color tab are pretty much identical to those present in Mac OS 9.1:

1. To establish a color profile for your Mac's monitor, select the model display you have or choose a generic profile from the Display Profile scrolling list. Then, click on the Calibrate button. Apple's Display Calibrator Assistant (see Figure 3.10) will be launched.

NOTE: *You can also find the Display Calibrator Assistant application in the Utilities folder, inside the Applications folder, if you want to access it directly and bypass System Preferences.*

---

2. Before proceeding, take a quick look at the introductory text in the Assistant's dialog box. For the most accurate color calibration, you'll want to click on the Expert Mode checkbox, if it's not already selected. Click on the right (forward) arrow to progress, and the left (back) arrow to review a setting. When you click on the right arrow, you'll move right to the Set Up screen (see Figure 3.11).

3. Use your display's brightness control to increase the brightness so the center shape is visible, but the two halves of the background square appear as one.

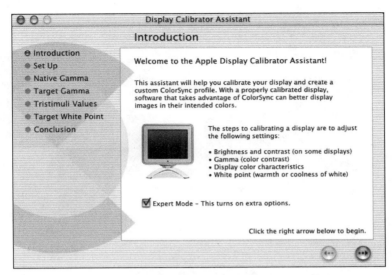

Figure 3.10   Apple's Display Calibrator Assistant helps you create a ColorSync profile for your monitor.

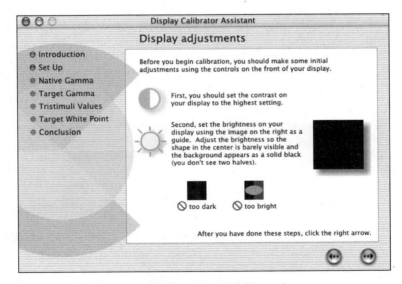

Figure 3.11   Adjust your Mac's optimal brightness here.

NOTE: If you have a regular CRT display, you'll need to redo brightness as the unit ages. Users of LCD displays shouldn't have to revisit these settings unless lighting conditions change substantially or you move to a different working environment.

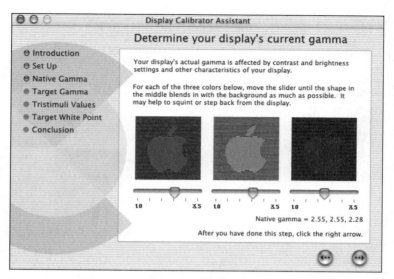

Figure 3.12   The gamma settings for each color are made here.

4. When you click on the right arrow, you'll see the Native Gamma screen (see Figure 3.12). This setting lets you calibrate the gamma (center point) for the three RGB (red, green, blue) colors of your display by moving the slider back and forth. At the proper setting, the color of the Apple picture within the squares will seem to almost disappear into the background.

TIP: It's a good idea not to sit too close to your display when making these adjustments. You get the most accurate view of gamma settings if you sit back from the display as far as possible. Otherwise, you might find that the inner and outer portions of the square never seem to come together.

---

5. A click of the right arrow brings up the Target Gamma setting (see Figure 3.13). Move the slider to configure the setting and observe the picture in the preview screen to see the end result. If you must live in a mixed-platform environment, you might want to choose the PC Standard setting. Otherwise, use Mac Standard.

6. We are near the finish line. Click on the right arrow to see the Target White Point screen (see Figure 3.14). The slider will set white point (or color temperature) for your display. D65, or 6500 degrees Kelvin, is normal. A setting of 9300 will brighten the display somewhat.

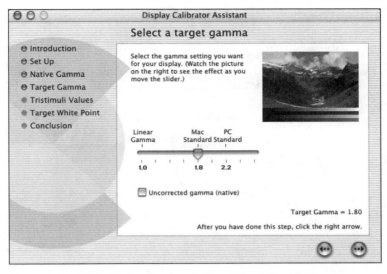

Figure 3.13   When Native Gamma is done, Target Gamma is next.

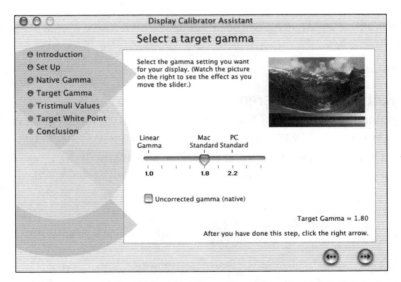

Figure 3.14   Choose the white point setting and you're almost finished.

7. A click of the right arrow takes you to the final stage of the process (see Figure 3.15). Name your profile (Calibrated Profile is the default). Then, click on Create to finish and close the Display Calibrator Assistant.

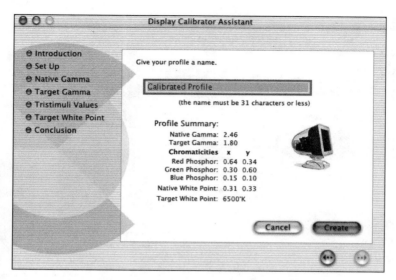

Figure 3.15   Name your calibration profile and click on Create to wrap up.

NOTE: *If you already have a profile using the same name, you'll see a prompt asking if you want to delete the profile. This is your choice; perhaps, you'd rather just pick an alternate setting in the event you want to switch from this to another for different purposes.*

Setting Dock Preferences

Apple's famous Mac OS X taskbar (see Figure 3.16) can be configured in several ways to adjust display. The settings are as follows:

• *Dock Size*—Move the slider to set the default size of the Dock. It will resize itself as needed to accommodate additional icons.

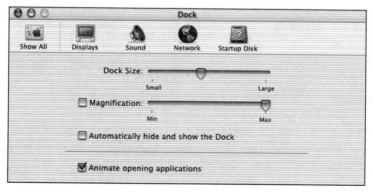

Figure 3.16   Adjust how you interact with the Dock here.

- *Magnification*—If you click on this checkbox, the Dock will magnify as you drag your mouse across it. This is useful if you have lots of small icons and need to see them more clearly, but it can otherwise be a bit ostentatious. You can move the slider to set the amount of magnification.

- *Automatically Hide And Show The Dock*—If you don't want to be disturbed by the Dock, click on this checkbox, and it'll only appear when you move your mouse to the bottom of the screen. Otherwise, it'll be hidden.

- *Animate Opening Applications*—When you launch a program, its icon will animate in the Dock. If you find this effect annoying, uncheck this box. I cover more Dock-related issues in Chapter 5.

Setting Energy Saver Preferences

The exact settings screen you'll see (shown in Figure 3.17) depends on the kind of Mac you have. With a regular desktop Mac, you're limited to three basic adjustments:

- The first setting puts the system into sleep mode after it's been idle for the preset period of time. The most recent desktop Mac models, beginning with the Power Mac G4, are designed to operate most efficiently by leaving the unit in sleep mode rather than actually shutting it down. You just move the slider to change it from the minimum of 30 minutes to Never (which deactivates the function).

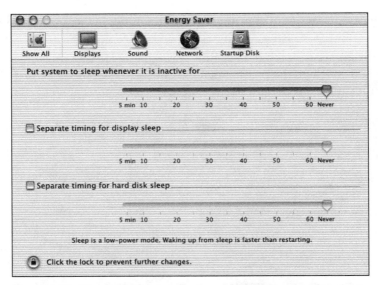

Figure 3.17   Use the slider to adjust your Energy Saver options here.

3. Mac OS X User Preferences

- The second setting lets you establish separate adjustments for your display, to preserve screen life and put it into sleep mode when not in use for a specific interval.

- The final setting puts the hard drive to sleep. To activate this or the previous option, select the checkbox, then drag the slider to the interval you prefer. If you have an iBook or a PowerBook, you'll have separate Energy Saver settings for AC Power and Battery; the latter settings can be used to maximize battery life.

WARNING! *Some older displays are not Energy Star-compliant and will not go into sleep mode, even though you've activated that setting. If you're not certain whether your display supports the feature, check the manufacturer's documentation, the shipping box, or the manufacturer's technical support division.*

NOTE: *Some programs make continuous demands on the hard drive, and thus putting the drive into sleep mode won't work efficiently. The best time to use this feature is when you do not intend to work on your Mac.*

Setting General Preferences

If you thought you'd see the Mac OS X equivalent of the General control panel from previous versions of the Mac OS, think again. What you see is the Aqua equivalent of the Appearance control panel, at least part of it, except for desktop backgrounds, which are set under Desktop and Dock preferences. I get to those in the next chapter.

You have three sets of appearance-related settings in the General pane (see Figure 3.18) from which to choose:

- *Appearance*—If the default Blue (or Aqua) color isn't to your liking, click on the pop-up menu to choose the Graphite setting to adjust the look of buttons, menus, and windows.

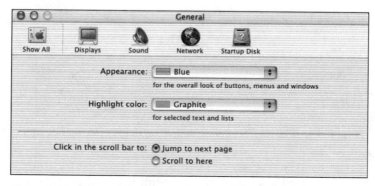

Figure 3.18   Choose your Mac's appearance settings on this panel.

WARNING! When you switch the appearance to Graphite, the colorful buttons at the left of a Finder or document window become gray when they can be used. The only visual indication of what they do will be a symbol within each clear button when the mouse is brought near.

- *Highlight Color*—This sets the color you see when you select text. Feel free to experiment with different settings to see which colors set off highlighted text to your liking.

- *Click In The Scrollbar To*—This sets the action that results from the click. Click on the radio box to jump to next page or scroll to here (return to the previously viewed page).

NOTE: *When you close some of the Preference panels, you'll see a message indicating you have to click on Save to store the settings.*

Setting International Preferences

Mac OS X is designed to be a worldwide operating system, with built-in support for some of the major languages. Under older system versions, you had to install separate modules for different parts of the world or, in fact, buy a different product. But Apple has moved to selling a single operating system version, and the preferences available here (see Figure 3.19) are designed to localize keyboard and

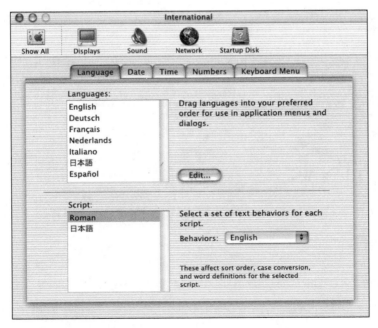

Figure 3.19   Choose your language settings on this screen.

language settings as needed. You have settings for Language and separate tabs to adjust display formats for date, time, and numbers. These options group together the functions of several control panels from older versions of the Mac OS. The final tab—Keyboard Menu—lets you choose whether to put up a menu bar label from which you can quickly switch from one keyboard layout to another.

Setting Internet Preferences

This settings pane (see Figure 3.20) is reminiscent of the Internet Control Panel from Mac OS 9.1, with the notable addition of a category for Apple's iTools feature. Click on a tab to enter a particular setup screen. Four are available:

- *iTools*—Put in your iTools member name and password. If you don't have an account, click on the Free Sign Up button and you'll be connected to Apple's Web site to set up your account.

- *Email*—These are settings you would have retrieved from Mac OS 9.1's Internet Control Panel. Specify which email program you want (Mail is the only Mac OS X-savvy program shipping with Mac OS X), the incoming and outgoing mail servers used by your ISP, the type of account, and the username and password required to log in.

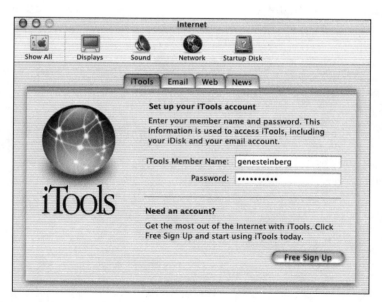

Figure 3.20   Enter the settings used when you access your ISP here.

TIP: If you failed to write down this information from your Mac OS 9.1 installation, you can launch any Classic application to bring up the Classic environment. After you switch to that application, you can use the Apple menu to get the settings from the Internet Control Panel.

- *Web*—Pick a browser, a home page, and a default search page. You can also select a default location on your Mac's drive where downloaded files are placed; the default, and probably the best locale, is your Mac's desktop.

- *News*—If you want to access Internet newsgroups, click on this tab, choose a news reading application, and then enter your ISP's news server information.

NOTE: For some ISPs, you'll have to enter your username and password as a registered user to access newsgroups. This is done to protect against relaying messages to post junk messages. EarthLink is one of the services to require authentication.

Setting Keyboard Preferences

These settings (see Figure 3.21) affect your Mac keyboard's Automatic Repeat modes. Here's the list of the available choices:

- The first option specifies the time you hold down a key before it repeats.

- The second option specifies the speed at which a key repeats.

Move the sliders to make the needed changes. You can also enter text in the textbox to get a feel for the changes you'll be making.

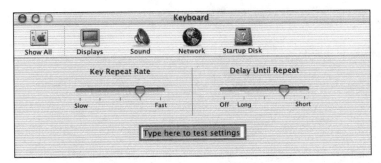

Figure 3.21   More likely than not, you won't visit the Keyboard preference panel all that often.

Setting Login Preferences

You use this setting (see Figure 3.22) in a fashion similar to the Startup Items folder under previous versions of the Mac OS. The programs that appear in this window launch when you log in. Click on the Add button to locate and select startup applications that will open when you boot or log in to your Mac, and click on the Remove button to delete a selected item.

Click on the Login Window tab if you want to display a login prompt when your Mac boots. If you want to set up your Mac for multiple users, you'll need to uncheck the Automatically Log In checkbox. I cover these settings in more detail in Chapter 6.

Setting Mouse Preferences

Most Macs ship with the Mouse panel in the middle setting, and that can be somewhat slow. However, the middle setting can be helpful for those new to personal computing and pointing devices and who need to get accustomed to a mouse's feel and movement. Generally, though, you will find that the standard speed setting is just too slow, especially if your Mac has a large screen display. The Mouse Speed slider (see Figure 3.23) adjusts the tracking speed; the Double-Click Delay setting is used to configure the ideal interval for a double-click to activate a Mac OS function. There is no correct setting. It's entirely up to your taste, and you can experiment with different adjustments to see which are most comfortable. You'll also find that the ideal

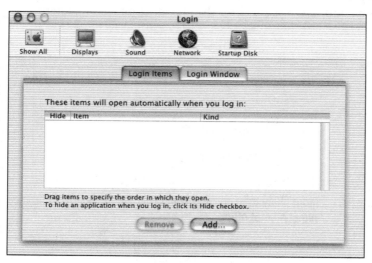

Figure 3.22   Add the programs that will launch when you boot your Mac.

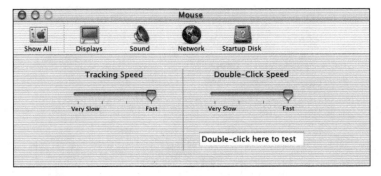

Figure 3.23   Set the mouse parameters here.

settings change as you move from one Mac to another, or to a differ-ent brand of pointing device. If you have an iBook or PowerBook, there will be a separate Trackpad tab for additional settings.

NOTE: Some non-Apple input devices, such as those from Kensington and Microsoft, come with special software to allow you to access extra button features plus custom tracking routines.

Setting Network Preferences

This configuration screen has four tabs (see Figure 3.24) that control various aspects of your network settings. There are two categories of settings you can make. One is for your internal modem, used for con-necting to your ISP. I cover those in more detail in Chapter 8. Under the Built-in Ethernet category, there are four tabs to configure differ-ent settings:

- *Configure*—The settings you make here, labeled Manually, BOOTP, DHCP, or No Connection, are for TCP/IP-based connec-tions, if you have one. They activate these services for a local network, cable modem, or DSL. They're very similar to those used in the TCP/IP control panel of older Macs. The required settings will come either from an ISP or network administrator.

NOTE: If you want to access a dial-up connection to the Internet, you'll make your user settings in the Internet Connect application, which is located in the Applications folder.

- *PPPoE*—Some broadband ISPs, such as those using cable mo-dems or DSL, use PPPoE (for PPP over Ethernet) software or settings. When you click on this tab, you'll be able to enter information for Service Provider, PPPoE Service Name, Account

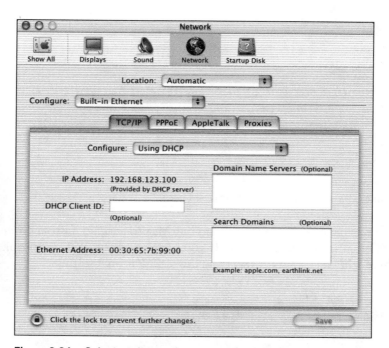

Figure 3.24   Select a tab to make a network-related adjustment on your Mac.

Name, and Password. There are additional options to save your password and a PPPoE Options button for settings that might be required by your ISP.

NOTE: *Your ISP is the source for updated information about the settings required for the PPPoE panel. The settings will vary from service to service.*

• *AppleTalk*—If you want to access Macs on a standard AppleTalk network, enter your computer's unique network name here. It can be anything you want, as long as there are no other computers on the network with the same name in your network zone. Select the checkbox to activate AppleTalk.

• *Proxies*—Depending on the requirements in your network or for your ISP, you might have to enter proxy settings to access the Internet or your local network. You'll need to contact your network administrator or ISP for the appropriate settings information.

After you've made your changes to your network services, you can click on the close box to leave System Preferences or move to another preferences panel. Either way, you'll see a prompt asking if you want to save your settings before you move on. If you don't click on Save, the network changes will be discarded.

Setting QuickTime Preferences

Apple's QuickTime is a multimedia standard around the world. Use this settings pane (shown in Figure 3.25) to establish five sets of user preferences:

- *Plug-In*—This setting determines how your Web browser works with the QuickTime plug-in. The first checkbox turns on a QuickTime movie as soon as it's downloaded. The second stores it in the browser's Web cache (not a good idea if it's a big file), and the third turns on Kiosk mode. This allows you to save movies and adjust your QuickTime settings from within the browser.

- *Connection*—Click on this tab to optimize QuickTime to work best with your specific ISP connection. Choose the speed at which you access your ISP and whether to allow multiple streams of net traffic (this one is best only with broadband Internet access). The Transport Setup button is best left to network administrators.

- *Music*—Use this setting to choose a music synthesizer package. You don't need to use it unless you've added such a package from a music program.

- *Media Keys*—Use this setting to store passwords to access secured multimedia files. Specify the fashion in which Mac OS X's built-in QuickTime features are used.

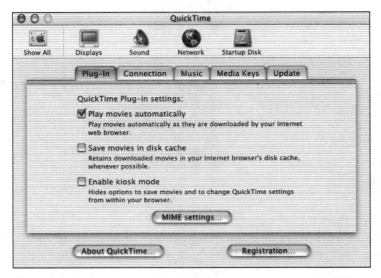

Figure 3.25   Choose your QuickTime user preferences on this pane.

- *Update*—The final tab lets you check for updates to QuickTime from Apple's Web site, or to enter your registration information, in the event you've opted to purchase QuickTime Pro (and get rid of those annoying messages about doing so when you try to view multimedia content on the Internet).

NOTE: *The upgrade to QuickTime Pro gives you more options with which to edit and export movies in the QuickTime Player application. It also allows you to save at least some of the movie trailers that you download from the Internet.*

Setting Screen Saver Preferences

If you've used Microsoft Windows, no doubt you've discovered that it has a built-in screen saver. Apple has finally delivered one of their own (see Figure 3.26). The setup screen is ultra-simple. Pick a module, and then click on the Activation tab to set the idle time before the screen saver activates. The intervals are in 5-minute jumps up to 60 minutes. The Hot Corners option lets you automatically activate a screen saver when moving the mouse to the selected corner.

NOTE: *You can opt to password protect your screen saver in the Activation pane, using your regular username and password to unlock it and dismiss the display. Otherwise, the screen saver remains active.*

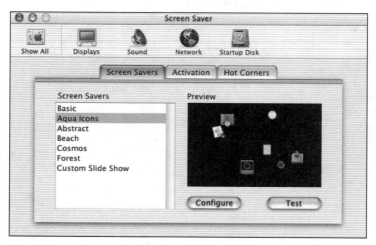

Figure 3.26   At last—the official Mac OS screen saver.

Setting Sharing Preferences

Peer-to-peer file sharing is one of the delights of the Mac OS. You
don't need a network administrator to set up a network over which
you can share files with other users. Once you've activated AppleTalk
in the Network pane, you just have to open this pane (see Figure 3.27)
and click on the Start button for file sharing and the Start button for
Web sharing (which uses the Apache Web Server software to let you
host a site). You also have the option to allow remote login (Telnet) or
FTP access to your Mac. The choices shown are grayed out if AppleTalk
isn't active. The final display shows your Network Identity (the name
you give your Mac) and its IP address for TCP/IP connections.

Setting Software Update Preferences

Starting with Mac OS 9, Apple offered a Software Update option, intended as a way to provide an effective way to check Apple's Web site
for the latest Mac OS X software updates (see Figure 3.28 for Mac OS
X's version).

You can opt to update your software manually whenever you want, or
select the Automatically option to have Apple's Web site checked on

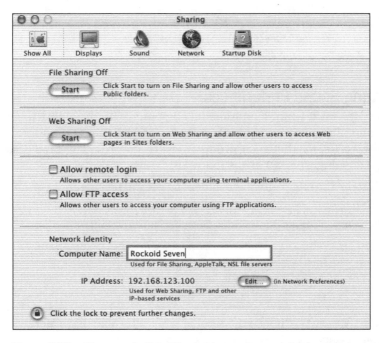

Figure 3.27   Choose whether file sharing and some sharing services will be
available on your Mac.

Figure 3.28   Update your OS using this panel.

a daily, weekly, or monthly basis for needed updates. The status display will show the last time you attempted the update. Click on Update Now whenever you want to recheck for updates.

NOTE: *The Software Update Control Panel under Mac OS 9 was not always as effective as it should be. It required several updates of Software Update itself to make it fairly reliable. However, Apple assures us that the version used for Mac OS X will deliver the goods. Regardless, you may want to check the **VersionTracker.com** Web site periodically to see if you missed a needed update for your Apple system software.*

Setting Sound Preferences

Your Mac is, at heart, a multimedia computer with the ability to create and play audio and video productions (with the right additional software for making such productions, of course). The Sound settings (see Figure 3.29) are as follows:

- *System Volume*—Move the sliders to get the best overall volume level.

- *Balance*—Adjust the balance between left and right speakers.

NOTE: *The Sound preferences you see depend on the kind of Mac you have. For example, if you have one of the slot-loading iMacs, you may see additional adjustments for use if you're using Harmon Kardon's iSub, a woofer module that enhances the sound reproduction on these models.*

- *Alert Volume*—Choose the level at which the Mac plays alert sounds, such as those warning you of a problem with your Mac. If the little beeps and blurbs are irritating to you, you can make them lower than the overall volume.

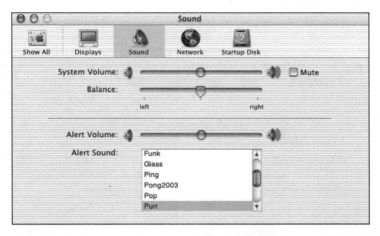

Figure 3.29 Set your volume, speaker balance, and alert sounds in this pane.

- *Alert Sound*—The final setting specifies the audible warning you get when an alert is displayed. When you select a sound from the scrolling list, you'll hear it played in your Mac's speaker.

Setting Speech Preferences

Some Mac programs support Mac OS X's Speech Manager, which allows you to activate Mac functions via spoken commands and have text read back to you. In this settings pane (see Figure 3.30), you can

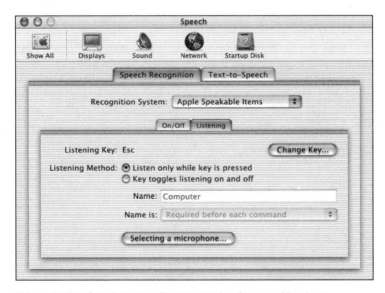

Figure 3.30 Speak to me. Choose a voice for your Mac here.

decide whether to activate the speech recognition feature. Click on On and then click on Listening to specify whether you can speak a command with or without a listening key (a keyboard shortcut that precedes the speech command). The standard setup calls for saying "computer" prior to a command. With recognition turned on, you'll be able to access the Speakable Items folder to see the available commands.

The Text-to-Speech tab brings up a screen from which you can choose a voice from a list, then specify the rate at which the voice is played back. As the rate increases, the pitch of the voice is raised, and the speed at which it reads to you is also increased proportionately. Moving the slider to a slower rate has the reverse effect.

NOTE: *It's not a good idea to be overly dependant on Apple's speech features. The "recognition" feature is limited to some simple commands and doesn't work terribly well in a crowded room. The Text-to-Speech feature will work, after a fashion, but many words will simply not be pronounced correctly. If you want to use speech recognition for dictation, look for the Mac OS X versions of IBM's ViaVoice Enhanced and MacSpeech's iListen.*

Setting Startup Disk Preferences

This setting lets you switch startup disks, if you have additional volumes with system software on them on your Mac. In Figure 3.31, you can see two selections representing the names of the volumes connected to my Mac when I wrote this book. For most of you, the change will be made to switch from Mac OS X back to Mac OS 9.1. To change the startup disk, follows these steps:

1. Click on the icon representing the name of the volume from which you want to boot your Mac.

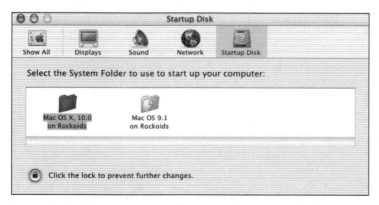

Figure 3.31   Click on a System Folder icon to select another startup disk.

2. Click on the Close button or choose Quit System Prefs from the Application menu to store your settings.

3. Choose Restart from the Apple menu to log off and then restart from another startup disk.

WARNING! For your Mac to boot properly from another startup volume, it must contain system software that's compatible with your computer. The Startup Disk preferences screen only displays the disks on which a Mac OS System Folder is present; it won't always know whether your Mac can run from it. Should your Mac not be able to boot from the specified volume, it will, instead, boot from another volume with a compatible version of the Mac OS (perhaps the one from which you just switched).

When you're finished setting your Mac's preferences, click on the red or close button to quit System Preferences or choose Quit System Prefs from the application menu. The changes you make go into effect immediately.

NOTE: If you've selected the Graphite appearance option, the lights will be gray, and the buttons will have visible symbols when the mouse is brought near. The close light will have an "X" symbol.

Setting Users Preferences

Bring up this screen if you want to change your login password or add additional users to your Mac, to take advantage of its multiple users features. To make the change, click on your username, then click on the Edit User button and enter the new password twice in the appropriate text fields and then the appropriate hint, if you want a reminder. Once you click on the OK button, your new password goes into effect. The Cancel button undoes the changes you've made.

Configuring a Printer

As mentioned at the start of this chapter, under all previous versions of the Mac OS, you would use the Chooser to select and configure a printer. With the departure of the Chooser, your printer choices are now made with an application called Print Center. You'll find it in the Utilities folder, within the Applications folder.

After you've located the application, follow these steps:

1. Go to the Utilities folder and double-click on the Print Center application icon to launch it.

Figure 3.32   Locate and select your Mac's default printer via the Print Center application.

2. If you have no printers selected, you'll see a dialog box (see Figure 3.32) asking if you want to add a printer. Click on the Add button.

WARNING! What happened to your networked printers? Before you can check an AppleTalk network, you need to make sure AppleTalk is turned on. It's a setting in the Network pane of the System Preferences application.

3. On the next screen, click on the Connection pop-up menu and select the network or peripheral connection on which you want to check for printers. Depending on the kind of Mac you have, you can choose from AppleTalk, LPR Printers Using IP, or USB. The Directory Services option can locate an enterprise printer located on your network. In the example shown in Figure 3.33, I chose AppleTalk to locate a printer on my Ethernet network.

4. If your printer is located in another network zone, click on the second pop-up menu to pick that zone.

5. Continue browsing for printers until they are all displayed.

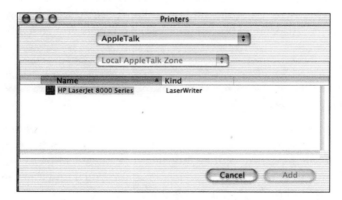

Figure 3.33   The author's laser printer as it appears in the Local AppleTalk Zone.

6. Click on the red button to close the window. At this point, all your available printers should appear in the main Printers window.

7. To select a default printer, the one normally selected when you want to print a document, click on the name of the printer to select it, then choose Make Default from the Printers menu (or just press Command+D). The name and icon of the printer will then appear at the very top of the Print Center window. However, you'll still be able to pick other printers connected to your Mac or your network, direct from the Page Setup and Print dialog boxes.

8. If you want to change your printer's custom settings, choose Setup from the Printers menu, and then select your printer's features from the dialog box. Depending on the kind of printer you have, you can configure extra paper trays, different printer resolutions, or perhaps the ability to print on both sides of the paper (also known as duplexing).

*3. Mac OS X
User Preferences*

NOTE: *Mac OS X didn't ship with PPD (Printer Page Description) files for printers other than Apple's, so you cannot configure the printer driver to recognize custom features on a PostScript printer unless you get those files. Once Mac OS X versions are available, simply locate the PPD folder. It's found within the system's Library folder, in a folder called, naturally, Printers. Without this file, the printer will handle regular letter-sized and several extra-sized pages from the default paper trays.*

---

9. You can remove a printer from the Printers window at any time by selecting the printer's name, then selecting Delete.

10. After you've completed setting your preferences, click on the close box or choose Quit from the application menu to close the program.

If you have no more printers to add, you will not see Print Center again until you actually print a document. Then, its icon will just show up in the Dock. Click on the Dock to bring up a status display of your printer queue, where you can monitor your print jobs and remove or reorder specific items. This window is very similar to the one shown in Apple's desktop printer window from earlier versions of the Mac OS.

NOTE: *The best setting for a networked printer is CPR. This setting is the one most compatible with PPD files and delivers the best performance. You'll need to consult your printer's configuration page or manual to see if you can use an IP number to access your printer.*

Chapter 4

Introducing the Mac OS X Finder

If you need an immediate solution to:	See page:
Setting Finder Preferences	81
Keeping Folder Views Consistent	81
Setting Viewing Preferences	82
Changing Finder List View Columns	84
Customizing the Finder's Toolbar	85
Using the New Finder on a Day-to-Day Basis	86
Moving a File	86
Copying a File	86
Making an Alias	87
Creating Favorites	87
Accessing Contextual Menus	87
Ejecting a Disk	87
Using the Show Info Window	88

In Brief

Although the Mac OS has been upgraded time and time again since it debuted in 1984, there has been one sole constant—the Finder, Apple's famous file access and management software. Although it has been enhanced and refined over the years, its basic look and goals have persisted substantially unchanged.

Not so with Mac OS X. The Finder (shown in Figure 4.1) has meta-morphosed into a totally new application, bearing more than a passing resemblance to the file viewer for the NeXT operating system and even some of the Mac shareware programs over the years. At the same time, however, it retains characteristics of the Finder we know and love, although some contents appear in a very different form.

NOTE: *Another application that offers a similar look in some respects is Greg's Browser. This file viewing or browsing program is produced by the folks responsible for Kaleidoscope, a popular shareware program that alters the entire appearance of the Mac with various themes.*

Aside from the function of the new Finder, there's plenty to be said about its form. Using Apple's Quartz imaging technology, the new Finder is carefully crafted from an artistic standpoint. You can drag it across the screen in realtime; the image is antialiased, with clearly defined corners that cast a shadow behind them as it is dragged across the desktop.

Despite the surprisingly new look and feel, however, you'll see that there is more than a passing resemblance to the traditional or "Classic" Mac OS Finder. The basic functions—viewing the contents of a hard drive, as well as opening, copying, and moving files—are, of course, little different despite the highly changed Aqua interface. However, in some respects, the way you look for files may be substantially changed, and as you'll see later on in this chapter, you have more options with which to customize its look and feel. To start with, look at the ways in which you can now view your files with Mac OS X's Finder. To change the display motif, simply click on one of the three small buttons at the right end of the Finder window. Here's what they do, from left to right:

- *Icon View*—This is familiar territory (see Figure 4.1); it's quite similar to the way you examine files with the original Mac Finder. Each Finder item is identified by a unique icon, ranging from the

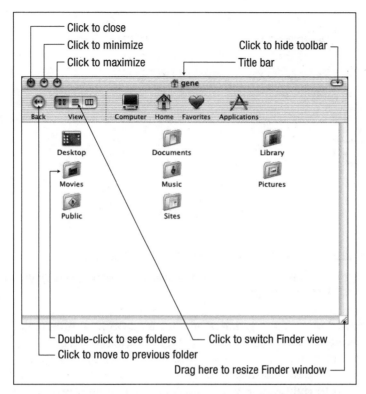

Click to close
Click to minimize
Click to maximize
Click to hide toolbar
Title bar

Double-click to see folders
Click to move to previous folder
Click to switch Finder view
Drag here to resize Finder window

Figure 4.1   The Mac OS X Finder has basic elements from the original Mac Finder, but in an entirely new uniform.

simple folder picture to a far more complicated rendering for some applications. You just double-click on any item to open it.

- *List View*—The icons in List View (see Figure 4.2) are small (unless you change the Finder option to make a larger icon, as explained in the section "Setting Viewing Preferences" later in this chapter). As with previous versions of the Mac OS, the contents of a disk or folder are displayed as a list, in four distinct categories. You can use the Finder List View preferences to add or remove categories. To open an item, just double-click on it.

TIP: It's easy to change the sorting order in List View. Just click on the title of the category under which you want the listings sorted. Normally, it's by name, but if you click on Date Modified or another category, the list will be organized in that fashion.

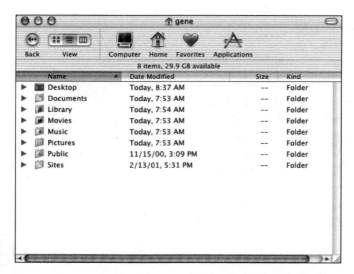

Figure 4.2   You get more items in a Finder window when you choose the List View option.

- *Column View*—This choice is new for Mac OS X, although as mentioned, it is not unfamiliar to users of the NeXTSTEP operating system or some shareware file browsing programs. It gives you a full hierarchical view of the contents of a folder, from left to right (see Figure 4.3). Just click on an item to see its contents, which are displayed at the right. If you click on a file

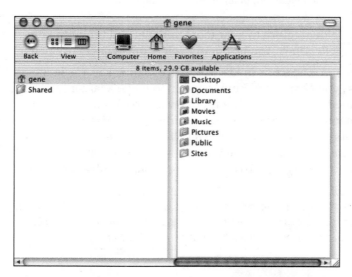

Figure 4.3   Click once on an item at the left to see the contents at the right.

or application icon, a graphic preview describing the item you selected is displayed. This viewing method is ideal for navigating deeply into nested folders without having to produce endless numbers of open folders on your Mac.

More Finder Navigation Features

After you've opened a folder, you can Command+click on the title bar to produce a pop-up menu to see the direction (path) of your folder navigation and access the higher-level folders through which you've traveled. This feature is a carryover from previous Mac OS versions. You can also move back through whatever folders you traveled through (regardless of path) if you click on the back arrow. In that sense, it works similarly to the back arrow of a Web browser.

Visiting the Finder's Toolbar

Another new feature of the Mac OS X Finder is a colorful customizable toolbar, which gives you one-click buttons (or icons) to provide fast access to specific folders, files, or other features (depending on what choices you make). We'll start with the four icons at the right of the separator bar, since the other two were explained earlier:

- *Computer*—This is the Mac OS X Finder's display for the disk icons that also inhabit the desktop (see Figure 4.4). When you click on this button, you'll see icons for available drives and a

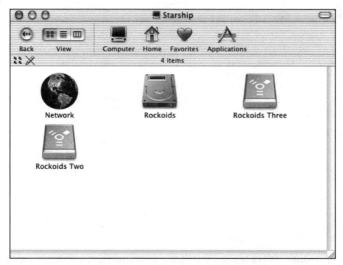

Figure 4.4   The Computer toolbar button takes you directly to your disks and servers.

Network icon, to access network or Internet-based services. The name on the title bar will reflect the name you've given your Mac.

- *Home*—The Home folder is part of the multiple-user feature of Apple's operating system. When you click on this button, you'll see the directory that contains your personal file folders. Figure 4.5 shows the standard layout, neatly categorized for convenient organization of your stuff. The Public folder is where you place files that you want to share across a network.

NOTE: *Each person who uses your Mac can get their own Home folder, as I explain further in Chapter 6.*

- *Favorites*—Probably the closest equivalent of what you could do with the late Apple menu, this locale can be used as a repository for items you want to access again and again. By default, it has aliases to your Home and Documents folders, but you can easily add more. I cover this topic in more detail in the "Immediate Solutions" section of this chapter.

- *Applications*—This folder, shown in Figure 4.6, is meant to be the repository for all your installed programs (although they can run if put elsewhere). This rigidity is useful from an organizational standpoint. This way, you don't have to go hunting all over your Mac's drive for a specific program.

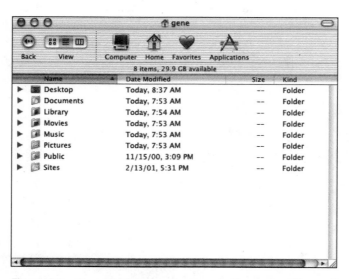

Figure 4.5   Several folders make up a user's personal Home directory under Mac OS X.

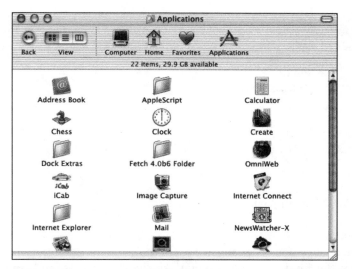

Figure 4.6   This Applications folder shows some of the standard
applications that are distributed with Mac OS X, plus a few
I've added.

NOTE: If you try to move an application from the Applications folder, it'll be copied instead. This new organization scheme can stay where they are and still function normally in the Classic environment.

TIP: Don't want the Finder's toolbar to intrude on your Mac's desktop? No problem. Just choose Hide Toolbar from the View menu, type Command+B, or click on the little oval icon in the upper right of the Finder window. If the toolbar has already been hidden, the View menu displays Show Toolbar instead; the keyboard combination stays the same. When you hide the toolbar, the Finder acts like a Classic Mac OS Finder, and double-clicking on an item spawns a new Finder window rather than producing it all in one window. Double-clicking with the Command key pressed produces the same result.

The New Finder Menus

The Mac OS Finder has had essentially the same display options from
day one. But with Mac OS X, certain elements have changed, and in
some respects, the changes are drastic. In this section, I cover the
new menu bar commands and how they differ from the previous versions of the Mac OS.

If you used the Mac OS X Public Beta, the first thing you'll notice
when you look at the menu bar is that the Apple menu has been restored (shown in Figure 4.7). In addition, the Application menu is
now situated at the left side of the menu bar rather than the right.

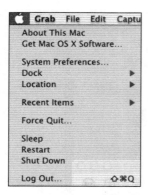

Figure 4.7   A familiar menu, but in a new guise.

Although the Apple menu looks the same, as you see from the contents, there are some big changes. Part of this is the result of the elimination of the Finder's Special menu. All the commands, and some extras, are now available system-wide in the Apple menu. This means you don't have to return to the Finder to activate these functions.

> **NOTE:** *In the initial release, it was not possible to customize the Apple menu in any way, as you could with previous Mac OS versions. This could be changed for future versions.*

Here's the list of the Apple menu features:

- *About This Mac*—Very little is different here. Choose this command to see a window displaying the Mac OS X version you are using, the amount of memory installed, and the kind of processor your Mac has. The big change is that the amount of virtual memory is no longer listed, because virtual memory is a full-time function and never turned off.

- *Get Mac OS X Software*—Select this command to be taken to a page on Apple's Web site where you can order new programs for your Mac.

- *System Preferences*—Access the System Preferences application from here.

- *Dock*—Configure the settings for the famous Dock, such as whether you'd like to hide it, magnify the icons when you pass the mouse over them, and so on. Chapter 5 covers the subject in more detail.

- *Location*—Location may be the watchword for realtors, but it's also a feature of Mac OS X that lets you customize network and Internet setups for different locales. This is especially helpful if you move your Mac from place to place (invaluable with an iBook or PowerBook). Chapter 8 covers this in more detail.

- *Recent Items*—A carryover from the Apple Menu Options software of previous Mac OS versions, it displays up to five recent applications and documents in the submenu, with no way to change these settings.

- *Special menu items*—The remaining five items—Force Quit—Sleep, Restart, Shut Down, and Log Out—are Special menu-type commands moved to the Apple menu for convenient access without returning to the Finder. You can also access Force Quit via the Command+Option+Esc keystroke.

TIP: *Commands with one or more letters beginning with the Command (or Apple) key are keyboard shortcuts you can use to access a feature without using the mouse.*

Following is a list of how the remaining menus have changed:

- *Application menu*—As mentioned, the application menu has been moved. In addition, the name of an application is now in bold (see Figure 4.8) for clear identification. When you click on the application menu, you'll see commands that apply to that program. Some programs also include a Services submenu (but not the Finder), which has direct links to programs that extend the features of the one you're using. You can use the various hide options to hide the program in which you're working or to hide other programs for a cleaner desktop. The biggest change is the Quit command; it has now moved from the File menu to what Apple feels is a more logical location—the application menu. the Empty Trash is also found under the Finder.

NOTE: *Older, or "Classic" Mac applications will still have their Quit commands in the File menu, and it's possible some of the Mac OS X-savvy applications will, as well, at least in their preliminary versions.*

Figure 4.8   The Finder's application menu has new features for Mac OS X.

TIP: *If you hold down the Option key while selecting another application's window, all windows for other programs are hidden from view; the exceptions are applications that run in the Mac OS 9 or Classic environment. The Show All feature in the Application menu reverses the effect. This feature works the same as in earlier versions of the Mac OS.*

- *File menu*—The Finder's File menu (see Figure 4.9) isn't much different from the one in Mac OS 9. The big change is the replacement of the Get Info window with the Show Info window. It has some of the same functions, plus some new ones I'll get to shortly. The other notable changes include: Command+N now produces a new Finder window, and the keyboard command for a new folder is now Command+Shift+N. To make an alias, you type Command+L (it was Command+M previously). You now use Command+M to minimize a window and consign it to the Dock. (Don't ask me to explain the wisdom of changing things in this fashion; I just work here.)

- *Edit menu*—Some things have remained nearly the same. The Edit menu, shown in Figure 4.10) is functionally identical to the Edit menu of older versions of the Mac OS.

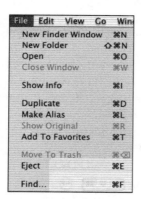

Figure 4.9   New keyboard commands and a new Show Inspector window highlight major changes to the Finder's File menu.

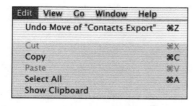

Figure 4.10   The contents of Mac OS X's Edit menu have not changed from the one in Mac OS 9.

- *View menu*—The first three options (see Figure 4.11) simply mirror those available in the Finder itself. You can select to view items as columns, as icons, or as a list. The other choices let you hide a Finder window's toolbar, customize the toolbar, or set view options. I explain the latter in detail later in this chapter.

- *Go menu*—This menu appears to inherit at least some parts of the original Apple menu in Mac OS X (see Figure 4.12). The first five choices mirror the standard toolbar options in the Finder, plus add the ability to bring up your iDisk, part of Apple's iTools feature. The Recent Folders option provides a submenu of recent Finder folders you've accessed. Another new command to the mix—Go To Folder—lets you type the actual path of a folder in order to bring it up. An example would be "/users/<*your username*>", which would immediately transport you to your Home directory. The Connect To Server option is used to access a shared volume, whether it's on a local network or on the Internet.

- *Window menu*—This menu is found in many applications. It first appeared in Mac OS 9.1 and has been carried over to X's Finder (see Figure 4.13). The first option—Minimize Window—shrinks an application or Finder window to the Dock. Bring All To Front

Figure 4.11 Choose the manner in which Finder contents are displayed from this menu.

Figure 4.12 This is a convenient jumping point for a number of areas on your hard drive, directly from the Finder.

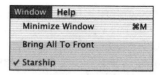

Figure 4.13   Adjust the display of Finder windows from this menu.

makes all open Finder windows accessible (you'll use this option if the windows were previously hidden from view). The items at the bottom of the display are the names of the Finder windows presently open. Select the one you want to bring to the front.

NOTE: *If the active application is the Desktop, the minimize command is grayed out.*

- *Help menu*—This menu is just what the name implies. Most of the information that Apple provides about Mac OS X is situated here, rather than in a printed document. (It's rather skeletal, but at least you have this book to learn the rest.)

Immediate Solutions

Setting Finder Preferences

As with any feature of Mac OS X, there's no need to customize or alter the new Finder in any way. You can continue to use it in its pristine form if you prefer, running applications on your Mac, surfing the Net, and so on without needing to alter the appearance. But there are many ways to customize the look and feel.

By default, the Mac OS X Finder displays its contents in single-window mode. You open the contents of a folder in the Finder, and it replaces the contents in the window with the contents of the opened folder. If you want to change this to how it worked with the previous Mac OS, where it would open a new Finder window, you can take any of the actions described in the following sections.

Keeping Folder Views Consistent

This preference setting establishes the default behavior when you double-click on a folder icon to open it. Just follow these instructions:

1. Choose Preferences from the Finder's application menu, which brings up the Finder Preferences window shown in Figure 4.14.

2. Click on the Keep The Same View When You Open A Folder In The Same Window checkbox at the bottom of the window.

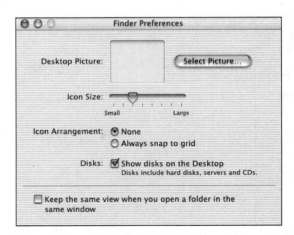

Figure 4.14 Select the way the Finder displays the contents of an opened folder.

3. Click on the red light button to close the window and save your preferences. From here on, all folder windows opened within a Finder window will inherit the same view setting, whether icon, list, or column view.

NOTE: *No, I didn't miss the other preference settings. I cover the rest of the Finder Preferences options in Chapter 5, since they relate to how the desktop is displayed.*

If you don't want to make a permanent change in the way an opened folder displays, just hold down the Option key to reverse the behavior when you double-click on a folder icon. That way, you can decide on the fly whether a new Finder window is opened.

Setting Viewing Preferences

As with the previous Mac OS Finder, you can set the way items show up in the Finder, but your options are far more extensive under Mac OS X. Settings can be made on a global basis, where they apply to all open Finder windows and all display categories or to a specific Finder window.

1. Go to the View menu and choose Show View Options, or type Command+J. The window shown in Figure 14.15 appears.

2. If it's not already selected, click on the Global tab, and then select Global Icon from the View pop-up menu. You have three categories of changes you can make to the Finder's display, as described in the following list:

Figure 4.15   Click on a tab to set the options under that category.

- *Icon Size*—By default, icons are fairly large—at least compared to older versions of the Mac OS. You can move the slider to change it as you look. The changes will be reflected in all open Finder windows.

- *Icon Arrangement*—Whether you like your desktop automatically arranged or not, the choice is yours. Just click on the appropriate radio button. The default—None—means you can place your disk, file, and folder icons as you wish, anywhere in a Finder window. The Snap To Grid option is similar to what you find in some drawing programs. The icons are spaced by an invisible grid, at fixed distances apart. The final option—Keep Arranged By—gives you a pop-up menu of sort sequences. Choose from Name, Date Modified, Date Created, Size, Kind, or Label.

- *Folder Background*—This Finder feature is new for Mac OS X. You can leave it at None if you prefer. Otherwise, you can give your Finder background a unique color by clicking on the Color radio box, then on the box at the right to bring up an Apple Color Picker (see Figure 4.16). After you click on the kind of color adjustments you want, moving the sliders with the mouse changes the selected colors. When you click on the final option—Picture—press the Select button to bring up the Open dialog box, where you can choose a picture instead.

After you've made your settings, you can click on the close button to activate the changes. Or, you can go to the next section if you want to make further changes.

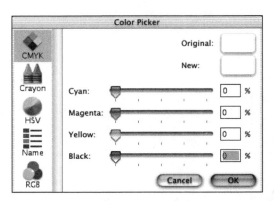

Figure 4.16 Drag sliders to produce a color scheme that suits your taste.

3. If you prefer the Finder's List View, you'll want to make some additional settings. Choose Global List from the View pop-up menu (see Figure 4.17). Then, select a checkbox that applies to the specific list item you want displayed or deselect the option you want removed. The final setting on this screen sets either a small or large icon size.

4. If you want to apply list preferences for a single Finder window, just select the Window tab, which brings up a List View window nearly identical to the one shown in Figure 4.17.

5. When you're finished setting Finder preferences, click on the Close button.

Changing Finder List View Columns

The new Mac OS Finder can be customized extensively in List View. In addition to adjusting preferences as to which categories are displayed, you can further modify it in two ways:

- *Resize Category Lists*—Move the mouse between the columns and you'll see the cursor change to reflect two opposite pointed arrows. Then, simply click and drag the column to resize it. The change you make is reflected in all new Finder windows.

- *Change Order Of Categories*—You can also move an entire category into a new position in the Finder window. Just click and drag the Finder category to its new location, and let go of the mouse button. This change can be made in all categories except

Figure 4.17   Select the view options you want.

name. After a category is in a new position, the change is reflected in all new Finder windows.

Customizing the Finder's Toolbar

In addition to hiding the Finder's toolbar, if you prefer the old ways of the Mac OS—the ability to open a folder and spawn a new Finder window—you can customize the toolbar in a variety of ways. Here's how it's done:

1. Choose Customize Toolbar from the Finder's View menu. This brings up a convenient window displaying lots of cool icons (see Figure 4.18).

2. To add an icon, drag it to the toolbar. You can use the Separator icon to categorize your selections.

NOTE: *If you add too many icons, you can drag the resize bar to the right to make the Finder window wider; otherwise, it will leave an arrow at the end of the toolbar that you can click on to access the remaining icons.*

3. If you want to limit the toolbar icon to either the icon or the text, make your choices from the Show pop-up menu at the bottom of the screen.

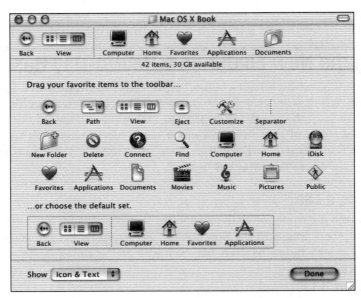

Figure 4.18   I've added a Documents icon to the toolbar.

TIP: *If you make a mistake and put the wrong icon in the toolbar, you can click and drag it to a new position.*

---

4. Click the Done button to complete the process.

NOTE: *To restore the toolbar to factory issue, you can click the default set on the Customize Toolbar screen and drag it to the toolbar. It'll replace the contents.*

TIP: *Don't fret if the icon you want to add isn't shown. You can drag and drop any application, file, or folder icon onto the Finder's toolbar to have it immediately added.*

After you've changed the toolbar, you can remove an icon by holding down the Command key and dragging the icon off the toolbar. The default toolbar icons, however, cannot be removed this way. They can only be removed when you bring up the Customize Toolbar screen.

TIP: *One useful icon in the Customize Toolbar screen is the Path icon. When you add that, a click on it will show the folder path of the item you've selected, which lets you quickly move to higher folder levels. Of course, holding down the Command key and clicking on the title of a Finder window gets the same result.*

Using the New Finder on a Day-to-Day Basis

After you have the Finder configured the way you want, you'll find that it's easy to get accustomed to the new way of handling your Mac's files and even the restricted organizational requirements. In the remaining pages of this chapter, I cover basic file management techniques. For the most part, you'll see they aren't terribly different from earlier versions of the Mac OS.

Moving a File

To move a file from one folder to another, simply click on it to select the file, then drag it to the new folder. You might need to open another Finder window to move between widely disparate folders.

Copying a File

To copy a file from one folder to another, hold down the Option key as the file is being dragged to its new location. This copying function is automatic if you are moving an icon from one drive's folder to a folder on another drive.

Making an Alias

An alias is a pointer to the original file that aids in file navigation (it's similar to a shortcut in Windows). You can put the alias where you want without having to depend on Mac OS X's organizational structure for applications and other files. Many Mac users place aliases for files on the desktop, putting them a double-click away from launching without having to burrow deep through nested folders.

To make an alias, simply select the item, then choose Make Alias from the Finder's File menu, or type Command+L. The alias can then be moved or copied to your preferred location.

TIP: *To make an alias of an item and move it at the same time, simply drag it to its new location while holding down the Command and Option keys.*

Creating Favorites

The Favorites folder is a great place to keep the documents you use over and over again. To make an item appear in that folder, just select it, then choose Add To Favorites from the Finder's File menu, or type Command+T.

Accessing Contextual Menus

This feature, which debuted with Mac OS 8, produces a pop-up menu related to the item selected. It's quite similar to the right-mouse feature of Windows. To access the contextual menu, just select an item and hold down the Control key.

NOTE: *Some third-party input devices have extra buttons that you can program to access the contextual menus. This will be familiar territory for Windows users.*

Ejecting a Disk

This function works the same as in previous versions of the Mac OS, with a small exception. The normal behavior is to drag the disk icon to the Trash. You can also type Command+E. The Put Away command (Command+Y) has been removed. When you drag a disk icon to the Trash, the icon for the Trash changes to an eject symbol.

Using the Show Info Window

In older versions of the Mac OS, you'd use the Finder's Get Info window to adjust a program's memory allotment and get information about a program's version. For Mac OS X, there's a Show Info window (see Figure 4.19) with one key feature no longer present: the ability to change the memory given to a program. That's no longer necessary under Mac OS X, because the operating system dynamically allocates the memory a program requires. Here are the basic features:

- *General Information*—This screen presents general information about a selected item, including its location. If you've selected an application, it shows the version information.

- *Application*— If you've selected a document, you'll see an Application menu, where you can change the application that opens that document.

- *Preview*—This feature only appears when you select a document icon. You can use it to view a preview image of the document.

NOTE: If the icon you've selected belongs to a Classic application, all you'll see is an enlarged picture of its icon.

- *Sharing*—Use this window to set access privileges to the selected item. That way, you can extend the range of users who can view that item via file sharing.

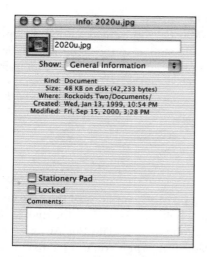

Figure 4.19   The Show Info window lets you access information about a file or change the application that will automatically open a document.

Chapter 5

Mac OS X
Desktop Management

If you need an immediate solution to:	See page:
Setting Dock & Desktop Preferences	96
Using the Dock	100
Making Your Mac OS X Desktop as Cluttered as Ever	101

In Brief

The Mac OS X desktop looks similar to the one from previous versions. There's a decorative pattern and, unlike the versions of the new operating system that were shown during the development process, the familiar icons for your hard drive are present. But something appears to be missing. Where's the trash? As you've probably noticed, it's migrated to the Dock, which, in part, forms the main subject to be dealt with in this chapter.

The pristine desktop is part of the normal behavior of Mac OS X, but as you'll see in this chapter, it's not necessary to keep things neat and clean. One of the rights of the Mac user is to arrange, even clutter up, a desktop to one's taste, and the new Mac operating system, as with the Classic Mac OS, gives you lots of freedom to change background images and clutter it with icons to a fare-thee-well.

The Dock Dissected

In previous versions of the Mac OS, there were several ways to access a file quickly, whether a document, a folder, or a program. Apple has merged a number of these functions into a single program—a colorful, almost cartoonish, and almost infinitely resizable palette of icons that resides at the bottom of your Mac's display. It's called the Dock (see Figure 5.1).

Here's what the Dock replaces:

- *Apple menu*—Although the original Apple menu (see Figure 5.2) was the former repository of frequently used items, Control Panel access and immense customization. It was customized fairly easily, but doing so required a trip to the System Folder, and then to another folder called Apple Menu Items. For Mac OS X, the Apple menu has gotten an overhaul, after disappearing entirely in prerelease versions (see Figure 5.3). It now incorporates the

Figure 5.1   The Dock is a single location where you check and open applications, documents, and folders. Note the white separation line to divide the Dock into two usually unequal parts.

Figure 5.2   The original Apple menu was infinitely customizable and was easily set to reflect the tastes of its user.

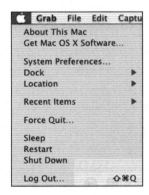

Figure 5.3   The new Apple menu is designed in a more rigid fashion, merging the old and the new, and replacing the functions of the Finder's Special menu.

functions of the Finder's Special menu, system-wide customization and just the core of the recent items features of the previous version. The list of recent folders has been moved to the Go menu, as explained in Chapter 4. Control Panels have been replaced by the System Preferences application, which consolidates the various system settings into one program; it gets a featured spot in the Dock. I covered this subject of setting your Mac OS preferences in detail in Chapter 3.

- *Control Strip*—Some Control Panel functions and settings for a number of applications were put in the Control Strip (see Figure 5.4), a floating palette that first debuted as a feature on the Apple PowerBook. It later spread to all Macs. Some of the functionality has been rolled into the System Preferences application and the Dock can accept extra modules (Dock Extras) that mimic the functions of Control Strip modules.

- *Application menu*—Part of the function of working with open applications stays in the menu bar, with the bold Application menu now at the left of the screen. The ability to switch between open applications is now a function of the Dock.

NOTE: *If you prefer something more akin to the Control Strip of old, don't despair. There are plenty of opportunities for independent programmers to get in the game. A shareware program, OpenStrip is meant to replace some of the functions of the original Mac OS Control Strip. It's also possible that Apple will ultimately adopt a shareware program of one sort or another as standard issue in Mac OS to add functions. Apple Menu Options, the menu bar clock, Extensions Manager, and the Window Shade feature were originally shareware before Apple acquired them in the mid-1990s for use with the Classic Mac OS.*

The Dock is divided into two parts, and some of the icons have clearly identifiable functions. Here's a description of how they work:

- *Left side*—Application icons, including those representing open programs, stay here (see Figure 5.5).

- *Right side*—Icons representing documents, folders, servers, Web sites, QuickTime TV channels, and the famous Mac OS Trash exist on the right end of the Dock (see Figure 5.6).

Figure 5.4   Depending on the programs you have installed on your Mac, the contents of the Control Strip.

Figure 5.5   The items at this end of the Dock consist strictly of applications. Those with the triangles beneath are open.

Figure 5.6   The rest of the icons you put in the Dock reside at the right, regardless of political content.

Figure 5.7   This icon represents the Finder.

- *Desktop*—Click on this icon to open a Finder window (see Figure 5.7).
- *System Preferences*—As part of the Dock when you've installed Mac OS X, this icon allows you to set your Mac's preferences (see Figure 5.8). It replaces the Control Panels, at least in part.

TIP: Missing an icon? Although several application and document icons are part of the standard installation of Mac OS X, it's easy to drag them off the Dock. If you want them back, just locate the original icon for that item, and drag it back to the Dock.

- *Mail*—This icon represents Apple's powerful new email software (see Figure 5.9). When you receive email, you'll see a display on the Mail icon indicating the number of unread messages waiting for you. I'll cover this program in detail in Chapter 21.
- *Document*—This icon represents a document that's been placed in the Dock (see Figure 5.10).

Figure 5.8   Click on this icon to launch the System Preferences application.

Figure 5.9   This icon represents Apple's Mac OS X exclusive email software.

Figure 5.10   When you add documents to the Dock, they'll look something like this.

**5. Mac OS X
Desktop Management**

- *Web Sites and Servers*—Another great feature of the Dock is the ability to store icons that link you to your favorite Web sites or provide direct access to a networked server (see Figure 5.11).

- *Minimized Window*—When you click on the minimize icon in an open document window, it shrinks to the Dock (see Figure 5.12). It remains here until you click it to restore or maximize the document window. Unfortunately the process is for effect only, and Apple's screen capture utility, Grab, isn't able to photograph it for us. A Command+M, by the way, will also minimize a window.

TIP: *If you want to see the ultraslow "genie effect" demonstrated at Macworld Expos by Apple CEO Steve Jobs, hold down the Shift key when minimizing a document. You'll see the reverse effect with the same keyboard shortcut when clicking on an icon representing a minimized document in the Dock.*

- *Trash*—The famous Mac OS Trash is no longer a resident of the desktop (see Figure 5.13). It now always sits at the right end of the Dock.

- *Dock Items*—The latest variation on those famous Control Strip icons, a file with the Dock extension can be placed in the Dock and provide immediate display of such things as monitor resolution, battery life for iBooks and PowerBooks, and signal strength for an AirPort network.

Figure 5.11   Whether a networked server or a favorite Web site, it's just a click away in the Dock.

Figure 5.12   The famous "genie effect" ends with the icon residing in the Dock.

Figure 5.13   The Trash gets a new home for Mac OS X.

- *Pop-up Menus*—Click on any item in the Dock and hold down the mouse button. In seconds, you'll see a pop-up menu related to that item. For a Dock item, you'll see control functions you can access, such as display resolution. The best effect occurs when you click on a disk or folder icon (see Figure 5.14). The end result is a menu with lots of submenus, similar in scope to what you used to see in the Apple menu. The display for a regular application is more pedestrian. Click on the icon and you'll have a Show in Finder command. If the application is open you'll be able to quit the program from the pop-up menu.

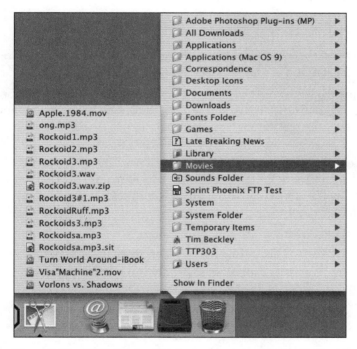

Figure 5.14   Up to five levels of pop-up menus can be displayed when you click and hold a folder or disk icon in the Dock.

Immediate Solutions

The Mac OS X desktop is ripe for changing, and you'll be pleased to know it's quite possible to organize it in many ways depending on your particular needs. In the following pages, I'll describe the various desktop preferences and then cover how you can tailor your Mac's desktop to resemble the one used in prior versions of the Mac OS, or in ways you might not have imagined before.

Setting Dock & Desktop Preferences

In Chapter 4, I covered the Finder portion of the Dock & Desktop preferences, and now I'll give you, as long-time radio broadcaster Paul Harvey says, the rest of the story. You can follow these steps to change the way your Mac's desktop and the Dock functions:

1. To change Dock settings, choose Dock from the Apple menu and select Dock Preferences from the submenu. This brings up the Dock settings pane from the System Preferences application (see Figure 5.15).

2. Set the following four Dock preferences:

   - *Dock Size*—This setting lets you configure the size of the icons by moving the slider back and forth. You're apt to find that the Dock is just too imposing on your Mac's screen

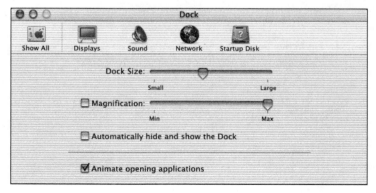

Figure 5.15   Change the look of the Dock here.

except for a very large display, so you'll probably want to make it smaller.

TIP: *You can also resize the Dock by clicking and dragging the bar on the Dock that separates applications from documents up or down. If you hold down the Option key while resizing the Dock, it'll default to fixed-sized icons, such as 32 pixels, 64 pixels, and 128 pixels. Otherwise, the adjustments are infinitely variable.*

- *Magnification*—Select this checkbox to make the Dock magnify the icons as you drag the mouse over them (see Figure 5.16). It looks flashy, but it may be a little bit much after you use it for a while. The slider bar lets you decide just how much the icons will expand.

- *Automatically Hide and Show the Dock*—The Dock sits above your open application windows, and you cannot grab anything beneath it, so this adjustment may be a great convenience. It's also a good way to save screen real estate. The Dock stays hidden unless you drag the mouse to the bottom of the screen to make it visible. You'll find this adjustment particularly useful for a smaller Mac's display.

TIP: *You can also make the Dock hide itself when the mouse isn't near by pressing Command+Option+D.*

- *Animate Opening Applications*—When this feature is shown at a presentation, it looks cool, but the idea of having an application's icon bounce up and down in the Dock may grow tiresome. You can switch it off here and just wait a while for programs to open for you without warning.

3. After you've set your Dock preferences, click on the close box to dismiss the System Preferences application.

4. To change Finder desktop settings, choose Finder Preferences from the Finder's application menu. The dialog box shown in Figure 5.17 appears.

Figure 5.16   The Dock's icons magnify when you drag your mouse over them.

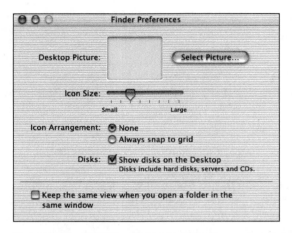

Figure 5.17   Alter the Mac's desktop appearance here.

Here you can make four types of changes:

- *Desktop Picture*—Similar to the feature available in earlier versions of the Mac OS, for this option, you just click on the Select Picture button to bring up an Open dialog box. Then you select the picture. Such standard graphic formats as GIF, JPEG, and TIFF are supported. When you select the picture, it magically appears on your desktop; smaller pictures are tiled to cover the entire backdrop. See Figure 5.18 for a telling example. Just click on the Remove Picture button if you prefer to return to the original design or choose an alternative.

- *Icon Size*—If the default icon size is too big for you, just click and drag the slider to change it to your taste. If you want to go back to the original size, however, you'll have to depend on memory alone. There's no "defaults" button.

- *Icon Arrangement*—Whether you like your desktop neat, cluttered, or somewhere in between, here's where you select how your Mac's desktop icons are arranged. The default radio button, None, allows you to place an icon anywhere on the desktop and have it remain there until it's moved. The second setting, Always Snap To Grid, automatically sets the icons on an invisible placeholder, at fixed distances.

TIP: An interesting arrangement is a hybrid setting, where you set some icons to a specific grid setting, then turn off the option under Desktop preferences so the remainder of your icons can be placed anywhere on the desktop you like.

Figure 5.18 I've selected this photo depicting a character in one of my science fiction novels.

• *Disks*—Leave the checkbox selected if you want to accept the Show Disks on the Desktop feature. This will place all disks, including your Mac's hard drive, networked volumes, and CDs on the desktop. Unchecking it will limit access to the Computer button on the Finder or the similar command in the Finder's Go menu.

5. If you want to go further and set the entire range of Finder preferences, refer to Chapter 4 for more information. When you're done, just click on the Close button to dismiss the Finder Preferences screen.

Using the Dock

In day-to-day use, the Dock is highly intuitive. It provides clear status messages about your open applications and documents, and it can be, as explained previously, customized in many ways for your convenience. Here are some basic hints and tips for getting the maximum value out of the Dock:

- *Adding icons*—Because the Dock expands dynamically to accommodate the number of icons you've added, all you need to do is drag the icon to the Dock to have it display (the actual file, of course, remains where it was). The left side of the Dock carries your application icons. The right side handles the rest, such as documents, folders, links to servers and Web sites, and QuickTime channels. You can't put the wrong icon in the wrong side; the icon will only be accepted in the proper side of the Dock.

> **NOTE:** *Icons in the Dock are not automatically sorted for you. You can click and drag them to new positions, depending on whether you prefer alphabetical order or some random sequence.*

- *Application switching*—As explained earlier, open applications are indicated by a black triangle below the application's icon in the Dock. Just click once on the icon of any opened application in the Dock to move directly to that program.

> **TIP:** *To hide all other open application windows when opening up a new one from the Dock, hold down the Command+Option keys while clicking on any application icon. Hold down the Option key to hide just the application window from which you're switching. The Show All command in the Desktop application menu brings them back.*

> **TIP:** *You can use the keyboard to switch between open applications. Just press the Command+Tab keys. Upon release, the next open application appears. To reverse the process, press Command+Shift+Tab.*

- *Single-click access*—Just like the Launcher in older versions of the Mac OS, you can access any item in the Dock with a single click.

- *Reordering icons*—To change the order of an icon in the Dock, click and drag it to its new position. You cannot, of course, put application icons on the right end of the Dock, but otherwise, feel free to reorder items as you prefer.

NOTE: *Did the application icon disappear? Some applications, such as Mac OS X's Print Center, only stay open as long as the print queue has a job being processed. After the processing is finished, the application automatically quits. It may take a few moments, however, for the actual document to finish, depending on the speed and the need for extra processing by the output device itself. The same vanishing effect holds true for the Classic environment; the Mac OS 9 icon vanishes when Classic has loaded (even though it remains active).*

- *Removing icons*—Did you change your mind? You can discard a Dock icon you no longer need. Just click and drag it away from the Dock. In just a second it'll disappear in a puff of smoke, like magic.

Dock Scripts

Among the handy features of the Mac OS is AppleScript, a way to add system-wide automation. In Chapter 9, I'll cover the subject in more detail. In the meantime, if you want to give it a try, consider checking Apple's AppleScript Web site (**www.apple.com/applescript**). There are several handy scripts available that will allow you to modify the Dock setup in several ways, including creating a brand new Dock Setup, which allows you to recall a specific set of icons at will.

Making Your Mac OS X Desktop as Cluttered as Ever

One of the good or bad features of Mac OS X, depending on your point of view, is the new desktop. Depending on your needs, it can be clean and uncluttered, when you remove those disk icons. However, if you leave them intact, you are well on your way toward producing the requisite degree of disorder.

My Mac's desktop, under Mac OS 9.1, traditionally has about 100 items on it, ranging from mounted drives and available desktop printers, to files I need to send to my son's computer for our joint writing projects, to folders containing recent downloads, and just files that I need to access…well, one of these days. Every so often, I put most of these files in another folder called, with no attempt at originality at all, Desktop Icons. The desktop is clear, at least for a few days, after which it becomes just as cluttered as before.

Apple has made a concerted effort to organize your desktop and file organization patterns under Mac OS X. The desktop is clear as water,

5. Mac OS X Desktop Management

unless you decide to pollute it with some icons. Here's how to return your Mac's desktop to its former glory:

1. In Mac OS X's rigid organizational system, applications are meant for the Applications folder and documents for the Documents folder. Mac OS X-savvy applications are meant to stay put, but if you hold down the Command+Option keys and drag the icon to the desktop, an alias is placed there.

NOTE: *The Command+Option shortcut also works with all files and Classic applications.*

---

2. After your application icons are on the desktop, go ahead and locate your favorite document files and place them there as well. A few minutes of clicking and dragging and, presto (see Figure 5.19), your Mac OS X desktop can be as cluttered as you wish, precisely as it was in previous versions of the Mac OS.

Figure 5.19   If your taste is for a busy Mac desktop, don't worry. Mac OS X will not prevent you from organizing it the way you want.

Chapter 6

Setting Up Mac OS X for Multiple Users

If you need an immediate solution to:	See page:
Setting Up Multiple-User Access	108
Editing a User Account	110
Setting Up Keychain Access	111
Checking and Using Your Keychain	113
Changing Keychain Settings	113
Running a Keychain on Another Mac	114
Coping with Problems Involving Keychains and Multiple Users	115
Setting Up Multiple Users for Use with Children	116

In Brief

Beginning with Mac OS 9, Apple introduced a Multiple Users feature. It was an outgrowth of AtEase, a no-frills security program that allowed the owners of Macs to create a simplified user environment for children and inexperienced users. The program was popular in the educational environment because it gave teachers and systems administrators the ability to restrict student access to certain files and disks on the Macs in their classrooms and computer labs.

NOTE: *In addition to being offered in workgroup form for network use, AtEase was bundled as standard equipment on many of Apple's mid-1990s consumer computers in the Performa series.*

Mac OS X extends the Multiple Users feature on a more professional level, allowing any Mac user with appropriate access privileges to easily configure his or her computer to offer a customized user experience. The great value of this feature is that it allows users to restrict access to system-related adjustments and even to restrict rights to read files or copy files to removable media. Each user can customize their Mac's desktop and Finder appearance to their needs without impacting the settings made by other users.

Mac OS X Multiple Users Features

Because it is based on Unix, Mac OS X is, at heart, a multiple-user system, and thus some of the features are similar to those introduced in Mac OS 9. Mac OS X has its own unique variation, which is that you cannot turn off the feature. However, once you get used to the differences, you'll find that Mac OS X provides a secure working environment with lots of options to help you set it up for all the people who will use your Mac.

NOTE: *Not all multiple-user features available in Mac OS 9 have been carried over to the new operating system. For example, the ability to create limited-function interfaces isn't present. Customization and access settings are limited to the standard Aqua user interface.*

Here are some of the basic features of Mac OS X that provide customized user environments and security:

- *Owner as administrator*—When you first install Mac OS X, you'll establish your user account as the administrator of the computer. After you've set up your username and password, you can add users to and remove users from your system, and you can unlock and use certain system preferences that are available to only the administrators (see Figure 6.1). These preferences include: Date & Time, Energy Saver, Login, Network, Password, Sharing, Startup Disk, and Users. You'll learn more about using these preference settings in Chapter 3.

NOTE: *Items in the System Preferences application that can be accessed by only the administrator are always identified by a padlock icon. In large installations, it is usually recommended that a dummy account, separate from the administrator's real user account, be created for systems administration.*

- *Keychains*—If you use a number of different passwords to access your Internet accounts, online ordering and banking services, and various applications and server connections, no doubt you have to keep a record or memorize many passwords. It's very easy to forget those passwords and thus lose your access to programs and services. With Apple's Keychain Access application (see Figure 6.2), located in the Utilities folder, you can store all those disparate passwords in a single location—called a *keychain*—and just enter a single password to access all of them. Only you or someone with your password can unlock those passwords. When they're unlocked, applications and services that need those passwords can get them as needed, but casual users cannot see them. When you finish using them, you just lock your keychain.

NOTE: *In order for a keychain to work, the application for which you want to store a keychain must support that feature. Not all do, so you'll want to check the appropriate documentation to see which Mac OS X features are supported before you attempt to use your passwords stored in a keychain.*

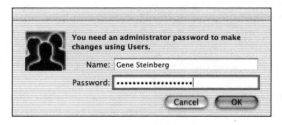

Figure 6.1   When you click the padlock icon, you must enter your administrator's username and password to gain access to certain Mac OS X features and System Preferences settings.

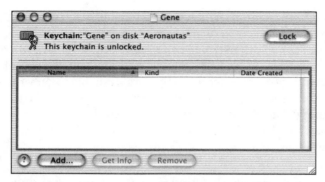

Figure 6.2   You can use the Keychain Access application to set up your personal account and store all your user passwords inside.

- *Shared folders*—All users who have accounts on your Mac have their own personal user folders for their own sets of applications, documents, system-related preferences, fonts, Internet accounts, and so on. These files are available to only the administrator or the individual user who logs into that user account, unless additional sharing privileges are granted. The Shared folder, however, serves as a place where you can put files and make them available to anyone who accesses your Mac. That way, those users do not need special access privileges. You can also establish a Drop Box folder, where other users can place files, but only the individual user (who created the Drop Box) or the administrator can access the files inside.

NOTE: *The Shared folder is also used as a location where users who access your Mac from across a network can send and receive files. You'll want to read Chapter 8 for information on how to configure network file-sharing privileges so that access to a Public folder is restricted.*

- *System logins*—When you log out, only a user with a valid username and password can use your Mac. That rule provides the maximum possible degree of security for system-related access. However, if you are the sole user of the Mac, and you have no qualms about letting others, perhaps family members or coworkers, work on your Mac, you can continue to bypass the Login prompt at startup. I'll explain more about this subject in Chapter 3.

WARNING! *Although you need the proper password to access a Mac under Mac OS X, there's nothing to prevent you from restarting your computer under Mac OS 9, or with a Mac OS 9 startup disk, and then gaining access to files in that environment. If maximum security is important to you, you'll want to set up the Multiple Users feature* *of Mac OS 9 as well so that users cannot casually access your Mac. Additionally, it would be a good idea to hide system startup CDs (and third-party utilities, such as Norton Utilities, come with bootable CDs too) so that access cannot be gained in that fashion.*

- *Dedicated security software*—Under previous versions of the Mac OS, a number of dedicated security programs were available from such publishers as ASD Software and PowerOn Software. Although these programs have not yet been updated for Mac OS X, no doubt there will be updates forthcoming from PowerOn. ASD has indicated that it is not planning to update its security software for the new operating system. Regardless of which program you choose, however, you'll find that it can totally lock out your Mac from access from different operating systems or from external or CD-based startup disks. For the highest level of security in a workplace, you might want to seek out further information about the availability of such programs.

Using Strong Passwords

If you are running your Mac in a family environment or in a small office, you might not have to be overly concerned about your choice of passwords, because it might not be a critical issue if another user in your environment works on your Mac. But if you need the maximum amount of security, you'll want to use a password that is difficult for others to guess. The best password is a random combination of upper and lowercase letters intermixed with numbers. That way, it would be extremely hard for anyone to guess your particular password, and thus you have the maximum level of security. Because of its Unix underpinnings, passwords in Mac OS X are limited to eight characters.

6. Setting Up Mac OS X for Multiple Users

WARNING! Once you set up your Mac with Mac OS X, there is no way to gain user access without the proper password. Even if you use the Login preference panel to bypass a password request at startup, many features will not be available to you until you can manually enter that password. Should you forget it, you will have to reset your password using the Password Reset utilitiy that is available on the Mac OS X Installer application. Chapter 19 explains how.

Immediate Solutions

Setting Up Multiple-User Access

Each user of your Mac can be given his or her own personal password and user environment. This allows each user to set, within the guidelines you establish, a custom set of fonts, user preferences, applications, and documents.

Follow these steps to create a new user account:

1. Launch the System Preferences application. You'll find it on the Dock or in the Applications folder.

2. Click on the Users icon to bring up the Users Settings panel (see Figure 6.3).

3. If the padlock is closed, click on the padlock to open it, and enter the username and password for your administrator account.

4. With the padlock opened, click on the New User button or press Command+N. This opens the dialog box shown in Figure 6.4.

5. In the Name field, type the actual name of the new user.

6. In the Short Name field, type a username (nickname). By default, Mac OS X will suggest a possible username based on a shortened version of the real name.

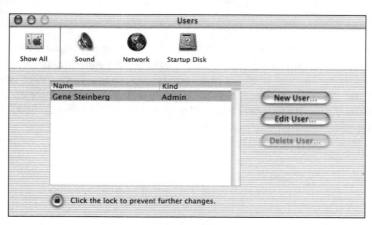

Figure 6.3   Establish a new user account from this dialog box.

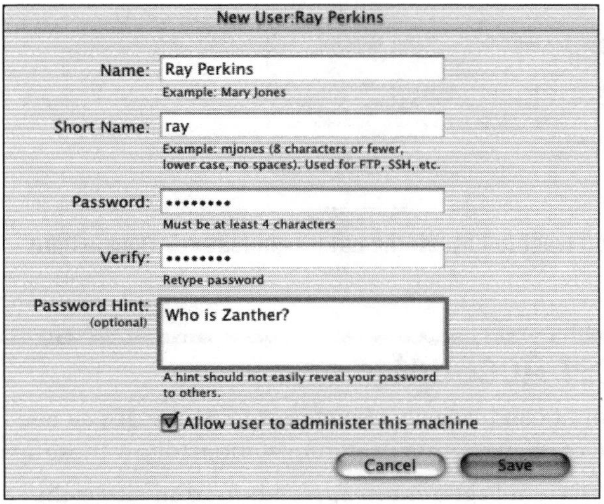

Figure 6.4   Create a new user account on your Mac here.

7. In the Password field, type a password of up to eight characters for the user. Then retype the password in the Verify field. If the password isn't accepted, retype it again. It has to be entered the same way in both places.

8. If you want a helpful reminder about a forgotten password, enter a question in the Password Hint text field (but don't make it so obvious that a third party can guess it).

9. If you want to give the user the authority to act as administrator for that Mac, click on the checkbox at the bottom of the dialog box.

WARNING! Before allowing another user to act as administrator for your Mac, consider carefully whether you really want to grant those access privileges to someone else (other than a family member, of course). Remember that any user who can log in as administrator will have the same authority that you do as owner of that Mac.

10. Click on Save to store the new user account. If you opted to use the auto-login feature, to avoid manually entering the username and password each time you boot your Mac, you'll see a dialog box (see Figure 6.5) where clicking on Yes will turn off the feature and clicking on No will let the new user log in at the next restart.

11. Repeat Steps 4 through 10 to add more user accounts.

12. Quit the System Preferences application by choosing Quit from the Application menu or by pressing Command+Q.

6. Setting Up Mac OS X for Multiple Users

Figure 6.5   Do you want to turn off the auto-login feature? Decide here.

Editing a User Account

A new user account can be easily changed at any time. If you need to reset a password or change other user information, follow these steps:

1. Launch the System Preferences application from either the Dock or inside the Applications folder.

2. Click on the Users icon to launch the settings panel.

3. Click on the padlock (if it's not already open), and enter the username and password for your administrator account.

4. With the padlock opened, click on a user's name. Then, click on the Open User button or press Command+O to access your user account information.

5. Make the appropriate changes to the user's name and password information and enter a password reminder question if you want.

6. If you intend to grant this user the authority to act as administrator for the Mac, click on the checkbox at the bottom of the dialog box.

7. Click on Save to save the edited user account.

8. Exit System Preferences by choosing Quit from the Application menu or pressing Command+Q.

If you need to remove a user account, follow these steps:

1. Launch the System Preferences application.

2. Click on the padlock if it's closed, and enter the username and password for your administrator account.

3. With the padlock opened, click on the name of the user account you want to delete.

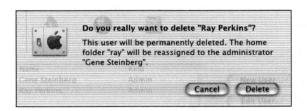

Figure 6.6 Are you sure you want to remove that user account?

4. Click on the Delete User button, and then click on Delete to respond to the acknowledgment prompt (see Figure 6.6). (Or, if you change your mind, click on Cancel instead to leave the user account.)

5. Quit the System Preferences application by choosing Quit from the Application menu or by pressing Command+Q.

Setting Up Keychain Access

The keychain, first introduced in Mac OS 9, is a valuable feature that helps simplify management of all your passwords by storing them in a single place.

NOTE: *To be precise, the keychain feature did appear previously in System 7.1.1, commonly called System 7 Pro, but that system version didn't quite catch on (it was a failure in the marketplace, actually), and it was several years before the feature returned.*

Here's how to use the feature:

1. First, you need to create a keychain so you have a place to store all those passwords. To do that, first locate the Keychain Access application, which is located in the Utilities folder inside your Applications folder.

2. Double-click on the Keychain Access application to launch it; this displays the screen shown in Figure 6.7.

NOTE: *When you set up a username, a Keychain under that name is already made for you.*

3. Choose New Keychain from the File menu to name your new keychain (see Figure 6.8).

4. Type a name for your keychain, and then click on the Create button.

6. Setting Up Mac OS X for Multiple Users

111

Figure 6.7   This message only shows up if there is no existing Keychain.

Figure 6.8   Give your keychain a name here.

5. On the next screen, type a user password, and then retype the password to confirm it. You'll want to use a strong password, as explained earlier in this chapter.

6. Once you've created a Keychain, it's time to populate it. If you have several keychains, there will be a Keychains menu; otherwise, your new keychain will be displayed. Click on Add, and type a name for the item you want to add. (Use a name that identifies the item's contents.)

NOTE: *If you are entering a Web site, be sure you include the exact access URL in the Name field. Otherwise, you won't be able to use that password to access the site.*

TIP: *A quick way to enter a complicated password is simply to access it via your Web browser and then copy the address in the URL field. You can then paste it into the Keychain Access application.*

---

7. Type the user password that you need for that particular program or service.

8. Repeat Steps 6 and 7 for each password you want to enter.

9. When you're finished using Keychain Access, quit the application by choosing Quit from the Application menu, pressing Command+Q, or clicking on the Close button.

NOTE: *You can easily create multiple keychains, with each storing a different set of user passwords. That may help from an organizational standpoint.*

Checking and Using Your Keychain

Once you've configured Keychain Access to store your user passwords, it's very simple to launch the program and check or use your passwords. Just follow these steps:

1. Locate Keychain Access in the Utilities folder, inside the Applications folder, and double-click on the program to launch it.

2. If you have more than one keychain, select the Keychain Access menu, and choose the keychain you want to open. If you have only one keychain stored, there will not be such a menu.

3. To unlock a keychain, click on the Unlock button, and then enter your keychain password.

4. If you want to learn about a specific password, click on Get Info and then click on View Password.

5. Click Allow Once to see the password.

6. Keep your keychain unlocked if you want to use it with your applications or services.

7. When you're finished working with your keychains, choose Quit from the Application menu, press Command+Q, or click on the Close button to close the program.

Changing Keychain Settings

The Keychain Access application has just a few settings, but you'll want to consider all the options to see what fits your work environment. Here's how to change the settings:

1. Launch the Keychain Access application.

2. Choose My Keychain Settings from the Edit menu (the words *My Keychain* will reflect the actual name of the keychain you want to configure). This opens the dialog box shown in Figure 6.9.

3. If you want to change your password, you can do so now. You'll have to confirm your password to make it active.

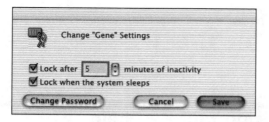

Figure 6.9   Choose your keychain settings here.

NOTE: *If you use a password that the software thinks isn't secure, such as a simple word or recognizable name, you'll get a warning prompt. If you need a strong password, I suggest you heed the warning and create a new password.*

---

4. You can also have your keychain lock automatically after a specified period of inactivity (you set the number of minutes) or when your Mac slips into sleep mode. Go ahead and check the settings you want.

5. To change the name of a keychain, choose Keychain List from the Edit menu, and then select the name of the keychain.

6. Type a new name for the keychain.

7. When you're finished making your changes, quit Keychain Access by choosing Quit from the Application menu or pressing Command+Q.

Running a Keychain on Another Mac

When you create a keychain on your Mac, the keychain is not limited to that one computer. You can easily access the very same keychain on another Mac. This is quite convenient if you need to access the same applications and services on home and office computers or on an Apple laptop. Here's how to work with a mobile keychain:

1. Locate your personal keychain file. You'll find it in the Your Keychains folder, inside the Library folder, within your Users folder. Your keychain file will be stored using the name you specified when you set it up.

2. Drag the file to a mounted disk to make a copy, or just make a copy in your Public folder by holding down the Option key when you drag the file to that folder.

3. On the other Mac, you can access the keychain file from across the network or from another drive simply by locating the file and double-clicking on it.

4. If you want the keychain to appear in another Mac's Keychain List, just drag the other keychain file into the Keychain List you have open. That will place the file on the other Mac as well.

5. Once the keychain is available to you, you can open it by entering the proper username and password.

6. When you're finished using the keychain, close the application by choosing Quit from the Application menu, pressing Command+Q, or clicking on the Close button.

Coping with Problems Involving Keychains and Multiple Users

The Multiple User features of Mac OS X are quite straightforward and usually work without a hitch. They just require a little attention to detail. But if you run into trouble, here are some likely problems and solutions:

- *Password isn't recognized*—Are you sure you entered the password correctly? Did you leave the Caps Lock key engaged by mistake? If you followed my suggestions about using a strong password, the keyboard combination might not be something you readily remember. It would be a good idea to write it down somewhere and put it in a safe place. Type it again, just in case you made a mistake the first time (which you wouldn't see because the only feedback on your screen are the bullets in place of the characters you type). If you cannot get your keychain or multiple-users password to work, you'll have to consider reinstalling Mac OS X and starting again, unless you can delete the individual keychain file or user account via your administrator's access using the Reset Password feature of the Mac OS X Installer.

- *Keychain doesn't work with a program*—Not all applications support keychains or other multiple-user features. You'll want to check with the software publishers about their plans to support these features.

- *User forgets password*—You'll want to login as administrator and recheck the user's account. You'll also want to keep a written record, in a safe place, of all user accounts so you can access the users' computers whenever necessary or simply give them a lost password. As administrator, you can easily log in via the Multiple Users feature, open the user's account, and reset the password with a new one, if necessary.

WARNING! From a security standpoint, when you set up an administrator's account, it's never a good idea to leave a password setting blank. If nobody else will access your Mac, or only friends and family, you can just as easily create a password identical to your username.

Suggestions for Setting up Multiple Users for Use with Children

Many new Macs are purchased for home or small business use, where they'll be frequently used by children, ranging from those barely out of the toddler stage to the teen years. Parents are often surprised that young people take to personal computers far more easily than they did. My son, for example, was actively trying to trash all my files from my Mac's desktop when he was three or four years old. But more seriously, they learn mouse skills, and develop good typing skills (with a little parental or school-based direction) far more speedily than the older generation. As a result, they can get on the Internet more easily and perhaps get into trouble more easily.

Here are some considerations for setting up Mac OS X for use with children:

- *Use Apple's iTools*—In Chapter 22, I'll explain how you can set up the KidSafe feature of iTools to restrict a child's access to unapproved or unsafe Web sites.

- *Keep passwords hidden and hard to guess*—Just as you would hide your password for outsiders, you'll want to consider making your user password difficult for them to detect as well. Today's kids have a remarkable ability to figure out such things, if you make your password too easy to guess. You will want to make sure they cannot log onto your administrator's account and do mischief (even if unintended). That way, they will be limited to system preferences that are padlocked or secured.

- *Consider AOL or CompuServe 2000 for a kid's Net access*—By the time Mac OS X appears as a final release, there will no doubt be a "savvy" version of AOL's software (and the software for its sister service). Figure 6.10 shows the expected user interface. AOL has a powerful set of Parental Controls that allow you to restrict your child's access to various features of the service, such as instant messages, email from strangers, and various Web sites. This family-friendly attitude approach is one reason why AOL has risen to the top of the heap in terms of online services (not to mention its hugely successful promotional campaigns).

- *Use email filtering*—Apple's Mail application and the other alternatives have filtering options that allow you to prevent email from specific locations to arrive. By extending these tools, you can restrict a user to receiving only email from approved locations, such as family members or friends. That way, unacceptable material doesn't arrive. Another ISP that will help you in this regard is EarthLink, Apple's default ISP partner. They inherited a feature called *Spaminator* when they merged with MindSpring. This feature automatically blocks email from known purveyors of junk mail. That, plus careful filtering, will go a long way toward protecting children from getting unacceptable email solicitations.

6. Setting Up Mac OS X for Multiple Users

Figure 6.10   Here is the expected AOL 5.0 for Mac OS X.

Chapter 7

Mac OS X's Search Feature

If you need an immediate solution to:	See page:
Searching for Files	124
Searching Files for Content	125
Indexing a Drive	126
Setting Sherlock Preferences	127
Searching the Internet	128
Finding People on the Internet	131
Customizing Your Information Request	132
Saving Your Custom Searches	135
Searching for Files in a Single Folder	136
Making Your Own Sherlock Channel	137
Installing Additional Search Modules	138

In Brief

Hard drives are constantly getting cheaper and bigger, which means you can store more and more of your stuff on them. However, with so much data, it gets increasingly harder to find the files you want. Additionally, the World Wide Web contains literally millions of sites, with content that dwarfs the largest libraries in the world. With so much material out there, just what can you do to find the information you want without spending endless amounts of time in the process?

For Mac OS X, Apple has enhanced its famous Sherlock search utility (see Figure 7.1) to run faster and more efficiently, using a plain-English language technique for making requests. This makes it much easier to find the information you want without having to know special search techniques or arcane instructions.

Figure 7.1   Apple's fancy search utility handles local, network, and Internet searching with aplomb.

Sherlock Searches Locally and Internationally

Where did you put that document containing information about a great new stock opportunity? Can you find the right news story about your favorite movie star? Are there online resources for searching for new homes in that city to which you've been transferred?

Before Apple created its highly flexible searching tool, there was no central resource to access this information. On your computer, you had to use its built-in search mechanism, and you had to get a third-party program to actually check the content of a file. On the Internet, there are a number of popular search engines, but knowing which one will work for your specific range of requests is a matter of trial and error. In addition, you have to learn the right search syntax for any but the most simple information requests.

Beginning with Mac OS 8.5, Apple introduced Sherlock, an all-purpose search utility that grew out of the original Find File application. Where once your searches were limited to drives connected to your Mac or from a network, Sherlock brought the Internet into the picture by allowing you to extend your search capabilities across the world. In addition, the ability to search the content of files was added.

For Mac OS X, Apple has made Sherlock faster and more efficient, yet the basic user interface from the Mac OS 9 version—Sherlock 2— is essentially the same, other than inheriting the Aqua look. Why mess with a good thing?

Sherlock divides its search feature into eight buttons, or *channels*, each of which accesses a different type of search routine. Here's a brief description of what they do; I'll cover all these features in detail later in this chapter:

- *Files*—This channel confines the search to files on a drive available to your Mac, whether attached to your computer or accessible by a local or Internet-based network. As you'll learn later in this chapter, you can also use this feature to customize the search extensively and even to search for the contents (text) in a file.

- *Internet*—Select from one or more popular Web-based search sites (see Figure 7.2) to search for almost any accessible Internet-based location.

Figure 7.2   Click on the checkbox to activate or deactivate a search site.

- *People*—Let your Mac replace your phone directory. This feature lets you look up people around the world by name or by email address.

- *Shopping*—This channel is a very useful feature of Sherlock, though only a small number of online merchants are supported. Just enter a word or phrase that describes the item that you seek, and Sherlock will not only search for it but also display a list of current prices so you can do instant comparisons.

- *News*—Before it reaches your daily paper, you can search several popular news-oriented sites for stories on the events of the day, business, technology, personal finance, lifestyle information, and more.

- *Apple*—Need more help with your Mac? Or do you just want to check out the latest models? This channel has direct links to several of Apple Computer's Web sites.

- *Reference*—Take advantage of online encyclopedias for general information, help with homework, or perhaps just the definition of that troublesome word. Do your online research courtesy of Sherlock.

- *My Channel*—This channel isn't populated yet. It's there for you to enter your own custom-selected search sites.

You can launch the Sherlock application, choose a category or channel, and then enter your search request in plain English. Sherlock will go to work finding the information you want. Whether it's your Mac's drive, an attached drive, a network, or the Internet, you'll be taking advantage of one of the fastest search tools available on a personal computer. But you can easily customize both requests and features of Sherlock. You'll learn how in the following section.

7. Mac OS X's
Search Feature

Immediate Solutions

Searching for Files

In seconds, you can easily locate a file on any drive connected to your Mac or accessed across a network. Whether it's a document, application, or folder, Sherlock can handle the job for you in seconds. Here are the simple steps to follow:

1. Launch Sherlock by clicking on its icon in the Dock or double-clicking on the Sherlock icon in your Applications folder.

2. If it's not already selected, click on the Files button (or channel).

3. Click on the File Names radio button.

4. Enter your search request in the text field.

5. Click on the magnifying glass. In seconds, Sherlock produces results that match your request (see Figure 7.3).

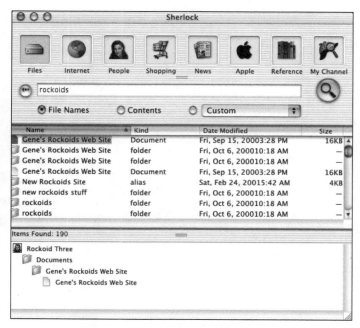

Figure 7.3   Sherlock has located files on my Mac's hard drive with names that match up with the request.

6. To see the location of an item that's been located by Sherlock, click on its name to select it, and you'll see the information displayed in the results pane at the bottom of the window.

7. If you want to open the item, double-click on its name. If it's an application or document file, the application itself will be launched, then, if necessary, the document itself. The process is the same as if you actually double-clicked on the original item.

8. If you want to move the selected item, drag it to an open Finder window. Remember that applications in the Applications folder cannot be moved, only copied.

9. To make a copy of the item, hold down the Option key as it's being dragged.

10. Should you want just an alias to the file, hold down the Command+Option keys as the item is being dragged to its new location.

TIP: If you want to delete selected items from the Sherlock window, press Command+Del. This action moves the selected item to the Trash, but it won't be emptied until you actually perform that action in the Finder's Application menu.

Searching Files for Content

It's not enough to simply find a file by its name. Sometimes, you need to find files that have a specific word or phrase. Fortunately, Sherlock can handle that chore as easily as any other search routine.

NOTE: Your startup drive is indexed automatically, but other drives you're using must be indexed separately. If you haven't indexed a drive, check the next section for information on how to perform this little procedure.

To search the text inside a file, follow these steps:

1. Launch Sherlock.

2. Click on the Files button.

3. Click on the Contents radio button to confine your search to strictly the text inside a document.

7. Mac OS X's Search Feature

4. If you do not find the information you want, refine your search by trying a different combination of words or phrases that are contained in the files for which you're searching.

NOTE: *The text parsing process isn't perfect. Sherlock should be able to search for the text in most documents from word processor, page layout, graphic, and Internet applications, but there's always that possibility that one program or another will be encoded in a manner that Sherlock can't read.*

---

5. After you've found the item you want, click once on the listing. Information on the contents appears in the results pane at the bottom of the Sherlock window.

6. When your search is done, quit Sherlock.

NOTE: *If your file and text search doesn't yield results, you might want to refine your requests still further. You'll want to read the section entitled "Customizing Your Information Request," later in this chapter.*

Indexing a Drive

To use Sherlock to examine the contents of a drive, you must first index it; the process is automatic only for your startup drive. When a drive is indexed, keywords to locate the text strings are all placed in a special file so Sherlock can access the information quickly. Here's how to begin the indexing process:

1. Launch Sherlock.

2. Select the drive you want to index from those listed in the Sherlock window.

3. Go to the Find menu and choose Index Now. The process begins. If a lot of data is on the drive, the process can take a considerable amount of time.

4. Repeat the process for each drive you want to index, or just select them all and they will progress in sequence, usually two at a time (see Figure 7.4).

WARNING! *Because a new index procedure can consume a large amount of time, as would an index of a drive on which lots of changes have been made, you might want to schedule the process for times when you're not using your Mac. Even though Mac OS X's preemptive multitasking feature can handle multiple tasks at the same time, you should do the indexing during a time when you're not apt to be changing the files that are being indexed.*

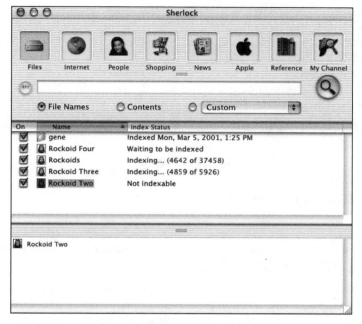

Figure 7.4   These drives are being indexed as we watch.

Setting Sherlock Preferences

You can configure Sherlock's indexing settings in the Preferences screen (see Figure 7.5). As with most Mac OS X applications, the preferences are located in the Application menu. Here are the settings you can change:

- *Automatically Index Items When Sherlock Is Opened*—This speeds up the index process of your Home directory. Unless the process seems to slow down your Mac, you should keep this option checked.

- *Automatically Index Folders When They're Added To The Files Channel*—Again, this process just speeds things up, particularly if you're adding extra folders for custom searches. I'll explain how to add folders later in this chapter.

7. Mac OS X's
Search Feature

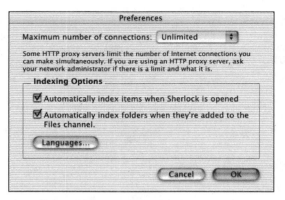

Figure 7.5   Click on the checkbox to change a setting.

Searching the Internet

As mentioned, Sherlock doesn't distinguish between local, network, and Internet-based searching. It can handle all with equal flexibility. Here's how to search for information on the Internet:

1. Log on to your ISP. (See Chapter 20 for information on how to configure Mac OS X to make your Internet connection.)

2. Launch Sherlock, then click on the Internet channel button or any other channel button that reflects the information you want to search online. A screen listing the search options available in that channel appears (see Figure 7.6).

NOTE: *By default, some of the search sites are checked and some aren't. Feel free to check and uncheck items as desired to refine the search to the sites that interest you.*

3. Make your search request. Enter the word or phrase that best describes what you're searching for in the text field. For example, if you are interested in buying a new Ford, just enter "Ford" or, more specifically, the model, such as "Ford Taurus".

4. Click on the magnifying glass to start the process.

5. After a short time, Sherlock produces a list of items that match your search request. Depending on the number of sites you've activated and the speed of the connection to your ISP, this may take anywhere from a few seconds to several minutes. A progress bar indicates the status. By default, items are listed in order of relevance, how closely they match your search query.

Figure 7.6   Click on the checkboxes to add or remove search sites.

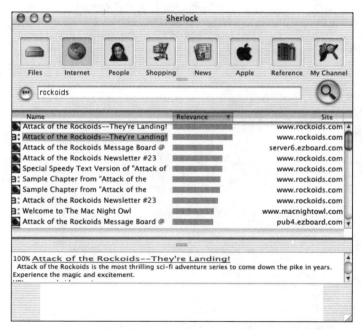

Figure 7.7   The bottom pane provides a summary of the selected
search result.

When Sherlock is done, click on any item in the search list to see more information in the results pane at the bottom of the Sherlock application window (see Figure 7.7).

NOTE: *Not all search requests will yield a positive result. If you don't receive any matches to your request, try refining the request a bit, perhaps by using a more descriptive phrase. I'll get to the process of customizing your search requests later in this chapter.*

---

6. If you've found an item you want to know more about, click on the link in the results list to open your Web browser. This takes you right to the page you've selected (see Figure 7.8).

7. Repeat the process to search for additional information.

8. Quit Sherlock when you're done using it.

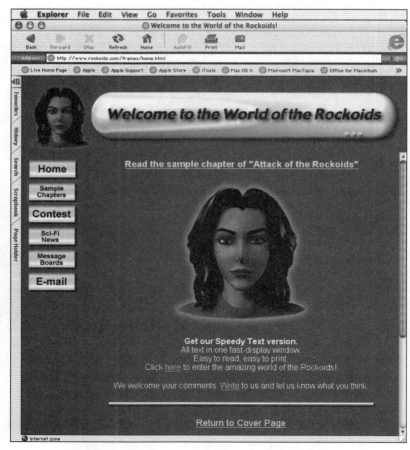

Figure 7.8 Success! Sherlock has found a site that has information that matches your needs.

Finding People on the Internet

In the old days, if you wanted to find out someone's physical address, you'd have to check a phone directory or call the telephone company for the information. Now, there's a new way to let your fingers do the walking, with the help of Sherlock—and you can find email addresses as well. To find someone on the Internet, just follow these steps:

1. Log on to your ISP in the usual fashion.

2. Launch Sherlock, then click on the People channel button.

3. Enter the name of the person you want to find in the text field. You can enter the real name or the email address, if you know it.

4. Click on the magnifying glass. Sherlock goes to work searching the Internet for the person you want to contact. A progress bar indicates the status of the search.

5. After you see a list of likely candidates, if any, click on the item to bring up a summary in the results pane of the Sherlock application window (see Figure 7.9).

6. If you don't find the right person the first time, continue to check likely candidates from the list.

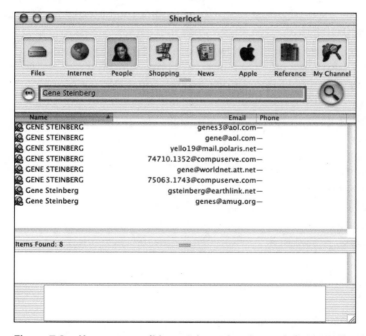

Figure 7.9   Here are possible matches when I search for-myself-with Sherlock.

7. Should your initial request not be successful, ask the question differently. Instead of the real name, try an email address or vice versa. If the person is listed on the Internet in some fashion, one technique or the other may produce a successful match.

NOTE: *I don't want to overstate the accuracy of "people" searches on the Internet. There are gaps in the databases, and sometimes information will be highly out of date or simply unavailable. I still find listings showing email accounts and ISP affiliations that I abandoned long ago; the items in Figure 7.9 are a prime example.*

---

8. When you're finished with the search request, make another or quit Sherlock.

Customizing Your Information Request

Not every request will be successful, and it's not always because you've done something wrong. There is so much information on the Internet that sometimes it's just necessary to fine-tune your request or try a few different ways of asking.

As mentioned, Sherlock works with plain English to send your requests, whether they're made locally, on a network, or on the Internet. There are ways, however, to fine-tune the information so you get what you need. Here are some suggestions:

1. If you want your search request to include all the words of a phrase, type a plus (+) character between each word. So if you're looking for that Ford Taurus, you might try Ford+Taurus, if the original request isn't specific enough.

2. If you want to exclude a word, you'd think you'd type a minus sign, right? Well, no; it's an exclamation point (!). So if you wanted to refine that request on Ford products to exclude the Taurus, you'd use Ford!Taurus. That way, the Taurus is eliminated from the search.

3. Now we get a bit more complicated. If you'd like to search for a group of items, put a parenthesis in them. You can even group items, yet exclude specific categories in this fashion:

(cars|Ford)! Taurus.

Again, we're excluding the Taurus.

NOTE: *That vertical bar character (which looks like a slash in some typefaces) is accessed by pressing Option+Shift+1.*

---

4. If the simple additions to your search request don't deliver what you want, you can customize your request still further, although the options I cover now are strictly confined to file-based searches, not Internet site searches. With the Files button selected, click on Sherlock's Find menu and choose More Options (see Figure 7.10). In the example shown, I've clicked on the Advanced Options arrow to bring up still more possibilities.

NOTE: *Is the Find menu grayed out? Make sure you've clicked on the Files button in Sherlock's window first.*

5. From the More Search Options window, select the checkboxes that cover your search category and enter the appropriate information, or click on the pop-up menu and make your selection. Here are the categories available:

NOTE: *The search criteria described next can only be refined when you first select the checkbox that describes that category. Otherwise, text entry fields and pop-up menus remain unavailable.*

- *File Name*—Click on the pop-up menu to decide whether the file name is included or excluded from the search request in several ways.

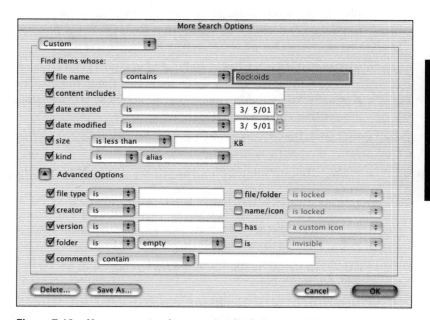

Figure 7.10   You can customize search criteria in a number of ways. I've checked all the categories in this screen for clarity.

- *Content Includes*—Refine your file search by making sure that a certain bit of text (a word or phrase) is included.

- *Date Created*—Decide how closely the search will look at file creation dates in making your request. You can click on a date, then use the up and down arrows to change it. Then, you can click on the pop-up menu and choose from the selected day, the previous day, or from a range of criteria that includes a fixed period from that day.

- *Date Modified*—The settings are the same as in the preceding item, except the search covers the modification date of the file.

- *Size*—This option limits or includes files of a particular size. It's especially helpful for content searches—particularly if you want to look at text in a small document but don't want to wait until large documents are also searched.

- *Kind*—Is the file an alias, a document, or a font, or does it fit into a wide range of categories? Choose the one you want from the pop-up menu.

- *File Type*—Under Advanced Options, this category lets you enter whether a file is a document created in a specific program. You can find out this information by selecting a file's icon, then choosing Show Inspector from the Finder's File menu and selecting Application from the Show pop-up menu.

- *Creator*—This is a more complicated category. The creator identifies the name of the application that made the file. Normally, you wouldn't know this code unless you have a file viewer that can read such attributes.

- *Version*—Here, you specify the version of a program or the program that made the file.

- *Folder*—In this category, you indicate whether the folder has files.

- *Comments*—Here you specify whether comments are included or excluded from the search. Comments are found in the Finder's Show Inspector window.

- *File/Folder*—Is the file/folder locked or not? You decide which applies here.

- *Name/Icon*—Is the name/icon locked or unlocked? Here's where you make your choice.

- *Has*—Does the file have a custom icon? Here's where you decide.

- *Is*—Is the file invisible or not? Some files are declared invisible by the Finder because they are system-related and not intended for general access. However, Sherlock lets you search for them anyway, although this is an option you wouldn't generally use often, if at all.

WARNING! A number of system-related files under Mac OS X are set in a specific way or located in a specific place because they are required for your Mac to run properly. Don't attempt to seek them out and manipulate them with Sherlock, or you might find that your Mac fails to run properly or will not even boot when you try to restart.

- After you've fine-tuned your information request, press the magnifying-glass button. Sherlock comes up with a list of results that match your request. If you find that it's not successful in getting you what you want, you can refine the searches still further.

- When you're finished using Sherlock, quit the application.

TIP: You can deselect all the checkboxes quickly in the More Search Options window simply by going to the Edit menu and choosing Turn Off All. Or press Command+T. The Edit menu is grayed out if no checkboxes have been selected.

Saving Your Custom Searches

With all those choices available to you to customize your file search, no doubt you'll want to reuse a complex search pattern more than once. If that's the case, you'll be pleased to know that it's possible to save a search routine for regular retrieval. Here's how:

1. With the More Search Options window opened, click on the Save As button. Then, give your search routine a name.

2. When a new search routine has been saved, it'll show up as a selection in the Custom pop-up menu on the opening Sherlock window.

TIP: You can also save a set of search preferences as a separate file. To do so, choose Save Search Criteria from Sherlock's File menu, then give your search routine a name. Once you've saved it, you can double-click on that file to activate Sherlock and your custom search setup.

7. Mac OS X's Search Feature

Searching for Files in a Single Folder

As you saw in the preceding section, Sherlock can be customized in an almost infinite number of ways to search for precisely what you want. If you just want to keep it simple, however, and look for files in a specific folder, here's a quick way to do it:

1. Launch Sherlock.

2. Click on the Files button.

3. Go to the Find menu, and select Add Folder (see Figure 7.11).

4. Drag a folder from a Finder window into this dialog box so that it's included in your Sherlock request. Repeat this action for each folder you want to add before clicking on Choose to close the dialog box.

5. Enter your search request, and then click on the magnifying-glass button to perform your search.

6. If you don't intend to search a folder again, go to the Files menu and return to Add Folders.

7. Select the folder you no longer need to search, and drag it to the Trash. Don't fret. This action won't actually delete the folder; it'll just remove the folder from Sherlock's list.

8. When you're done, quit Sherlock.

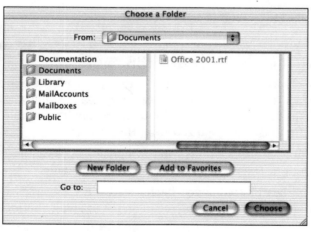

Figure 7.11   Drag a folder icon to this screen to search it via Sherlock.

Making Your Own Sherlock Channel

As explained at the beginning of this chapter, Sherlock's application window has eight buttons that access the various channels. The last, labeled My Channel, is one you can customize to your taste. You can even add additional channels, but you'll want to widen Sherlock's window to accommodate the extra entries. Here's how to create or customize a channel:

1. Launch Sherlock.

2. Go to the Channels menu and select New Channel, which brings up the dialog box shown in Figure 7.12.

3. Give your channel a name, or just rename the one that's opened.

4. Choose an icon from the list. You can move the arrows up and down until you see the icon you want.

5. Select the type of channel you want from the Channel type pop-up menu. You can choose from Searching, People, Shopping, and News, depending on what you want to do. Be certain of what you want, because you can't mix and match and you cannot change the category without deleting the channel. If necessary, make an extra new channel.

6. Adding a search site is simple. Just open another channel that has the search site you want, hold down the Option key and then drag that to your new channel's button. Once again, only the items in the category you've created can be added.

WARNING! If you fail to hold down the Option key when transferring a search site, it will be removed from the source channel (not just copied).

7. If you want to rename a channel, click on the Channel button.

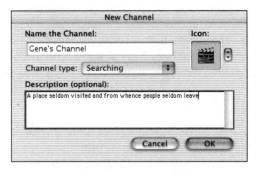

Figure 7.12   Name your channel, and you're ready to begin.

8. Go to the Channels menu and pick Edit Channel.

9. If you want, enter a description to explain the purpose of your channel, then click on the OK button to save your changes. From here on, the new or modified channel appears in the Channels window (see Figure 7.13) and as a button in the Channels menu.

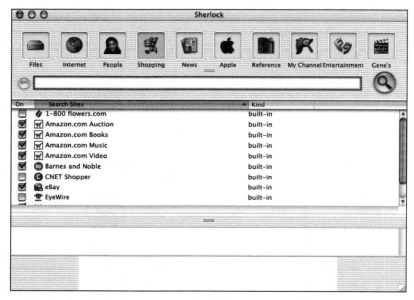

Figure 7.13   The author's custom channel now gets its own spot in the Sherlock search window.

Installing Additional Search Modules

Mac OS X comes with a small selection of search sites, but you're not limited to the offerings. You can add additional search areas to further extend the reach of Sherlock. You'll find additional plug-in modules for Sherlock at Apple's Web site, **http://www.apple.com/ sherlock/plugins.html**. Here's how to install a new module for Mac OS X:

1. Download the module to your Mac's drive.

2. Make sure the file is not compressed. It will be named with an .src extension if it's ready to use. Then go to your Home directory by clicking on the Home button in the Finder.

3. Locate the Internet Search Sites folder. It's located in the Library folder in your Home directory. You'll find the folder has additional folders, each identified by channel. Drag your Sherlock plug-in to the correct channel's folder.

TIP: If you want to install a Sherlock plug-in in more than a single folder, select the plug-in's name, hold down the Option key, and drag it to another folder so that it's duplicated, not moved.

Once installed, the search site appears in the appropriate channel when you launch Sherlock again.

NOTE: Modules can be removed simply by taking them out of the folder in which they were installed, but you'll want to do it after you quit the Sherlock application. The changes will appear the next time you launch the program.

---

7. Mac OS X's Search Feature

Chapter 8

The Networking Overview

If you need an immediate solution to:	See page:
Sharing Files with Mac OS X	147
Connecting to Shared Macs Under Mac OS X	152
Using Internet Connect for Dial-Up Networking	155
Verifying Connectivity	159
Using Apple's Location Manager to Create Custom Setups	160
Accessing a Drop Box	161
Correcting Network Access Problems	162
Protecting Your Network from the Internet	163

In Brief

Although the Macintosh was originally designed as a computer that empowered the individual, easy networking was always a part of the picture. The first example of simple networking was the ability to set up a network-capable laser printer in just a minute or so simply by plugging it in, turning it on, and selecting the driver that worked with the output device in the Chooser. The same easy networking extended to more powerful printers. Even imagesetters, used in the printing industry for high-quality output, could be hooked up to a Mac just as easily as the cheapest laser printer. If you wanted to network Macs with each other, however, you needed special software.

> **NOTE:** *There was one no-cost exception to the rule of having to buy commercial sharing software, such as Apple's own AppleShare. A free program, produced but unsupported by the former Claris division of Apple, allowed for limited file sharing. It was called Public Folder, but its value ended when Mac users moved past System 6.*

When Mac OS 7 came around in 1991, Apple made a logical extension of networking by offering built in support for personal file sharing. This support allowed Mac users on a small network to activate peer-to-peer file transfers, without special software, by attaching cables among the computers and turning on file sharing. In minutes, the shared Mac's drive was visible in the Chooser as an AppleShare volume available on your network (see Figure 8.1).

For larger setups, it was easy to use the Get Info window to set user access privileges for file sharing. Using this limited set of user controls, you could restrict access by those connected to a Mac as far as the files they could see or modify. As file sharing evolved, Apple also added the capability of sharing a Mac across the Internet with almost the same ease as connecting to a Mac on a local network.

For Mac OS X, Apple has advanced its networking architecture, using industry-standard technologies to provide faster performance, greater reliability, and better cross-platform compatibility. The Darwin core of the new operating system includes the BSD networking stack, which includes TCP/IP, the protocol used to power the Internet. You don't have to abandon your existing techniques for getting connected, either; there's native support for PPP connections, so you can access your ISP as easily as before, perhaps more easily. (I'll cover the sub-

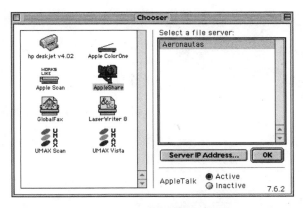

Figure 8.1   The late and definitely not lamented Mac Chooser was used to access printers and networked Macs.

ject of Mac OS X's Internet features in Chapter 20.) AppleTalk is also supported, so you don't have to do anything extra to access your existing Mac printers, although TCP/IP is required for file sharing.

Accessing Networked Macs from Mac OS X

When you look over your new operating system, you'll see that something's missing. There's no File Sharing Control Panel.

The answer to these abandoned features is closer in concept to the Network Browser application that first appeared under Mac OS 8.5 (see Figure 8.2). Networked Macs appear in the Connect To Server dialog (see Figure 8.3), available from the Mac OS X Finder's Go menu. Your network installation, whether local or Internet-based, is divided into *neighborhoods*, each of which consists of a set of networked Macs.

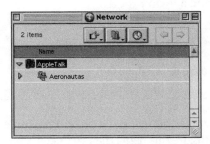

Figure 8.2   The Network Browser application could access local and Internet networks.

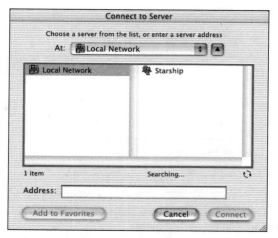

Figure 8.3   The Connect To Server feature in Mac OS X's Go menu is the
new method of taking advantage of file-sharing features.

NOTE: *This new Mac OS X nomenclature should seem familiar if you've used Microsoft Windows. Each network neighborhood is analogous to a zone under the Classic Mac networking arrangement.*

A Different Way to Share Files

With older versions of the Mac OS, the normal situation was to share an entire disk or folder. For Mac OS X, the normal routine is to place items you want to share in the Public folder. That way, everyone who uses your computer can have access to the files without having to log in to your user accounts. That folder can also be used as a repository for the files you want to share or to receive across your network. In the "Immediate Solutions" section of this chapter, I'll explain how to establish access privileges so that only the users you specify can connect to your Mac without requiring a login process.

TIP: *If you want to share a large number of files in other parts of your Mac's drive and see other files on your Mac's drive, create an alias for each of those items and place them in your Public folder. That will provide access to these items for users who access your Mac directly or across a network.*

You can limit file access even further by using the Drop Box folder within your Public folder. You configure this using the Privileges screen in the Show Info window, as explained later in this chapter. Once the Drop Box folder is set up, those who access your Mac across the network can deposit files there, but cannot see any files in that folder or anywhere else on your Mac other than the Public folder.

A Look at Mac OS X's Networking Components

The tools to network your Mac require settings in two System Preferences panels and a dialog box. I'll describe them here, and then, in the "Immediate Solutions" section, I'll discuss how they're used.

- *Network*—This settings pane (see Figure 8.4) is used to configure both your Ethernet and modem connections, all from a single set of screens. This helps ease the setup process. Moreover, most of the setups are essentially the same as the ones you used in the Classic Mac OS. There's even a Location Manager feature, which can automatically switch network settings when you move your Mac to different locales.

NOTE: If you are working in an organization where a systems administrator handles network-related issues, you'll want to consult with that person before you attempt to change any of the existing network settings on your Mac.

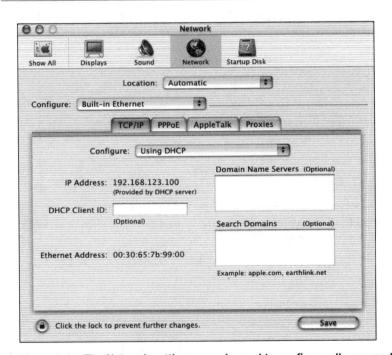

Figure 8.4   The Network settings pane is used to configure all your modem and network hookups.

- *Sharing*—You'll use this settings pane (see Figure 8.5) to switch file and Web sharing on and off. Web sharing uses the features of the famous Apache Web server software to let you run an Internet site from your Mac. You can also allow others to access your Mac via FTP or Telnet (remote login)—an option that adds to the flexibility of the new networking features.

- *Connect To Server*—This dialog box, available from the Go menu, is used to access all shared volumes (again, see Figure 8.3). You'll notice that aside from the Aqua user interface and a few additions, it bears more than a striking resemblance to the Network Browser application from the Classic Mac OS.

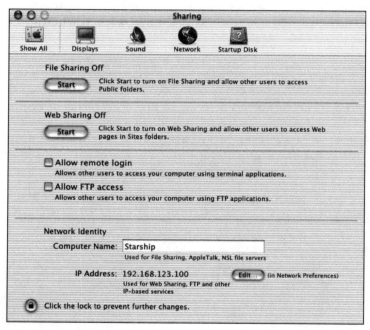

Figure 8.5   The Sharing settings pane is used to switch sharing services on and off.

Immediate Solutions

Sharing Files with Mac OS X

If you want to share files with a Mac running Mac OS X, prepare for some changes. Things have been implemented a little differently, even though setup screens appear very similar. For one thing, you will only be able to share files via TCP/IP by entering the IP addresses of the computers with which you want to exchange data. The standard AppleTalk connection via either printer or Ethernet port isn't supported, nor can you configure Apple's AirPort wireless networking hardware via Mac OS X for the initial release (Apple expects you to return to Mac OS 9.1 for that process), although you can access and monitor an AirPort network with no problems. There are apt to be changes as Apple updates the new operating system, but it's something you will want to keep in mind.

With these differences in mind, here are the basic steps to follow to activate file exchanges with Mac OS X:

1. On the OS X Mac, open the System Preferences application, and then click on the Network pane and choose Built-In Ethernet from the Configure pop-up menu (see Figure 8.6). I'll discuss the modem option in the section on setting your Mac up for Internet access later in this chapter.

2. If the padlock is locked, click on its icon, and then enter your administrator's username and password. If the login window shakes, it just means that you entered the wrong username and/ or password, so try again.

NOTE: If you do not have the username and password handy, please consult with your network administrator, if applicable. There's no way to access the protected features of Mac OS X without entering this information. If you don't set up your Mac for multiple user access, the lock can remain open for your use.

3. In the TCP/IP tab, select Using DHCP from the Configure pop-up menu.

NOTE: The PPPoE tab is used strictly for hooking up to certain broadband ISPs that require that feature to connect to their services. If such a setup is required, your ISP will provide the information you need to enter into the setup pane.

8. The Networking Overview

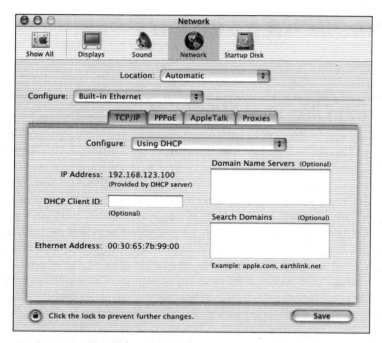

Figure 8.6   Change your network setups here.

4. Click on the AppleTalk tab and click on the Make AppleTalk Active checkbox (see Figure 8.7). If you want to change the name of your Mac for network access, you'll need to move on to the Sharing pane.

5. Click on the Save button to store your settings. If you forget, you'll see a reminder prompt, where you can click the Save button.

6. Now click on Show All to display the other settings panes in System Preferences.

7. Go to the Sharing pane, and click on the Start button to activate file sharing. Note the Network Identity of your Mac, because the Computer Name and IP Address are both needed to access your computer from elsewhere on the network. You can change the name of your Mac before sharing is activated, by the way. Once sharing is activated it may take a few minutes for it to start up.

NOTE: You don't need to concern yourself with Telnet or FTP access settings unless you expect to use your Mac as a Web server, exchange files via FTP, or allow users to log onto your Mac using Telnet across a network. Bear in mind, however, that if you allow FTP access, users can gain access to all files on your Mac for which access privileges are available.

Figure 8.7 AppleTalk is activated when you select the checkbox.

8. Access privileges can be changed only for the contents of an active user's folder, not for your entire drive (unless you have administrator's access). If you want to set custom access privileges for that folder, or another disk volume on your Mac, return to the Finder or desktop, click on the icon, and then click on the name of the item you want to share.

9. Choose Show Info from the Finder's File menu (the Mac OS X equivalent of Get Info), and then choose Privileges from the Show pop-up menu (see Figure 8.8).

10. The Privileges window offers three sets of access privileges, in a fashion very much like previous versions of the Mac OS. These are:

- *Owner*—This is the name of the owner or administrator of the files on this Mac. The normal access setting is Read & Write, which gives the owner the ability to access and modify files. By design, you can restrict your own access to files, but one wonders why you'd want to do that.

8. The Networking Overview

149

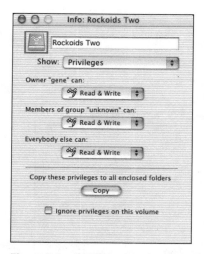

Figure 8.8   Set file access and sharing privileges in this window.

- *Members Of Group*—Each selected user of your Mac can be given a specific set of access instructions. Click on the pop-up menu to change privileges, choosing from Read & Write, Read Only, or Write Only. The Write Only setting lets the user place files in a Drop Box folder within the Public folder, but not actually see any of the other files.

- *Everybody Else*—The settings here are identical to those for a group, except that when you set them here, anyone who connects to your Mac as a guest can have that level of access, even if he or she hasn't been given specific user privileges.

Set your access privileges settings. They are activated as soon as they are changed. If you want to keep the same settings for all the files and folders within a folder, click on Copy to incorporate the settings. Even if you have a large drive, you'll find that the settings are copied almost instantaneously, compared to several minutes with the Classic Mac OS.

NOTE: *Depending on your needs, you may prefer to establish separate settings for individual files and folders, so use the Copy function with caution, because it will only duplicate the permissions you've established for the main folder or file.*

11.   The next step requires setups on the other Macs on your network. Assuming the other Macs are using Mac OS 9.1 or earlier, go to one of the Macs from which you want to access the Mac OS X computer, and open the TCP/IP Control Panel (see Figure 8.9).

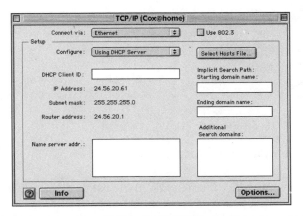

Figure 8.9 The old Mac OS TCP/IP Control Panel must be set up to allow for file sharing.

12. Choose Configurations from the File menu.

13. Pick any active setup, and then click on the Duplicate button.

14. Rename the duplicate setting to something that'll make it identifiable later, such as Mac OS X File Sharing.

15. Click on the Make Active button.

16. In the Connect Via pop-up menu, choose Ethernet, if it's not already selected.

17. In the Configure pop-up menu, choose Using DHCP Server.

18. Leave the DHCP Client ID field empty. You'll normally use that text field when you have a cable modem or DSL and you need to enter your router or modem's ID information.

19. Click on the Close box, and then click on the Save button to store your settings.

20. To access the Mac OS X computer from the other Mac (if it's running Mac OS 8.5 or later), launch the Network Browser application (it should be in the Apple menu), as shown in Figure 8.10. Otherwise, you need to use the Chooser.

NOTE: Be patient here. Each step might take up to a minute to complete, because it takes a while for the Mac to find that other computer.

21. Click on the right arrow next to Network to display the name of your Mac OS X computer.

8. The Networking Overview

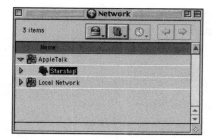

Figure 8.10   You'll see your shared Mac listed here.

22. Double-click on the other Mac's name in the list to display the standard file-sharing password prompt. After you enter the information, you'll see a list of shared volumes that are just a double-click away from access.

Connecting to Shared Macs Under Mac OS X

For Mac OS X, the Go menu becomes a neat substitute for the Chooser and the Network Browser application. To access other shared computers, follow these steps:

1. Return to your Mac's desktop.

2. Choose Connect To Server from the Go menu to open the dialog box shown in Figure 8.11.

Figure 8.11   Your available network shared volumes are shown here.

3. From the pop-up menu at the top of the screen, choose the type of server you need to access. The normal option is Local Network, but this may change depending on the number of network zones available to your Mac and whether the item you want to share is available via the Internet.

4. You see a list of available network neighborhoods in the Connect To Server dialog box. Unless you have a network with several zones, however, there will be just one network neighborhood, as in the example shown in this book. The network we have here is Local Network, typical for a setup where shared Macs are in a single office using just one zone. The pop-up buttons at the top of the screen can be used to connect to recently accessed servers and create a list of favorites.

5. If the computer you want to connect to isn't displayed, enter its IP address in the Address field, and click on Connect. After a few moments, it should appear in the window alongside the others.

6. Now double-click on the name of the networked computer you want to access.

WARNING! *In order to see a Classic Mac OS Computer from Mac OS X you must enable TCP/IP file sharing in that computer's File Sharing Control Panel. It's not available prior to Mac OS 8.5.*

7. In the login window, enter the username and password needed to access the Mac's shared volumes. When you choose guest access, your choices are usually limited to the Public folder.

NOTE: *You may need to check with your systems administrator to get the login information for the other computers on the network. The Options button also lets you attach a password to your Mac's keychain. Chapter 6 covers the subject in more detail.*

---

8. In the next dialog box, double-click on the name of the volume you want to access or just select it and click the OK button.

If you've shared files on previous versions of the Mac OS, you're now in familiar territory. You'll see one or more icons representing the volumes you've shared on your Mac's desktop (see Figure 8.12). They're also added to the Finder's display when you click on the Computer folder.

Now just double-click on any disk icon to see a Finder window of its contents (see Figure 8.13). To remove the drive from your Mac, just drag it to the trash.

Figure 8.12   Once a volume is shared, its icon appears on your Mac's desktop.

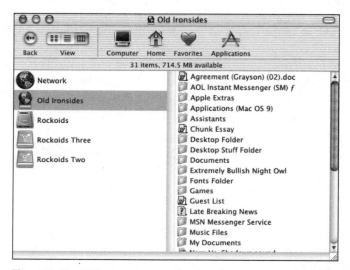

Figure 8.13   A Finder window showing the contents of a shared volume accessed via file sharing.

NOTE: If the shared volume is no longer accessible because either sharing has been turned off on the other Mac or there has been a system crash or restart, you'll see a prompt saying the file server has closed and when it happened.

Related solution:	Found on page:
Setting Up Keychain Access	111

Using Internet Connect for Dial-Up Networking

In the days of Apple Remote Access, you could actually call up your Mac from a remote location in order to access or send files. Your modem was used to hook up to the other computer's modem, and then—within the limits of dial-up file transfers, of course—your remote Mac was as easy to access as one connected to your local network. There is no Remote Access Control Panel for Mac OS X. Instead, you will make your connection with the Internet Connect application, with more than a little help with the settings in the Network pane of the System Preferences application.

NOTE: *Depending on your ISP, these settings might be made courtesy of an installer. You had the chance to install them when you ran the SetupAssistant right after you installed Mac OS X. I'm covering the process here in case you didn't enter the settings then, or you want to change them now.*

Here's how it's done:

1. Launch System Preferences from the Dock or from the Applications folder.

2. Click on the Network pane and make sure the Internal Modem (or Modem) option is chosen from the Configure pop-up menu (as shown in Figure 8.14).

NOTE: *One of the reasons for being able to enter separate settings for network and dial-up TCP/IP access is to allow you to do both at the same time. In theory, you can handle several configurations at the same time under Mac OS X, but obviously just one with your Mac's modem.*

---

3. If it's not already selected, make sure you've clicked on the TCP/IP tab.

4. Make sure the Using PPP option is shown in the pane's Configure menu. The second setting, Manually, is only used for specialized situations that may be required by your network setup.

5. If required by your ISP, enter the correct numbers in the Domain Name Servers field.

6. Under Search Domains, input the proper information. Again, this setting may not be needed by your ISP. The example shown in Figure 8.14 has the regular settings for making a dial-up connection to EarthLink, Apple's ISP partner.

8. The Networking Overview

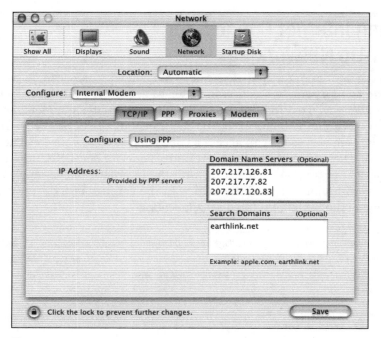

Figure 8.14   Enter an ISP's settings here.

NOTE: Where did these settings come from? In Chapter 2 I suggested that you obtain your setup from the Remote Access and TCP/IP Control Panels. Here's where they go. If you don't have the information, contact your ISP directly.

---

7. Click on the PPP tab to enter your dial-up information (see Figure 8.15).

8. Enter the telephone number, account name, and password for your account. When you click the Save Password checkbox, the password will be stored, but you can skip this process and enter it manually if others may have access to your Mac.

NOTE: You don't have to enter an alternate number, but it's a good idea, because then you have a choice if the first number is busy. You'll want to put the name in the Service Provider field just for identification, or to help you choose the proper option if you've created multiple Location setups (that's coming in the next section).

---

9. If you want to fine-tune your session, click on the PPP Options button and enter the appropriate information in the dialog box (see Figure 8.16). All the items shown are defaults, except for the first, which I checked. This one, Connect Automatically

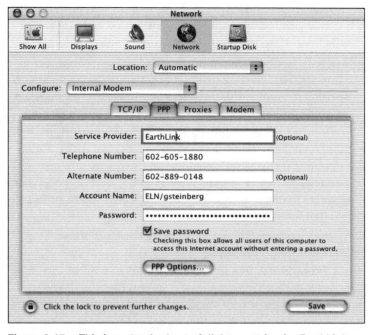

Figure 8.15   This is a standard set of dial-up entries for EarthLink.

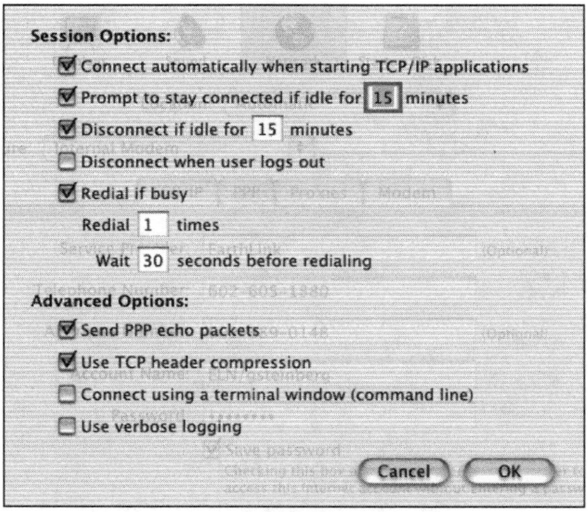

Figure 8.16   Choose special connection options here.

When Starting TCP/IP Applications, will log you in to your ISP whenever you launch applications such as your browser or email client. Here are the options from which to select:

- *Session Options*—In addition to making your connection when you launch your Internet application, you can also get a warning prompt if you've been idle for a while, or automatically disconnect after a selected interval. There's also an option, which is checked by default, to redial your ISP in the event of a busy signal.

- *Advanced Options*—Depending on the needs of your ISP, you may have to select one or more of the options beyond those already checked. Your ISP or network administrator can give you this information.

10. Once your settings are made, click on the OK button.

11. If you want to double-check your modem setup, or if you're not using a standard Apple Internal Modem, click on the Modem tab (see Figure 8.17). Modem scripts can be selected from among a wide variety by clicking on the Modem pop-up menu.

12. When you're done, click on Save to store your setup. Now you're ready to get connected.

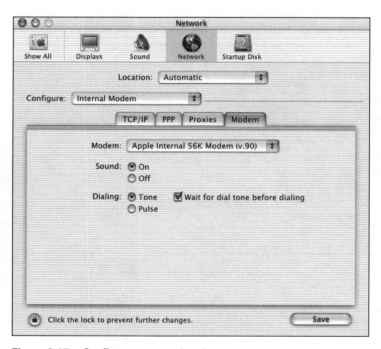

Figure 8.17   Configure your modem here.

Verifying Connectivity

Once you've established your dial-up settings, you'll want to try logging onto your ISP and making sure that everything works properly. Here's where you'll see Apple's replacement for the Remote Access Control Panel. To get connected, follow these steps:

1. Locate the Internet Connect application, which you'll find in your Applications folder.

TIP: If you intend to use Internet Connect frequently, drag its icon to the Dock. That way, it'll be just a click away whenever you need it. You can also make it a startup application by using the Login Items screen in the Login pane of System Preferences; with Mac OS X's efficient preemptive multitasking, you don't have to worry about keeping an extra application open for convenience.

2. Launch Internet Connect (see Figure 8.18). It'll have the name of your modem. You'll see that the settings you made for your ISP are displayed here. If you didn't enter a password, the Password field will be blank for you to type that information.

NOTE: You can redo the settings from the Internet Connect application simply by clicking on the Edit button. It'll launch the Network pane in the System Preferences application for you to reconfigure your setup.

3. Click on the Connect button to establish your connection. A status window will appear, indicating when your connection is established.

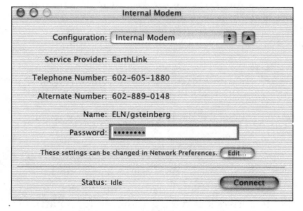

Figure 8.18 The settings previously made in the Network pane are duplicated here.

4. When your online session is done, click on the Disconnect button (which toggles to Connect). The process is no different from the way it was done under the Classic Mac OS.

NOTE: *Internet Connect will work even if your Internet application runs from the Classic environment.*

Using Apple's Location Manager to Create Custom Setups

As with the Classic Mac OS, there are times when you want to move your Mac to different places, particularly if it's an iBook or a PowerBook. Apple's location feature lets you create custom AirPort, modem, and network setups for each particular location. That way you can easily connect to the right local network and access the proper ISP without having to do the settings all over again. As you move from one place to another, just choose the correct location from the Network pane in the System Preferences application. Frequent travelers will treasure these features. Here's how it's done:

1. Launch the System Preferences application and click on the Network pane.

2. Under Configure, click on the Advanced option, which brings up the settings screen shown in Figure 8.19. You will see your present setup.

3. To create a new location, click on the Location pop-up menu and choose New Location.

4. Type the name for your new location and then click on the OK button.

5. Enter the Ethernet and modem and connection settings for that location, and click on the Save button to store them.

6. Repeat the above process for each location that you want to create.

7. To switch locations, choose Location from the Apple menu and select the name of the location you want to use from the submenu. The default is Automatic, which simply accesses whatever available network service is required for a particular purpose.

Figure 8.19   This is your setup for a typical Mac.

NOTE: *The Default Setting is smart enough to sort out most routine differences in network setups as you move from location to location.*

Accessing a Drop Box

Here's the problem. You attempt to copy or write files to the Drop Box folder on an AppleShare IP Server. But instead of seeing a progress bar to indicate that the files are being copied, you see a warning: "The operation cannot be completed because you do not have sufficient write privileges." The solution is to make sure that you only attempt to send files to a shared volume that has read/write privileges established. If you cannot change access privileges, contact your network administrator.

Correcting Network Access Problems

One of the hallmarks of the Mac operating system has been easy networking. You plug one Mac to another, or to a printer, network hub, and so on, and with a few simple setups, you are sharing files and printing without any great amount of difficulty. Should your network installation not work, however, you'll want to look into these possible solutions to the problem:

- *Recheck your settings*—Your first troubleshooting step should be to verify your setups in the Network pane of the System Preferences application. Remember that you will need to click on the Save button for changes to become effective (fortunately you'll be reminded of that with a prompt). One common problem is the failure to turn on AppleTalk, which means that standard network printers may not be available.

NOTE: *Don't assume Mac OS X is at fault. You'll also want to recheck the settings on the other computers involved in the network connection. If the setup is good, see if your Mac OS X computer can work with a different computer or printer. By checking this, you will be able to isolate a probable source for your problem.*

- *Examine your networking hardware*—Consider rechecking the networked cables and your hubs. Whenever there's a complete connection to the network hub or switch, one or two green lights will appear on that jack on a hub to indicate a proper connection is being made. If there's no green light, consider swapping cables to see if the problem transfers itself to the other computer or printer to which the cable was placed. If the problem travels, replace the cable. If it still doesn't work, consider whether your hub, itself, might not be defective.

- *Use the Network Utility application*—Mac OS X supplies a handy tool that can help you examine the status of your network in a more sophisticated fashion. You'll find the application (see Figure 8.20) in the Utilities folder, inside Mac OS X's Applications folder. After you launch the application, click on a tab to access your network scouring features. The most common one for you to check whether a network connection is being made is Ping, which sends a signal to the target Mac and then records whether the signal has been returned to you. Just enter the IP number of the Mac, click on Ping, and see if you get a result on repeated probings. Click on the Stop button when you're finished. If the

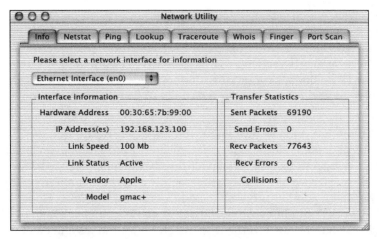

Figure 8.20 Apple's Network Utility can perform a variety of network-related diagnostics on your Mac.

probe doesn't yield a successful result, you'll want to return to your network hardware and configuration to be sure you didn't miss anything.

Protecting Your Network from the Internet

More and more folks these days have high-speed Internet connections. From cable to DSL, homes and businesses are joining the fast lane. I cover these and other fast access options in Chapter 20. An always-on connection, however, doesn't just deliver convenience. It means your Macs are vulnerable to attack from Internet vandals who might want to play pranks with your computers, or attempt to retrieve passwords and other personal information. Nobody is immune from such intruders. Even Microsoft was the victim of highly publicized network attacks on the secured servers that contain the source code for some of their software. Here are some ways to protect your network:

- *Use a hardware router to share connections*—There are several companies who manufacture Internet router products that will feed your Net connection across an Ethernet network to other computers (Macs and PCs). They include Asante, Farallon, LinkSys, and MacSense, to name just a few. These products are all designed to distribute the connection, and some include a hub or network switch. Most of these products also offer a built-in firewall, which sets up a secured barrier to prevent outsiders from entering your network. The common form of security employs an NAT (Network Address Translation) feature that, in effect, manages requests to and from the network, and hides the true IP numbers of your workstations. As a result, network intruders will find it far more difficult to invade your systems.

- *Software firewalls*—If you use a software router to share your connection, such as Sustainable SoftWorks IPNetRouter, or your Internet connection has no other means of protection, you'll want to buy a program that sets up a firewall. Current entrants in the Mac marketplace include Symantec's Norton Personal Firewall (based on another program called DoorStop from Open Door Networks) and Intego's NetBarrier. Both programs will help to block unauthorized traffic from reaching your Macs and can be adjusted to selectively allow certain traffic, as needed.

NOTE: *Symantec has also bundled Norton Personal Firewall with Norton Anti-Virus and Aladdin's iClean (which deletes old cache files and other items) to form an integrated package called Norton Integrated Security. Mac OS X versions of these programs and those from Intego were announced but not available when this book was written.*

- *Restrict distribution of administrator passwords*—Many of you have heard the horror stories about vengeful former employees of a company stealing confidential files and other proprietary information. While you may have legal remedies to get this material back, the cost in manpower and legal action can be tremendous with no guarantee of real success after years of effort. The best thing to do is to be careful about who gets access to passwords in your company, and perhaps to consider a non-disclosure agreement if employees have access to company secrets that will put a competing company at an advantage if they acquire the information. You'll also want to follow through with my suggestions to use strong passwords when setting user accounts to further help protect your network.

Chapter 9

The New AppleScript

If you need an immediate solution to:	See page:
Locating Mac OS X's AppleScript Collection	171
Choosing Mac OS X's Sample Scripts	171
Using Script Runner	173
Making or Editing Your First AppleScript	173
Running a Script from the Unix Command Line	176

In Brief

A lot of the work you do on your Mac is manual, despite the powerful operating system and incredible processing power. Every step requires an operation of keyboard and mouse. You locate a document in a specific folder with the Finder, and then double-click on the document to open it in the appropriate application. You then examine or edit the document. As necessary, you'll save it, print it, and proceed to the next document.

When you navigate the World Wide Web, you might enter a site's address or select one from your list of Favorites. During the course of a day, you'll be carrying out a number of repetitive steps.

What if you could make your Mac carry out a complex set of steps just by running a single application or by dragging and dropping files upon a little application? What if the tools to provide all that complex functionality didn't cost an extra cent and didn't require installing additional software? A dream? Is it something only a skilled computer programmer can do? Read on.

For years, the Macintosh operating system has had a built-in feature that lets you automate complex tasks. It's not something that's reserved for computer programmers and highly technical power users. The capability is in use today in the graphic design departments of major companies around the world. It's a feature used for creating print publications, editing videos, producing Web content, and automating everyday tasks, such as copying and printing files.

Did I say it was free? In fact, its origins can be traced way back to Mac System 7 in 1991. It's called AppleScript, and it's a powerful feature that's already on your Mac and that has no equal in the Windows world.

NOTE: *To be perfectly technical, one can use batch files and third-party programs to script Windows-related tasks. But AppleScript is far more user friendly than a batch file, and it's a standard part of the Mac OS.*

What AppleScript Can Do

The word *script* connotes an arcane language that is apt to confound and befuddle all but the most experienced Mac users. Yet AppleScript, while not quite plain English, is close enough to make it possible for folks like you and me to create scripts. What's more, with the scripts already available, you might be able to get all or most of the desktop automation you want without having to make anything at all.

In effect, AppleScript lets Mac programs communicate with one another and with the operating system. The scripts you make tell these programs what to do. For example, you might want scripts to automatically copy a file from one disk to another, to batch-process a series of images and apply certain Photoshop filters to them, and to save and print documents. And that's just the beginning. Many of the most popular Macintosh productivity programs depend on AppleScript to exploit some of their most useful features.

NOTE: *If you want to learn what sort of support an application has for AppleScript, check the application's documentation. AppleScript's uses range from the simple to the complex, and all variations in between.*

In the "Immediate Solutions" section of this chapter, you'll discover some of the tools Apple has already provided to let you exercise AppleScript. For now, here's a brief idea of what you can do with AppleScript:

- *Automate use of the Mac OS X Finder*—Many common Finder functions can be scripted. That means, you can use complex file-management features by launching a single script.

- *Automate Mac OS system functions*—From searching the Internet, to automatically adjusting a specific set of settings, AppleScript can handle operations that require repeating steps.

- *Automate workflow*—This is where AppleScript comes into its own in a working environment. Users of the popular desktop publishing application QuarkXPress, for example, can create scripts that access specific templates for pages, flow in text, import images, and scale and crop the images. In Adobe Photoshop, a script can be used to open all the images placed in a single folder, apply a specific set of program filters to them, and then save the images in a specific file format. Imagine if you had to do all this work manually, one step at a time.

- *Record your actions*—You don't have to write all your scripts from scratch. Many programs (and the Mac OS X Finder) let you record a series of actions, using Apple's Script Editor application. After the steps have been recorded, you can save them as a script, and then have them run the same as any other AppleScript.

AppleScript, however, is not the only desktop automation feature. Some commercial programs, such as CE Software's QuicKeys, perform similar functions, but have the added advantage of working with all Mac software, not just those that can be specifically scripted. As this book was being written, QuicKeys for Mac OS X was announced (see Figure 9.1). It might be available by the time you read this book.

What Doesn't Work in Mac OS X

Some features of the Mac OS X version of AppleScript might not be completely functional. An example is the Folder Actions feature, which allows you to attach specific functions to a folder when it's opened. AppleScript features are works in progress, and more features will be added over time. Fortunately, your existing scripts ought to work pretty much the same under Mac OS X as they did under the Classic Mac OS. In addition, printing and network scripting and program linking were not initially supported.

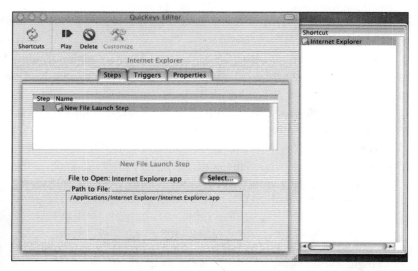

Figure 9.1   A long-time favorite, QuicKeys is making the migration to Mac OS X.

Apple suggests, however, that when you create scripts you should identify the operating system version, in case problems arise when switching from one to the other. That'll make the process of testing and removing bugs from the script easier.

Mac OS X Script Features

When you get started with AppleScript, you'll find that a number of Mac applications support a feature and thus will provide quite a degree of exposure to what this valuable tool can do. These include such standard applications as QuickTime Player, Sketch, and TextEdit. In addition, AppleWorks 6.1, which has been rewritten to support Mac OS X, can be scripted, as can Casady & Greene's MP3 program, SoundJam MP.

The Tools for Using Scripts in Mac OS X

Aside from the built-in functions of some programs that use AppleScript behind the scenes, an AppleScript can come in several forms—as an applet, as a fully compiled script, or as a text file containing the script commands. Which form to use depends on the program you're running, but the most common form of script is the applet. An applet is a small application you can double-click on to start it or on which you can drag and drop an item that is subjected to the scripting action.

NOTE: *In addition to double-clicking and dragging and dropping, you can place an AppleScript applet in the Dock so that it can be activated with a single click. Later in this chapter, you'll learn about some custom AppleScripts that directly affect the functions of the Dock. There's even one that can quit the Dock, in case you would rather not use it.*

In Mac OS X, Apple has included a convenient way to run your scripts. It's an application called *Script Runner*, which allows you to execute any number of scripts from a single floating palette (see Figure 9.2). I tell you how to set it up in the "Immediate Solutions" section of this chapter.

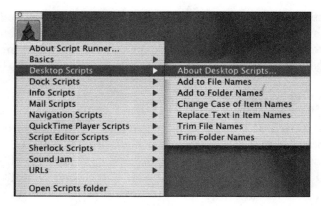

Figure 9.2   The Script Runner in this picture has already been loaded with a number of useful scripts for Mac OS X.

AppleScript: The Future

The future of AppleScript is wide and vast. Apple has made no bones about the fact that the present iteration of its system-wide scripting language works just fine with both the Carbon and Cocoa environments, so it doesn't matter whether software developers use either. In addition, AppleScript continues to function with Classic applications, so there's no fear about losing the functionality of scripts made with such programs as Adobe Photoshop and QuarkXPress.

NOTE: *Both Adobe and Quark have committed to bringing their applications into the Mac OS X environment. You'll want to check with these publishers for estimated timetables. It appears that QuarkXPress will be updated later rather than earlier. They have indicated that the version they were working on when this book went to press would first appear as a Classic application.*

What's more, Apple plans to extend AppleScript support for the Unix environment as well. You'll get an indication of how AppleScript works in the "Immediate Solutions" section of this chapter, where I show you how to run a script from the command line.

Immediate Solutions

Locating Mac OS X's AppleScript Collection

Before you get started making a script of your own, you might want to try using the ones Apple has provided. You'll get a good idea of what an AppleScript can do, and by examining the script in the Script Editor application, you'll learn the scripting language; this will go a long way toward helping you develop your own scripting skills. To locate the scripts, follow these steps:

1. Open the Applications folder.

2. Double-click on the AppleScript folder.

3. Open the Example Scripts folder, and then open the folder that contains scripts in the category you want to try.

After you've located the scripts you want, you'll need to install them in Apple's Script Runner application.

Choosing Mac OS X's Sample Scripts

As explained in the previous section, Apple has assembled a small collection of useful AppleScripts that you can use to learn how it works. Here's a list of the script folders and some of the scripts provided:

- *Basics*—These scripts are designed to help you discover the basics of preparing your own AppleScripts. The scripts provided will transport you to the AppleScript pages at Apple's Web site, launch the Script Editor application, and give you a tour through the handy Help menus on the subject.

- *Finder Scripts*—These scripts are designed to work with the Finder. They can alter file and folder names in various ways, from changing case to searching and replacing the names of files in a folder. In addition, file and folder names can be trimmed to look more readable in a Finder window.

- *Info Scripts*—The sole script provided with Mac OS X lets you change your Date & Time setting.

9. The New AppleScript

- *Mail Scripts*—There's just one entrant in this area, but it's a useful one. You can use this script to set an address and a subject line for an email message. Once you enter this information (you have to set a default address first), the script will automatically open the Mail application and then populate a new message window with this information.

- *Navigation Scripts*—These scripts are designed strictly to work with the Finder. They will activate a new Finder window pointing directly to a specific folder. There are scripts for the Applications, Documents, Favorites, and Home folders.

- *Script Editor Scripts*—These all have a single purpose—to help you write a script that runs properly. Each is designed to test a particular script function, such as checking for syntax errors.

- *Sherlock Scripts*—The sole entrant when this book was being written allowed you to use Sherlock's handy Internet searching features. You'll learn more about Apple's superb search application in Chapter 7.

- *URLs*—The scripts in this folder are designed to access specific Web sites. These scripts contain the examples I use when I show you how to modify or create your own scripts.

- *Dock Scripts*—These scripts can be used to control the way the Dock functions. One of the scripts—Quit the Dock—can be used to eliminate the Dock entirely if you no longer want to use it. The other scripts allow you to perform such actions as changing the Dock's preferences and resetting it to its factory configuration.

NOTE: *This script (Quit the Dock) and the next are not a part of the standard Mac OS X collection, but you can find this and other scripts for you to try at Apple's Web site. Just point your browser to **www.apple.com/applescript/MacOSX/OSXBeta.02.html**, and you'll get the latest information and sample scripts.*

- *SoundJam*—This set of scripts is designed to work with the Mac OS X version of Casady & Greene's popular MP3 application, SoundJam MP Player for Mac OS X. These scripts can be used to control various aspects of the application and the way in which it handles your sound files and play lists.

NOTE: *As you might know, SoundJam is the predecessor of Apple's iTunes jukebox software. iTunes not only inherited some of the programming code of SoundJam, but the lead programmer, Jeffrey Robbin (also the author of Conflict Catcher, a system extension management program), also rejoined Apple to continue working on iTunes development. The Mac OS X version of iTunes is available separately as a download from Apple's Web site.*

Using Script Runner

To get started with AppleScript in Mac OS X, you'll want to set up Apple's Script Runner application, a program that can be used to both organize and run your scripts (see Figure 9.3). Here's how to work with Script Runner:

1. First, locate your copy. Script Runner is in the Applications folder.

2. Double-click on Script Runner to launch it.

3. To get started, click on the button on the little Script Runner floating icon, and select Open Scripts Folder from the pop-up menu.

4. In the Example Scripts folder, Apple has provided some sample scripts to get you started. Drag them all to the Scripts window.

5. Click on the close button of Script Runner to close it. Now, launch Script Runner again. Your newly added scripts are now available from this little program.

6. Removing a script is a simple matter of dragging the script from the Scripts folder. The next time you launch Script Runner, the script will no longer be available.

Figure 9.3   Script Runner is a convenient way to access all your scripts from a single interface.

Making or Editing Your First AppleScript

Although AppleScript is a plain-English language, there are some basic commands you need to use to make your scripts work. In this section, I'll show you how to create your first script, just to give you an idea of how it's done. Using these techniques, once you learn the syntax, you'll be able to make scripts as easy or complex as you want.

NOTE: *I am not trying to minimize the learning curve for AppleScript. It takes time, study, and some practice to become flexible in writing reliable scripts. If you want to learn more about the subject, visit the AppleScript Web site at **www.apple.com/applescript**. There, you'll discover sample scripts and online tutorials where you can learn both simple and complex scripting skills.*

In this script, you will tell Microsoft's Internet Explorer to access a Web site—in this case, mine. Here's how to make your first script:

1. Locate the Script Editor application, which is in the Utilities folder inside the Applications folder.

2. Double-click on the program to launch it (see Figure 9.4).

3. When the program is running, a blank script window ought to be on your screen. If it's not, choose New Script from the program's File menu.

4. The first element in our script is a property. The property defines the item you will be acting on in the script. In this case, the URL that's named **www.macnightowl.com** will be accessed. So, type the following text and then press the Return key (don't worry about writing commands in bold as you see them in a completed script; it's not necessary):

```
property target_URL: "http://www.macnightowl.com/"
```

5. Now, type the following commands, which tell the script to ignore how an application responds to the command:

```
ignoring application responses
```

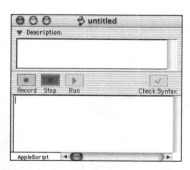

Figure 9.4   Creating an AppleScript starts here.

6. In the next set of commands, specify the application that you want to script, tell it what action to perform, and then close this set of commands:

```
tell application "Internet Explorer"
Activate
GetURL target_URL
end tell
end ignoring
```

7. We are almost at the finish line now, and your Script Editor window should look much like the one in Figure 9.5. The next step is to make sure the script was written properly. Click on the Check Syntax button. The script you just wrote will be checked for errors. AppleScript is very literal-minded, so if a single letter in a command is wrong, you'll see what it is and what you need to do to fix it.

TIP: *When a script is examined for syntax, it will take on the text formatting shown in Figure 9.5, with bold commands. Before you do that, it's all straight text.*

---

8. If the script has an error, now's the time to recheck the script and fix the problem. If the script checks out, choose Save As from the File menu.

9. Type a name for your new script that corresponds to its purpose, choose Compiled Script as the format, and specify the location where the script will be saved. (The best place to save the script is in the Scripts folder so it'll be recognized by Script Runner.)

10. Click on the Save button.

Figure 9.5 Here's the completed script ready to check for bad syntax.

11. To make sure your script truly does what you want, go ahead and run it. Launch Internet Explorer. If the script to access a specific URL was compiled correctly, it'll access the Web site you specified (see Figure 9.6).

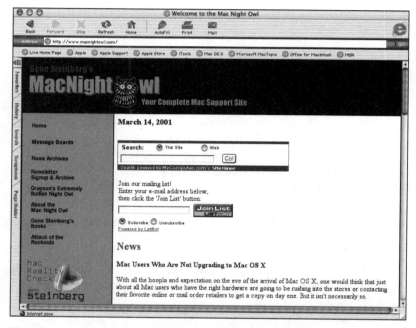

Figure 9.6   Success! The author's Web site was opened, courtesy of the script you created.

Running a Script from the Unix Command Line

If you want to try running an AppleScript from Mac OS X's Unix command line, here's what to do:

1. Locate the Terminal application in the Utilities folder, within the Applications folder.

2. Double-click on the Terminal application to launch it.

3. In the command line, type "osascript" and then type the name of the script.

4. Press Return to activate the script. If you enter the correct file name, the script should run precisely the same as if it were accessed via Script Runner.

Chapter 10

Installing Programs Under Mac OS X

If you need an immediate solution to:	See page:
Handling Complex Application Installations	182
Using an Installer	182
Using a Disk Image	182
Making a Startup Application	184
Using the New Open Dialog Box	185
Using the New Save Dialog Box	187
Using the Services Menu	189
Troubleshooting Software Installation Problems	191

In Brief

Way back when, you could install an application on your Macintosh simply by dragging the application's icon from a floppy disk to your hard-drive icon. In a few moments, the program would be on your Mac, a double-click away from running.

Over time, however, things have gotten a lot more complicated. A single application might consist of hundreds of files, and not all those files are placed in the same folder. Some go into disparate locations inside the System Folder. More often than not, it isn't even readily apparent which file belongs to what. So, the installation is handled by an installer that is designed to sort all this out for you and, if necessary, to restart your Mac.

Removing an application can be totally frustrating unless the installer has an Uninstall option. There's even a third-party program—Spring Cleaning, from Aladdin Systems—that is designed to remove all vestiges of a program.

Introducing the Package

Beginning with Mac OS 9, Apple came up with a better idea for Mac users (though it's not unique to the Mac)—the *Package*. A Package is simply a folder that contains an application and all its support files, whether one or a thousand. But all of these elements are hidden from the end-user. The Package appears on your Mac as a single icon that you can double-click to launch the application that is located within the Package folder.

Installing is a dream—a throwback to the earliest days of the Macintosh. Just drag the application's Package to the appropriate folder and run it.

Removing an application involves the same process. You drag it to the trash and empty the trash, and all elements of that program are removed. It's remarkable that the best way to install and remove a program was the way it was done originally, back in 1984 when the first Mac appeared on the scene.

The Microsoft Way

Microsoft, which has paid more attention to the Mac platform in recent years, has been featuring drag-and-drop installation of its software since Office 98 came out in 1998. The process involves dragging a folder to your Mac's hard drive. However, you still have a visible folder containing a lot of separate files, and you still have to open that folder to run any of the applications you've installed.

Also, when you first launch any recent Microsoft application, it will populate the older Mac OS Extensions folder with a bunch of files, and these have to be manually removed if you decide to uninstall the software. So, Microsoft's drag-and-drop installation is only part of a solution, but it's a step in the right direction.

Exploring New Application Features

As I explain throughout this book, any application written to support Mac OS X inherits a bevy of beautiful interface features and Unix-based reliability. In addition to preemptive multitasking and protected memory, you'll see visible differences to enhance your computing experience. These differences include:

NOTE: *Although older, Classic Mac applications can run under Mac OS X, they do not inherit any of the features about to be discussed. These are all the province of programs developed for the Carbon or Cocoa programming environments.*

- *Services*—Available in the Applications menu of many applications, the Services command produces a submenu that makes it possible for you to access the features of another application. This feature allows you to select text or a picture in your document and then go to the Services menu, choose a command from another application, and have that command executed in that program. In effect, this lets you send the text from one program to another without having to launch the second application, drag text between them, or use Export and Import features.

- *Open dialog box*—The venerable Mac Open dialog box has been one of the most confusing features of the operating system. It can be difficult for folks to navigate through large collections of nested folders and various disks to find a file. Although the Open dialog box was updated in Mac OS 8.5 with a new scheme, called *navigation services*, this was only part of what needed to be done. For Mac OS X, Apple has redesigned this dialog box yet

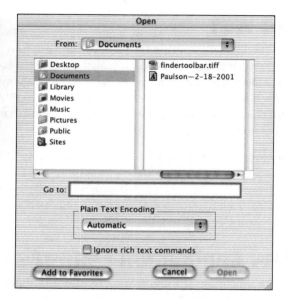

Figure 10.1   The new Open dialog box makes it easier for you to locate the file you want to use.

again, and the new version (see Figure 10.1) simplifies navigation tremendously. In addition, it's non-modal, which means that it doesn't prevent you from doing something else on your Mac until it's dismissed. You can bring up the Open dialog box and then switch to another application, and the Open dialog box will still be there when you return; the operation of your Mac is not affected.

TIP: *Users often overlook the Open dialog box. A prime example is the common practice of many Mac users to double-click on a file's icon to open it, even if the application used to make the file is already open. Apple has had to do its homework here, and it has made things much better for Mac OS X.*

- *Save dialog box*—Another bugaboo of the older versions of the Mac OS was the Save dialog box. When you wanted to save your document, where were you putting it? How often did you waste time figuring out the correct place (if there was one) to put a file? The Mac OS X version of the Save dialog box opens as a sheet in the document window in which you're working (see Figure 10.2). There's no question as to what you're saving, and the simple elegance of its interface makes it easy for you to specify precisely where your document is going so you can easily locate it later— without a headache or constant use of the Sherlock file-search utility.

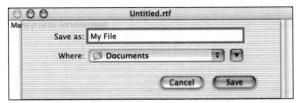

Figure 10.2   A new way to simplify the process of saving your document.

- *New location for the Quit command*—This is not a critical issue but is one of logic. Instead of putting the Quit command in the customary place in the File menu, it goes in the application menu. The logic is that the command affects the application, not the file (except indirectly, because files are closed before an application is closed). If nothing else, logic wins out here.

TIP: *Regardless of the location of the Quit command, pressing Command+Q still activates this feature. Some things never change, thank heavens.*

- *Font panel*—Not all applications designed for Mac OS X will inherit this feature, but those that do use the Font panel will enjoy enhanced abilities to access fonts and manage a font library. As described in Chapter 16, Mac OS X has native support for PostScript, TrueType, and OpenType fonts, plus the original bitmap fonts that date back to the original versions of the Mac OS. With the Font panel (see Figure 10.3), not only can you select your fonts, but you can preview them in the sizes you want and create special collections to ease font management.

Figure 10.3   The Mac OS X Font panel, when available in your application, eases font handling.

Immediate Solutions

Handling Complex Application Installations

Mac OS X's Package feature greatly simplifies the installation and removal of applications, but some programs have, for one reason or another, more complex installation processes. This can happen when you're trying to install a Classic application. The following sections describe some of the installation options.

Using an Installer

The normal way to install an application—when you're not using Mac OS X's new techniques—is to load a CD and double-click on an installer application. After an installer is launched, read the prompts and other on-screen instructions. Should the installer application ask for a location for the application, specify the Applications folder for ease of organization.

At the end of the installation, you might see a Restart prompt. Click on it to restart your Mac. After the restart, you'll be able to use the application normally.

Using a Disk Image

Another way to distribute software is to use the disk image. The disk image has the virtue of being a copy of the original distribution disk for the software, so you can use it without needing to have the disk media present. A disk image can consist of just the installation files or the full installation CD.

NOTE: *Just about all of Apple's software files are distributed in disk image form for convenience, and many other publishers are using a similar technique.*

To use a disk image, follow these steps:

1. Locate the disk image file. It will usually be identified by a file name with the extension .img or .smi. Double-click on the file's name. Over the next few seconds, the file will be checked to make sure it isn't damaged. If it turns out to be damaged, you will have to get another copy (download it again, for example).

TIP: *If the file was compressed for distribution to save download time from the Internet, the file may come as a compressed archive, which sports an .sit or .hqx extension. If you have a file of this sort, double-clicking on it ought to be sufficient to activate the decompression software (StuffIt Expander, which comes with Mac OS X). StuffIt Deluxe 6 and StuffIt Expander 6, available from Aladdin Systems, include improved support for Mac OS X. The latter is free, so you'll want to consider downloading it from the publisher's Web site at* **www.aladdinsys.com.** *The installation information contains special instructions about using the program with Mac OS X.*

2. When the file opens, it'll put a disk image icon on your Mac's desktop. Double-click on the icon to reveal its contents (see Figure 10.4).

3. If the file contains an installer, double-click on the installer to proceed.

NOTE: *When you open the contents of a disk image file, you'll want to see if there are any ReadMe files. If there are ReadMe files, open them to see if you need to follow any special instructions to install the application or prepare for the installation.*

4. Should the disk image contain the actual file or files to be installed, look for instructions on how to proceed. Microsoft's Office and Internet software include a text description on the disk image or on the CD itself explaining what to do (usually just drag the installation folder to your Mac's hard drive).

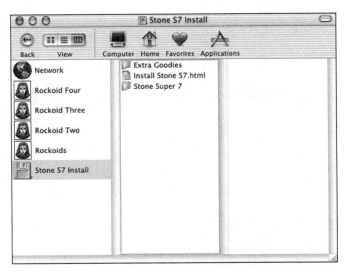

Figure 10.4   A disk image's contents appear in the Finder window.

5. When the installation is done (and you've restarted the Mac, if necessary), you can proceed with using the new software.

Making a Startup Application

If you want to have your application launch as soon as you boot your Mac, follow these steps:

NOTE: *In Mac OS X, there are no system extensions. The alternative is to run your program as an application that starts up with your Mac. Some installers might set this up for you behind the scenes. These instructions tell you how to do it yourself.*

---

1. Locate the System Preferences application icon in the Dock, and click on it, or double-click on its icon in the Applications folder.

2. Click once on the Login pane to open the Login Items window, shown in Figure 10.5.

3. Click on the Add button.

4. In the Open dialog box that appears next, select the application or file that you want to open when you log in as a user on your Mac (see Figure 10.6).

5. Click on the Open button to store the file in your Login Items window.

6. If you want to hide the application (so its window is available only from the Dock), click on the Hide checkbox.

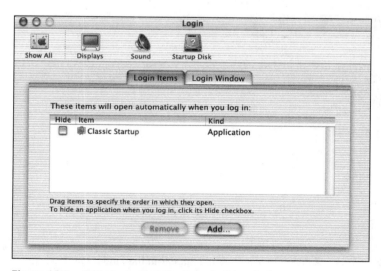

Figure 10.5   Add startup applications in this window.

Figure 10.6   Select your startup application in this dialog box.

7. Choose Quit from the Application menu, or press Command+Q, to quit System Preferences (or press the close button). Then next time you reboot your Mac and log in under that username, the selected application will launch.

NOTE: *Startup applications apply strictly to a single users account. Each user of your Mac can select from a different range of startup applications.*

Using the New Open Dialog Box

If you're used to double-clicking on a document to open it, rather than going through the Open dialog box, here's Mac OS X's better way:

1. Launch the application in which you want to open the document.

2. Choose Open from the File menu or press Command+O. This produces a dialog box much like the one shown in Figure 10.7, featuring a Finder-type column display. The pop-up menu lists the folder hierarchy from bottom to top, also easing navigation.

NOTE: *Open dialog boxes include options that apply to a specific application. I used AppleWorks 6.1 for this illustration. You will find that some choices are different for other Mac OS X applications.*

---

3. Click on a folder's name to reveal its contents.

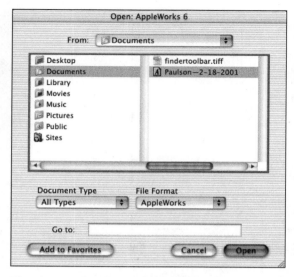

Figure 10.7   Easily locate the document you want to open.

4. Should you want a document added to your Favorites, select its icon and click on the Add To Favorites button before opening the document.

5. If the document you want doesn't appear, see if your application's Open dialog box has a pop-up menu listing alternate file formats supported, and use these to see if the document appears.

TIP: *If a document's name is grayed out, it means that the program you're using cannot open it.*

---

6. When you locate the document you want to open, either select it and click on the Open button, or double-click on the document's name.

TIP: *If a document you open is a template or was created in an older version of a program, you might see a new, untitled document on your screen, rather than the name of the one you selected. If this is the case, you can simply save the document with the original name to replace it, or give it a new name and store it in a new location, if necessary.*

---

7. If the document you wanted to locate isn't shown, click on the Cancel button or press Command+. (period) or the Esc key to dismiss the Open dialog box. Then, use Apple's Sherlock search application to find the document. You'll find more information about Sherlock in Chapter 7.

Using the New Save Dialog Box

On the surface, saving a new document ought to be an especially easy process, but it hasn't always been thus in the Mac OS. The new Save dialog box for Mac OS X offers both basic and advanced options to help you quickly find a place to put your document, so you can easily locate it later. Here is how to use this feature to its best advantage:

1. When you're ready to save your new document for the first time, choose Save As from the File menu. A virtual sheet will drop down from the document's title bar (see Figure 10.8).

NOTE: *When the Save dialog box is displayed, you can move on to another document in the active application or to another application on your Mac. The dialog box will stay put, connected to the original document's title bar, so you can save it later without storing the wrong document by mistake.*

2. Type a name for your document in the Save As text field. It's always a good idea to be as clear as possible when creating a name, so you can easily recognize the document when you need to open it again.

NOTE: *Although, in theory, Mac OS X supports file names with a total of 256 characters, you'll want to keep a file name to a reasonable length.*

3. To select a location for your document, click on the pop-up menu to the right of the Where field. The default location is your Documents folder, inside your personal user's folder, but you can click on the menu and specify another location.

4. To see more locations and additional choices, click on the down arrow at the right of the Where pop-up menu. You'll then see the expanded view reminiscent of the Finder's column view (see Figure 10.9).

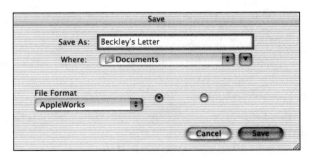

Figure 10.8   Where do you want to put your document?

Figure 10.9   You have additional choices as to how to handle your new document.

NOTE: *When you choose an expanded Save dialog view, the selection will usually stick for that particular application until you switch to the standard, simplified display by clicking on the up arrow to the right to the Where field.*

---

5. Click on a folder in the left column to see the contents in the right column.

6. If you want to put your file in a new folder, first choose the location for the folder from the column display, and then click on the New Folder button, which will open the New Folder dialog box (see Figure 10.10).

7. Type a name for the new folder.

8. Click on the Create button. The new folder will be placed in the location selected in the Save dialog box.

9. You can also make the document a favorite so that it'll appear in your Favorites folder for fast access. To do this, click on the Add To Favorites button.

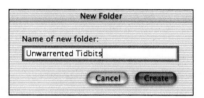

Figure 10.10   Name your new folder.

10. When your save options are selected, click on the Save button to store the file. If the document name you selected is already in use, you can either replace the document with the duplicate name or give your new document a different name; the document you are replacing must be closed for this to work.

WARNING! Once you replace a document with the duplicate name, the replaced document is history, so consider carefully which choice to make if you run into this situation.

NOTE: If the column display isn't big enough to show a thorough view of the contents of your Mac's drive, click on the resize bar at the bottom-right corner and drag to expand the Save As window.

Using the Services Menu

Wouldn't it be nice if applications could easily communicate with one another without your having to go through the confusing processes of cutting and pasting and dragging and dropping? The Services menu for Mac OS X helps to minimize this problem. Here's an example of how it can be used to make two programs work together:

NOTE: This example is for demonstration purposes only. I use TextEdit and OmniWeb, a Web browser described in Chapter 20. But any Web browser that accesses the Services feature can accomplish the same task. You can download a copy of the latest version of OmniWeb from www.omnigroup.com.

1. Open a word processing or text editing program. For the sake of this exercise, I'm using TextEdit, the replacement for Apple's SimpleText.

2. Type the URL for your favorite Web site.

3. Select the URL.

4. Go to the Application menu, choose Services, and scroll to OmniWeb, where the submenu will read Open URL (see Figure 10.11).

When you select this option, the selected URL will open in OmniWeb (see Figure 10.12). Depending on the program you're using and the kind of text or picture objects you've selected, the Services menu will display different choices, and different commands will be available to apply to the selected material.

Figure 10.11   It takes longer to describe than to show.

Figure 10.12   OmniWeb now displays a Web site whose URL was selected in TextEdit.

Troubleshooting Software Installation Problems

Mac OS X makes software installation easy, but there are times when things simply won't work. Here are some common problems and solutions:

- *The application won't launch*—Is it a Mac OS X application? If not, it might not work in the Classic environment. If the program is Mac OS X-savvy, consider restarting your Mac to see if it makes a difference. If it doesn't, reinstall the application. If this doesn't work, contact the publisher about possible compatibility problems.

NOTE: *It's a sure thing that most any application that is designed to work with specific hardware, such as scanning software, will not function in the Classic environment. You will need to wait for a Mac OS X version.*

- *The application keeps quitting*—Usually, this is an installation or compatibility problem. Your first line of attack is to try launching the application again. Mac OS X's protected memory will close down the memory space with the application (unless it runs in the Classic environment). If that doesn't work, restart your Mac. You might also want to consider reinstalling the program. Otherwise, consult the documentation or the publisher's support department or Web site for information about possible bugs.

NOTE: *Since you're running a brand new operating system, discovering applications that fail should not be unexpected. You'll want to check with the publisher about possible updates. In particular, you'll find that the Classic environment sometimes won't quit or will quit very slowly.*

- *The application is installed in the wrong place*—Drag the application icon or folder to the Applications folder.

If you continue to run into problems with an application, whether newly installed or not, check Chapter 19 for more information about troubleshooting Mac OS X.

Part II

Mac OS X and Hardware

Chapter 11

Hardware Management

If you need an immediate solution to:	See page:
Installing New Hardware	199
Maintaining Your Mac on a Daily Basis	200
Buying a New Mac	202
Looking at Extended Warranties	204
Solving Hardware and Software Problems	205

In Brief

The arrival of Mac OS X greatly simplifies the process of handling your system and application software. Ease of installation, simplified file management, and improved performance and reliability are hallmarks of the new operating system and the programs that come with it.

Most of the other chapters in this book deal primarily with the software, except for the ones devoted to adding new hardware accessories and using a Mac on the road.

But there is yet another important factor on the road to setting up and maintaining a Mac system and that's the Mac itself. In this chapter, I cover the basics of surviving a new Mac hardware installation, some of the special features Mac OS X provides to support that hardware, and some of the problems you may encounter and their solutions.

A Look at Two of Mac OS X's Special Hardware Features

It's not just the system software that provides the performance advantage and reliability for Mac OS X. The new operating system has special support to harness powerful features you might already have on your Mac.

Here are two of the main capabilities that can make your Mac more powerful and productive:

NOTE: *To truly exploit these powerful technologies, you need to run Mac OS X-savvy applications. Your older programs will run with good performance in the Classic compatibility environment, but no faster and no more reliably than they did before. If any of these applications crashes, it will bring the entire Classic environment down, although not affect the rest of the system. There could, in some cases, even be somewhat of a performance hit.*

- *Advanced Graphics Management*—The Quartz imaging layer has built-in support for technologies such as PDF, OpenGL and QuickTime. The superlative visual display of the Aqua interface, with shadings, shadows, transparency, and realtime object dragging, is one of the features that maximizes the potential of the graphics chips in your Mac. Even the first-generation iMac with a 233Mhz processor and entry-level graphics chip from ATI Technologies can provide speedy performance, but these work best in the thousands of colors mode. Of course, if you have a top-of-the-line Power Macintosh computer with an NVIDIA graphics chip, you will realize the maximum possible benefit from the new features regardless of resolution settings.

WARNING! If you do not have a Mac with a graphics chip from ATI, IX Micro or NVIDIA, you will have to contact the manufacturer about driver updates to address Mac OS X compatibility. This problem could be difficult if you have a graphic card from a defunct maker, such as 3dfx Interactive, but you might want to check such software information sites as VersionTracker.com to see if any outside parties will provide updates.

- *Symmetric Multiprocessing*—Some Macs come with more than a single processor chip. While previous versions of the Mac OS and a very few applications (such as Adobe Photoshop) offer limited support for multiprocessing, as a practical matter, the extra brainpower doesn't do much good, except to help Apple's marketing department push new Macs. This changes, however, with Mac OS X, which has built-in support for multiprocessing and can efficiently parcel tasks between processors to speed up performance. Any application that can handle multiple threading or tasks can also take advantage of multiprocessing, so that you get the maximum level of performance from all the extra processor.

NOTE: *Multiple threading means, simply stated, that a program can handle more than a single chore at the same time.*

Together, these features can take the same Mac that served you well under previous versions of the Mac OS and make it seem almost as if you bought a new computer. Your Mac will start faster, launch applications faster, and won't seem to bog down at inopportune times when you're trying to make it do two things at once.

NOTE: *Multiprocessing isn't a panacea. Other systems on your Mac, such as your graphics card and hard drive, can conspire to put limits on overall performance.*

With preemptive multitasking, the operating system parcels out the tasks among programs (not the programs themselves), so your Mac will be able to play a QuickTime movie, download software from the Internet, and print documents without slowing down or coming to a screeching halt.

TIP: *One way to test the effects of Mac OS X on your Mac is to pull down a menu while performing all the functions labeled above and see if performance changes. Then, try doing the very same thing under Mac OS 9, one of the more reliable Mac operating system versions, and see how long it takes for multiple processes to come to a stop.*

11. Hardware Management

Immediate Solutions

Installing New Hardware

The arrival of a new Mac in your home or office can be a special event. It may be your first Mac, or your tenth, but you'll want to get it up and running right away. The promise of getting on the Internet in 10 or 15 minutes flat is tempting. But here are some things to consider first before you deploy that new computer in a production setup:

1. Check it for obvious damage first. Macs are packed pretty carefully by Apple and their dealers, but sometimes they just don't survive the trip to your home or office. If the box has severe visible signs of damage, let the shipper or dealer know right away. Then, open carefully and see if the computer itself also seems damaged. If so, don't use it. Wait for a thorough diagnosis or replacement.

NOTE: This has happened to me. Shortly before this book went to press, I was assigned to review a snow-white iMac DV SE for CNET, a large online tech news resource, and when the computer arrived at my home office via overnight carrier, the box was a mess. When I opened it, the top of the case was cracked. Such a thing has only happened once to me, but it was a jarring experience.

2. Assuming your computer looks fine, follow the instructions carefully about hooking it up. If you intend to connect it to a network and/or hook up a bunch of peripherals to it, it's a good idea to first run the new Mac system all by itself, with just mouse, display, and keyboard, and a modem or other Net connection to handle registration.

NOTE: On a rare occasion, a Mac with no visible damage will still be dead on arrival. If the Mac refuses to boot properly, or crashes constantly even before you can perform simple functions, you should stop using it and contact your Apple dealer or Apple Computer about repair or replacement. Most dealers (even The Apple Store) will replace a DOA unit.

3. Turn on the Mac and follow the setup prompts to store your user settings and register the product. Registration from the Mac requires that you connect to Apple's Web site to send the information.

NOTE: *If there's no ready Net access, check the documentation with the new Macs for a registration card that can accomplish the same task via the post office.*

---

4. Once the Mac is registered, try running a few programs and see if everything works.

5. Should the Mac be running all right, you should connect your peripherals and/or network connections and see if everything functions normally.

6. If the computer seems to work, but you run into problems with one accessory or another, be sure you have installed the latest drivers for those products. I cover the subject of adding extras to your Mac in Chapter 12.

If your Mac comes through like a champ, you're ready to deploy it for production purposes.

Maintaining Your Mac on a Daily Basis

If your Mac runs fine, you may be tempted to use it day in and day out and never concern yourself about proper hardware maintenance. While a personal computer is nowhere near as sensitive to lack of proper care as the family car (where a missed oil change or two, or the failure to change worn breaks or tires can be catastrophic), you should periodically give your Mac a once over (or two or three) just to keep it purring. Here's a simplified maintenance schedule:

• *Check the Hard Drive Regularly*—Every week or so, you should have Apple's DriveUtility or your favorite hard drive diagnostic program check all the drives connected to your Mac. Directory damage has a habit of creeping up on you. First, there are reports of simple problems, and then they grow worse, finally resulting in lost files or the inability of the drive to mount. But if you perform regular diagnostics, you'll be able to fix problems before they become too serious.

WARNING! Many older hard drive diagnostic problems are not designed to work with Mac OS X, even if you restart your Mac from the Mac OS 9 environment. You should check with the publisher directly about compatibility issues. The file structure under Mac OS X is different enough for bogus reports of disk problems to appear, and attempts to fix those problems could create real ones.

- *Keep It Clean*—I live in a Southwest desert state, so I have a chronic problem of dust buildup. In just a few weeks, the surface of the Macs in my home office can become dusty, and don't ask about the interior of the computers. On a regular basis, it's a good idea to dust the case with a soft cloth (not abrasive). Stay away from caustic cleaning solutions, but sometimes a light dose of a window cleaning solution on a soft cloth is useful. If your display has become dusty, check the manufacturer's instructions about cleaning. Be especially careful with the soft surface of an LCD display. Damage can be mighty expensive. Every few months, you might want to open your Mac (powered off of course) and blow out the dust. Excessive dust buildup could affect the integrity of the items, such as RAM, connected to the logic board or the expansion bus (PCI or AGP). It can also hurt the performance of a cooling fan, or even block the convection cooling vents on the iMac and PowerMac G4 Cube.

NOTE: *Excessive dust inside your Mac can cause performance anomalies. I once visited a client who had chronic crash problems. His software seemed up to date, and he had recently reformatted the drive, yet the problems persisted. Before sending him to the repair shop and an expensive bill, I opened the Mac. A cloud of dust filled the room. A dose of a compressed air canister, placed just close enough to do some good, cleared out the Mac in short order. After removing and reseating the RAM and expansion cards, I closed up the Mac. It ran perfectly; no more chronic crashes.*

- *Optimize Sparingly*—The process of optimizing (or *defragging*) a hard drive rewrites all the files and puts them adjacent to each other, rather than spread across the drive as they are normally (though Mac OS X's advanced file system is more efficient in this regard). In theory, if there's enough defragmentation, performance might suffer. In practice, it takes an awful lot to make a difference. Besides, Mac OS X's improved file handling can reduce the problem. If you are, however, removing and reinstalling huge numbers of files, which is common in the graphic arts industry, you might find a slight speed boost if you optimize. Video capture performance can be especially affected by such problems.

- *Check for Driver/Software Updates*—Software and device drivers are all in a constant process of evolution and change. You'll want to stay in contact with the manufacturers about needed updates for better support of Mac OS X. A good resource for such information is the VersionTracker.com Web site (see **www.versiontracker.com**).

- *Check Your Mac After a Power Failure*—If a weather or power company problem has resulted in loss of power at your home or office, you'll want to check your computers carefully when power is restored. Normally, when you restart or shut down your Mac, there is a "housecleaning" process that writes cached files to the drive and updates the drive's directory. If the process is interrupted, files could be damaged, and drive directory problems might occur. Run Drive Utility's drive checking function or your favorite hard drive program to make sure everything is all right before you get back to work.

- *Shut Down Everything Before You Install Something Inside Your Mac*—The delicate electronic components in your Mac, from the logic board to the processor, can easily be damaged by static electricity or a short circuit. If you need to add or remove a peripheral card or RAM, touch the power supply (with the plug in) to get rid of any static charge you might have. Some of the better memory and peripheral card dealers will even supply a wrist strap to help the process. You may feel like a surgeon beginning an operation while thus equipped, but the benefit is that your installation can be done with the maximum degree of safety and the maximum protection to the delicate internal workings of your computer.

NOTE: *If you remove RAM or a peripheral card from your Mac, try to store it in one of those static-resistant bags. You may just want to keep them around for warranty service or for storing old hardware.*

Buying a New Mac

How many of you have been to someone's home or office and seen one of those original compact Macs still purring away in the corner, working almost as reliably as the day it was purchased.

While it's possible to keep a Mac for many years without encountering more than the customary range of system crashes and reinstallations, there are times when you might just want to give the old computer to the kids, or donate it to your favorite charitable institution.

Here's what to consider when you decide if your Mac should be retired:

- *It's Too Expensive to Fix*—You've encountered problems that appear to be hardware related. While there are dealers who can supply used or reconditioned logic boards, RAM, graphics cards and hard drives, do the addition before you take this route. It could be time to give your Mac a well-deserved permanent vacation.

NOTE: *One of my clients has an older Mac, a Mac OS clone computer from Motorola, upon which he has lavished attention and considerable expense. Between paying my fees for troubleshooting and installation, and buying the parts themselves, he has long since covered the cost of a new computer. But still he persists; however, the arrival of Mac OS X and its great user interface and the promise of greater performance and reliability is tempting him to upgrade so he can run the new operating system.*

- *It Won't Run Mac OS X*—This is a judgment call. Just because you can't run the latest and greatest doesn't mean your Mac will stop working and play dead. It could take years before most major applications are updated for Mac OS X. Even the initial updates will most likely be Carbonized, which means the application will work under both Mac OS X and the Classic Mac operating systems from 8.1 and on. That means, you can use that updated program now on the older Mac, and then have it work great with Mac OS X when you buy a new computer. You can compare this to some degree to the so-called "fat" applications of the early PowerPC Mac era. Such programs contained both the older 680x0 Mac code and PowerPC code, and thus could be easily transported from a computer with one processor to the other and work just fine. That's why software publishers are taking Carbon so seriously.

- *It's Slow and Won't Run the Latest Software*—Do you really need to use AppleWorks 6 if ClarisWorks 3 works all right? That's just one example, and it's a significant one. You may find that you're perfectly happy with the older version of a program and you don't want to learn new tricks. While older software will work on a newer Mac, if you're happy with your old computer and happy with the applications, don't let this book or the flashy "Think Different" ads you see from Apple deter you.

- *You Just Have to Have Mac OS X*—All right, that's a good reason to upgrade, but before you do, consider whether you'll also have to update your favorite programs before you make the jump and how much those upgrades will cost. If the applications you want are not yet Mac OS X-savvy, you won't get much advantage from the new operating system, because you'll still see the old interface much of the time and not enjoy the joys of Aqua. On the other hand, Mac OS X does include programs you can use to surf the Internet, so that may be partial compensation. In addition, while new Macs or recently discontinued models are lots cheaper than the older models, you'll want to consider what you're going to do with the computer to see if the upgrade is justified.

NOTE: *One of my clients, a semiretired hairdresser, pretty much restricts his first generation PowerMac to sending and receiving email and occasionally surfing the Net. He has no interest in the G4 or the G4 or even Mac OS X, and will probably continue to run his old Mac till it gives up. On the other hand, he does look longingly at closeout deals on recently discontinued iMacs, and says he's tempted to switch—one of these days.*

Looking at Extended Warranties

Whether you buy a new Mac from a local store or a mail order house, before you finish your order, it's quite likely the salesperson will ask you to consider just one more purchase—an extended warranty. Apple's computers, as of the time this book was written, had a one year limited warranty on parts and labor, with just 90 days of free telephone support. If you plan on keeping your new Mac for a while, the prospect of extended support might be tempting.

Consider this, though: Dealers might often rely on the sale of the extended warranty to shore up their profit margins, particularly in times where sales of new computers have stalled. More often than not, a hardware failure will occur early in an electronic component's life, during the warranty period. As with any insurance policy, you need to weigh the possible expense of an out-of-warranty repair against the certain expense of the extended warranty.

If you are using an Apple iBook or PowerBook, however, such a warranty might be a good idea. Laptop computers are subject to far greater potential abuse than desktop computers, because they are being dragged around so frequently. Having that extra protection might be worth the expense.

WARNING! *If you opt to buy an extended warranty, double check with the dealer whether the warranty is Apple's, known as AppleCare, or comes from another company. I have seen instances where customers ordered AppleCare and got something else. When checking into such a program, you'll want to compare the cost and benefits before signing on the dotted line.*

Solving Hardware and Software Problems

This is an eternal question. Your Mac crashes constantly, and you've gone through all the possible software troubleshooting you can, following the steps outlined in Chapter 19. But still your Mac misbehaves. Here are some additional choices to consider, along with areas where you might want to have the Mac's hardware serviced:

- *Chronic Hard Drive Errors*—Every time you check your hard drive with DriveUtility or one of the commercial hard drive programs, it comes back with reports of directory damage that needs to be fixed. Sometimes, you'll even see a message that the repairs can't be done. Should this happen, first try restarting your Mac with a System CD or one of the CDs provided with the commercial drive utilities. If you continue to run into problems that occur all over again or can't be fixed, back up your data, and reformat the drive. Leaving directory damage unfixed can eventually result in a loss of files or the inability of your Mac to recognize your drive.

WARNING! *If you see a prompt on your Mac's display offering to initialize your hard drive, don't do it! That's a destructive act that will erase the data. While it may be sometimes possible to restore a drive with a program such as Norton Utilities or with an expensive trip to a drive recovery service, you should try other diagnostic methods before going this route.*

- *Hard Drive Doesn't Work Properly After It's Reformatted*—You bit the bullet and reformatted your hard drive, yet problems still occur. You continue to get reports of hard drive directory errors, or the worst happens and the drive isn't showing up on your Computer directory. From here, you will want to have both the drive and your Mac checked by a technician. It's possible one or the other has failed.

- *Mac Makes Startup Sound, But the Screen is Dark*—If you just installed Mac OS X and you're using a graphics card that isn't from ATI, IX Micro or NVIDIA, you'll want to consult the manufacturer about Mac OS X support. You may need to restart with an Apple-approved graphics card to install updated software.

NOTE: *At press time, 3dfx Interactive, manufacturer of the Voodoo graphic cards available on the Mac platform, was in the process of dissolving, after selling its assets to NVIDIA, a rival company that has since released their own Mac products. This doesn't create much confidence in the possibility that this card will ever be updated to work under Mac OS X, unless a third party enters the picture and manages to come up with a compatible set of drivers.*

- *Mac With Upgrade Card Fails to Boot*—Mac OS X requires a Mac that shipped with either a G3 or G4 processor. If you have an older Mac and upgraded the processor, don't expect it to work or support from Apple. You may, however, want to check with the manufacturer of the upgrade cards just to see if they have a way to make them run. If you cannot make it work, your only alternative is to install Mac OS X on a Mac that meets Apple's requirements.

NOTE: *Even genuine G3 Macs with a G4 processor upgrade might have trouble. As this book went to press, manufacturers of such processor upgrades were looking into compatibility problems, particularly with Blue & White PowerMacs upgraded from G3 to G4 status. Additionally, one of the major processor upgrade companies, Newer Technology, went out of business, and it wasn't certain whether any of the other companies would pick up support of the products.*

- *Mac Fails to Boot, and Doesn't Make a Startup Sound*—Recheck the power cord, the power strip, and the devices attached to your Mac. If you recently installed a new peripheral card or RAM upgrade, go ahead and remove each, in turn (closing the Mac each time) and see if you can get the Mac to run. If removing one or the other fixes the problem, reinstall the item and try again. Should the problem return, contact the manufacturer for repair or replacement. If you cannot get the Mac to run, it's time for a trip to the dealer's service department.

NOTE: *Another potential cause of a Mac failing to boot is a defective peripheral card, particularly the graphics card. You'll want to shut down, and remove and reseat the video card and see if it brings your Mac back to life.*

- *Mac Fails to Boot with Peripheral Device Attached*—The blame should be placed on the device itself. Make sure it's powered on, if a SCSI device, before you boot your Mac. One key point of testing here is removing the device (after powering down), and then if your Mac works all right, you have a good idea as to the culprit.

- *Mac Crashes Constantly Early in the Startup Process or Right After Restart*—Follow the software diagnostics covered in Chapter 19. If a reinstallation of Mac OS X fails to fix the problem, consider backing up and reformatting your hard drive. From here, continued problems could be traced to bad RAM, a faulty hard drive, or your Mac's logic board. Take it to your dealer for diagnosis.

NOTE: *Can you do your own hardware diagnostics? Possibly. MicroMat's TechTool Pro (and the TechTool Deluxe application that comes with Apple's AppleCare service warranty) can test the various systems on your Mac. A number of new Macs also include an Apple Hardware Test CD that can also be used to perform a basic set of hardware tests. However, if you see a report of a potential problem, let a technician make the final call.*

- *You Smell Smoke or See a Spark from Your Mac*—What can I tell you? While laser printer toner can sometimes smell a little smoky, if you see symptoms of this sort, don't try to use your Mac. Let a dealer's service representative do a diagnostic first.

NOTE: *Of course a slight spark could just be static electricity. If you have thick carpeting or you're in a particularly dry climate, you may find that walking around builds up static electricity. If you touch a metal object, you may see a slight spark.*

11. Hardware Management

Chapter 12

Hooking Up Accessories

If you need an immediate solution to:	See page:
Installing a New Scanner	218
Installing New Storage Devices	219
Installing Digital Cameras, eBook Readers, Palm OS Handhelds, and Other Products	220
Determining What to Do If It Doesn't Work	221

In Brief

Your Mac isn't an island. Even if you have an iBook or PowerBook, there are times when you'll want to add extra devices to enhance its capabilities. Fortunately, the promise of the Macintosh operating system that has endeared it to millions upon millions of customers is easy...well, fairly easy...plug-and-play ability. That means you can attach a peripheral device and have it function with the absolute minimum of fuss and bother.

Mac OS X will continue to fulfill this promise. The initial release doesn't support a large number of add-ons, however. Only a small collection of drivers from Canon, Epson, and HP shipped with the CD. From ink jet printers to CD writers, you might find that you'll have to wait for the manufacturer to produce a driver update so that it'll function.

However, once the drivers are all in place, the combination of easy installation and the powerful system management of Mac OS X makes it possible to get the maximum value from any peripheral you want to buy.

In this chapter, I cover many of the types of devices you can buy and how to install and use them as speedily and efficiently as possible.

A Review of Mac Peripheral Ports

In the old days of the Macintosh, you attached your input devices to an ADB port, a printer to the printer port, a modem to the modem port, and an external storage device to the SCSI port. All that changed, however, with the arrival of the computer in 1998 that's credited with Apple's resurgence—the iMac.

The iMac begat a new peripheral standard on the Mac (although it wasn't new in the personal computing world) and eliminated some of the ports that were considered standard issue. Here's a brief rundown of the various peripheral standards present on Macs that can run Mac OS X and where they fit in the overall picture:

- *ADB (Apple Desktop Bus)*—This was an early standard input port for input devices, such as the keyboard and mouse you use on your Mac, or a trackball and joystick, and, additionally, such extras as digital cameras. Even some modems used this port. However, it can only support a very few devices, performance tends to be slow for demanding accessories, and the plug-and-play aspect is a little murky. You have to restart your Mac to remove and add devices, or you risk damage to the computer's logic board. It vanished with the arrival of the iMac and later new models, both desktop and laptop, and was replaced with USB (Universal Serial Bus), a much more flexible standard.

- *Serial ports*—Some Macs had two serial ports, and some PowerBooks had just one. On a regular desktop Mac, there was one port for printers (it doubled as a LocalTalk port) and another for modems. PowerBooks combined the two and added built-in modems so there was no conflict or need for a switch to allow you to use an extra device. These ports are, in theory, plug and play. You can usually switch devices without a restart, although it's recommended you restart when you can. As far as performance is concerned, it's more than adequate for printing and for modems. But networking speed is a fraction of that available for Ethernet, and thus the process of transferring files can be cumbersome if the files are too large.

- *SCSI ports*—Except for the very first Mac (which used the floppy drive port to add a hard drive), this was the original standard for adding storage devices, scanners, and some specialty printers to your Mac. This is the closest thing to plug and *pray* on your Mac, because SCSI can be problematic, especially when the SCSI chain is large. For regular SCSI, you can connect up to seven devices, daisy chained. Each device has a unique ID number, from 0 through 6, and the last physical device on the chain (regardless of ID number) must be terminated. With large SCSI chains, sometimes devices won't work properly or your Mac will crash frequently. The diagnostics include reordering devices (observing proper ID numbering and termination), swapping cables, taking two aspirins, and trying again. But with millions of SCSI devices out there, Mac users still need to employ this peripheral standard, although better ones are available.

- *Ethernet*—This is a high-speed networking standard in use in homes and both large and small offices. The standard Ethernet protocols in use on Macs are 10Base-T and 100Base-T, and the latest generation of desktop Power Mac G4s add Gigabit Ethernet. At its maximum speed, Ethernet can deliver networking throughput nearly as fast as a big hard drive. This is a true plug-and-play standard. You can connect multiple devices to a central connecting point, such as a hub or switch, and remove and reconnect as needed. Ethernet devices aren't limited to computers and printers. You can also add network routers and special modems for broadband Internet, such as cable and DSL.

12. Hooking Up Accessories

- *USB (Universal Serial Bus)*—This is the low- to medium-speed serial port that is standard issue on all shipping Apple computers. Most Macs, except the iBook, have two USB ports (the iBook has just one). To add additional devices, you need hubs. In theory, you can hook up to 127 devices with full plug and play, except for the need of installing driver software for many products and unmounting a storage device first. Up to 12 megabits per second speed is shared on a single USB bus, which is enough for input devices, low-cost scanners, digital cameras, and storage devices where speed is not a concern.

- *FireWire*—This is an Apple invention, a high-speed peripheral port that puts the kibosh on SCSI for all practical purposes. It delivers up to 400 megabits in performance, coming closest to all but the fastest SCSI standards. Devices can be daisy chained, and there's a high level of plug-and-play compatibility, including hot-plugging. Drivers are needed on some devices, and storage devices must be dismounted from the desktop, but that covers most exceptions. FireWire devices include digital camcorders, which makes all recent Macs ideal desktop video editing computers. There are also storage devices and scanners.

NOTE: *This is not to say that FireWire is free of conflicts. I once installed a FireWire scanner, and it had to be the last item on the peripheral chain. Otherwise, weird startup problems, problems copying large files to FireWire storage devices, and occasional system crashes resulted. The file copying problems persisted after Mac OS X was installed, so it wasn't a driver issue (there were no drivers available at the time). So, I never say never.*

Adding a Missing Port

What do you do if you want a peripheral, but your Mac doesn't have the correct port? For desktop Macs with expansion slots, there's relief, in the form of PCI-based peripheral adapter cards. They come in many shapes and sizes, offering the following:

- *FireWire*—Two or more FireWire ports can be found on a single expansion card, sometimes more. Best of all, such cards usually don't need any special software (aside from Apple's FireWire extensions for Mac OS 9) and can cost less than $50.

- *USB*—With so many USB products available, it would be nice if older Macs could use them. All it takes is a peripheral card that costs less than $50. You just need to make sure Apple's USB extensions are installed if you're using Mac OS 9.1 (USB capabilities are standard issue with Mac OS X).

- *High-speed Ethernet*—Although the newest Mac desktops offer Gigabit Ethernet, you don't have to feel abandoned with an older Mac. There are expansion cards that fill this gap as well, but they're costly.

- *Combo cards*—If you don't have enough slots, take heart. There are combination cards that offer both FireWire and USB. Now, you don't have to choose just one.

- *SCSI cards*—If you need to find a home for your existing SCSI devices, you'll find a ready collection of SCSI cards with various price points and speeds. The cheapest cards, at roughly $50, are up to twice as fast as the built-in SCSI on most Macs, and it gets much faster beyond that.

- *SCSI-to-FireWire converter*—This is another way to have the best of both worlds. Several brands of such converters are available that allow a single SCSI device to hook up to the FireWire ports on your Mac. Being single devices, there are no issues of termination and ID to consider.

- *Serial-to-USB converters*—These modules are used to allow you to attach products that work on regular Mac serial ports, such as older ink jet printers and modems, to a newer Mac's USB port. The major limitation is the occasional software conflict and the inability to work with LocalTalk devices, such as AppleTalk printers that attach to a standard Mac printer port.

- *SCSI-to-USB converters*—This type of product would appear to be a blessing, with the ability to continue to use those old SCSI products on a Mac that only has USB, such as the iMac. However, because USB is slower than SCSI, the conversion seems to work best for a scanner or low-speed storage device (such as a Zip drive or tape drive).

- *LocalTalk-to-Ethernet bridge*—If you have an older Mac where Ethernet is an option or a network printer that only has a LocalTalk port, this device allows you to continue to use these products on your Ethernet network. You won't get any faster speed, but you won't have to buy a new printer or spend extra money on buying a peripheral card for an old Mac that is near the end of its useful life.

- *ADB-to-USB adapter*—If you still cherish that old keyboard, mouse, or trackball, fear not. You can still use it on your new Mac with this type of adapter. On the other hand, many terrific input devices are available for Macs these days, particularly Apple's new Pro Keyboard and Pro Mouse (I love these and use them all the time), that ship standard on new Macs and are available from the Apple Store for older models. You may find the money better spent acquiring something new.

WARNING! Not all peripheral cards work seamlessly with Mac OS X. Before you purchase one of these products, contact the manufacturer or check its Web site directly to see its plans. For example, older Adaptec SCSI cards are not guaranteed to run with Mac OS X (which does not, of course, mean they won't). If you have an older product, you can try it at your risk, and keep your fingers crossed.

- *Expansion cards for PowerBooks*—PowerBook users shouldn't feel abandoned by the new peripheral buses either. There are both USB and FireWire PC cards that will add this capability to just any about any PowerBook that can run Mac OS X.

NOTE: *Unfortunately, the iBook and the iMac were conceived as inexpensive consumer computers and thus lack extra expansion ports and the ability to add them. So, you have to live with the ports you have should you be using one of these models.*

Peripherals Available for Macs

Just what do you need? Although some folks decry the availability of products for Macs, they aren't really paying attention to the product lists in today's Mac mail-order catalogs or the shelves in stores that specialize in the platform.

Literally thousands of Mac products are available. Many, in fact, are cross-platform. The very same product is available for both Mac and Windows users, with the sole difference being the driver software or the label on the box.

NOTE: *Some companies with cross-platform products will, for some unaccountable reason, only put their software drivers on their Web sites, rather than on the CD that comes with the product. If a product seems to work only under Windows, check the box and the manufacturer's Web site, in case you get lucky.*

Here's a short list of the kinds of products you can add to your Mac to help harness the great power of Mac OS X:

NOTE: *This listing is meant for information only, to give a sampling of the sort of products that you can connect to your Mac. Check with a particular manufacturer as to whether a special upgrade is needed for Mac OS X. Some of these products will just plug in and run, regardless of whether you have Mac OS X or Mac OS 9.1.*

- *Scanners*—Once the desktop scanner was the province of the professional graphic artist. They were expensive, with color models of reasonable quality running from one to two grand. Although there are still products in that price range, literally dozens of models are available for less than $100 up to around $200. A scanner allows you to capture and digitize artwork and photos and even convert printed material to text that you can edit in your favorite word-processing program (with special optical character recognition software). Once the artwork is scanned, you can convert it into a format that you can use on your Mac for word processing or desktop publishing, or just to send to your friends and business associates. Scanners are available in FireWire, SCSI, and USB form, with some models supporting more than one peripheral standard.

- *Digital cameras*—Is film obsolete? Perhaps not, but digital cameras offer a convenient way to take a picture and not have to wait for it to be taken to the processor lab and developed. Although the cheapest models provide pictures that hardly rate in comparison with those offered by even a low-cost film camera, a few hundred dollars can now get you a digital camera that can compare favorably to traditional models. Some of the more expensive models match film cameras with special features, such as single-lens reflex viewfinders (where you see the same image picked up by the camera's lens), and even the ability to do limited motion videos. Most of these products store data on small memory cards.

- *Hard drives*—This type of device can be essentially the same as the one in your Mac now, except that it's in an external case. They come in FireWire, SCSI, and USB formats, with the first two providing the highest degree of performance. In terms of speed, there should be no difference between external and internal. The Power Macs, except for the Cube, sport extra drive bays for additional internal storage devices, in case you want to put everything on one case.

- *Removable drives*—As I explain in Chapter 17, backing up your data is of critical importance. Even though Mac OS X is a superbly stable, industrial-strength operating system, problems can happen to a drive's directory, and individual applications can still fail. That, plus the possibility of external dangers, such as a burglary, natural disaster, or weather-related problems, makes it imperative that you keep regular backups of your most valuable material. A removable drive is a convenient backup tool and just

12. Hooking Up Accessories

as convenient a tool for moving files to another location, particularly files that are just too large to send online. Two handy removable formats are the venerable Zip drive, which has found its way into millions and millions of computers, and the Imation SuperDisk, which also reads older-style floppy disks.

NOTE: *Although the SuperDisk drive is quite handy and the technology seems robust enough, such drives are usually found in the closeout bins these days. The main manufacturer, Imation, has apparently given up the fight competing with the Zip drive, but they still make regular floppy drives for those who need them.*

- *CD writer (or burner)*—This is the type of product that only became standard equipment on a Mac in early 2001. The closest equivalent is the DVD-RAM drive on some older Power Macintosh G4 models, which records on a special DVD-based medium with a capacity of up to 5.2GB. A CD writer, or "burner," lets you make a CD of data or music. Such devices are ubiquitous and available in FireWire, SCSI, and USB trim (also ATA for use in a present-day desktop Mac's internal drive bay). There are two basic types of CD formats for writing data. One is the CD-R, which can only be recorded once. The other is CD-RW, which can be rewritten up to 1,000 times (but the disk can't be read on all drives). Although a CD drive is slower than a regular removable hard drive, it has the added benefit of permanence. A CD can last for many years without suffering damage or possible loss of data, unless given ultra-severe abuse.

NOTE: *There are actually two basic types of CD-R media. The data type is designed to record any kind of data from a computer. The music CD consists of the same media, but higher priced, to cover the royalty paid to artists whose material you are copying.*

- *Wireless networking*—Apple's AirPort wireless networking modules are available for all new Macs. They allow Macs to network with each other at near standard Ethernet speeds at distances of up to 150 feet. The AirPort Base Station lets you share an Internet connection.

NOTE: *If you have an older Mac without AirPort capability, there are other choices for wireless networking. One of these is SkyLINE from Farallon, which uses the same industry standard protocols as AirPort and can work as part of the same network. Also remember that, at least for the initial release, the AirPort must be configured under Mac OS 9.1, although the AirPort network can be accessed from Mac OS X.*

- *Loudspeakers*—Yes, most loudspeaker systems you add to a computer plug into your audio output or earphone jack, but some speakers hook up directly to your USB port. These include the Harman Kardon iSub and SoundSticks. This allows them to take advantage of the Mac OS's own sound control features to adjust volume, balance, and tone.

- *Handheld computers*—There are the popular Palm OS products from Handspring and Palm, and dedicated electronic book readers, such as the Rocket eBook. They aren't designed to be attached to your Mac all the time, but they need to interface with your computer for installing and removing software, or just synchronizing information. Then, you'll need special software to allow this connection to work.

Although installing an accessory on your Mac is fairly easy, you should always take a few extra precautions to make sure everything is set up properly. This is particularly important if you are setting up a complicated peripheral device, such as a scanner, where some extra steps might be necessary. In addition, because many products come with very sparse documentation, these steps will help you get things working without extra fuss or confusion.

In the next section, I cover some basic recommendations on installing a peripheral device on your Mac and how to cope with problems should they arise.

12. Hooking Up Accessories

Immediate Solutions

WARNING! Before you install any software for new hardware, be sure to consult the documentation or contact the publisher about Mac OS X compatibility. Even if you bought the product long after the new operating system was released, don't assume the unit is compatible unless there is specific information in the package or on the product's label about the subject. If you can't find this information, check with the publisher about the issue.

Installing a New Scanner

After unpacking the device, check the manual or installer card for basic setups and follow these basic guidelines:

1. Locate the lock on the scanner. It might be identified by a padlock icon, and unlocking can be done with a screwdriver or just by turning a latch. This is critical, because you risk damaging a scanner should you attempt to run the device while the optical mechanism is locked.

NOTE: If you plan to move your scanner to a new location outside your workplace, remember to lock the optical mechanism first to protect the unit.

2. If another user has logged into your Mac, you'll need to use your administrator's account. Installing anything that requires system-wide access can only be done in this fashion. If you're not logged in, just choose Log Out from the Desktop application menu, then log in under your administrator username and password.

3. Install the software. It should be on a CD somewhere that shipped with the scanner. Some scanners include an integrated installation process, which handles the scanner drivers, image-editing software, and other extras. Others offer each element as a separate, clickable install. Follow the prompts about selecting installation options. Depending on the installer, you may or may not have to restart your Mac.

WARNING! If, for some reason, there's an old-fashioned floppy disk installer, you can be assured the scanner drivers aren't compatible with Mac OS X. Contact the manufacturer about this problem, or just use it under the Mac OS X environment until a new version of the software is available.

4. Connect the scanner to your Mac. If it's a SCSI product, shut down your Mac and attach SCSI devices first, then restart after the hookup. For FireWire and USB, it's not necessary, because of the plug-and-play nature of these two peripheral standards.

NOTE: If you are installing a SCSI device, make sure there are no duplicate ID numbers and that termination switches on the product are turned on or off as needed for your installation.

5. Launch your scanning software and run the scanner through its paces for scanning and processing images. If there are problems, consult the documentation (it might be on the CD) for further assistance.

NOTE: Some scanner drivers don't work separately from a photo-editing program. So, you'll need to see if there's a copy of Adobe Photoshop or a similar program on your Mac and use that program's Acquire feature to activate the scanning driver.

Installing New Storage Devices

Depending on the sort of storage device you have, there may be no need to add any extra software. Here are the basic steps to follow:

1. Consult the documentation or look for a CD to see if special software needs to be installed.

NOTE: Mac OS X has built-in support for some popular removable devices, such as Imation SuperDisk drives, Iomega Zip and Jaz drives, and a number of FireWire storage devices. You can run them without adding any extra software and have them function normally. If you are installing a device in the same category, you may, as an experiment, just want to hook it up and try to make it run before you attempt to use the software, because it's possible the drivers aren't updated for Mac OS X.

2. If software is required, make sure it's Mac OS X-compatible, then log in as administrator on your Mac. As explained in the previous section, the fast way to get to the login prompt is to use the Log Out command in the Desktop application menu.

3. Launch the installer application and follow the prompts.

4. If needed, restart your Mac.

5. Connect the drive to your Mac. If you're hooking up a SCSI device, make sure that your Mac and attached SCSI devices are turned off first; you can safely restart after hookup.

NOTE: *Don't forget to check for SCSI ID and termination settings before powering up.*

---

6. Verify that the drive works properly. If it's a hard drive, you'll want to copy files to and from it. For a removable device, insert the removable media and run it through its paces.

WARNING! On a CD drive, it's worth wasting one CD-R disk just to be sure that you can copy data satisfactorily. You do not want to back up critical data and then find out, too late, that there was a problem reading the CD.

Installing Digital Cameras, eBook Readers, Palm OS Handhelds, and Other Products

The process of setting up a device that's not connected full time to your Mac is essentially the same as hooking up a device that's always hooked up. Here are the steps to follow:

1. Unpack the device and check for interface plugs. If there's no USB or FireWire cable, check to see if a serial cable is available. Depending on the kind of Mac you have, you might need an interface adapter, such as a serial-to-USB converter, to make it run.

2. After verifying Mac OS X compatibility, locate the installer CD and install the software.

3. Check the device for proper operation, and then attach the unit to your Mac as instructed.

4. Consult the instructions about synching or interfacing with your Mac.

5. If the product doesn't run as expected, check manuals or the manufacturer's support Web site or telephone support line for further advice.

Determining What to Do If It Doesn't Work

Despite some of the concessions to mass production and competition to keep prices low, it's a rare product that will fail out of the box. Usually when something doesn't work, you can take steps to address the problem.

Here are some items to check in case the accessory you've bought for your Mac isn't working as you expected:

- *Is the device compatible with Mac OS X?* Even if the box or documentation says it is, don't expect seamless compatibility in every case. You may need to double-check with the manufacturer to see if additional updates are required. If the box or documentation doesn't specifically address the issue, assume the product won't run unless there's built-in support under Mac OS X. Except for a limited number of products, the answer is probably no.

NOTE: The promise and non-delivery of Mac OS X compatibility information was brought home to me just before this book went to press. I bought a new software product whose box had a sticker promising details about a Mac OS X upgrade inside. I checked and I checked, and there was no information whatsoever on the subject. A call to the manufacturer yielded the worst news of all—the label was a mistake. They hadn't made any decisions about when such an upgrade would be available and in what form.

- *Have you installed the wrong software?* New products are apt to have different installers for Mac OS X and for the Classic Mac OS. Double-check to make sure that you ran the correct installation. You might want to do it again and see.

- *Did you forget to restart?* It may or may not be necessary, but if a product won't work, this last step is worth it just to make sure the proper drivers load.

- *Are you experiencing peripheral application crashes?* Even though the Darwin core of Mac OS X is highly robust and crash-resistant, this doesn't mean that individual programs aren't going to crash from time to time. Fortunately, protected memory means that an application can quit and you can still continue to use your Mac. Should the program continue to quit or freeze, contact the manufacturer about needed updates.

- *Is the device plugged in?* Even if the AC adapter is connected to the wall socket or a power strip, you may have to tear through a spaghetti-like maze of cables to see if everything is hooked up properly. Cables sometimes separate during Spring cleaning.

12. Hooking Up Accessories

NOTE: *This issue isn't as obvious as it seems. I once got a frantic call from a client who wondered why her printer had stopped working. I asked her to double-check her cables, and she assured me everything was plugged in. But when I visited her office to check, I discovered the loose printer cable lost behind a mass of similar-colored wiring that was extremely difficult to sort out. Apparently, a cleaning person had mistakenly pulled the cable from a USB hub in a futile attempt to make the wiring mess look neat.*

- *Is there a bad or broken cable?* It's not always easy to see such a problem, because of the sometimes thick shielding on a cable. Try another cable, if you have one, as a test. Frayed or otherwise damaged cables should be replaced right away. Naked wires could cause a short circuit, which would "fry" the delicate electronic circuitry in the component itself.

- *Is the device faulty?* Perhaps it's not your Mac or something you did at all. Sometimes, new products just fail out of the box or shortly after they're placed in service. That's the purpose of the new product warranty, and don't hesitate to read the fine print and find out what you need to do to get the unit repaired or replaced. Some companies will replace a product that's dead on arrival, by the way.

You may hope that you can continue to work full time in Mac OS X, although this is apt to be difficult with the initial release of Mac OS X. However, there will no doubt be situations where a product just won't run under Mac OS X, even if there's the claim of compatibility. If this is the case, bite the bullet and return to your old operating system.

Chapter 13

Taking Mac OS X on the Road

If you need an immediate solution to:	See page:
Computing on the Road	227
Using the Battery Monitor	227
Getting the Maximum Amount of Battery Life	228
Using an Apple Laptop Travel Kit	230
Getting the Most Efficient Online Performance	234
Missing Laptop Features from Mac OS X	235

In Brief

The rise of mobile computing means that you can truly take it with you—your laptop, that is. That way, you can sit on the beach and finish up that business proposal, or write your great American novel while on a Caribbean cruise. Apple Computer even ships an iBook and PowerBooks with DVD drives, so you can catch your favorite flick on that cross-country or cross-continent flight and not have to depend on the often mediocre fare the airline selects for you.

With Mac OS X, Apple Computer has made your portable computing experience even more pleasant, with clever touches that will make your iBook or PowerBook run faster and more efficiently.

Exploring Mac OS X Tools for Laptops

Laptop computers nowadays are extremely powerful, in many respects on a par with desktop computers. A particularly notable example is the strikingly distinct Titanium PowerBook G4, which offers a brilliant 15.2 inch LCD display and great processor performance. In addition, using the built-in peripheral ports, you can easily attach a keyboard and mouse, and on PowerBooks, an external display, and use the computer for double duty as a stationary desktop computer. If you need to take your work on the road, disconnect the laptop, pack it in a case, and you're ready to roll.

Superior Power Management

Year after year, as computer processors get more powerful, they also require less power. So, today's iBook and PowerBook can crunch numbers with the best of them, yet the low power requirements of their microprocessors and Mac OS X's power management features allow you to maximize the amount of time your computer can run without the need of a battery recharge or a nearby AC outlet.

Integrated Mouse Control Panel

Under Mac OS X, a separate system setting for trackpad speed is no longer present. When you launch the System Preferences application and click on the Mouse settings pane (see Figure 13.1), you'll be able to adjust trackpad speed and double-click speed directly. You may, with some models, see a separate Trackpad tab, though.

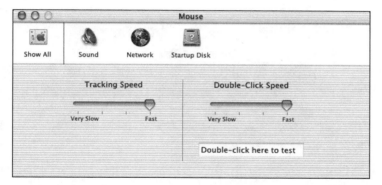

Figure 13.1   The Mouse settings pane handles trackpad settings for your
                Apple laptop.

Superfast Sleep and Awake Features

In the old days (before there was a Mac OS X), when you put your
PowerBook to sleep, it would take a few seconds for your Mac to do
its disk drive and network housecleaning chores before going into
idle mode. The reverse process could take even longer, up to a minute
for your Mac to return to its normal operating mode after the computer is brought back to life.

*NOTE: The slow process of awakening from sleep mode has been sped up for Mac OS 9.1, but
it's still not as fast as in Mac OS X.*

For Mac OS X, Apple has made both processes ultraefficient and su-
per-quick. Just choose Sleep from the Apple menu, and your iBook or
PowerBook will close down almost immediately. Best of all, you can
bring them back to life almost instantaneously by either pressing any
key on the keyboard or, with most models, opening the case. It almost seems as if they were never placed in sleep mode to begin with.

Editing Vacation Videos on the Road

If your iBook or PowerBook has FireWire capability (and all the recent models do), you'll be able to edit the videos of the family vacation or presentation on the road, using Apple's marvelous iMovie
software (see Figure 13.2) or any video editing tool you prefer.

*NOTE: The initial release of Mac OS X, reviewed as this book was being written, didn't include a
new version of iMovie; however, that application can be downloaded from Apple's Web site by the
time you read this book.*

Figure 13.2   iMovie is the flexible yet super-simple desktop video-editing program that's free with many new Macs and a low-cost downloadable application otherwise.

After you have shot your videos, you can easily copy them to your iBook's or PowerBook's hard drive and then edit the footage the way you like, adding special effects and sound effects. Then, after the movie has been prepared, you can save it in a variety of formats, including QuickTime, which allows for easy online distribution.

In addition to making and editing videos, you can also use programs such as AppleWorks 6 and Microsoft Office to make slide shows. After you're finished, you can attach your Apple laptop to a TV or projector and use it for a portable presentation.

TIP: *Apple iBooks equipped with FireWire have an AV output port that you can use to attach these cute laptops even to a regular TV with composite video or camcorder ports. The PowerBook's output capabilities include S-video.*

NOTE: *Because video fills a large amount of drive storage space, you might want to consider bringing an extra drive with you if you intend to capture a large video. Remember that USB-based drives are very slow and usually unsuitable except for lower-resolution video capture and playback. Expansion bay, FireWire, and SCSI-based devices can provide sufficient speed for good performance.*

Immediate Solutions

Computing on the Road

Some day in the future, it's possible most computers will be mobile devices, designed to work efficiently on the road, yet ready to plug into a desktop docking system at a moment's notice. Apple flirted with this sort of setup some years back with the Duo system, but the product never truly caught on as they expected. In the meantime, however, it's possible to enjoy a remarkably flexible Mac computing experience with the iBook, the PowerBook, and, of course, Mac OS X.

An Apple laptop comes complete with all the ingredients for performing the computing tasks you need when you're not at your home or office. The latest models include a built-in modem and Ethernet networking ports, and most models have a reasonable array of expansion ports so you can add extra devices to fill in the gaps. Only the iBook and Titanium PowerBook G4 lack such niceties as a high-speed expansion bay for storage devices.

Before you take your iBook or PowerBook on that trip, however, you'll want to be prepared for the worst and for the most effective computing experience whether you're visiting someone's home, staying in a hotel, or camping out. With a little advance preparation, you can get the most value from your Mac computing experience regardless of your destination.

Using the Battery Monitor

With older versions of the Mac OS, you could check the state of your laptop's battery courtesy of a Control Strip module or as an optional icon on the menu bar clock. For Mac OS X, Apple's new solution is the Battery Monitor application (see Figure 13.3).

Where is Battery Monitor? Just go to Mac OS X's Applications folder, and then open the Pack Extras folder. You'll find Battery Monitor inside.

When you launch the program, in addition to the Show Info panel, you'll see a graphical display in the Dock (see Figure 13.4) indicating

Figure 13.3   Battery Monitor's information panel showing just how long the battery on my iBook will run before shutting down.

Figure 13.4   The Battery Monitor sits in the Dock, alerting you to approximately how much battery life is left.

estimated battery life. You access the floating panel simply by choosing Show Info panel from the Battery application menu, or by typing Command+I. After it appears, the command will change to the Hide Info panel, although it can be just as easily dismissed by clicking on the close button on the top left of the panel itself.

TIP: Place Battery Monitor in the Dock and it'll work like a Control Strip module.

Getting the Maximum Amount of Battery Life

Whatever you do, your iBook or PowerBook won't run forever before the battery is spent. If you have an AC outlet and your power supply nearby, this may be a minor convenience at most. But if you're in a plane or power is otherwise unavailable, you'll want to find ways to stretch your battery as far as you can.

Here are some suggestions to get the most from your Apple laptop's battery power:

- *Let it sleep.* When you're not using your laptop, let it drift into sleep mode. Mac OS X will bring it to life in just a second when you're ready to use it again. While in sleep mode, all your applications remain open with your settings intact. Only your online or network connections will be deactivated.

- *Use the Energy Saver preference pane.* Launch System Preferences, and open Energy Saver (see Figure 13.5). You'll be able to adjust the intervals for system, display, and hard drive sleep. The settings are separate for AC power and your laptop's Battery. Because the hard drive can use a lot of extra juice, letting it go to sleep after a brief period of inactivity might conserve battery life far beyond the normal level.

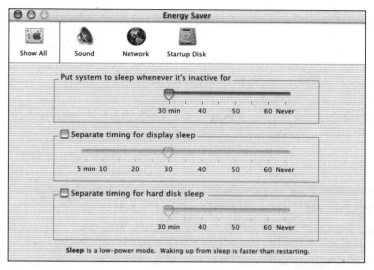

Figure 13.5   Use Energy Saver to give your battery greater longevity.

NOTE: Some applications tend to cause a lot of hard drive activity when running, so a sleep setting won't save battery life. In addition, if your Apple laptop doesn't have a large amount of RAM, Mac OS X's advanced virtual memory feature will swap data to and from the hard drive frequently, again limiting the effectiveness of this setting.

- *Turn down the brightness.* You probably like a brilliant picture, but the brighter the setting, the more power is required. If you can reduce brightness and not suffer too much from the dimmer screen, you might buy some extra time from your battery power.

- *Don't use the modem.* If you don't have to surf, your iBook or PowerBook won't need to draw as much current from the battery. Hence, you'll get longer life.

- *Remove expansion bay devices.* These devices are powered by your PowerBook's battery and thus will reduce battery life. Just remember, if it's a storage device, you need to eject the disk icon first by dragging it to the Trash before you disconnect the device itself.

NOTE: The Titanium PowerBook G4 and iBook lines do not have expansion bays.

- *Avoid PC Cards.* Don't use a PC Card expansion module if you can help it, because that too will require additional juice.

- *Use headphones for audio.* Headphones draw less power, and you can turn the volume lower and save on precious battery life. The side benefit is that bystanders won't be annoyed if your sound, game, or musical preferences differ from theirs.

- *Forget the DVD.* When it is finally supported under Mac OS X, it's nice to be able to watch your favorite flick on the road, but it can sharply reduce battery life. It's a trade-off, but one you might find with sufficient entertainment value to be worth the sacrifice.

Using an Apple Laptop Travel Kit

When you take your iBook or PowerBook and Mac OS X on your next trip, you should consider adding a few items to your packing list so you can get the maximum level of convenience that portable computing has to offer. Here's a short list of items to take with you and the preparations to make:

- *Traveling bag*—You can pack your iBook or PowerBook into a suitcase, well cushioned with clothing, and it should survive the trip just fine. But you should consider buying a dedicated laptop travel bag. Such products usually have extra pouches and special storage compartments for removable media, extra drives, batteries, cables, software, and other items you might need for your work. There's also usually a shoulder strap in case the entire package gets a little heavy for you. In buying such a bag, consider a product that has a well-cushioned area to protect your laptop from the rigors of such things as airline turbulence and driving on rocky terrain in a sport utility vehicle.

WARNING! Some older laptop cases aren't large enough to contain the latest iBooks or PowerBooks comfortably. Although the new Apple laptops tend to be lighter than many older models, the larger LCD displays make them physically wider or deeper. I ran into this very problem when trying to fit an iBook into my favorite carrying case, although the ultra-wide Titanium PowerBook G4 fit just perfectly.

- *Protection from the elements*—As rugged as those laptops are in normal use, if you're going to be outside in a damp environment or you're at sea, make sure your computer is well protected. Please check with your dealer about getting a case that can protect your laptop, particularly in a damp environment.

WARNING! Don't expect your iBook or PowerBook to run perfectly on your favorite ski slope or in the midst of a blizzard. According to Apple's spec sheets, the normal operating temperature is 50 to 95 degrees Fahrenheit. So if you bring your laptop in from the cold, be sure to give it enough time to warm up before you use it.

- *Backups for key files*—You plan on getting some work done on the road, but your laptop's hard drive fails. Although these little computers are built to survive a reasonable amount of abuse, the fact is that storage devices fail at unexpected moments. It's easy for a repair shop to replace the drive, but recovering data from a defective drive can be costly, with no guarantee of total success. In addition to taking backup media for your most important files, you may want to include a copy of your laptop's system installer and restore disks in case you have to replace everything on a new hard drive.

TIP: You might also want to take with you a backup for your home or office system. That way, should something happen at either location during your trip, you'll still be able to get up and running again upon your return.

NOTE: Having a hard drive fail on a notebook computer isn't as unusual as you might think. Just before I left to attend the Macworld Expo in San Francisco in January 2001, the drive on my iBook Special Edition began to make a frightening clicking sound and quickly failed. Fortunately, I made a CD of the files I needed to continue writing this book, and I was able to borrow another laptop from a colleague and continue working with minimal delay.

- *Extra storage devices*—Whether your Apple laptop has a built-in expansion bay port or not, there are plenty of convenient storage devices that are small enough for packing away in a PowerBook case. A number of external FireWire and USB storage devices, from such companies as Iomega, LaCie, and VST Technologies, are bus powered (meaning they are powered by your Mac's ports). That means, you don't have to deal with power bricks and finding extra AC outlets in your hotel room. If you can put up with the little appendage, you can even use these devices during airline travel.

- *Diagnostic or repair CDs*—In addition to Apple's Disk First Aid, you might want to bring along an emergency CD for such programs as Alsoft's DiskWarrior, Symantec's Norton Utilities, or MicroMat's TechTool Pro or Drive X (due to be released by the time you read this book). These programs offer an extra measure of protection against drive directory problems and, in the case of TechTool Pro, for potential hardware issues.

WARNING! Some disk diagnostic programs won't work properly under Mac OS X, but they will function properly when you boot under Mac OS 9.1. Before using any of these programs to diagnose a possible disk-related problem, check the compatibility information from the publisher.

- *Extra input devices*—Not everyone loves the feel of a laptop's keyboard; I have been hot and cold about the PowerBook G4, although the iBook seems nice for my purposes. Such a keyboard might be perfectly fine for occasional use, but if you have to pound a keyboard or do lots of mousing around during your trip, you might want to pack a full-sized keyboard and mouse in your carrying bag. If you're into computer games, or the kids are part of the trip, you might also want to consider buying a trackball or joystick, both of which are recommended for superior computer gaming.

- *Patch cables*—Need to hook up to a network, a phone jack, or an external drive or scanner? Don't forget to bring the proper cables, along with your laptop's AC power supply. Even if you're not 100 percent certain you'll need a specific cable setup for a specific purpose, having an extra cable isn't likely to weigh down your carrying bag very much.

TIP: Don't assume that the phone in your hotel room is in a convenient location. It might be next to the bed, but you want to work on a table. It's a good idea to get a long telephone cable for just this purpose.

- *Consider a wireless connection*—Apple makes it possible to network or explore the Internet with the iBook and recent PowerBooks without a direct connection cable using its AirPort wireless networking system. You can install the AirPort module in your laptop and attach a base station to a phone. Then, you can stay connected for a distance of up to 150 feet (sometimes more). In a sense, you can lounge on a patio or a beach, and surf the Net with your Apple laptop without having to run a long cable.

- *Special connection cables*—For trips overseas or when you are staying in a hotel or other locale where a convenient modem data port isn't available, you'll have to be creative to find a way to get connected. One useful resource is a company called TeleAdapt (**www.teleadapt.com**), which makes connection cables and power adapters for a variety of installations around the world. You'll be able to cope with foreign power connections, portable power supplies, and various forms of telephone hookups with the right connection kit. Although nothing is perfect, if you need to stay in touch, this might be an option to consider.

- *Portable printer*—The major manufacturers of ink jet printers, such as Canon, Epson, and HP, all have smaller models that are designed for travel. What they lack in terms of print quality and speed is more than made up for in size and convenience.

- *Insurance*—Laptop computers are theft magnets. The convenient carrying handle of the iBook, for example, makes it tempting to just carry it in your hand and leave the rest of the accessories in your suitcase or laptop accessory bag. But it can also attract thieves who'd just love to separate you from your computer. Be wary of tight crowds at the airport and deliberate distractions, and definitely don't put your computer down somewhere, even for a moment. Professional thieves know all the tricks. The best preparation you can consider, however, is simply to get a good insurance policy so you can replace the computer in case the worst should happen. Some major insurance companies offer computer coverage, including units taken on the road, as part of homeowner's and small-business policies.

TIP: *If your insurance agent can't cover your computers, you might want to consider Safeware (see **www.safeware.com**). They have been in business for years, they're listed favorably with the Better Business Bureau, and many laptop owners, both PC and Mac users, swear by them.*

- *Airport X-rays*—Through the years, I've dutifully put my iBooks and PowerBooks under the airport security X-ray machines and haven't suffered any losses of data or computing power. Just let them do their job. If you are still concerned, however, you can ask for a personal inspection. Just remember to put your laptop in sleep mode rather than shut it down to speed up the inspection process. The security personnel primarily want to see the computer's desktop display so they know it's really a computer. Imagine their surprise when they see how quickly Mac OS X starts up.

- *Games for the kids*—If you are taking your clan on a long trip, you may want to bring along some of their favorite computer games for relaxation. This can keep them from getting into your hair, plus they can help you get the most value out of your iBook or PowerBook. The latest generations of both products are, in fact, pretty decent game machines, with fairly good performance on high-action 3D games.

13. Taking Mac OS X on the Road

Getting the Most Efficient Online Performance

Today, it's getting more and more difficult to stay away from your email, unless you are willing to get away for a while and can afford to let the mail sit unopened until your return. Fortunately, if you must keep up with the messages, there are ways that you can stay in touch, even if your ISP isn't available in the area you're visiting.

Here are some considerations to help you track your email in the event you need to surf the Net:

- *Check your ISP's access.* Such services as AOL, its sister service CompuServe, EarthLink (Apple's recommended ISP), and other large services have access numbers in most major cities around the world. Before leaving, you should retrieve and print out a listing of the phone numbers in the cities you plan to visit. If your itinerary should change along the way, you can usually go online and look for additional numbers. If you're using a local service, however, you may have to consider other options. One possible solution is the EarthLink Mobile Broadband service, which uses a special high-performance wireless model to deliver speeds of up to 128KBps. Many services, such as AOL and EarthLink also offer Web-based email options to retrieve your messages), or you can sign up for a free email account from such services as Microsoft's Hotmail or Yahoo. That way, if you can get online from, say, a public library, you can still retrieve your email. If you intend to travel to an out-of-the way locale without convenient online access, you might want to check with the hotel or airline or travel agent for suggestions. On the other hand, it was once possible to survive on a trip without cellular telephones or email, so you may find that you can live without the luxury.

TIP: Another way to stay connected while away is to consider joining a free ISP for travel. Although your online visits are accompanied by floating ad palettes, you'll still be able to access your favorite Web sites and check your messages. For Mac users, free services were not readily available, but the option is worth exploring.

- *Send messages to yourself for backup.* If you plan on getting some work done on the road, consider sending copies of your documents via email so you can retrieve them when you return to your home or office. That way, if something happens to your laptop during the trip, you'll still be able to get the files when you return.

NOTE: *Some ISPs have strict limits on the size of file attachments you can send with your messages. For AOL, it's 2MB outside the service and 16MB within the service. Other online services, such as EarthLink and Excite@home (which powers many cable-based ISPs), limit the size to 10MB. Apple's iDisk, part of their iTools service, affords you 20MB of storage for your personal stuff, and more if you are willing to pay a fee for the extra capacity. If you need to handle larger files, consider trying to compress them, or just bring along extra disks and a removable device for storage.*

- *Use a fax machine for a printer.* You can also use your computer's fax modem to print a document by sending a fax to yourself. If you're using the hotel's fax machine, you may want to check the hotel's fees beforehand, because some have simply outrageous per page charges amounting to several dollars each. Or perhaps you can find a local business or travel office who'd be willing to lend a hand. Another way to get printed output is to visit a print shop that can provide output for your files.

Missing Laptop Features from Mac OS X

The initial release of Mac OS X wasn't quite complete from a feature standpoint. This is to be expected, because Apple set a strict deadline for itself in releasing the new operating system, and they had to cut a few elements that weren't ready in time. These features were expected to be available as updates some time after the initial release:

- *DVD Player*—One of the neat features of recent Apple laptops, the built-in DVD capability, wasn't supported, so don't expect to enjoy your favorite movie on that long flight unless you're pre-pared to return to Mac OS 9.1. Because Apple thoughtfully provided Mac OS 9.1 as part of the installation, this is, at best, a minor inconvenience, because it's hardly certain that you will want to watch a DVD at the same time as you're doing actual work on your computer.

- *Third-party peripherals*—While many third-party drives and other peripherals are supported under Mac OS X, particularly from the larger makers, you might need special drivers for your particular product. This is especially true for PC cards. The best thing to do is to check with the manufacturer about compatibility issues, or just go back to Mac OS 9.1 during the times you truly need to use these products.

Part III

The Software Review

Chapter 14

Mac OS X-Savvy Applications

If you need an immediate solution to:	See page:
Introducing AppleWorks for Mac OS X	251
Using AppleWorks Starting Points	251
Using Tables in AppleWorks	252
Introducing Create for Mac OS X	254
Using the Inspector	254
Starting a Web Page in Create	255

In Brief

Mac OS X has a host of new interface elements and features that can provide a more productive, enjoyable, and reliable computing experience. But to be able to use those features, you have to run software that is specifically compiled to run under Mac OS X.

The situation is very similar to what prevailed back in 1994 when Apple moved to PowerPC processors. There was an emulation mode that let you run older software at reduced speed, but it took months and in some cases a few years for most Mac software companies to move their products over to the new architecture.

The Two Forms of Mac OS X Applications

Back in the days when the first iteration of Mac OS X was announced (it was then known as *Rhapsody*), Apple announced that it expected software publishers to totally rewrite their products in a new programming language to be compatible. This, of course, fell on deaf ears in the major companies, who didn't want to invest years and millions of dollars in the effort, so Apple went back to the drawing board.

They came up with two ways to provide programs that would be compatible with Mac OS X:

- *Carbon*—This is Apple's trump card. Carbon is a special set of application programming interfaces (APIs) that can be used to modify an existing Mac program and make it support all or most of the features of Mac OS X. Rather than having to do all the work from scratch, only 10 to 20 percent (on average) of the program's code needs to be updated to support the new system architecture. Even better, most of these very same applications can run normally on Macs equipped with Mac OS 8.1 through the various versions of Mac OS 9.1, by virtue of a system extension called *CarbonLib*. Depending on the program, the job could take days or months, so check with a specific publisher about their plans.

NOTE: *By "all or most of the features of Mac OS X," I mean that some capabilities, such as the Font Panel (described in Chapter 16) are optional. Check with a specific publisher about which features they choose to support and which they do not.*

- *Cocoa*—A native Mac OS X application can use either Sun Microsystems' Java programming language or one descended from the original NeXT-based Objective C to deliver applications for Mac OS X. These programs will yield full support for all the core features of Mac OS X, but they won't run under the regular Mac OS. For new programs, it's a lot faster to build a program from scratch this way, but with existing publishers who have to rewrite up to millions of lines of code, it's not the best alternative.

The best thing about the way Mac OS X is set up is that you don't have to concern yourself with the choices made by a publisher to make their products compatible with Mac OS X. You can just install and use the program and take advantage of the features and improved performance and reliability.

Key Mac OS X Software Profiled and Previewed

As of the time this book went to press, literally hundreds of new or updated applications were announced for Mac OS X. Some were actually out, and others were promises of what was to come in the future. The initial release of Mac OS X includes several offerings to sample the possibilities.

In this section, I profile some of the significant programs. In the "Immediate Solutions" section, I cover some useful features you'll want to try from two of the available Mac OS X-savvy programs— AppleWorks 6 and the Stone Design Suite.

Microsoft

One of the first publishers to declare support for Mac OS X was, believe it or not, Apple's former adversary, Microsoft. The Public Beta included a Carbonized version of its Internet Explorer browser (see Chapter 20), and a Preview edition appeared with the final release of Mac OS X. In addition, their free email application, Outlook Express, was expected to be updated for the final release of Apple's new operating system. A Mac OS X version of Office 2001 for the Macintosh has also been promised, but not immediately. It requires updating some

26 million lines of code, with final release not expected until the Fall of 2001, according to the timetable Microsoft released at the Macworld Expo in January 2001.

The new version of Office will include revisions for Entourage, their new email client and personal information manager, in addition to support for Mac OS X's robust features. They had not announced whether the other components of the business software suite—Excel, PowerPoint or Word—would sport any feature changes.

Apple Computer

The standard installation of Mac OS X includes a number of utilities for you to try. These include the Mail application described in Chapter 21, plus the old standbys, such as the Calculator, Disk Utility (a combination of Disk First Aid and Drive Setup), Key Caps, QuickTime Player, Script Editor, Sherlock, and Stickies. In addition, Aladdin's StuffIt Expander is along for the ride, so you can open compressed files created in a variety of formats (even those from the Windows and Unix environments).

But there are quite a few new contenders as well. Following is a brief description of some of the most interesting new programs from Apple:

- *Clock*—This program (see Figure 14.1) is intended as a suggested replacement for the popular menu bar clock. It can also put a floating clock palette on your desktop. You have a choice of analog or digital clocks.

TIP: *If you prefer the menu bar clock, no problem. You can continue to use both. But if you prefer to eliminate the one on the menu bar, launch System Preferences, click on the Date & Time pane, and click on the Menu Bar Clock tab. Uncheck the option labeled Show The Clock In The Menu Bar.*

Figure 14.1   Clock is a different answer to putting a clock on your Mac's screen.

- *Console*—As you use your Mac, you might, from time to time, see some strange error messages because of a printing problem or system-related issue. The Console application (see Figure 14.2), keeps a log of those messages. They may not be directly useful to the average Mac user, but you can use the information to help a software publisher figure out what went wrong with their product; you don't have to remember the arcane messages or prompts anymore with this utility handy, in the Mac OS X Utilities folder.

- *CPU Monitor*—Get a visual indication (see Figure 14.3) of how your Mac's processor is being accessed by Mac OS X. If you have a Mac with two processors, as I do, you get a separate display of each, just to see how both are handling the load.

- *Grab*—So, what does this grab? A screenshot of your Mac, useful in providing illustrations for documentation. It replaces such keyboard shortcuts as Command+Shift+3 under previous versions of the Mac OS. There are options to capture the entire screen, a selected window, or a timed capture, where you have 10 seconds to set things up before the shutter goes off.

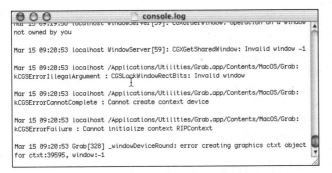

Figure 14.2   Now you can see the strange error messages that might help you troubleshoot a problem on your Mac.

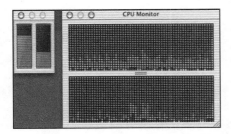

Figure 14.3   Two processors share tasks, and these little windows show what they're up to.

NOTE: *Thanks to Grab, which has no user interface to speak of to illustrate here, I was able to capture all of the Mac OS X illustrations used in this book.*

- *ImageCapture*—Found in the Applications folder, this application can download files from some, but not all, digital cameras (see Figure 14.4). The program is designed to work with your existing software for your camera to speed access to your pictures.

- *Internet Connect*—This application (see Figure 14.5) incorporates some of the elements of Remote Access, with a direct link

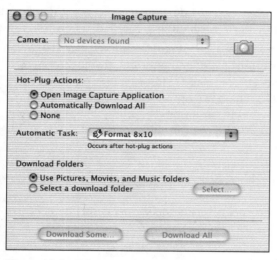

Figure 14.4   When enough support is available, you might be able to use many digital cameras on your Mac without having to get software updates.

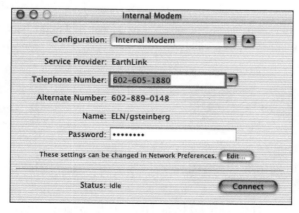

Figure 14.5   Use Internet Connect to dial up and log into your ISP.

to the Network pane of the System Preferences application to help you set up your dial-up access. It gets you online with a full status report in a few moments. The subject is covered in more detail in Chapter 8.

- *Mail*—Email is often the most used feature on the Internet, and Apple has delivered a brand new application for the purpose (see Figure 14.6). Mail will handle most of your email accounts, and provides a bevy of features that includes the ability to import your messages from several other email programs, multiple signatures, email rules, scheduled retrieval of messages, and a Finder-like interface where you can change the toolbar icons to meet your needs. I cover the subject in more detail in Chapter 21.

- *Network Utility*—Just what's happening on your network? Are you encountering a problem connecting to a shared computer or printer, or is your Net access not functioning as you expect? This application (see Figure 14.7) can be used to perform such functions as **ping** (contact and return, like sonar) or **trace** to find the source.

- *Terminal*—Apple has gone to great lengths to bury the native Unix command line for Mac OS X. As a result, Mac users can continue to use the new operating system without taking a gander at the core, but for Unix mavens, there's Terminal (see Figure 14.8), which gives you full access to the command line and a chance to explore the underpinnings.

14. Mac OS X-Savvy Applications

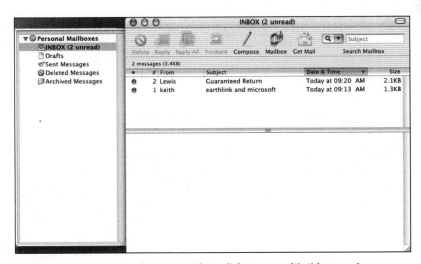

Figure 14.6   Manage a full range of email features with this speedy little application.

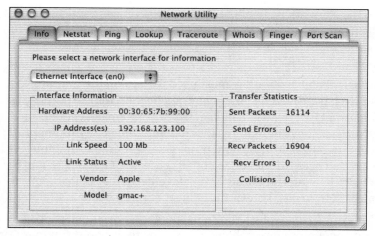

Figure 14.7   You can use this application to examine the condition of your local network or Internet connection.

```
●  ○  ○                        /bin/tcsh (ttyp1)
Desktop               Music                    Sites
Documents             Network Trash Folder     TheVolumeSettingsFolder
Library               Pictures
Movies                Public
[localhost:~] gene% cd documents
[localhost:~/documents] gene% ls
5Y_8400.pdf           ListBot Code        Thoth Files        XV-5080Cat.pdf
Gene's List           Mac OS X Book       Update Installers  dvi-to-adc.pdf
[localhost:~/documents] gene% cd applications
applications: No such file or directory.
[localhost:~/documents] gene% ls
5Y_8400.pdf           ListBot Code        Thoth Files        XV-5080Cat.pdf
Gene's List           Mac OS X Book       Update Installers  dvi-to-adc.pdf
[localhost:~/documents] gene% cd /applications
[localhost:/applications] gene% ls
Address Book.app      Image Capture.app   Sherlock.app
AppleScript           Internet Connect.app Show Desktop.app
Calculator.app    I   Internet Explorer   Stickies.app
Chess.app             Mail.app            System Preferences.app
Clock.app             NewsWatcher-X       TextEdit.app
Create.app            OmniWeb.app         Utilities
Dock Extras           Preview.app         iCab
Fetch 4.0b6 Folder    QuickTime Player.app thoth-1.0.6
[localhost:/applications] gene%
```

Figure 14.8   Experience the guts of Unix with this application.

WARNING! Unix is not a tool for the casual user. The wrong commands can get you in trouble and invoke the wrong functions or cause performance problems. Before you explore the ins and outs of the command line, you'll want to visit this Web site: http://public.sdsu.edu/Docs/unixf/basic_unix_f/basic_unix.html. Feel free to explore the Unix environment within the constraints of this brief online tutorial, and you'll be less apt to get into difficulty.

Just to give you a gander at what Terminal does, launch the application (it's in the Utilities folder), and then type the command **ls**. This will list the contents of your Mac's drive. To move to an individual folder, type the command **cd <name of folder>**, which switches you to the specified folder. Now an **ls** command will list the contents of the folder. All those text listings, even if they don't really change the way your Mac works, will also look very impressive to your friends.

By far, the most interesting Mac OS X application, however, is not one of the handy utilities that are bundled with the new operating system, but an upfront and personal example of the potential of Carbon. This program was originally released for users of Mac OS 8.1 or later, but when the Public Beta came out, Mac users learned that the popular software suite had built-in support for Mac OS X. The program? AppleWorks 6 (see Figure 14.9), a major upgrade to the venerable program suite from Apple. I cover AppleWorks in more detail later in this chapter.

NOTE: *If you bought an iMac or iBook released since the Spring of 2000, you'll find a copy of AppleWorks 6 is already present, in your Applications folder, at no extra cost, but a more compatible version is available from Apple's Web site.*

Although its interface seems simple and uncluttered, there's a lot of power packed into this program. I tell you more about it in the "Immediate Solutions" section.

FileMaker

Apple's spin-off, which handles development of FileMaker Pro, promises to produce a Mac OS X version. FileMaker Pro is a cross-platform database program (one that is available in both Mac OS and Windows versions) that has existed since the early days of the Mac.

Adobe Systems

When Apple CEO Steve Jobs first demonstrated Mac OS X's Aqua interface in January of 2000, he produced an early development version of Adobe Photoshop to show the potential of Carbon. The unique aspect of this application was the fact that it was all done by a single Adobe programmer, working in his spare time, without actually seeing what Aqua looked like. The end result was rough, but functional. Adobe has committed to bringing all of its current graphics programs to the new operating system.

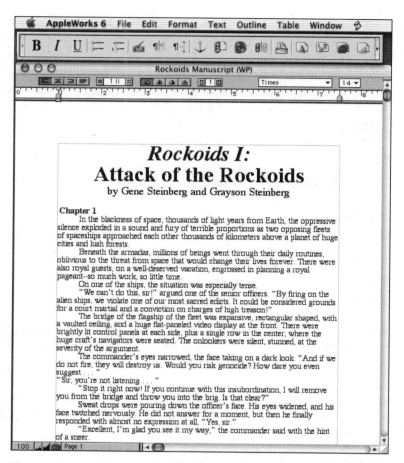

Figure 14.9 AppleWorks shows off the flexibility of a Carbon application.

Alias|Wavefront

One of the most significant developments for Mac OS X users is the arrival of brand new programs on the Mac platform. The $7,500 3D animation program, Maya, is one of the new entrants. While the program isn't quite a household name, the work done with Maya has been upfront and present in a number of very popular movies. Maya has been used to create spectacular effects for films such as *Star Wars I: The Phantom Menace, The Hollow Man,* and *A Perfect Storm.* A number of the major production houses have this application doing duty in their special effects labs.

Macromedia

Program for program, many of Macromedia's offerings are in direct competition to those from Adobe. It comes as no surprise, then, that Macromedia will also be in the forefront of Mac OS X development, promising to deliver new versions of their flagship products, such as Dreamweaver, Flash, and FreeHand.

Quark, Inc.

The flagship program from this company, QuarkXPress, is in line to be developed for Mac OS X. This highly sophisticated page layout application is a standard for both advertising agencies and publishers. The built-in PDF feature of Mac OS X's Quartz imaging layer should be especially helpful in expanding the scope of Quark as it migrates to the new operating system.

Stone Design

This publisher has migrated from the NeXT world and has embraced Mac OS X. Among their most useful applications is Create (see Figure 14.10), an integrated illustration program that also incorporates elements of HTML authoring and page layout. Create treats every element, from text to pictures, as an object, which can then be dragged and dropped onto other objects to create some very sophisticated illustrations.

14. Mac OS X-Savvy Applications

NOTE: *The various Stone Design applications stand as evidence of the power of Apple's Cocoa development environment. A great amount of work on these programs was done by one person, Andrew Stone. Using traditional developer tools, it would have taken a programming team to create software of this level of sophistication in a reasonable amount of time.*

AOL

The world's largest online service is not ignoring Mac OS X. At press time, they had committed themselves to developing a Mac OS X-savvy version of their software, so you'll be able to dial up your AOL account in the same fashion as before, under the Classic Mac OS. Whether the new version would include the features of AOL 6 or reflect the earlier version, 5, with a few cosmetic changes, hadn't been determined.

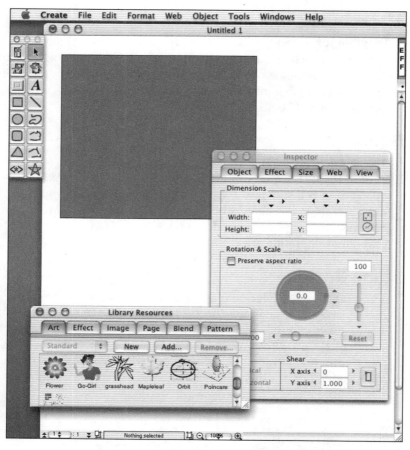

Figure 14.10   Create is the centerpiece of Stone Design's Mac OS X
product line.

Immediate Solutions

Introducing AppleWorks for Mac OS X

What's the good of having a modern operating system if there are no programs to exploit its wide-ranging capabilities? Apple's integrated application suite, AppleWorks, underwent a huge change with version 6. But the biggest change of all was only hinted at if you checked a file placed in the System Folder after the installation—CarbonLib. This little file is designed to allow Mac OS X applications that use the Carbon API to run on a Mac using Mac OS versions 8.1 through 9.1.

Here's a brief run-through of this cleverly designed program, the first Carbon application from a major publisher, in fact (which is fitting).

NOTE: *Starting Points has had some influence in big places. The Project Gallery featured in Microsoft Office 2001 is highly reminiscent of the feature.*

Using AppleWorks Starting Points

When you first launch AppleWorks, you'll be greeted by the program's Starting Points (see Figure 14.11), a floating tabbed palette. From here you can create new documents or open recent ones. Here is a brief description of what you get when you click on each tab:

NOTE: *The following information applies strictly to version 6.1 of the program. If you're using an earlier revision, you'll want to access the latest from Apple's Web site. You'll also notice that the Aqua interface isn't all there yet.*

Figure 14.11   Use Starting Points to originate or open documents in AppleWorks.

- *Basic*—Access any of the six AppleWorks modules just by clicking once on the kind of document you want to make. Depending on what you select, the user interface will vary in terms of menu bar commands, toolbars, and features.

TIP: Where's Starting Points? If you don't see it, choose Show Starting Points from the File menu.

- *Assistants*—AppleWorks is designed for users of all skill levels, from novices just setting up their first Mac to power users. The Assistants palette provides step-by-step guidance in setting up a new document in several useful categories, from a business card to an envelope.

- *Recent Items*—This tab provides a fast way to open a document you've worked on previously. When you click here, you'll see a list of up to dozens of documents you've created in the program, sorted alphabetically.

- *Templates*—To help get you started with a brand-new document, you can choose from a fairly decent collection of document templates. Just click on a preview icon to bring up a blank document with the template ready to roll.

- *Web*—Apple keeps an updated collection of clip art, templates, and tips about AppleWorks 6 at its Web site. When you click on this tab, you can access a current list of what's available. If you're logged onto your ISP, a single click in the listing automatically downloads the templates to your Mac.

- +—You can use this tab to make your own custom palette, then drag and drop items to fill it in.

Using Tables in AppleWorks

One of the biggest new features of AppleWorks 6, aside from the user interface and Mac OS X support, is the Table tool. You can easily add tables to any AppleWorks document, and easily resize the tables to fit your needs. To use this handy feature, follow these steps:

1. Launch AppleWorks 6.
2. Start a new document.
3. Make sure the program's toolbar is open. If it's not visible, go to the program's Window menu and select Show Tools (see Figure 14.12).

Figure 14.12   The toolbar you see in AppleWorks changes depending on the kind of document you're creating.

Figure 14.13   Easy table creation in AppleWorks starts here.

4. Locate the table frame tool (see Figure 14.13) and select it.

5. Place the cursor in the location on your document where you want to put a table, and then drag the mouse in a diagonal direction to set the approximate size of the table. This can be changed easily.

6. In the Insert Table dialog box that appears (see Figure 14.14), type how many rows and columns you want to put in the table. This, too, can be changed easily.

7. Click on OK to finish the table setup process.

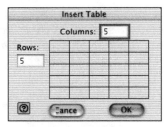

Figure 14.14   Choose how many rows and columns with which to populate your table.

Once you have set up the raw essentials of your table, you can easily adjust the table as you see fit. The entire table or rows and columns can be resized by clicking and dragging. When you're working in a table, a new Table menu shows up on the menu bar that you can use to add or delete rows and columns.

Introducing Create for Mac OS X

Stone Design's clever illustration suite, Create, is an all-purpose illustration program that has elements of several applications rolled into one. In addition to being able to produce simple or highly complex drawings in its uncluttered interface, you can create special effects, manage complex text stylings, and build your own Web site.

Using the Inspector

A lot of the work you do in Create is directed by the Inspector window. It's a mélange of buttons, checkboxes, sliders, and text entry points where you can originate the look and feel of your document.

NOTE: *The Inspector feature available with Create is not the same as the Finder's Inspector. It provides services strictly for the application, and not for the rest of the Mac OS.*

To access the Inspector, follow these steps:

1. Launch Create.
2. Go to the Tools menu and choose Inspector (see Figure 14.15).
3. Click on the tab that represents the type of project you are working on.

With the Inspector active, you'll find an easy way to manipulate your artwork, configure Web pages, and apply and change color selections.

TIP: *You can use another terrific feature of Create—the Resources palette—for clip art and document templates. If the Resources palette isn't present, choose Library Resources from the Tools menu to bring it up.*

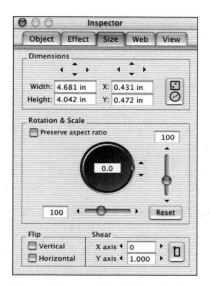

Figure 14.15   The Inspector has many faces, depending on the tab you select.

Starting a Web Page in Create

In addition to being a pretty flexible object-oriented illustration environment, Create lets you generate a fully professional Web page. Here's how to get started setting up a Web page in this program:

1. Launch Create. A new Untitled document window appears, along with, by default, the Resources and Inspector windows.

2. Type your text and place your pictures in the document.

3. When you're ready to enter URL links to other pages or sites, click on the area of your document where you want to place the link.

4. Now, click on the Web tab of Inspector, as shown in Figure 14.16.

5. Enter the URL. If you want to specify custom options for this link, click on the Use Custom option.

6. When your Web page is finished, choose Create Web Pages from the Web menu and name your file. When you click on Save, you'll see the page opened in the Web browser set as an Internet preference in the System Preferences panel, so you can check to see how it'll look when it's published on the Web.

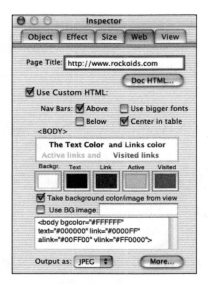

Figure 14.16   The multipurpose Inspector lets you configure your Web page.

Chapter 15

Using Older Programs with Mac OS X

If you need an immediate solution to:	See page:
Launching Older Mac Programs	263
Running Classic as a Startup Application	264
Getting Reliable Performance from Classic Applications	266
Keeping Your Mac OS 9.1 System Folder Safe and Sound	269
Solving Classic Environment Problems	270
Returning to Mac OS 9.1	271

In Brief

When Apple Computer released the first Macintosh computer with a PowerPC processor in the early part of 1994, the landscape was lonely. Although these computers offered the promise of far greater levels of performance, it would only happen when programs were ported (or updated) to support the new chip architecture.

There were, however, thousands of Mac applications that were designed to run on the older 680x0 Motorola processors. With this in mind, Apple devised a plan to allow Mac users to continue to use the vast majority of these programs with decent performance, and then gradually migrate to the PowerPC versions as they were released. The ROMs for PowerPC Macs came with an emulator (extensively updated via patches to the system software). The emulator, shorn of the complex programming techniques involved, would, on the fly, emulate a 680x0 processor. It would thus allow those programs to run with good compatibility—except for software that required a Mac with an FPU chip for special math-related functions. At first, the speed of the emulator barely kept up with 68030 processors, let alone the fastest 68040 processors that were produced before the PowerPC took over. But as the emulator got better and the new chips got faster, performance of the older programs was so good, it was sometimes hard to see a significant difference.

Introducing the Classic Environment

For Mac OS X, the changes are far greater than the switch to the PowerPC's RISC code. The underlying structure of the operating system would seem, in comparison, to be from an alien world. It's Unix-based—the same operating system that powers some of the most powerful Internet servers—and thus the situation is somewhat more complex.

However, Apple has an inventive solution: the Classic Compatibility environment (see Figure 15.1). It's not an emulator, such as the one used for PowerPC Macs, nor is it in the tradition of software that emulates Windows on a Mac, such as Connectix Virtual PC.

The closest description would be that Classic runs as a sort of virtual machine in which Mac OS 9 runs as a separate process or application within Mac OS X, but without inheriting the Aqua user interface nor

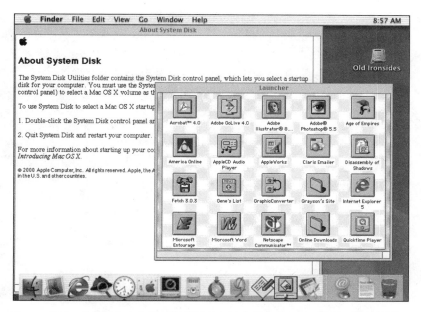

Figure 15.1   Yes, this is truly Mac OS 9.1, only it's running within Mac OS X.

the robust operating system features of the Darwin core. Basically, when you run a Mac OS 9 program, the old menu bar, Apple menu, Control Strip, Launcher, and most features of the older operating system take over your screen (see Figure 15.2). However, when you switch out of a Classic application, you're back in Aqua.

NOTE: *An actual Mac OS X version of Microsoft Office was promised for the fall of 2001. In the meantime, having 9.1 included with Mac OS X will be of great value, since there are so many older programs you're likely to use.*

Classic Environment Limitations

As seamless as switching to a Classic application may seem (and I'll explain the best ways in the "Immediate Solutions" section of this chapter), there are limits to compatibility, more so than with the switch from 680x0 to PowerPC. Although you can run most of your applications with good performance, some programs just won't run until updated for the new operating system. Here's the short list of potential problems:

- *It still crashes a lot.* The Classic environment doesn't inherit the robust features of Mac OS X, such as preemptive multitasking and protected memory. It has the same limitations of the original Mac OS, which means that if a single application crashes, you will

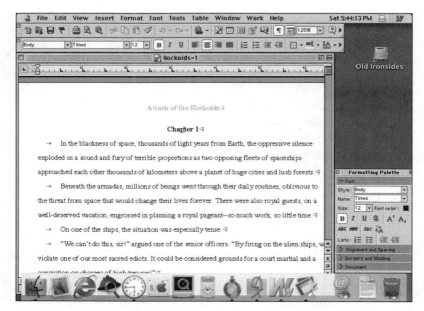

Figure 15.2   This is Microsoft Word 2001, the Classic version, running under Mac OS X, but with the Mac OS 9.1 look.

need to restart Classic. However, because it operates in its own protected memory space, that memory is walled off from the rest of the system, so you can continue to use your Mac OS X applications without a problem. If Classic crashes, just run it again.

- *Many system extensions don't run.* Mac OS system extensions that access hardware functions are probably going to fail, or they'll only run with limited compatibility. I'll explain ways of cleaning out your Mac OS 9 user environment for best performance in the "Immediate Solutions" section of this chapter.

- *CPU-intensive applications are slower.* Adobe Photoshop and other programs that tax the Mac's processor to the limit may run somewhat slower in the Classic environment. The amount performance suffers depends largely on the speed of your Mac's processor, hard drive, and graphic hardware. However, other functions, such as launching and screen refreshing, will seem not altogether different from a regular Mac OS 9 Mac.

- *Certain Mac peripherals fail.* Any product that requires special drivers to run is likely going to fail under Mac OS X, even if run from the Classic environment. Although it's possible that some of these devices will work after a fashion, don't expect consistent compatibility. Among the affected products are CD burners,

DVD-RAM burners, digital cameras, removable storage devices (except for Imation and Iomega products), FireWire devices (except for a handful of drives from such companies as LaCie and VST Technologies), scanners, tape backup drives, and peripheral cards that provide such features as extended audio editing or video capture. Even graphics cards that were not provided by Apple's graphics chip partner, ATI Technologies, IX Micro (which is now defunct) or NVIDIA, won't function unless the company who makes the product has produced drivers for Mac OS X. The best source of information about what works and what doesn't is the manufacturer of these products.

NOTE: *At press time, Formac, a German-based manufacturer of high-performance graphics cards for Macs, was working on Mac OS X drivers. In addition, NVIDIA, a new entrant in the Mac arena, will provide Mac OS X compatibility for any Mac products they manufacture, such as the chips used in the 2001 Power Mac G4 desktops. 3dfx Interactive, which announced that the company was going out of business in late 2000, never updated drivers for its Voodoo cards for Mac OS X, though it's possible third parties might find a way to do it.*

- *Some printers won't work.* You can continue to use most laser printers by using the Print Center application of Mac OS X. But some special laser printers that do not have Adobe PostScript installed or that use the USB rather than Ethernet ports may not work without driver updates. The same holds true for those ever-popular ink jet printers that have captured a large portion of the printer market. Most of the makers of these products were expected to have Mac OS X software ready, including such companies as Canon, Epson, HP (some of these are on the Mac OS X installer disk), and Lexmark. Such updates will probably be available direct from the manufacturers' Web sites.

- *Certain hard drive formatters won't work.* Any device that provides low-level support to storage devices probably won't work until a special Mac OS X version is delivered. Apple's own Drive Setup can handle most—in fact, probably all—ATA drives and many recent SCSI drives. Otherwise, you have to wait for the third-party manufacturer to come through for you.

NOTE: *FWB Software, publisher of Hard Disk ToolKit, informed me that its Mac OS X version of the popular drive utility application would be "late," meaning that you may want to consider trying Apple's disk formatter for the time being if you need to run a drive under Mac OS X.*

- *Some Windows emulators are not yet compatible.* Connectix Virtual PC will not work under Mac OS X. The company was working on a compatible version when this book went to print. The other major contender, FWB's SoftWindows, will run with decent performance, but since it has been officially discontinued, do not expect updates if problems arise, unless another company chooses to pick up the product.

• *Internet software compatibility is a mixed bag.* If you have a high-speed (broadband) Internet connection, you may be all right, but dial-up connections had problems of one sort or another. AOL is expected to have a Mac OS X-compatible version of its access software available shortly after the first regular release of Mac OS X.

• *Some classic games won't work.* Although Mac OS X is designed to be a gamer's paradise, the realization of that promise isn't going to happen until games are truly ported to the new operating system. In the meantime, you can run many older games in the Classic environment, but do not expect stellar performance. Frame rates, for example, will not be quite as high as you experienced under Mac OS 9.

Immediate Solutions

Launching Older Mac Programs

You don't have to do anything special to run your Classic Mac applications within Mac OS X. The operating system is clever enough to sort it all out for you and give you the proper environment for the program you run. To launch an older Mac program and have it work, just do the following:

1. Locate the document or program on your Mac's drive.

2. Double-click on the application icon or a document created with the application.

3. If the Classic environment isn't running, it will go through its regular boot process (see Figure 15.3).

4. The first time you launch Classic from Mac OS X, you'll see a dialog box notifying you that some resources (extensions) need to be added to the Classic System Folder to continue the startup process. You must click on OK to accept the installation and continue running Classic. Otherwise, click on Quit and the process will stop.

5. If you click on the disclosure triangle in the Classic window, you'll see a standard Mac startup screen (see Figure 15.4), but it happens within an application window within Mac OS X. Clever! Once the Classic environment is running, the application you launched will be opened as well. Then your document will appear on the screen, surrounded by a user interface that is essentially the same as what you experienced under Mac OS 9.1.

NOTE: When Classic is launching, its icon will appear in the Dock and will (assuming you haven't changed the option) bounce up and down rhythmically as the environment is loading. You'll also see an icon representing the Mac OS 9.1 application you opened.

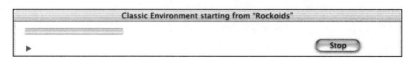

Figure 15.3   This progress bar shows that the Classic environment is starting up.

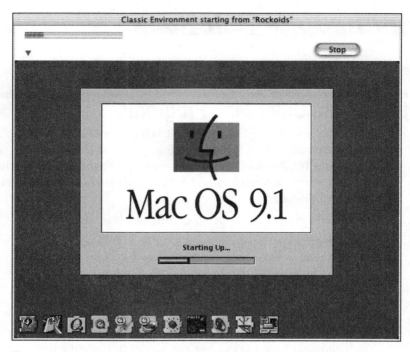

Figure 15.4 If you click on the disclosure triangle, you'll see the standard Mac OS 9 startup screen.

TIP: Another way to start Classic is just to go to Mac OS X's Applications folder and double-click on the Classic icon. It'll do the rest.

Running Classic as a Startup Application

It's highly likely that, at least during the early stages of Mac OS X's rollout, you'll have to spend plenty of time in the Classic environment to run your older programs. Therefore, it may be a good idea to have Classic as a startup application so you don't have to wait for it later on when running those programs. Here's how to make it a startup program:

1. Launch the System Preferences application (it's normally in the Dock).

2. Click on the Classic icon. The Classic preference pane, shown in Figure 15.5, appears.

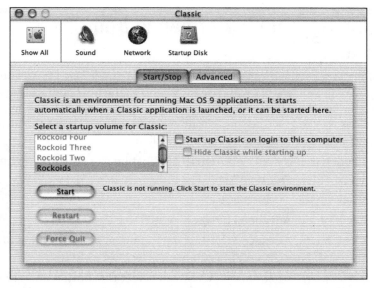

Figure 15.5   The Classic preference pane is used to set up the environment
as a startup process.

3. Choose the startup volume that contains the Mac OS 9.1 System Folder from the scrolling list.

4. Click on the checkbox labeled Start Up Classic On Login To This Computer. Whenever you log in to your Mac OS X user account, Classic will be launched. You can still quit the environment in the normal fashion later on, but you'll be all set when you're ready to run your older software.

5. If you want to begin Classic right away, just click on the Start button.

6. Click on the Close button to quit the System Preferences application.

NOTE: *I'll cover the settings found in the Advanced Classic settings pane, which will help you tailor performance and reduce potential hang-ups, in the next section.*

Getting Reliable Performance from Classic Applications

Making it possible to run older Mac programs under Mac OS X is one of the main factors that will ease migration to the new operating system. Rather than fret over what works and what doesn't, the most efficient way to run Classic right now is bare bones. Here's the ideal way to set it up for maximum compatibility:

1. Launch the System Preferences application (it's probably in the Dock unless you removed it).
2. Click on the Classic pane.
3. Click on the Advanced tab (see Figure 15.6).
4. Click on the Advanced Options pop-up menu and select one of the configuration options you want. They are as follows:

   - *Turn Off Extensions*—When you select this option and click on the Start Classic button, Mac OS 9.1 will reboot with extensions off. This offers maximum compatibility, at the risk of losing access to system extensions needed to run specific programs (such as Microsoft's). Video acceleration in Classic mode is also turned off, so screen refresh will slow considerably.

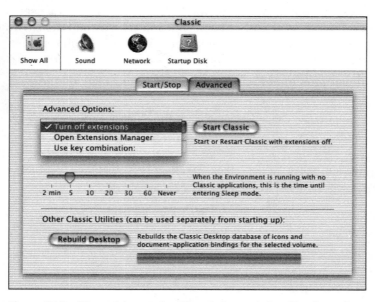

Figure 15.6   These Advanced settings help you tailor Classic performance and compatibility.

- *Open Extensions Manager*—When you select this option and click on the Start Classic button, as Mac OS 9.1 boots, the Extensions Manager application will open, giving you a way to fine-tune your extensions lineup to remove items that may cause performance hits or incompatibilities. I'll cover this more detail shortly.

- *Use Key Combination*—When you select this option, you'll need to enter a keyboard combination in the data field that will appear below the pop-up menu to trigger Classic.

5. The easiest management technique is to select the Open Extensions Manager option. When Classic starts, it'll be the equivalent of holding down the spacebar at startup under Mac OS 9.1. The Extensions Manager window appears, as shown in Figure 15.7.

6. Choose the Mac OS 9.1 Base set from the Selected Set pop-up menu.

7. Go to the File menu and select Duplicate Set. A window appears allowing you to name the set, as shown in Figure 15.8. This simply makes a copy of the Base set you've already selected.

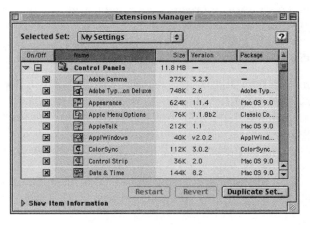

Figure 15.7   Apple's Extensions Manager helps you set up Classic for the best performance.

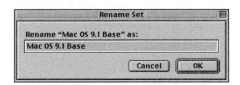

Figure 15.8   This is a copy of the Base set extensions set.

8. Name the copy of the Base set something that will identify it for the purpose, such as "Mac OS X Classic Set."

NOTE: If you run any recent version of Microsoft's Internet programs or any Microsoft Office application while using this Mac OS X set, a number of system extensions required by these programs will be installed the first time any of those programs are launched. There's no reason to be concerned about this; the installation is normal.

---

9. Close Extensions Manager to save your set. From here on, whenever you want to start your Mac under Mac OS X, make sure you activate this special "lean and mean" set for Mac OS X.

NOTE: You can perform essentially the same operation if you use Casady & Greene's Conflict Catcher to manage your Mac OS 9.1 System Folder.

WARNING! On occasion, you may have to reenter the serial number for Conflict Catcher when switching between Mac OS 9.1 and Classic under Mac OS X. This appears to be a problem related to that program, so keep your serial number handy just in case.

Once this special set has been created, you might want to consider adding a few of your cherished extensions and see if Classic continues to run efficiently. There's no reason to abandon your normal extensions set; just switch over before you install or run Mac OS X.

In my experience, a lean and mean Classic environment is a good way to get the most out of the Mac OS X without a wasting a lot of time seeking out possible extension conflicts. If you need to return to Mac OS 9.1, after restart (see "Returning to Mac OS 9.1" later in this chapter), hold down the spacebar until the Extensions Manager (or Conflict Catcher) window appears. Then switch back to your regular extension set (this will probably bring up a dialog from Conflict Catcher stating that it will restart your Mac yet again). That way, you can enjoy the best of both worlds.

NOTE: If you switch extension sets with Conflict Catcher, on occasion, you'll see a prompt indicating that you need to restart your Mac again. This happens if some of the extensions that were activated must boot before Conflict Catcher. It is perfectly normal behavior.

Keeping Your Mac OS 9.1 System Folder Safe and Sound

Another way to protect your Mac OS 9.1 System Folder is to use another startup drive for your regular workaday setup when you're not using Mac OS 9.1. This way, you don't have to fret over special startup sets, extra extensions in the System Folder from Mac OS X, or other possible problems that might result from the switching process (although it should, in theory, work all right). Here's how to get the most value out of this multiple System Folder scheme:

1. Before you install Mac OS X, back up and reformat your Mac's hard drive into at least two partitions.

2. Install the version of Mac OS 9.1 you want to use with Mac OS X on your first partition.

3. Install the System Folder you want to use for regular work on the second partition.

4. Proceed with your standard installation of Mac OS X, as described in Chapter 2.

5. When the installer proceeds to the dialog box where you select a disk for installation, choose the one on your first boot partition. Be sure not to check the box to erase the partition; otherwise, you'll wipe out the data on that drive.

6. Continue with the Mac OS X installation. For now, whenever you wish to use Classic, you'll choose the Mac OS 9.1 System Folder on the first partition. When you want to work full-time in the older operating system, you'll simply select the System Folder in the second partition.

15. Using Older Programs with Mac OS X

TIP: If you find that one or the other System Folder isn't being recognized for startup, or by the Startup Disk pane in the System Preferences application, open that folder, then close it again. This has the effect of "blessing" the System Folder, making it possible to boot your Mac from it.

Related solution:	Found on page:
Installing Mac OS X	28

Solving Classic Environment Problems

If you follow the steps in the previous sections, you should be able to continue to use your Classic Mac OS applications with decent performance and the maximum-possible level of compatibility. However, if you choose to abandon the simple setup to add some extra extensions, you may encounter some troubles along the way. Here are likely causes and solutions:

- *A slow startup of the Classic environment*—If it seems to take a long time to access a Classic application, consider this remedy: Pare down Mac OS 9 system extensions to the Base set, then create a new Mac OS X set from it. The startup process should be much faster now, and your problems fewer.

- *Classic startup applications switch back and forth*—I have observed this phenomenon when the Launcher and Spell Catcher played a game of dueling launches. The immediate solution is to click on the menu bar and quit the Spell Catcher application, but the long-term remedy is to disable one or the other. Spell Catcher's compatibility under Mac OS X is questionable, and it wasn't certain when this book was written whether the publisher, Casady & Greene, would update the program, particularly since its author, Jeffrey Robbin, has gone to Apple to work on iTunes (which is descended from SoundJam).

NOTE: *Spell Catcher is a terrific interactive spell-checking and thesaurus utility. It runs in virtually all programs and will flash warnings if you make an error. Its Ghostwriting feature stores keystrokes, in case you lose a file as a result of a system crash. It would be nice to see this program continued under Mac OS X, but author Evan Gross says it is doubtful he'd do it, particularly because it would have to be rewritten from scratch as a Cocoa-based application, because the tools he needs to make it work aren't supported in Apple's Carbon APIs.*

- *A nasty startup crash when returning to Mac OS 9*—More than likely, you will need to restart under Mac OS 9.1 for one reason or another, unless the Mac on which Mac OS X is installed is devoted to testing and nothing else. Shortly after the startup process begins, before extension icons appear, all or part of a blank bomb screen will bring the whole process to a halt. The probable cause is that you ran a Classic Internet program and it tried to make a connection to the Net, particularly when you were running Mac OS X's PPP Connect application. The solution is to restart with system extensions off (hold the Shift key down at startup), then trash the TCP/IP Preferences file in the Preferences

Folder inside the System Folder. Then it'll be safe to restart normally. You'll need to re-create the settings (or just keep a backup around just in case).

TIP: *One way to avoid this annoying symptom is to remove your standard TCP/IP Preferences file and keep it for safekeeping. Upon restart, a new, empty file will be created. With no data entered, it is less apt to become corrupted when you try to run your old Mac Internet software from the Classic environment. Another way is to lock your settings, so they cannot be modified. This is done by changing the user mode to Administration (the ability to do that is accessed via the File menu). Once you're in Administration mode, you can lock down any setting.*

- *Launching Internet programs doesn't get you connected*—If you have dial-up access to the Internet, you need to launch the Internet Connect application first and then connect. You can then use any Carbon or Cocoa Net program. If you're using a program that does its own dialing, such as AOL or CompuServe 2000, you'll need to check for Mac OS X updates to their client software.

Returning to Mac OS 9.1

There is no reason not to switch back to Mac OS 9.1 to run programs and hardware that isn't ready to work under Mac OS X (that's why it's part of the Mac OS X package). To return to your former environment, just do the following:

1. Launch the System Preferences application.
2. Double-click on the Startup Disk pane (see Figure 15.9).

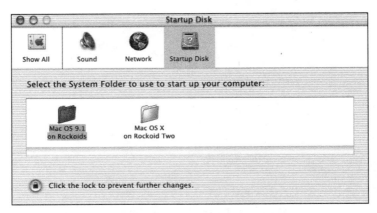

Figure 15.9   Choose your startup disk from this screen.

3. Click on the padlock icon (if it happens to be closed), and then type your correct username and password to get access to changing the startup disk.

4. Click on your Mac OS 9.1 startup disk.

5. Click on the Close button to close System Preferences.

6. Choose Restart from the Apple menu. In a few moments, your Mac will restart under Mac OS 9.1.

NOTE: *If you followed my recommendation to establish a special set in Extensions Manager or Conflict Catcher to use when running Mac OS 9.1 in the Classic environment, be sure to hold down the spacebar when starting under Mac OS 9.1. This will bring up your startup manager's screen, and you can then switch to your preferred Mac OS 9.1 startup set for regular use and enjoy all of your favorite system extensions.*

---

15. Using Older Programs with Mac OS X

Chapter 16

Mac OS X Font Management

If you need an immediate solution to:	See page:
Installing Fonts Under Mac OS X	281
Using the Font Panel	281
Adding Font Favorites	283
Using Favorites	283
Creating a Font Collection	284
Choosing Custom Font Sizes	285
Checking the Characters in a Font	286
Avoiding Too-Small Fonts in TextEdit	287
Handling Mac OS X Font Problems	288

In Brief

The desktop publishing revolution is credited with giving the Macintosh platform credibility. Where you once had to use an artist's table, dedicated typesetting computers, and high-cost output devices to produce artwork for a brochure or publication, the Mac made it possible to do it all on your desktop at relatively low cost, even in your own home. Page layout applications, such as Adobe PageMaker and QuarkXPress, low-cost fonts, and relatively high-quality laser printers combined to bury much of the traditional typesetting industry, except for extremely specialized work.

However, the availability of thousands of fonts has proven to be the bane of the Mac user's experience, because it creates new concerns and sources of confusion.

There Are Fonts and There Are Fonts

It would be nice if fonts all came in just one format and were easy to install, but the situation has been otherwise. There are multiple font formats, and fonts of different types with the very same name. Where does one begin?

Font Formats Defined

Before you even select a font to use in your document, you are faced with choices of installation and organization. Here's a list of the types of fonts commonly used on Macs:

- *Bitmap fonts*—These fonts are designed for printing and display in a single size. If they are scaled in one size or another, the quality of the image deteriorates in proportion to the size difference, and the image can become an almost unreadable collection of pixel shapes when printed or viewed at a very large size.

- *PostScript fonts*—This is the scalable font format developed by Adobe Systems in the mid-1980s.

- *Scalable fonts*—These fonts can be printed in any available point size at the full resolution of the printer or other output device. However, the fonts come in a form that tends to confuse many Mac users. The scalable fonts, called variously outline fonts or printer fonts, are separate from the fonts that generate images on your Mac's display, the screen fonts. This is a carryover from the way fonts were organized in the days of traditional typography, where font sets were also divided into two parts for width or space values and for output. But it also causes confusion because the lack of the screen font means your font won't show up in a font menu and the lack of a printer font means it won't print at full quality.

- *TrueType fonts*—In 1990, to avoid having to pay license fees for use of PostScript fonts, Apple (with help from Microsoft) developed a new scalable font format. TrueType fonts include the screen font and outline font in a single file. For that reason alone, they are easier to handle. However, there are downsides. One is that you should not try to use a PostScript and TrueType font of the same format. At worst, printing of the document will be inconsistent or it'll be output in the wrong font. Or letterspacing may be distorted. The other problem with TrueType is that printers and service bureaus with high-resolution output devices may not fully support the format, particularly if they are using older hardware.

NOTE: *Though originally introduced on the Mac platform, TrueType fonts are the standard font format for Microsoft Windows. On the Mac platform, however, PostScript remains the font format of choice for the publishing industry, as the high-resolution output devices used may not always support TrueType (although this has been largely fixed with newer devices). New Macs, however, and the Mac OS, all ship with TrueType fonts.*

- *OpenType fonts*—A recent entrant in the font arena, the OpenType font format can combine elements of PostScript and TrueType fonts in a single file, along with more extensive character sets, but it hasn't quite caught on yet, although it's fully supported by Mac OS X.

Font Organization under the Mac OS

Before Mac OS X arrived, Mac users had to rely on extra software for flexible font handling and, in fact, for the user to actually use fonts with some printers. Here's a list of the options and what they did:

- *Adobe Type Manager (ATM)*—Originally introduced in 1989, this program (shown in Figure 16.1) is designed to provide clear screen display of PostScript fonts in all available sizes on the Mac's display. It also had the side effect of allowing non-PostScript printers, such as ink jet printers, to use PostScript fonts and deliver the maximum quality they were capable of. An

Figure 16.1   ATM Deluxe manages your font library and provides clear display of fonts, all in the same program.

enhanced version of ATM, ATM Deluxe, also allows you to activate and deactivate fonts that are not installed in the System Folder, check for duplicates and damaged fonts, and print font samples.

NOTE: *Although a Mac OS X version of ATM hadn't been announced by Adobe when this book was written, you'll still want to keep it at hand for clean display of PostScript fonts used in the Classic environment.*

- *Alsoft's MasterJuggler*—MasterJuggler is one of the early font management programs. As with ATM Deluxe, it's used to activate and organize a font library. It does not, however, do anything about font rendering, so you still need to have the basic version (now free) of ATM for that purpose.

- *DiamondSoft's Font Reserve*—This program provides a unique way to store and manage fonts. It places all fonts outside the System Folder in a database file, so you don't have to concern yourself with placing them in any particular location. There are various sorting features, as well as the ability to print samples of your library. Again, ATM is needed for font rendering.

- *Extensis Suitcase*—The original font manager, which has passed through several software publishers (such as the late Fifth Generation Systems and Symantec) before finding its current home with the popular publisher of add-on graphics utilities. It is somewhat similar to MasterJuggler in terms of its focus and features, but you still need ATM for clean display of PostScript fonts.

Mac OS X's New Font-Handling Scheme

When developing Mac OS X, Apple Computer realized that font management was confusing for a great many Mac users and often the source of trouble in preparing and outputting documents. The response is the Apple Type Solution (ATS). This mechanism, which works with the Quartz 2D imaging layer of the new operating system, delivers system-wide handling of all the major font formats— PostScript, TrueType, OpenType, and even the original Mac bitmap fonts.

ATS handles font rendering of all the formats using Mac OS X's Portable Document Format (PDF) mechanism (which uses Adobe's popular open standard for creating electronic documents), so there's no need for ATM for PostScript font display. In addition, there are built-in tools for organizing font collections and displaying samples, which may, to some extent, reduce or eliminate the need for a font management program.

NOTE: *As you'll see in the pages that follow, the ATS font system isn't a panacea and it doesn't work with all programs, nor will its font-handling features appeal to everyone. This is apt to leave plenty of room for third-party publishers to update existing font managers or develop new programs to provide needed features lacking in the core operating system.*

Additionally, fonts are available in two ways to users of Mac OS X:

- *System-wide*—Fonts can still be placed in a Fonts folder, but the folder itself is in a new location. You'll find it in a folder labeled Library, where a number of folders related to system settings and preferences are located. Fonts located in this folder are available to all users of that computer. Changing fonts or anything else on a system basis, of course, requires that you log in using your administrator's account name and password.

- *User-specific*—Each user can have a separate library, stored in the Fonts folder, in his or her personal Library folder. The Library folder is located within the Users folder, which bears the user's name. Those fonts are only available to that user, but they behave transparently to Mac OS X otherwise and are indistinguishable in the font menu.

NOTE: *Another advantage of Mac OS X is the number of fonts you can use. Under Mac OS versions prior to 9, the limit was 128 font resources, meaning bitmap and suitcase files. Some users would drag and drop font suitcases atop one another to combine them and get around this limitation. The limit went to 512 fonts under Mac OS 9, but with Mac OS X, there is no practical limit to how many fonts you can install, other than the size of your Mac's drive and the agony you want to experience in looking at an endless font display.*

Introducing the Font Panel

Apple has made a significant stride toward more efficient font management with Mac OS X's Font Panel (see Figure 16.2). This handy feature not only simplifies selection of fonts, but also allows you to organize your collection, regardless of size, according to your needs.

In fact, the Font Panel may even, in part, replace the need for a separate font management program—except for one serious limitation. When software publishers Carbonize their applications to work under Mac OS X, they have a number of choices to make. One is just to make the program run in the new environment and be compatible with the basic features, such as preemptive multitasking and protected memory. This entails less work on the part of a publisher's programming team. However, Apple also provides tools to exploit the features of Carbon should the publisher undertake the extra work, and one of those features is the Font Panel (and support wasn't yet available for the initial release of Mac OS X). That means that an application that otherwise fully supports Mac OS X will have a plain-Jane font menu. Unfortunate, but true.

However, if the publisher has developed a Cocoa application, you'll find a flexible way in which to manage your font collection. If the font feature isn't supported, you'll see an ordinary type of font menu instead (see Figure 16.3).

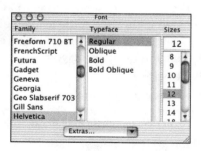

Figure 16.2   Choose, sample, and organize your font library here.

16. Mac OS X
Font Management

Figure 16.3   This particular application, though Carbonized for Mac OS X, only yields an old-fashioned font menu.

Special Font Features of Mac OS X

If an application supports the Font Panel, it also inherits some additional system-wide font features that used to be available only in separate programs. When you call up a font menu in a Mac OS X program that offers the expanded font features (see Figure 16.4), you'll see a number of those additional features (some will vary from program to program) in addition to the normal range of font formatting choices. They include the following:

- *Kern*—Used by graphic artists, *kerning* is the process of adjusting the spacing of letter combinations that would otherwise be wide apart visually. For example, in the word *To*, kerning tucks the lowercase *o* closer to the letter *T* for a more pleasing appearance and better readability. Mac OS X lets you use the kerning features of a font. You can also adjust the overall spacing between characters, which is sometimes called *tracking* or *range kerning*.

- *Ligature*—In high-quality books and ads, *ligatures* create single, integrated characters of such combinations as *fi* and *fl*, by joining the tops of the characters, such as fi and fl. The conversion is done automatically when you type a character.

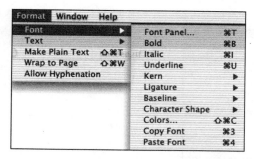

Figure 16.4   This submenu shows additional font management options
for Mac OS X.

NOTE: *Such programs as QuarkXPress and Adobe InDesign, two popular page layout applications, can convert ligatures on the fly. Mac OS X lets you do it with all programs that support all of its superior font-handling features.*

With all of the great font-handling features of Mac OS X, you may begin to cherish the ease with which you are able to manage your library, whether it includes a few dozen or a few thousand fonts. In the next section, I'll cover the ways you can install or use fonts under the new operating system.

Immediate Solutions

Installing Fonts under Mac OS X

As explained at the start of this chapter, fonts can be installed on a system for everyone who uses your Mac or on an individual-user basis, where only that user can access them. Here's how to use both features:

1. To install a font on a system-wide basis, you must first log in as the administrator of that Mac or a user with administrator's rights. If another user has logged in, use the Log Out command in the Apple menu and then enter your username and password in the Login prompt.

2. Locate your Mac's Library folder, which is located on your Mac's startup drive.

3. Copy the fonts directly to the Fonts folder. The fonts will be recognized by your newly opened applications. If they don't appear right away, restart your Mac.

The other way to install fonts is for the individual user only. Here's how it's done:

1. Log in under the individual user's account.

2. Locate the Users folder, then the folder with that user's name.

3. Locate the Library folder, then copy the fonts directly to the Fonts folder. Fonts installed in this fashion should show up immediately in your font menu. If not, follow the steps in the preceding list and restart your Mac.

WARNING! Fonts installed under a user's account are only available to an individual user. If you expect that more than one user will work with a font, it's better to install the font on a system-wide basis.

Using the Font Panel

Mac OS X's Font Panel provides a feature-laden way to organize and access the fonts in your library, regardless of the size. In the next few pages, you'll learn how to harness the power of this font handling feature.

Here's how to use the Font Panel:

1. From within an application that supports the feature, go to the Format menu, and choose Font. Then select Font Panel from the submenu. The window in Figure 16.5 appears. A faster method is just to type Command+T.

2. Under Family, select the font you want to use.

3. If the font has several styles, choose the one you want from the Typeface column.

4. Pick the size you want from the Sizes column (or just type the size in the text field at the top of the column to get a size not listed in the display).

> **TIP:** *If the Font Panel is too large to be comfortably placed on your Mac's screen in addition to your document window, just resize it by moving the resize bar as you want. Fonts are also organized into Collections. If you expand the width of the Font Panel, you'll see one more column, Collections, from which you can select a different group of fonts.*

5. Close the Font Panel screen and continue to work in your document.

> **TIP:** *If you plan on switching fonts back and forth, feel free to keep the Font Panel window displayed so you can return to it quickly from your document.*

> **NOTE:** *Common available weights of a font, such as bold or italic, can be selected directly from the Font menu without invoking the Font Panel, although purists say you'll get better printing results if you choose the correct font weight from the panel itself.*

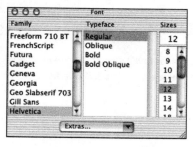

Figure 16.5   Many Mac OS X-savvy applications support the Font Panel.

Adding Font Favorites

Another great feature of the Font Panel is the ability to store fonts as Favorites for fast retrieval. Here's how to set them up:

1. From within an application that supports the feature, activate the Font Panel. Or just press Command+T.

2. Select the font family, style, and size you want.

3. Click on the pop-up menu labeled Extras (see Figure 16.6), and select Add To Favorites.

4. Repeat the process for each font you want to use as a favorite. Favorites will list not just the typeface, but also the exact size you specified.

Using Favorites

To access a font from your Favorites listing, just follow these steps:

1. Activate the Font Panel. Click on the size bar and extend it to the right, to expand the width of the Font Panel.

2. From the Collections column, click on Favorites, which will show the display seen in Figure 16.7. The Favorites listing will also show the selected fonts in their actual size and style.

NOTE: *If you used the Mac OS X Public Beta, you'll probably recall that the Font Panel included a preview of all selected fonts. For the final release, this has been confined strictly to the display of a font after it's selected under Favorites.*

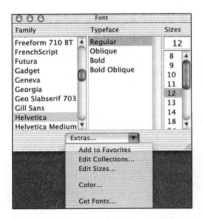

16. Mac OS X Font Management

Figure 16.6   Additional commands are available for you to organize your font collection.

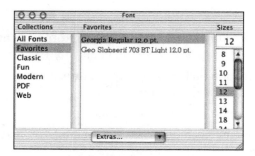

Figure 16.7   Choose your Favorites from this listing.

3. To remove a font from your Favorites listing, just select it, then choose Remove From Favorites from the pop-up menu.

Creating a Font Collection

One of the more useful features of Mac OS X for managing a large font library is the ability to create a custom collection to match your specific needs. That way, you can have one font collection for personal use and another for business. If you're a business user, you can subdivide fonts by the name of your client, your document, or the type of fonts you're using, such as serif and sans serif, or title and text, to name a few.

The Collections feature of the Font Panel makes easy work of this. Just follow these steps:

1. Activate the Font Panel.

2. Click on the pop-up menu below the font sample area and choose Edit Collections (see Figure 16.8).

3. In the Collection column, press the plus symbol, which produces a brand-new collection with the name New-1, or New-2, depending on how many you've made.

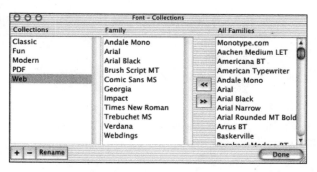

Figure 16.8   Manage and create new font collections from this window.

4. Click on the Rename button to give the collection a more appropriate name, if you wish.

5. With the new collection selected, locate the font you want in the All Families column at the left, and press the left-pointing arrow to add it to your collection.

6. Repeat the process for each font you want to add to that collection.

7. If you want to remove a font collection, just press the minus key.

WARNING! There is no warning prompt if you press the minus key when selecting a font collection. So be certain you want to remove that collection before pressing the button. This is a feature that may or may not be fixed in the final release of Mac OS X.

8. Click on Done when you're finished making your collections.

9. To add that particular font as a Favorite, choose Add To Favorites from the Font Panel's pop-up menu.

10. When you're finished creating your font collections, close the Font Panel.

11. When you need to use a specific collection, just access the Font Panel and click on the collection's name in the Collection column.

12. Select your font in the same fashion described at the beginning of this section.

Choosing Custom Font Sizes

The Font Panel includes a standard set of popular display sizes, but if your needs require more fine-tuning, follow this process:

1. Activate the Font Panel from a program that supports the feature. Or just press Command+T.

2. With the Font Panel on display, choose Edit Sizes from the pop-up menu. This brings up the screen shown in Figure 16.9.

3. Under New Size, enter the size you want to include in the Sizes list, and press the plus button. Alternatively, you can choose the Adjustable Slider button, and move a slider to select the various font sizes.

4. If you want to remove a font size, select it and click on the minus button.

5. Click on Done when you're finished. You'll be returned to the Font Panel.

16. Mac OS X Font Management

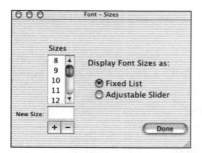

Figure 16.9   Add new font sizes here.

Checking the Characters in a Font

Some things never change, and the way you look for the extra characters in a font under Mac OS X is the same as in previous versions of
the Mac OS, with Key Caps (see Figure 16.10).

To use Key Caps, follow these steps:

1. Locate Key Caps in the Utilities folder, and double-click on the
   program's icon.

2. Go to the Font menu and select the font you wish to use.

3. The keyboard layout displays the characters available. Press
   the appropriate modifier key, either Option or Option+Shift, to
   see the character you want.

4. Type the character by clicking on the key with the mouse or
   pressing the appropriate key on the keyboard. That character
   shows up in the display window above the keyboard layout.

5. To use this special character, select it, then copy it. You can
   then paste it into the text-entry point in your document.

Figure 16.10   Key Caps is still part of the Mac OS, and its functions remain
              essentially the same.

16. Mac OS X
Font Management

Avoiding Too-Small Fonts in TextEdit

Apple's replacement for SimpleText, TextEdit (shown in Figure 16.11), can be used as a simple word processor, with full management of fonts with the Font Panel. However, it can be quirky in an important respect, because you cannot specify an exact line width in the same fashion as a regular word-processing program. Instead, it uses the width of your document window to determine the size, and the line breaks made in the document on your Mac's display will match those in your printout.

However, if your printout uses a page width smaller than the screen, the font's size will be scaled down in proportion, and under some circumstances, it can get downright small. There is, however, a simple solution to this dilemma:

1. Go to TextEdit's Format menu.

2. Select the Wrap To Page option. When this feature is active, lines will wrap on the basis of the page size selected in the Page Setup box. No more ultra-small (or ultra-large) letters, and the size that's printed will be the exact size you selected in the document itself.

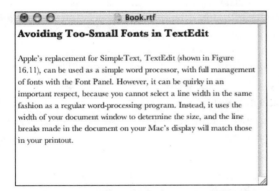

Figure 16.11   TextEdit is meant to be a less modestly featured replacement for the famous SimpleText application.

Handling Mac OS X Font Problems

The new, more robust font-handling features of Mac OS X usually make it far easier to handle a font library, whether small or large. But because of the interaction between Mac OS X and the Classic environment, for example, you may still run into problems.

Here are some common Mac OS X problems and the standard range of solutions:

- *Fonts not in font menu*—If a font was installed in a user's folder, it won't be available to any other user on your Mac. If you want more than a single user to access a font, install it under that user's account as well, or system-wide. If you did install the fonts in the proper fashion, try restarting your Mac just to make sure that they are recognized by the operating system.

- *Fonts appear in some applications and not in others*—Could the fonts have been installed in Mac OS 9.1's Fonts folder? That would explain why it's not there. The solution is just to reinstall the fonts under Mac OS X, as described in "Installing Fonts under Mac OS X."

- *Garbled or bitmapped font output*—This is probably a font conflict, similar to those that afflicted earlier versions of the Mac OS. The best way to handle this is to make sure you have installed only one version of the font, and not both PostScript and TrueType versions. Another possible cause is installing two or more fonts of the same name from different sources. The operating system won't be able to sort them out.

- *Poor letterspacing*—Check the previous item just to be sure you do not have fonts that are in conflict. Another possible problem is a damaged font suitcase or TrueType font, which may not provide the right letterspacing information.

- *Missing font collection*—Are you sure you didn't delete it by mistake? You get no acknowledgement if you press the minus key by error. Otherwise, make sure that the fonts added to a collection were not part of another user's account. That would explain why it's not there when you try to access the collection.

Chapter 17

Performing Backups

If you need an immediate solution to:	See page:
The No-Frills Daily Backup Plan	302
What You Need	302
Performing No-Frills Backups	303
The Special Software Backup Plan	303
What You Need	304
Performing Your Regular Backup Routine	304
Tips and Tricks for Robust Backups	305

In Brief

You might remember that old TV commercial with the motto "nobody can eat just one." Although the comment applied to potato chips, the same theme can be carried over to the files you create on your Mac. Nobody should depend on just one.

There is no telling what might happen to your files during your day-to-day Mac computing experience. Although Mac OS X offers a robust computing environment, about as free of potential system crashes as the state of the art allows, some programs will still fail under normal use. When a program fails, it could conceivably harm the document you're working on. In addition, hard drives, being mechanical devices, can fail unpredictably, even though they are supposed to have lengthy mean times between failures, sometimes up to 500,000 hours and more.

There are all sorts of potential issues beyond that of your Mac and computing environment that could also conspire to cause loss of your data. They include such things as weather-related problems such as hurricanes or tornadoes, or natural disasters such as earthquakes and floods, along with potential disasters like fire and theft. In addition, any factor that might cause a power outage or power spike, even if caused by a problem at the power company, can result in a damaged file or hard drive directory damage if it occurs at the wrong time.

Even if all of your computing equipment is protected by insurance (and it should be, especially if used for business purposes), insurance cannot re-create the files you lose. However, if you have recent backups of all of your critical data, you will be able to resume operation without having to re-create this material.

A Survey of Backup Software

Depending on your setup and requirements, there are different methods to perform backups. The easiest is just to copy your critical files to another drive by dragging the files or folders to the drive's icon. If you don't have a lot of files to handle, this may be the perfect and highly practical solution, as long as you remember to do so on a regular basis.

NOTE: *All Macs of recent vintage have a Software Restore CD, which allows you to return the Mac to its shipping condition (minus the files you've added, of course). In addition, the vast majority of software shipped nowadays comes on a CD. So even if you only back up the documents you create, you can restore your Mac's hard drive without a full backup, though at the expense of losing your user settings, such as those required for Internet access.*

The other method is probably more reliable, because you don't have to remember to make those backup copies. It's done for you on a more or less automatic basis, and it involves using dedicated backup software.

I'll list several of the popular backup applications here. No doubt, as Mac OS X continues to gain in popularity, additional backup options will be available to suit a variety of needs.

An Overview of Retrospect

What most regard as the most popular backup program for the Mac is Retrospect from Dantz Development (check **www.dantz.com** for more information). This program is bundled with a number of backup drives, which makes the choice automatic. It's also sold separately and is available at most Apple dealers. Besides its market share, the various forms of Retrospect routinely get top reviews from the Mac magazines.

NOTE: *If you want to read one of my published reviews of the program, point your Web browser to **http://macuser.zdnet.com/mu_1097/reviews/retro.html**. I gave Retrospect a five-mouse review in the last issue of that magazine before it merged with Macworld (and, no, that wasn't the reason it failed).*

Depending on your needs, there are three versions of Retrospect to consider:

- *Retrospect Express Backup*—Consider this the no-frills version of the program, though it doesn't scrimp on important features that you need for regular, robust backups. You can use its EasyScript feature to create a custom backup routine by simply answering a few basic questions about the sort of backups you plan to do and how often you want to do them. Based on this information, Retrospect Express will build an automated backup routine that suits your needs. Say, for example, you want to back up your Mac at 4:30 P.M. each afternoon, using your Jaz 2 drive. You just place your backup medium in the drive and leave the drive and your Mac on. At the appointed hour, Express will launch itself, and then run your scripted backup precisely as you specified. The program has its own compression feature to reduce the size of backup sets. Hundreds of fixed and removable storage devices are supported, including CD-R/RW and DVD-RAM. Backups are stored in *sets*, which are special files containing all of the data you've backed up. You can perform full backups and incremental backups (just the files that have changed). The Express version of the software only lacks networking backup and support for tape drives. It may be all the backup you need, however, for a small home or business office setup.

TIP: *A particularly useful feature of Retrospect is multiple snapshots, which are, in effect, different backups of your Mac taken at different points in time. This gives you the power to access different versions of the same document, or documents that may have been trashed between the initial backup and later backups.*

- *Retrospect Desktop Backup*—This version of Retrospect (see Figure 17.1 for a prototype of their promised Mac OS X version) has all the features of Express, including EasyScript. It adds support for a large variety of tape drives (including the hardware compression offered by these drives) and the ability to expand support to networked Macs and Windows-based PCs via Retrospect Client. These are programs that allow the files on each Mac on a network to be backed up to the same set of storage devices, in a single or separate backup session. Because Retrospect is also available for the Windows platform, cross-platform backups are

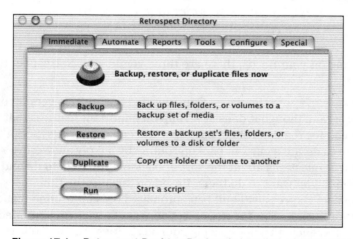

Figure 17.1   Retrospect Desktop Backup is bundled with a number of backup devices and also sold separately.

possible. This version of Retrospect can also be configured to send backup status reports to you via email.

NOTE: *All versions of Retrospect include a robust security option. This allows the backup sets to be encrypted, so only those with the correct username and password can access and decrypt the backups or retrieve files from them.*

- *Retrospect Workgroup Backup*—This is a fully packaged solution for automatic backups. The program comes with the standard Retrospect application and thus supports the entire set of features. You also get Client software (see Figure 17.2) for up to 20 networked computers.

NOTE: *The pictures shown here are based on prerelease versions of the Mac OS X version of Retrospect. The final version was due for release sometime after release of the new operating system.*

An Overview of ASD Personal Backup

ASD Software (see **www.asdsoft.com**), publisher of several popular Mac security products, targets Personal Backup for single users or small offices (see Figure 17.3). The program supports standard removable media, but it doesn't work with tape drives. In addition, there is no network client option.

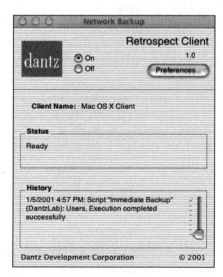

Figure 17.2   The Client version of Retrospect offers a simple interface that displays backup status.

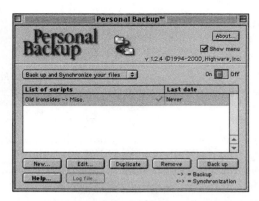

Figure 17.3   Easy configuration and keystroke backups are hallmarks of Personal Backup's feature set; the Mac OS 9 version is shown here.

NOTE: *At the time this book was written, ASD Software hadn't committed to developing a Mac OS X version of their backup application. They did say it was a good possibility, although they had no plans to update their Mac security software for the new operating system. That is why I included a description of the program here.*

Following are Personal Backup's features:

- *Single control-panel–type interface*—The program's features can be accessed from a single, simple control-panel–like application. There are only a small number of setup dialogs to configure the program's various features.

- *Easy scripting*—You can schedule multiple sets of automatic backups without scripting knowledge simply by clicking on the dates, times, and options you want.

- *File synchronization*—You can compare the files you create on your desktop Mac with the ones you make on your iBook or PowerBook (or any other Mac you might use to work at a different location), so that you always have the latest versions on both systems.

- *Finder format backups*—The files you back up are in regular Finder format for easy access without your having to use a special restore feature.

- *Text backup*—Personal Backup can be set to record your keystrokes as you type. If you lose the original document because of file corruption or a system crash, you can easily retrieve the text (but not, of course, a program's special formatting).

Other Backup Programs

The choices listed in the preceding sections are not the only ones available. Here are some other choices:

- *Iomega's QuikSync 3*—This program is easy to set up for on-demand or scheduled backups. The new version overcomes the limitation of the previous edition, by supporting storage devices not manufactured by Iomega. Among the features of QuikSync 3 are:

  - *Easy setup*—A convenient setup wizard guides users through the process of setting up an unattended backup without their needing to understand scripting or complicated setups.

  - *Automatic copying*—You can specify certain folders on your Mac's hard drive for automatic backup. Files that are copied or moved to those folders will be automatically duplicated in the "sync" location, which is usually (one hopes) an external storage device.

  - *Multiple revisions*—By being able to save more than a single revision of an individual file, you can view documents in progress at different stages, and restore the ones you need to use.

  - *Enterprise implementation*—As with Retrospect, QuikSync 3 can be administered from a central location, making it easy for IT managers to set up the program on a network system.

- *Connectix's CopyAgent*—Several years ago, Connectix released a system-enhancement utility, SpeedDoubler, designed to boost performance in three basic ways. Two of the features, the 680x0 emulator for older Mac software and the disk cache component, were eventually supplanted by superior methods from Apple. With the release of Mac OS 9, the entire program was no longer compatible. Connectix took the faster copying element and expanded it into CopyAgent. In addition to handling scheduled backups, Connectix claims its program is capable of doubling network copying performance. That claim was made under Mac OS 9, not X, however, so it remains to be seen whether this claim is true for the new operating system.

- *Power On Software's Rewind*—You install something new on your Mac and suddenly it appears as if the computer is possessed. You can, of course, troubleshoot the problem and perhaps remove the application. But wouldn't it be easier just to turn back the hands of time? Rewind does that, by keeping a reference file of changes you've made to your Mac and then, when called into action, restores your Mac to the condition that existed before the event that triggered your problem. You can also use this clever application to recover a lost file, by going back in time to the point before you actually deleted the file. Although there are file recovery utilities, this may be a more robust way to regain lost ground.

NOTE: *At the time this book was being prepared, Power On Software was committed to updating several of their programs, which include security and personal information managers, to Mac OS X. An updated version of Rewind wasn't available for me to examine, however, so I'm summarizing the features of the Classic Mac OS version.*

In addition to the commercial programs, there are several shareware offerings that promise many of the basic features of the commercial options. When you decide which program to deploy in your environment, you'll want to consider the features offered and how they fit your situation.

An Overview of Internet Backups

Beginning with Mac OS 9, Apple attempted to make Internet networking as transparent as connecting to a local area network (LAN). Mac OS X's user interface is designed to further blur the differences between the location of shared volumes, so it no longer makes a difference whether it's located at the other end of your room or at the other end of the world (except for file transfer speed, of course).

The ease of Internet networking and the lack of standard backup drives on some new Macs have resulted in a search for other backup methods. One of those methods harnesses the power of the Internet as a repository for your backed up files. Following are descriptions of two Internet-based backup resources. One is free, direct from Apple. The other comes with a modest monthly charge and requires special software.

- *iTools (**www.apple.com/itools**)*—Beginning with Mac OS 9, Apple introduced a new feature, iTools, which allowed for expanded access to their apple.com Web site. The initial features included a custom mac.com email address, special KidSafe Internet access controls, the ability to create a personal home page, and iDisk (see Figure 17.4), which sets aside 20MB of storage space for your files. iDisk is easily accessed as a disk icon, which you can use in the same fashion as a volume connected directly to your Mac or your local network. iDisk is useful

Figure 17.4 Apple's free iDisk feature gives you 20MB of free Internet storage to use for backups or to make files available to your Internet contacts.

as a limited, fairly robust backup solution. It allows you to store your files in a private area, free from public access.

NOTE: *Apple Computer offers more storage space as an extra-cost option. Check the iTools Web site for current pricing and capacities.*

• *BackJack (www.backjack.com)*—This Canadian-based company claims top ratings from Mac support Web sites. It offers a dedicated program that will provide automatic, unattended backups to their 128-bit secured Web servers. They also use StuffIt compression technology to maximize the number of files you can send in a given amount of storage space. Pricing plans depend on the amount of storage space you need.

Although Internet backups are a reliable method of backing up critical files, and they offer the added benefit of being offsite, they have some decided disadvantages. Chief among them is throughput and capacity. Transferring even a few megabytes of files via a standard

56Kbps modem connection can be a tedious process. Worse, if you are disconnected during the transfer process (a fairly common occurrence), you must go through all or most of the process all over again to make sure all of your files were sent. You will want to consider broadband access, such as cable modem or DSL, if available in your area, should you choose this backup solution.

TIP: *Even if you have broadband Internet service, don't be surprised if your upload speed is throttled to a level far below that of download speed. Typically, cable modems limit uploads to 256Kbps or less, even though they promise download speeds from 1 to 2Mbps.*

The other shortcoming is capacity. iDisk limits you to 20MB total storage (unless you buy the extra storage space). Commercial Internet backup resources such as BackJack offer standard plans with fixed storage capacities (theirs is 40MB and 100MB), and additional per-megabyte charges for larger storage capacities. Even if you had the capability of sending large amounts of data in a speedy fashion to such a service, the costs of backing up a fairly full hard drive in a new or recent Mac (with several gigabytes of files) on a regular basis can be considerable.

An Overview of Backup Media

A number of storage mediums are useful for backups—some more robust than others. When choosing a product, you should consider your specific needs, such as the amount of data you wish to back up and how robust the medium is for long-term storage, if that's one of your requirements.

NOTE: *I have made no attempt to cover older, discontinued removable devices, such as SyQuest drives. Any of these products can be judged compared to the products mentioned here in terms of speed, capacity, and reliability. You should consider, however, whether it's a good idea to trust your backups to an obsolete product with little or no customer support.*

- *Floppy drive*—This was the original backup medium. It isn't terribly robust; floppy disks are known to develop disk errors even after being used just a few times. Worse, capacity is extremely limited. Even if you have an older Mac with a floppy drive, or you're using HD-style floppy disks on a SuperDisk drive or external floppy drive, you'll find this medium works best for small documents or pictures, when transferring them from one location to another.

- *SuperDisk drive*—This product is earmarked as a floppy drive replacement. It has the benefit of reading and writing to HD floppy disks at a speed greater than a standard floppy; it's most noticeable if you have the "2X" SuperDisk product. This allows support for legacy media (except for 800KB and 400KB floppies, of course). The SuperDisk media itself is a 120MB disk that, at first glance, looks very much like a floppy. Although the product hasn't been on the market terribly long, it appears to be robust, and the medium is relatively inexpensive. Such drives are not particularly fast, however, which makes them less efficient for larger files, and the user base is still relatively small, despite the relative popularity of such devices as accessories for the iMac and other USB-based Apple computers.

NOTE: *Sad to say, the SuperDisk drive has been discontinued, although media is still available and the devices may still be found in closeouts. But they couldn't compete with the Zip "juggernaut."*

- *Zip drive*—This is Iomega's most popular product; they are found in many business environments. The medium resembles a fat floppy disk, and it uses a mixture of floppy and hard drive technologies to provide storage capacities of 100MB and 250MB. Zip drives have been standard issue on many of Apple's desktop models, and there are millions of drives out there, so it makes it easy to find compatible drives at other locations. The drives and media are considered quite robust, standing the test of time, beyond some early reliability concerns on the mechanisms themselves.

- *Jaz drive*—The Iomega Jaz drive is, essentially, a portable drive using traditional hard drive technology. It comes in 1GB and 2GB formats (the latter product is called the Jaz 2), with media to match. It has the benefit of being relatively fast—about the equivalent of a slower hard drive. Long-term reliability of the media is also somewhat of a question mark, although the drive seems solid enough for part-time use and archiving.

- *Castlewood ORB drive*—This product has superficial similarities to the now-departed SyQuest drives, perhaps because the founder of Castlewood was also the founder of SyQuest Technologies. The drive uses low-cost 2.2GB cartridges and employs a variation of standard hard drive technology called magneto-resistive, now increasingly common on modern fixed drives. Its long-term robustness is not known, because the product has been on the market only a relatively short time at this writing. A review in

17. Performing Backups

Macworld magazine, however, suggested there might be some reliability concerns with the product.

- *Portable hard drive*—Because this standard hard drive is in a small case, it is suitable for easy transportation. Such drives are available in all the popular storage technologies, including FireWire, SCSI, and USB. Some notable examples include a FireWire product line from VST Technologies (see **www.vsttech.com**), which uses the FireWire bus for power. That and its Hot Plug feature make such drives easy to set up and move from workstation to workstation.

- *CD/CD-RW*—These products use special CD-based media, offering a high degree of longevity. The standard recordable CD technology is write-once, meaning that you cannot erase or replace the data already recorded. However, the medium is very cheap, so this isn't a serious problem. The more expensive CD-RW products let you rewrite data up to 1,000 times, but the discs themselves do not work on some regular CD drives, particularly older models. The shortcoming is speed, although newer 12x and 16x CD recorders promise to record a complete 650MB CD in just a few minutes.

NOTE: *The figures 12x, 16x, and so on refer to multiples of the normal CD record speed, which takes approximately 74 minutes to write to a 650MB disc. In addition to the basic speed in recording data, you have to add the time it takes to read back the completed CD for verification (although that process is much faster, because standard CD readers on the Mac reach and exceed speeds of 32x and third-party drives are even faster).*

- *DVD-RAM*—This product uses a variant of the newer high-density DVD form to reach a storage capacity of up to 5.2GB. Recording speed is equivalent to the fastest regular CD recording devices, and thus this is a useful method for backing up large amounts of data for long-term storage.

TIP: *Apple no longer ships the high-end PowerMac G4 with a DVD-RAM drive, but it's available as a build-to-order option. In addition, a number of third-party peripheral companies, such as LaCie and Que, offer drives using this format. However, the format is unfinished enough that the media recorded on one drive may not work on another brand.*

- *Tape drives*—Such drives come in several forms, using tapes that are roughly similar in setup to a cassette deck. Tape drives are not cheap, but the medium is. You can buy DDS tapes for around $10 apiece or more, with storage capacities of up to

40GB (depending on the ability of the tape drive or software to compress data). Larger capacities are available for some tape drive formats. Tape drives tend to be slower than the other media, except for CDs, and the technology doesn't offer random access. Therefore, restoring files located in different locations on a tape can take a while. In addition, although tapes are subject to wear and tear, the media is easily and relatively cheaply replaced.

* *Network volume*—You may also back up your data to a drive on another computer (a Mac or a Unix- or Windows-based server), located on your local network. Such techniques are useful for each individual workstation, but the volume to which you are backing up should also receive a regular backup routine to ensure the highest amount of protection for the files.

Immediate Solutions

The No-Frills Daily Backup Plan

This plan doesn't require special backup software. All it requires is a commitment to a regular program so you don't face the loss of crucial files in case of an emergency.

What You Need

Before you begin your backup, you need the following elements:

- *Backup media*—Use a separate drive or networked volume (local or Internet-based). The "In Brief" section covers a number of backup products you might want to consider. You should also make sure you have backup media with sufficient capacity to store all the files.

- *A plan*—Create a small word processing document listing the files and folders you want to back up on a regular basis.

TIP: *To keep track of your backups, you might want to include a list of dates and times on your backup list, along with an underscore or checkbox where you can easily mark your backups as you complete them.*

- *Logically named folders*—Create folders on the backup drive to easily identify the files you are backing up. If you plan to keep separate copies of each generation of your backup files, you should consider putting a date on each folder or other identification information that will help you quickly locate the files you need at a later time.

- *Reminder device*—It will help to have an alarm clock, clock radio, reminder program, or other means to notify you of the time of the scheduled backup.

- *Easy access to your original system or application CDs*—As mentioned earlier in the chapter, new Macs come with a Restore CD, which can put the computer back in the form in which it shipped (at the expense of losing application and system updates and preferences).

TIP: *The standard user license for most every program allows you to make a single backup copy. It is a good idea to make a backup of your software CDs and store them off site, in the event of theft or damage at your original location. Remember that if you are backing up a bootable CD, follow the instructions in the CD software to make your copy bootable as well.*

Performing No-Frills Backups

Once you've got the raw materials set up, follow these steps:

1. Make sure you set your notification device to alert you of the appointed time for the backup.

2. Have your backup medium ready. If you're using a removable drive, such as a Zip drive, be sure that a disk is in the drive, ready to roll.

3. Refer to your backup list for the files and folders you need to copy.

4. Drag the files to the appropriate folders.

5. Once the files are copied, put a note on your backup list confirming the day's backup is complete.

NOTE: *If your Mac is set up for multiple users, you may want to establish a single backup folder to which all users have access. That way, each user does not have to run separate backup sessions (a potentially confusing, awkward process).*

These steps allow you to easily keep track of your daily backups, to make sure that you or one of your employees has performed the task as scheduled.

TIP: *If you are working on a mission-critical document that will take you a long time to re-create in the event of loss or damage, you may also want to perform frequent backups of the files throughout the work day. I do this regularly when I'm writing a book, because re-creating even a single chapter or portion can be an annoying, time-consuming process.*

The Special Software Backup Plan

The following steps are based on using one of the backup programs described in the previous section, "An Overview of Backup Media." I'm assuming you will be installing the software according to the publisher's instructions and that you will be setting up your backup media as indicated.

17. Performing Backups

What You Need

First, you'll want to take steps to prepare for your regular backup regimen:

- If you're using a removable device, be sure the disks or cartridges are inserted into the drive and ready to run at the appointed time.

NOTE: *If you expect your backups to fill more than a single disk or tape, you should have spares available in case additional media is requested. You may, of course, recycle media if you want to discard older backups that are no longer useful.*

- Make sure that the backup software is properly installed.

- Use the program's scheduling features to create a regular backup routine that meets your needs. You may schedule full backups once a week and incremental backups (which cover only the changed files) each day.

- If your backups are likely to consume more than a single disk, be sure someone is available to insert extra media, if necessary.

- If your backup software includes automatic notification of problems via email, be sure the program is configured to contact you or your systems administrator at a location at which they're likely to be at the time the backups occur. This may, for example, include the email address you use at home. If you have email service on your pager or mobile phone, that might be a convenient option to use for offsite notification.

WARNING! If your Macs are located in an office, take the time to explain to your staff your backup schedule and advise them to try not to use their Macs while files are being backed up. Files created or left open during the backup process may be copied in incomplete form or not at all.

Performing Your Regular Backup Routine

Once your backup program is in place, here are the steps you'll follow to make sure the process is done correctly:

1. Schedule your backups to occur at least once every workday, usually at a time when your Macs are not in use, so as not to interfere with your work schedule.

TIP: *Although some firms run backups at the end of the day or during the early morning hours, backups can also be conveniently done during lunchtime or at any time when all or most employees aren't present, if they can be completed within that time frame.*

---

2. Before the scheduled backup is to begin, be sure the backup drive or drives and media are ready so the process can occur (where possible) unattended.

3. Make sure that the backup drive and all the computers from which files will be retrieved are left on and ready to run at the appointed time.

4. If the backups are unattended, check your software to see if it produces a log of the backup (Retrospect offers this feature). If a log is available, consult it regularly for information about possible problems with your scheduled backup.

Tips and Tricks for Robust Backups

Once you get accustomed to a regular backup routine, you'll appreciate the added security it offers. Consider the following additional procedures to customize your backups:

- *Store additional backup disks off-site*—Financial institutions, ISPs, and other companies store backups at other locations. That way, if something happens that damages or destroys equipment and media at the original location, the valuable files are still available to be copied onto replacement equipment. A bank vault is one possible location. Although it may not be convenient to store all of your files off-site, those most valuable to you should be considered as candidates for such storage.

NOTE: *A particularly tragic example occurred during the bombing of the World Trade Center some years ago. Some firms impacted by the tragedy were reportedly put out of business because they failed to make offsite backups.*

- *Test your backups*—Don't assume you will be able to restore your files even if the software reports the backups were successful. You should from time to time do a test run to make sure you can easily retrieve files should it become necessary.

- *Use the automatic backup or autosave features from your software*—A number of Mac programs include the ability to save documents at a regular interval or make extra copies. Check a program's preference dialogs or documentation for information about these features. Among the programs that offer one or both of these features are AppleWorks 6, Microsoft Word 98, Word

2001, and QuarkXPress. Financial programs, such as Intuit's Quicken 2000 and Quicken 2001, also can create backup files of your financial records.

- *Perform extra backups of work-in-progress*—Whether you are compiling a financial profile, writing a novel, or creating an illustration for an important ad, it's a good idea to create extra copies from time to time. You can simply drag a copy of your document to a backup location, so there's always an extra one in case the original is damaged.

WARNING! Although using the Save As feature is a possible method of making an extra copy, the end result is that you will end up working with the new document rather than the old, which means the original won't be updated.

- *Save often*—The best protection against loss of a document in case of a crash or power outage is to have a copy on disk. Consider saving the document each time you make an important change and certainly after you create a new document.

- *Get file recovery software*—Even if you take extra steps to make sure you do regular backups, it's always possible you will trash a necessary file by mistake. Programs such as Micromat's TechTool Pro, Power On Software's Rewind, and Symantec's Norton Utilities are able to restore files you delete by mistake. They work best when you install them first, as they are able to track files as you trash them.

TIP: *If you delete a file by mistake, try to recover it right away with one of the programs mentioned. When a file is trashed, it is not actually erased. The portion of the drive on which the file is located is simply marked as available, meaning new data can be written there. If you don't create new files, there is a greater possibility you'll be able to recover the file.*

- *Use a program's incremental backup feature*—Backup software will handle a backup in two ways: a full backup, in which all of your files are copied, and an incremental backup, in which only the files that are changed are added to your backup. The most effective, time-saving routine is to use a mixture of both. The initial backup should include all the files that need to be backed up, and the subsequent backups should be limited to changed files until the backup medium is filled. Then you will want to begin from scratch. In either case, you will probably want to do a complete backup once a week if you have a steady flow of files, or once every two weeks otherwise.

WARNING! Backup programs that use tape-based media may restore files much more slowly if they have to check for a large number of new or changed versions of files when retrieving files. So you should use this feature judiciously at best, particularly with tape media.

- *Double-check your network setups*—In order for a networked backup to work, you need to make sure that your networked volumes are accessible when the backup is being performed. Pay particular attention to such issues as access privileges and whether your backup software is properly installed. You'll also want to make sure that your medium is large enough to handle the available files. If not, an unattended backup won't be a good idea. If you run into problems in getting a useful network backup, you'll want to examine your network configuration from stem to stern and also look at the backup logs made by your software to see what errors are being reported. Basically, if a shared volume is available for exchanging files, it should work fine for a networked backup.

17. Performing Backups

Chapter 18

Computer Viruses and Mac OS X

If you need an immediate solution to:	See page:
Choosing a Mac Virus Program	314
Micromat's TechTool Pro	314
Intego's VirusBarrier	315
Network Associates' Virex	317
Symantec's Norton AntiVirus	318
Choosing Personal Firewall Software	320
Open Door's DoorStop Personal Edition	321
Intego's NetBarrier	321
Intego's ContentBarrier	322
Hardware Firewalls	322

In Brief

Even if you use your Mac at home or in a small business, you are not immune from the potential of catching a computer virus. You've no doubt read the reports of email and macro viruses and felt that perhaps they were only threatening to users of other computing platforms and that folks who use Macs don't have to fret over such things. After all, the majority platform has been the victim of literally thousands of computer viruses, and programs are updated frequently to combat the latest strains. Therefore, it's often believed that the pranksters who create such viruses have no time to do their dirty work with Macs.

Of course, as those who have worked on Macs for many years may realize, this just isn't so. There have been several dozen Mac viruses over the years, some just annoying, others causing crashes and possible loss of data.

NOTE: *I have seen two serious instances of mass virus infections on Macs. In the early 1990s, there was a virus called WDEF that infected the desktops of Macs running System 6. More recently, in 1998 and 1999, many Macs were infected by the AutoStart virus, which even managed to turn up on a few commercial CDs—ones quickly withdrawn, I might add.*

Worse, the proliferation of macro viruses that affect Microsoft's Office software haven't totally left our favorite Mac computing platform alone. Although such viruses won't cause some of the dire effects that may be prevalent in the Windows variations, such things as damaged documents and problems with document templates have been legion.

NOTE: *I can tell you that folks tend to be a little too overconfident about a Word macro virus. I have seen them in documents from software publishers who ought to know better (names omitted to protect the guilty).*

In addition, the growth of high-speed or broadband Internet connections, such as cable modems and DSL, and the recent support for Internet-based file sharing, have made Macs more and more vulnerable to direct attacks against the computer itself from the Internet.

18. Computer Viruses and Mac OS X

An Overview of Mac Viruses

It's common for movies to portray the use of computer viruses as something that's good, a clever scheme to beat the bad guys and win the day, or even save the world, depending on a particular situation. From *Independence Day* to *The Net*, the underdog who is smart enough to be able to write a virus manages to snatch victory from the jaws of defeat.

But in our real world, the author of a computer virus isn't the hero, and the victims of such viruses are not the villains. They are folks like you and me who just want to compute in comfort, without having to concern ourselves with invasions to our privacy and to the sanctity of our personal computing experience.

Types of Computer Viruses

There are two basic types of computer viruses, but extensive variations exist among each group:

- *Virus*—The standard form of computer virus is a piece of code that's attached to a program or other file. When the file is opened, the virus is activated. It can, in turn, be spread to other files as part of its function. Such a virus may be a simple joke, putting up a silly message on the screen. Others may cause system crashes or even damage files and perhaps the hard drive directory itself.

- *Trojan horse*—This is the worst sort of virus-related affliction, because, on the surface, it appears to be a file or program that has a useful, productive function. However, like the Trojan horse of old, embedded within that file is a malicious application that's ready to wreak havoc on your Mac once it's unleashed. A recent example was the Graphics Accelerator or SevenDust virus. It was sent as a system extension, called Graphics Accelerator, that was supposedly designed to enhance video performance. The virus would actually erase files on a Mac's drive. Complicating matters is that there is indeed a Graphics Accelerator extension that was provided with older versions of the Mac OS to support models equipped with ATI graphics chips. Later on, that extension and its associated files were renamed with ATI prefixes, so they are easy to identify and there's less source for confusion.

Viruses and Mac OS X

No doubt it will be a while before virus authors find ways to infect Macs running Mac OS X because of its UNIX underpinnings. However, because you will initially spend a lot of time running programs

18. Computer Viruses and Mac OS X

in the Classic environment, there's the potential for infection of your older applications and files. So there is no way to escape the need to use a virus program to ensure that you're protected. At this writing, the available programs are designed strictly to run in the Classic environment, but that is expected to be remedied some time after the release of Mac OS X.

In the next section, I'll describe the popular virus detection programs available for Mac users. Because they include both applications and system extensions, you'll want to boot your Mac under Mac OS 9.1 before you run them rather than use "Classic".

If you are cautious in your personal computing habits, you should be able to get the maximum amount of protection with the least amount of interference.

Broadband Internet and Invaders from the Outside

Another possible threat stems from the fact that more and more Mac users have upgraded to high-speed Internet services. Whether it comes by way of a cable modem, DSL, or a wireless connection (such as Sprint Broadband Direct or satellite), the primary difference between this sort of connection and regular dial-up is that you spend far more time online. It's rare for someone to be connected via a modem 24/7, but with a broadband connection, you're almost always connected to the Internet, in the same way that you may be connected to a printer or shared Macs or Windows-based computers on a local network.

In addition, Macs can share files via the Internet, a feature of Mac OS 9 and Mac OS X. Such networking, combined with a high-speed connection, can, in effect, minimize or eliminate the difference between a local and Internet-based network. This means that your Mac may be more vulnerable to another form of attack, from outsiders who try to take control of your Mac via your TCP/IP-based Internet connection.

To protect yourself from such invasions, consider getting a firewall program. Such programs monitor Internet traffic and warn you or even block attempts to access your Mac from outside.

NOTE: *A firewall program puts, in effect, an armed guard on your Mac, monitoring traffic coming to and from your computer and preventing unauthorized access.*

Even before there are Mac OS X-savvy applications to seek out viruses, you can continue to use your existing software and have it function just fine in the Classic user environment. If you want to learn more about how older programs interact with Apple's new operating system, please check Chapter 15.

In the following pages, I'll profile four programs designed to protect your Mac against computer viruses and two programs that are designed to act as software firewalls. You'll want to contact the individual publishers of these programs to see whether you need a special version to support Mac OS X.

Related solutions:	Found on page:
Launching Older Mac Programs	263
Getting Reliable Performance from Classic Applications	266

18. Computer Viruses and Mac OS X

Immediate Solutions

Choosing a Mac Virus Program

In the early days of the Mac platform, a number of commercial and shareware virus detection programs were available. Over time, many of these programs were acquired by other publishers or just discontinued. Shareware virus offerings included VirusDetective, which was continued until the early 1990s, when its author decided that payments were just too small to continue. Here are the currently available commercial Mac virus protection applications.

> **NOTE:** *One of the early Mac virus programs, Rival, continues to be developed and supported in the European market but has never returned to the United States.*

Micromat's TechTool Pro

This is an all-in-one application (see Figure 18.1) that not only checks for Mac computer viruses, but can also handle hardware and hard drive diagnosis. Here's a quick look at the basic feature set of TechTool Pro 3:

> **WARNING! Some features of this program will not work under the Mac OS X environment until an upgrade comes from the publisher. For example, hard drive examination will be done by a companion program, Drive 10, which was due for release shortly after the release of Mac OS X.**

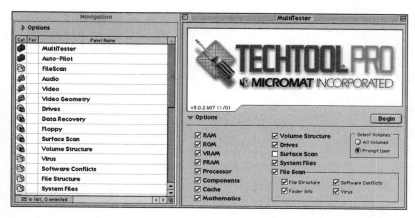

Figure 18.1   TechTool Pro performs a wide spectrum of analysis of your Mac.

- *Hardware diagnostics*—Does the problem lie in the RAM, the hard drive, or the logic board? TechTool Pro runs your Mac through a full diagnostic to determine whether all the systems on your computer and its attached peripherals are functioning properly.

- *Hard drive diagnostics and repairs*—Once Drive 10 or a Mac OS X-compatible version of TechTool Pro is out, you can use that program to check your Mac's hard drive for possible problems and repair them. This program can also optimize a hard drive, which may, in theory at least, speed up performance somewhat.

- *Software conflicts*—Although this problem is less of an issue under Mac OS X, the consequences of application or system extension conflicts have been the bane of the Mac user's experiences for years. This program can check your installation for possible problems and report on the steps you should take to eliminate them.

- *Virus scans*—This powerful component of TechTool Pro can scan your Mac for the presence of viruses. As with the competition, you can opt to perform scans in the background as you use your Mac, and at scheduled intervals for more comprehensive scans. TechTool Pro can repair or move an infected file or just leave it alone (your decision). To speed performance, you can configure the program to only scan files that have not been previously checked. You can also check for online updates to address program changes and newly discovered virus strains, but this process isn't done automatically.

Intego's VirusBarrier

The newest entrant to the antivirus application arena comes from the publishers of NetBarrier, a firewall program that will be dealt with later in this chapter. VirusBarrier has a particularly unique user interface that puts configuration panels in a drawer that can be opened and closed as needed, as shown in Figure 18.2.

NOTE: *As with the other virus programs described here, it's best to contact the publisher before attempting to run it in the Mac OS X environment. It should, however, continue to run normally when your Mac boots under Mac OS 9.1.*

18. Computer Viruses and Mac OS X

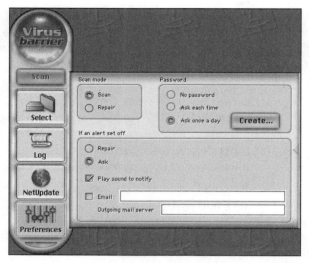

Figure 18.2   **Click on a button to open a drawer that offers additional settings.**

Here are the features of VirusBarrier that will help provide the maximum degree of virus protection:

- *Simple interface*—Unlike the other programs described in this chapter, the Classic Mac OS version of VirusBarrier consists of just one file, a control panel, where all features are activated. The other programs are an amalgam of applications, control panels, system extensions, and so on. This doesn't mean they are any less effective or more complex to use, but it's something you should consider when making your purchase decision.

NOTE: *At the time this book was written, Intego announced that a Mac OS X version would appear before the third quarter of 2001. Because Mac OS X doesn't support control panels, it would have to appear in an application format.*

- *Automatic repairs*—You can opt to have infected files repaired automatically by the program, a feature that matches up with the capabilities of the other contenders. A system log will report on such episodes, so you can see what was fixed and why and also if the file couldn't be fixed.
- *NetUpdate*—This feature allows the program to scan the Internet for program upgrades on a regular basis, or whenever you want to do a manual check. If an update is available, it'll be downloaded automatically. Unlike other programs of this type, when

new virus detection capabilities are added, the actual control panel will sometimes (but not always) be updated, too.

- *Doesn't intrude on software installations*—Although it's best to disable a virus program before performing a software installation, VirusBarrier is designed to allow such processes to run without interfering.

- *Doesn't affect boot or system performance*—Because virus scans may slow your Mac's performance, VirusBarrier promises fully transparent operation, so you won't notice its presence unless a virus infection is found.

Network Associates' Virex

One of the older Mac virus programs, Virex (see Figure 18.3), has had a checkered history as far as having a steady manufacturer is concerned. It has gone through several software publishers, finally ending up in the hands of the McAfee division of Network Associates. This should not, of course, deter you from buying Virex; it continues to be developed and supported with regular program and detection string updaters. The version shipping at the time this book was printed was 6.1.

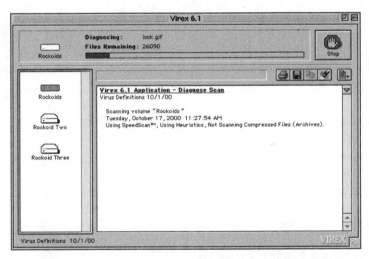

Figure 18.3   Virex continues to be updated to support newly discovered virus strains.

Here are the basic features of Virex:

- *Scans file downloads*—The Universal Scan-at-Download feature checks the files you retrieve from the Internet or a networked computer for possible virus infections. Among its capabilities is the ability to examine files within compressed archives for the presence of viruses.

NOTE: *Although being able to scan compressed files is good for bragging rights when listing features, a virus in an archive cannot infect your Mac until the archive is expanded or the file containing the virus is executed. Then any virus program will catch the offender, as long as the detection strings can find it.*

- *Advanced cleaning*—This feature essentially tries to remove the infection from a file and restore it to its normal condition. Once again, it's not a feature that differs materially from the competition.

- *Checks for viruslike activities*—In addition to using detection strings to detect the presence of known virus strains, Virex can scan for what it considers to be viruslike activity. This way, Virex can help protect you against virus strains not already discovered.

- *Automatic updates*—Virex has a NetUpdate feature that's supposed to check the publisher's Web site for the presence of program or detection string updates. However, to be perfectly frank, I've not had great success in getting this feature to work with any consistency.

- *Scheduled scans*—In addition to scanning your Mac and attached drives automatically, you can schedule automatic scanning operations at times when you are not using your Mac, so that all the work is done for you when you return to work.

- *SpeedScan*—This feature stores a reference record of all the files it scans. When a new scan is done, only files that are added or modified are checked. This speeds the rescan process so that a process that normally would take several minutes to complete may only take seconds.

Symantec's Norton AntiVirus

Once upon a time, the most popular Mac Virus program was SAM, short for Symantec Anti-Virus Utilities for Macintosh. To keep the naming similar to the Windows version, the publisher reinvented the program as Norton AntiVirus. The version shipping when this book was printed, 7.0, (see Figure 18.4) can scan Mac OS X systems, but only when you boot the computer from Mac OS 9.

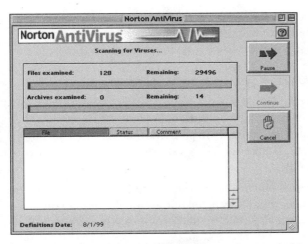

Figure 18.4   Norton AntiVirus in action looking at my drive for potential virus infections.

Following is a brief list of the major features of Norton AntiVirus; you'll see that Symantec and Network Associates have added similar feature sets to their programs, leapfrogging one another as new versions appear:

- *Scans email*—One of the most irritating areas where virus infections have developed is within email. You receive a letter, supposedly from someone you know, and it contains a file that can infect your computer. Fortunately, the strains discovered so far have afflicted the Windows platform, but that doesn't mean problems won't occur for Mac users as well. This feature is unique among Mac virus programs, at least for now.

- *Scans downloads*—As with Virex, Norton AntiVirus can scan files as they are being downloaded to protect you against infections contained in incoming files. Additionally, Norton AntiVirus can check for the presence of viruses in compressed files, again matching a corresponding feature in Virex.

- *Installer-aware capabilities*—If you attempt to install software, Norton AntiVirus displays a dialog box offering to disable itself until the installation is done.

- *Checks suspicious files*—This feature appeared in SAM, the predecessor to Norton AntiVirus, first. It lets the program check for system activities that may indicate the presence of a computer virus. Several levels of protection can be configured in the program's preferences. Keep in mind, however, that if made too robust, this feature can cause a number of annoying messages for tasks that really don't appear viruslike at all, such as expanding a compressed file that contains a system extension that is, in fact, not infected.

- *LiveUpdate*—This feature is shared with another Symantec program, Norton Utilities. As a result, it'll seek out updates for both programs in a single operation. You can configure it to access the Internet regularly in search of the updates or only when you want. Unlike the Virex variation, this feature appears to work consistently.

- *Scheduled scans*—In addition to scanning files as they're downloaded or when you mount a disk either locally or via your network, you can schedule regular scans so you are ensured of the maximum level of protection.

- *Fast scanning of new or changed files*—As with Virex, Norton AntiVirus will not scan files that haven't been changed, to speed subsequent scans of the same drive.

NOTE: I suppose the limitation of a feature of this sort would be a virus that infected a file but somehow managed to give no indication that the file had been modified in any fashion.

Choosing Personal Firewall Software

With so many folks getting always-on Internet services, it stands to reason that there is a far greater vulnerability to potential invasions from the Internet. Although this would seem a fairly unlikely source of trouble, in fact, there have been some well-publicized instances of so-called "denial of service" attacks, where personal computers are commandeered by Internet vandals and used to flood popular Web sites with meaningless data, which prevents real access by visitors to those sites.

Up until now, those problems haven't affected Macs, but that doesn't mean our preferred computing platform is immune. Although large companies often seek hardware solutions to such problems in the form of network routers, there are some relatively inexpensive Mac programs that can offer good protection for homes and small-business users.

Open Door Networks' DoorStop Personal Firewall

This publisher's Shareway IP software was used by Apple Computer in Mac OS 9 to offer Internet-based file sharing. DoorStop Personal Firewall (see Figure 18.5) offers simple, solid protection against attacks from Internet vandals. You can configure several elements of protection, from Internet-based connections to your Mac, to FTP file transfers. The program displays a warning if an attempt is made to connect to your Mac via the Internet (I get several of these a day when I'm connected via cable modem), and it logs all access attempts.

NOTE: *As this book went to press, Open Door Networks licensed DoorStop to Symantec, where it has reemerged as Norton Personal Firewall. Additionally, the program is packaged with Norton AntiVirus and Aladdin Systems's iClean to form Norton Internet Security. Subscribers to EarthLink's DSL service are eligible for a copy of this application at no cost. You will want to check with EarthLink or Symantec on how to get a copy of the program.*

Intego's NetBarrier

This is the program that made this publisher's reputation. NetBarrier (see Figure 18.6) shares a uniquely different interface with VirusBarrier. It lets you set several levels of protection, depending on the level to which you want to limit access to and from your Mac via the Internet.

Among the program's powerful feature set is the ability to protect against browser plug-ins and Java applets that may house hostile code.

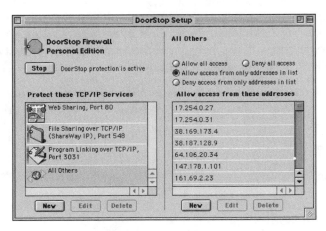

Figure 18.5   DoorStop Personal Edition has flexible configuration options to ensure that you get the maximum level of protection against Net intruders.

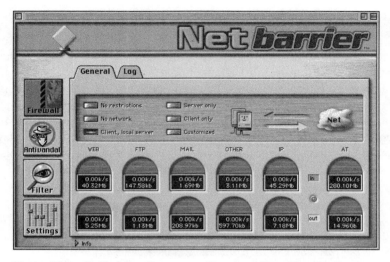

Figure 18.6   NetBarrier offers several levels of firewall protection.

There are also built-in protections against access of personal information on your Mac, such as passwords and credit card information.

Intego's ContentBarrier

The programs described so far will protect your Mac against outside Internet-based invasions or virus infections. Intego's ContentBarrier, on the other hand, is designed to monitor Internet access. It works for both home users and businesses, by allowing you to filter content that might be unacceptable to those using your Mac. Additionally, you can block Internet access at specific times of the day so children don't waste time surfing rather than doing their homework assignments and household chores. It also helps increase employee productivity, as less time is wasted on unproductive pursuits.

ContentBarrier also logs Internet access and settings can be password protected, so only those with access privileges can change program settings.

NOTE: *As this book was being written, Intego had announced a new software suite, Internet Security Barrier, which includes all the features of ContentBarrier, NetBarrier, and VirusBarrier.*

Hardware Firewalls

Another route to firewall protection is hardware-based. There are several Internet sharing hubs, which distribute an ISP connection across a network. The products, from such companies as Asante, Farallon, and MacSense, usually include something called network address translation (NAT) firewall protection. As a result, the IP numbers of the computers on your network are hidden, and thus outsiders cannot see them. This provides a high level of security.

TIP: One way to test the resiliency of your firewall protection is to use a set of Web-based tools from Gibson Research called Shields Up. You can access the tools via ***www.grc.com***. Although the company primarily makes software for the Windows platform, their Web-based firewall tests will function with the Classic Mac OS and Mac OS X.

---

18. Computer Viruses and Mac OS X

Chapter 19

Troubleshooting Mac OS X

If you need an immediate solution to:	See page:
Solving Installation Failures	329
Solving System Crashes and Freezes	331
The Application Won't Quit	331
Applications Refuse to Launch	332
The Classic Environment Fails to Run	333
Solving Network Access Failure	333
Solving Shaking of Login Window	334
Desktop Folder Contents Not Visible under Mac OS 9.1	335
Mac OS X Can't Boot after You Deleted a File by Mistake	335
Performing a Clean Installation of Mac OS X without Reformatting	336
Solving Other Common Mac OS X Problems	338
Performing System-Level Diagnostics	340
Resetting Root Access	342
Monitoring System Use to Check for Conflicts	343

In Brief

It's a normal part of the life of every personal computer owner to have a program suddenly quit or to find the entire computer frozen, totally unable to function. Such problems are not restricted to either users of Macs or Windows-based PCs. They are both quite capable of failing at unexpected moments, usually when you need to complete an important document and time is short. In fact, it has been said that if your everyday automobile had the same reliability as your computer, you could barely make it to the supermarket without brakes failing or the car just stopping with neither rhyme nor reason.

The long-term experience on a personal computer is littered with system troubleshooting, reinstallations, and endless searches for program updates that address one problem or another. Beginning with Mac OS 9, Apple introduced a System Update control panel that was designed to periodically check its support Web site in search of necessary system updates. Even third-party publishers have gotten into the act. Programs from Intego, Network Associates, and Symantec have built-in features to seek out updates.

Mac OS X promises to begin to liberate Mac users from regular diets of system-related troubles. Like Unix servers, which can run for days, weeks, or months without suffering breakdowns, the revolutionary new version of the Mac operating system is designed to be as resilient as possible to the trials and tribulations of daily computing.

Mac OS X's Crash-Resistant Features

Whether you surf the Internet, use heavy-duty graphics programs such as Adobe Photoshop or QuarkXPress, or use database software that must perform a lot of sorting and organizing, there are times when your Mac will be susceptible to problems. Here's a look at what Mac OS X has to offer to provide greater reliability:

- *Protected memory*—Every time you run an application under Mac OS X, it gets its own memory partition, dynamically allocated by the operating system and walled off from other programs. Should that program quit or crash, the memory allocated to it is reallocated as part of the memory available to your Mac. You can continue to run your Mac safely without having to restart; try that under any previous version of the Mac OS without risking a serious crash. Although there is still a Restart command, now in the Apple menu, you will find yourself using Force Quit more often. Apple doesn't expect you to have to restart except when installing a new program or leaving Mac OS X to return to Mac OS 9.1.

- *Advanced memory management*—Under previous versions of the Mac OS, an application received a specific portion of available memory. If this wasn't enough to run the program efficiently, you had to quit, open the Finder's Get Info window, and allocate more. In addition, if there wasn't enough free RAM to open a program, it would not run, or it would run so inefficiently that you risked poor performance, an out-of-memory error, or perhaps a system crash. Mac OS X dynamically allocates the memory a program needs, and if need be, it provides virtual memory too. Therefore, in theory, a program can never run out of memory.

NOTE: *Don't assume that a Unix-style virtual memory system is a panacea and that there's no downside. It's always better to have enough RAM to run a program, and if the operating system has to use virtual memory instead, performance slows down. There's no free ride.*

- *Preemptive multitasking*—Can a superior way to manage multiple applications improve reliability? Very possibly. Some applications simply hog available processor time, making it difficult for other programs to run efficiently. Too many programs competing with one another can indeed create the potential for a system crash. With Mac OS X, the operating system is the task or traffic manager, making performance better, sometimes much better, when multiple programs are performing complex tasks, such as downloading files, rendering a multimedia presentation, and printing at the same time.

NOTE: *One of the clever demonstrations Apple uses just to show how resilient Mac OS X is involves running a special application that repeatedly attempts to crash the operating system while a movie trailer continues to play, flawlessly.*

Keep in mind, however, that although Mac OS X is resilient and reliable, this doesn't mean that your Mac will never crash, or that programs will never quit. As long as software is written by human beings, there's the potential for conflicts. In the next section, I'll show you how to cope with common problems and how to get the most reliable performance from your Mac.

The Software Update Application

Beginning with Mac OS 9, Apple added a useful new feature, Software Update. Similar to some third-party applications that search for updates, such as the LiveUpdate utility that ships with Symantec's Mac utility programs, Norton AntiVirus, Norton Utilities, and Norton SystemWorks, Apple's utility checks the system-related files on your hard drive and seeks out updates at Apple's support sites on the Internet.

This utility continues in essentially the same form under Mac OS X (see Figure 19.1), but has migrated to the System Preferences application. When you activate this pane, just click on the Update Now button to have it check Apple's Web site for updates. If they're available, they'll be listed in a dialog box. Just check the ones you want, click on the Install button, and the program takes care of the rest, from downloading to installing. You just have to restart your Mac for the changes to take effect.

Figure 19.1   The Software Update pane from System Preferences will find needed Mac OS X updates for you.

Immediate Solutions

Solving Installation Failures

In Chapter 2, I covered the simple installation process for Mac OS X. For most users, everything should proceed quite normally. In some situations, you will encounter problems, warnings, or errors that prevent the process from continuing.

Following is a list of potential problems and solutions:

• *The firmware isn't up-to-date.* Recent Macs have a small boot ROM that's used to start your computer and perform small diagnostic checks. This firmware is updated from time to time to address hardware-related problems. If you receive a warning that the Mac OS X installation cannot proceed until you install the update, visit Apple's support Web site and see which updates apply to your model. The update site is located at **http://asu. info.apple.com/**.

• *The hard drive cannot be repaired.* At the very start of the installation process, the target volume (the one on which you're installing Mac OS X) is examined by the installer. If there's minor directory damage, it'll be fixed before the installation starts. If the damage cannot be fixed, you'll see a prompt on your screen about the problem. If this happens, the installation will stop dead in its tracks. At this point, you can try other options to repair the drive. Once you restart in your Mac OS 9.1 environment, you can try using the version of Disk First Aid that came with the Classic Mac OS or one of the hard drive diagnostic programs described in Chapter 2. Should none of these remedies succeed, your remaining choice is to consider backing up your files and formatting the drive. Unless there's a hardware problem with the drive, that final drastic step ought to solve the problem and allow you to install Mac OS X.

• *The hard drive cannot be updated.* During the installation process, the installer attempts to update the hard disk device driver. If the drive is already formatted with Apple's Drive Setup utility, this should not present a problem. Drive Setup works with any ATA-based drive and many SCSI drives. But if you have a hard drive that didn't come from Apple, it's highly likely the drive was formatted with a different program, such as FWB's Hard Disk

ToolKit or LaCie's Silverlining. You only need to make sure that the program used is compatible with Mac OS X. Otherwise, you should update the drive with the right version of your disk-formatting program. In these two cases, the message can be ignored.

***WARNING!** It's not a good idea to ignore messages about drive problems or to allow installation on a drive not formatted with a Mac OS X-compatible utility. The consequences can be serious—damage to your hard drive's directory and possible loss of data.*

- *Your Mac can't be restarted after installation fails.* When you run the Mac OS X Installer, it changes the Startup Disk selection so that it'll boot from the new operating system. Should something happen to abort the installation, you need to change the setup manually. This can be done by starting your Mac with your Mac OS X CD. Just restart and hold down the C key to boot from the CD. Once you're running from the CD, the first installation screen will appear. Go to the Installer's application menu and choose Open Disk Utility. With Disk Utility launched, click on the name of your target volume, and then the Repair button. Let Disk Utility examine your Mac's hard drive for disk-related problems. If you get a clean bill of health or any drive problems are fixed, go ahead and reinstall Mac OS X. Should that installation fail, restart with your Mac OS 9.1 CD, again holding down the C key. At this point, locate the Startup Disk Control Panel (in the Utilities folder) and select your Mac OS 9.1 System Folder to restart your computer. At this point, you may want to consider backing up and reformatting your Mac's hard drive before attempting a new installation.

***NOTE:** I am assuming that before you began the installation, you verified that your Mac is compatible with Mac OS X, and that it has the right amount of memory and storage space. While it may be possible to install Mac OS X on a non supported model, it's definitely not something I'd recommend unless the manufacturer of a third-party peripheral (such as a processor upgrade card) is willing to provide support in case of problems.*

- *You can't log in.* This is not as difficult as it may seem at first glance. Being a Unix-based operating system, Mac OS X expects you to enter the correct username and password unless the option to bypass the login panel is left selected in the Login pane of the System Preferences Application. If the problem just affects an individual user of your Mac, you can log in as administrator, then open the Users System Preferences panel and change the user's password. Should you be unable to access the administrator's account, restart with your Mac OS X CD, by holding down the C key. When the Installer launches, go to the Installer's application menu and choose Reset Password. In the Password Reset application window, click on the drive for which you want to reset the password, then choose the name of the user's password you want to reset from the pop-up menu. Type the new password in the first text field, then verify in the second. Click on Save to store the new password and then quit the application. You'll be returned to the Installer application, where you can restart by quitting Installer and then pressing the Restart button in the "Are you sure?" prompt. When you have rebooted your Mac, the new password should be in effect.

NOTE: *It's not uncommon for someone to activate the Caps Lock key by error, which means that the password would be typed in all caps. Look at the Caps Lock light on the keyboard to be sure when typing or creating a password.*

Solving System Crashes and Freezes

You may have hoped that Mac OS X would represent salvation from constant system crashes, but in the real world, it doesn't work that way. From time to time, you will encounter programs that behave as badly as they did under Classic system versions, but you'll be able to exit far more safely under Mac OS X.

Following are some common problems and solutions.

The Application Won't Quit

Whether the Quit command is in its accustomed place in the Application menu or in the File menu, as in Mac OS versions of old, you hit a blank wall. The application won't quit. It seems to be active, and you may even be able to open, edit, and save documents, but you cannot quit the program.

The solution is the famous Mac OS Force Quit feature, done as follows:

1. Choose Force Quit from the Apple menu or Press Command+Option+Escape.

2. On the Application List dialog box that appears (see Figure 19.2), scroll to the application you want to quit.

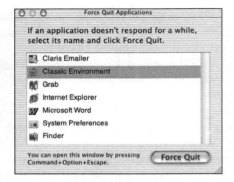

Figure 19.2 You can force quit one or more applications when this screen appears.

NOTE: *The new Force Quit feature, with its ability to selectively choose any open application, is not unique to Mac OS X. Even Windows works this way.*

---

3. Click on Force Quit. The selected applications will proceed to quit (well, usually).

Once the application is forced to quit, you can continue to use your Mac in the normal fashion. Mac OS X's protected memory allows programs to crash or be forced to quit without affecting system stability. Now you can try running the application again and see if it works all right. If it still misbehaves, you may want to contact the publisher for technical assistance.

NOTE: *On some rare occasions, you may actually need to force quit an application twice before it "takes." Such are the vagaries of software bugs even with an industrial-strength operating system.*

Applications Refuse to Launch

If the problem you encounter involves just a single application, you may want to consider trying again. If that doesn't work, you might need to reinstall the application.

If all of your applications fail to run, however, just restart your Mac and try again. Usually the restart will successfully fix the problem. If not, restart from your Mac OS X CD, and reinstall the operating system. The installer will not harm your existing documents, as long as you don't specify erasing the drive used for installation.

The Classic Environment Fails to Run

Do you have Mac OS 9.1 or later installed? The Classic feature simply doesn't support any earlier version of the Mac OS. In addition, many third-party system enhancements won't run in this setting. The best way to run a Classic System Folder is to configure it to be lean and mean. I cover the subject in more detail in Chapter 15.

If setting up an Apple-only System Folder fails to resolve the startup problem, you might consider reinstalling Mac OS 9.1 using the original system CD that came with Mac OS X or your Mac.

Solving Network Access Failure

Although Mac OS X has enhanced networking capability, it doesn't mean everything will work perfectly all the time.

Here are some ways to handle common network problems:

- *Settings don't change.* You should not have to restart your Mac whenever you switch network configurations, but doing so doesn't hurt. In addition, you may just want to redo the settings in the Network pane of the System Preferences application, just in case you missed something the first time out. Chapter 8 has more information on this subject.

- *Networked Macs and printers are not available.* Reopen your Network pane and make sure that AppleTalk is turned on and that you've given your Mac a name that's unique on your network. If everything is properly configured, check your network cables and hub configuration. Also make sure the other Macs on the network can recognize your Mac or other devices on the network. If other Macs encounter similar problems, complete network troubleshooting is in order. For a large system, you may want to contact your network administrator for further assistance.

- *Windows networking software doesn't run.* If you're using such programs as Thursby Systems' DAVE or MacSOHO, you should contact the publisher directly about support for Mac OS X; they were working on that update when this book was being written.

Solving Shaking of Login Window

If you enter a username and password and the window shakes when you try to log in, it means that the name or password you entered is not correct. The solution is just to reenter the login information and make sure that each keystroke is accurate. If the symptom happens with another user, you may just need to reset his or her password.

Here's how to do it:

1. Launch System Preferences, and then open the Users' pane.

2. Click on the padlock icon and enter your administrator username and password.

3. Click on the name of the user whose password you want to change, and click on the Edit User button. The dialog shown in Figure 19.3 appears.

4. Enter the new password, and then close the window to store the settings.

5. Choose Quit from the System Preferences Application menu, or press Command+Q.

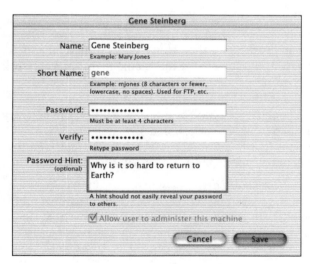

Figure 19.3   Edit a user's password here.

Desktop Folder Contents Not Visible under Mac OS 9

You place a file or folder on Mac OS X's desktop, but when you reboot under Mac OS 9, the item is not there. What's wrong?

The answer is that the desktops for the two operating systems are totally separate. The contents of one are not mirrored on the other. If you've installed Mac OS X on the same volume as Mac OS 9.1, you'll find a workable solution. There's an alias on your Mac's desktop labeled Desktop (Mac OS 9). When you open that folder, you'll see a folder called Private. Your Mac OS 9.1 desktop items are located inside. Unfortunately, this little trick doesn't work if you installed Mac OS X on a different volume than your Classic Mac OS. Then, your alternative is to reboot under Mac OS 9.1 and view any items you wish and, if need be, move them to another folder. If you're in Mac OS 9.1, you can find the Mac OS X desktop in the Mac OS X Users folder. The folder is labeled Desktop, and it's in that user's Library folder.

Mac OS X Can't Boot after You Deleted a File by Mistake

When you run your Mac under Mac OS 9, you'll see the following files at the top or root level of the hard drive on which Mac OS X is installed:

- Applications
- Library
- Mac OS 9 (on drives with a previous System Folder and their contents)
- mach
- mach.sym
- System
- Users

You can delete any files inside the Mac OS 9.1 folder if you want, though you should proceed with caution on System Folder items. If you delete something from the Mac OS X Applications folder, that application is no longer available. In addition, deleting a user's folder removes that user from the system. If you attempt to delete any of the other items, Mac OS X probably won't run. Should that happen, run your Mac OS X Installer CD to reinstall the system. The regular installation will preserve your system-related settings.

Performing a Clean Installation of Mac OS X without Reformatting

The standard installation of Mac OS X is pretty much the equivalent of the Easy Install procedure under previous versions of the Mac OS. Your core system components and bundled programs will be reinstalled, but system-related settings and user accounts won't be touched. If reinstalling in that fashion doesn't resolve your problem with Mac OS X, there's yet another way to accomplish this mission, and it requires a clean installation, which will require removing all vestiges of Mac OS X.

Unfortunately, some of the files included with the operating system are "invisible," meaning they are present but not visible under Mac OS 9.

Here's how to accomplish this "impossible" task:

WARNING! The installation method I'm describing here will remove all of your Mac OS X applications and settings. In effect, you're starting from scratch, so you'll need to follow the steps in Chapters 2 and 3 about installing and setting up Mac OS X all over again.

---

*NOTE: First, you will need a program that can view invisible files. One promising utility is File Buddy, which can be used to view and edit invisible files. You can get a copy from the publisher's Web site at **www.skytag.com/**. Another program, not easily obtainable, is DeskZap, a shareware application from the early 1990s that remains compatible with Mac OS 9.1.*

---

1. Assuming you're using File Buddy, launch the application.
2. Choose Find Invisible Files from the program's Cleaning menu. The screen shown in Figure 19.4 appears.

WARNING! Make sure only to remove the folders I've listed in this chapter. Removing the wrong item may affect other aspects of the way your Mac functions. Depending on the revision level of Mac OS X, some of these items may no longer be present.

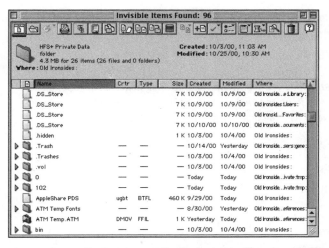

Figure 19.4   File Buddy can display invisible files on your Mac. Use it with care.

3. Select the following items, and click on the Trash icon in the File Buddy window:

- .DS_Store
- .hidden
- .Trashies
- .vol
- bin
- cores
- dev
- etc
- mach_kernel
- Network
- private
- sbin
- usr
- vmr

4. With the files removed, quit File Buddy, and then trash the following items on the top or root level of your hard drive:

   • Applications

WARNING! *I must remind you that when you trash this folder, all of your installed applications go with it, unless they are located in a Mac OS 9.1 installation. That means you'd have to reinstall these programs.*

   • Library
   • mach
   • mach.sym
   • System
   • Users

5. Empty the Trash. This may take a little time, because lots of files are being removed.

6. Restart with your Mac OS X and follow the instructions in Chapters 2 and 3 about installing and configuring the new operating system.

Solving Other Common Mac OS X Problems

Here are other problems you might encounter with Mac OS X. There are usually solutions, but some may not be as easy as you'd prefer:

• *Kernel.* White on black text splashes on the top left of your Mac's desktop. What's wrong? This is due to a system-level crash of some sort and you've been exposed to the command line. Press the "r" key to restart; you may need to do it a second time. Usually things will be all right after restart. If not, you'll need to force a restart, using the appropriate reset key on your Mac (signified by a back arrow icon).

• *The screen remains dark when booting from the Installer CD.* Mac OS X only supports graphic cards and chips from ATI Technologies, IX Micro, and NVIDIA. If you're using a graphic card from such companies as Formac, contact the manufacturer directly about a Mac OS X compatible version. You may also see this problem if you're using a Blue and White Power Macintosh with a G4 upgrade card. That, too, will require an update from the manufacturer.

NOTE: *If you are using a Voodoo graphic card from 3dfx Interactive, you may be out of luck. With the departure of the company after selling its assets to rival NVIDIA, the likelihood that driver updates will be produced are very slim. Fortunately, Mac OS X compatible graphic cards are not terribly expensive. The ATI Radeon, which outdoes the fastest Voodoo card in virtually all respects, was selling for less than $200 when this book was written.*

- *The printer isn't recognized.* Most laser printers should be recognized by Mac OS X. However, ink jet printers and some USB-based laser printers require special drivers to work. There are drivers for some Canon, Epson, and HP ink jets provided with Mac OS X. You'll need to contact the manufacturer about the availability of driver updates for unsupported models. If none are available, the devices will only run if you boot under Mac OS 9.1 and earlier.

- *The scanner doesn't scan.* The issue is the same as the printer not being recognized. It is up to the manufacturer to deliver a device driver that will function. If you cannot locate a Mac OS X-compatible version for a specific make and model, you may want to see if the software for a similar product in the manufacturer's line runs. Quite often, scanner drivers recognize a number of different models.

- *You cannot burn a CD.* The manufacturers of CD burners generally use software from such companies as Adaptec and CharisMac. You'll need to check with the manufacturers or software publishers about support for Mac OS X. If your Mac came with a built-in CD burner, however, support should already be present, assuming Apple's planned update arrives.

- *You can't use a digital camera.* To work with a camera or memory card, a special application is needed. Check with the manufacturer about when it will support Mac OS X.

- *Input device features are not recognized.* Mac OS X has built-in support for the second button and the scroll wheel on some input devices, but others require special software. You'll need to contact the publisher about compatibility issues.

- *Not all drives are recognized.* There is standard support for many popular removable and fixed storage devices, such as Imation and Iomega drives and devices from LaCie, Maxtor, and VST Technologies. If the product you want to use won't run, the manufacturer is your best resource for assistance.

- *Multimedia Keys on Apple Pro Keyboard Not Recognized.*
  Nothing much you can do about this limitation until it is addressed in a future Mac OS X update. For now, speaker volume
  settings may need to be done in the Sound pane of the System
  Preferences application and mounted CDs must be dismounted in
  the usual fashion, dragging the icons to the trash.

- *Cursor disappears under Classic.* This is a known problem with
  the first release of Mac OS X. Move the mouse to a point on your
  desktop that would appear to be over the Mac OS X Finder or any
  Mac OS X application and click on that window. Usually this will
  bring the cursor back and it should be available again under
  Classic (I ran into this very same problem while writing this
  book). Should that not work, open System Preferences, choose
  the Classic pane, then click on the Restart button. You'll have to
  acknowledge Save prompts via keyboard (Command+S).

- *Can't find files downloaded with a browser under Classic.*
  Normally, the files you download go right to your Mac's desktop.
  But if Mac OS 9.1 is located on a different drive volume, the files
  will appear in the Desktop folder on the 9.1 volume instead, and
  you may need to reboot under Mac OS 9.1 to find them. Another
  way around this is to open the Internet Control Panel under
  Classic and designate another location for downloaded files.

- *Can't install Classic applications.* If you get a message that you
  don't have the proper access privileges for such an installation,
  you will need to log in as administrator of your Mac to perform
  such an installation. Another route around this is to put Mac OS
  9.1 on a separate partition.

Performing System-Level Disk Diagnostics

The arrival of Mac OS X brings with it a tremendous number of changes
in the way your Mac runs. Although some functionality will no doubt
change further as Mac OS X continues to be developed, there will be
some constants, such as the underlying Unix core, which are just waiting to be explored by power users who want to see what makes the
new system tick.

Hard disk management is done with a new, combined application
called DiskUtility, found in the Utilities folder. It combines Disk First
Aid and Drive Setup. Unfortunately, the version offered with Mac OS

X cannot repair damage to the startup drive. Another way to perform a disk diagnostic is to reboot with your Mac OS X CD, and access DiskUtility from the Installer's application menu. If you don't have your system CD readily at hand, here's another alternative—a disk checking process that allows you to explore the depths of Mac OS X and have your Mac run in a fashion you never expected.

Here's what to do:

NOTE: *There's no way to actually provide illustrations of this process with the standard screen shot. The information provided, however, should be clear enough. Just don't be alarmed by what you are going to see. This is the way Mac OS X is designed.*

1. Restart your Mac.

2. As soon as the restart process starts, hold down the S key. What you see is only vaguely reminiscent of the DOS prompt accessed under Microsoft Windows. You see a true Unix command line, and if you thought DOS looked different, it doesn't hold a candle to what you see here.

3. With the command line displayed, a mélange of text appears. At the bottom of the text is a localhost# prompt. Just type the following command (and don't forget the space before the -):

```
fsck - y
```

4. Press Enter. Over the next minute or two, a series of status messages appear that are not dissimilar from those you'd see in Disk First Aid. These messages indicate the progress of the disk check. There is also an indication that the disk is being repaired, if this is necessary. When the disk check is done, the localhost# prompt returns.

5. Now it's time to restart and return to the comfort of the familiar Aqua interface. Type the following:

```
reboot
```

6. Press Enter. The screen darkens, and the Mac's startup chord sounds. Then the familiar Mac OS X startup screen appears.

NOTE: *I remember a line that Sean Connery uttered in one of the early James Bond movies when shown something unexpected during one of his save-the-world trips: "Shocking."*

Setting Root Access

Some Mac OS X installations require that you access the "root" or top level of your system under the Terminal application. Usually the administrator's password is sufficient to gain this access, but the password will be rejected unless you enable this feature.

To solve this problem, follow these steps:

1. Go to the Utilities folder and launch the NetInfo Manager application (see Figure 19.5).

2. Go to the Domain menu, choose Security, and select Authenticate from the submenu.

3. In the password prompt, enter the administrator's username and password and then click on OK.

4. With access gained, now return to the Security command in the Domain menu and choose Enable Root User from the submenu.

Figure 19.5   The NetInfo Manager is a useful network administrator's tool.

5. Enter the password for the root user in the password prompt. Once this is entered, root access will be enabled or reset for your Mac, and you'll be able to use the full scope of available administration tools.

WARNING! Some Unix mavens say enabling root access presents a security risk, so use this process only as a last resort.

Monitoring System Use to Check for Conflicts

Although Mac OS X may be quite a robust operating system, it isn't perfect, and many applications less so. From time to time you'll need to examine how your Mac is running to help a software publisher find a source of a conflict.

Here's a way to see just how programs are using system and memory resources, using the Terminal application:

1. Go to the Utilities folder and launch Terminal.

2. With Terminal open, type the command *top* and then press the Return key. You'll see an interactive display showing how resources may be using CPU or RAM on your Mac (see Figure 19.6). This information can help a software publisher see if there's the potential for trouble.

```
                        /bin/tcsh (ttyp1)
Processes:  42 total, 3 running, 39 sleeping... 129 threads      09:45:01
Load Avg: 0.03, 0.12, 0.15    CPU usage: 7.5% user, 8.8% sys, 83.6% idle
SharedLibs: num =   94, resident = 15.5M code, 784K data, 4.23M LinkEdit
MemRegions: num = 2431, resident =  135M + 5.18M private, 34.2M shared
PhysMem:  28.7M wired,  147M active, 69.6M inactive,  245M used, 11.2M free
VM: 1.79G + 43.4M   9852(0) pageins, 1170(0) pageouts

  PID COMMAND      %CPU   TIME    #TH #PRTS #MREGS RPRVT  RSHRD  RSIZE  VSIZE
  292 Grab        71.1%  0:08.28   3   128    94  11.7M   4.37M  14.9M  59.8M
  289 top         10.5%  0:45.31   1    19    14   180K    204K   400K  1.31M
  284 tcsh         0.0%  0:00.13   1    17    14   248K    432K   576K  5.57M
  283 Terminal     0.0%  0:04.05   4    76    57  1.41M- 4.37M  4.52M  49.9M
  281 Internet E   0.0%  1:13.04   8   118   203  14.2M  12.2M  21.8M  71.4M
  280 writeconfi   0.0%  0:00.64   1    28    18   412K    200K  1.27M  1.68M
  279 System Pre   0.0%  0:03.36   3   118    99  2.38M   4.64M  5.85M  50.9M
  277 TruBlueEnv   3.5% 40:27.74  18   234   221  82.3M   1.03M  83.1M  1.05G
  275 DocklingSe   0.0%  0:00.53   1    56    35   612K   2.26M  1.20M  30.0M
  274 Dock         0.0%  0:02.33   2   108    95  1.36M   3.58M  3.14M  42.5M
  273 Finder       0.0%  0:18.46   3    85   390  15.4M  14.6M  23.8M  84.2M
  272 pbs          0.0%  0:01.88   3    99    65   776K    860K  1.52M  15.4M
  268 slpd         0.0%  0:00.05   4    21    19    92K    180K   156K  2.93M
  266 loginwindo   0.0%  0:23.03   2   102    65  1.14M   2.86M  2.16M  45.1M
  263 cron         0.0%  0:00.02   1    10    14    64K    188K    88K  1.50M
```

Figure 19.6   Terminal is used to access Mac OS X's Unix core directly.

3. Now launch Console, also located in the Utilities folder. This program will display a log of system activities (see Figure 19.7) that can be used by a publisher to trace the possible cause of a crash or other performance problem. The log can be saved or printed for later review.

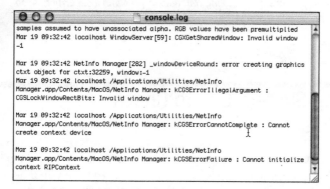

**Figure 19.7   Console logs system operations and is a useful tool to
diagnose software conflicts.**

Part IV

Taking Mac OS X Online

Chapter 20

Surfing the Net

If you need an immediate solution to:	*See page:*
Deleting Browser Caches	358
Killing the Cache in Internet Explorer	358
Killing the Cache in iCab	359
Configuring the Cache in OmniWeb	360
Determining Whether a Larger Cache Is Necessary	361
Using Bookmarks to Get There Faster	362
Solving Internet Connection Problems	362

In Brief

Since Apple began coming back from the brink in 1997, it has focused more and more on using the Mac for Internet access, to reflect the growing number of personal computer users who need to get online. In fact, the "i" in the names iMac and iBook is designed to reflect the idea that these consumer computers can get you hooked up to the Internet within minutes after you install them for the very first time.

In short, the ability to surf the Net easily and efficiently is a prime need for any personal computer, including the Mac. In this chapter, I focus on maximizing your Internet experience.

The Coming of Broadband Access

You hear it in the newspapers, on radio and TV, and when you're online: Broadband Internet access is coming to your neighborhood, and your online experience will never be the same. You've no doubt seen offer after offer filled with promises of huge speed increases over the conventional modem. Claims such as, "Experience full-motion video and high-quality stereo sound" and "Retrieve files in seconds" abound.

But when you try to have those new features installed in your home, something...well...doesn't quite jibe with the promises. For one thing, there is the fine print; perhaps such high-speed services aren't available everywhere. In fact, they may not be available at your home or office because you are too far from the telephone switching center or the upgraded cable TV lines that allow you to get onto the super-charged Internet highway.

I can't promise that I can help you get broadband any faster, but in this section, I'll cover the various technologies you'll be able to access on your Mac with Mac OS X.

NOTE: *Getting online at high speed is only part of the equation. If you already have an ISP, you may or may not be able to continue to use the service when you switch to high speed. Some of these ISPs don't offer faster access, and others are still fighting with cable TV companies for open access (this was a big issue in the government's review of the merger between AOL and Time Warner that was concluded in January 2001). You may have to use another ISP, and end up changing your email addresses, when you move to broadband.*

Following are the technologies currently available, as well as those that may become available in the future:

- *DSL*—Short for Digital Subscriber Line, this service allows your phone line to do double duty. First, it handles phone calls and faxes just as it does now. But it can also carry high-speed digital data to and from your Mac, without affecting the use of your phone in any way. Compared to what you get with a 56Kbps modem (which actually connects at speeds from 28.8Kbps to 53Kbps—and the latter very, very seldom), DSL starts at around 256Kbps and generally delivers up to 1Mbps (megabits per second); higher with business-oriented services. One consumer-oriented variant, ADSL (the "A" is for asymmetric), throttles the upload speed to something far less—usually around 256Kbps. The reasoning behind this is that most folks, except those who need to send large files all the time, perform a lot fewer upstream tasks than downstream tasks, and hence, they won't suffer much from the speed sacrifice. DSL service hooks up to a standard Mac Ethernet network, using a special device that acts like a modem to retrieve digital data from your phone line.

- *Cable modem*—Via the same cable from which you receive cable TV broadcasts, you can get high-speed Internet access. Speeds are potentially even higher than DSL, up to 3Mbps and more in some situations. However, the access to the cable is shared among a group of several hundred users on a single node or segment. If a lot of folks are accessing the Internet the same time as you are, expect performance to nosedive to speeds that may not be much greater than regular DSL. Upload speeds are usually throttled to 256Kbps. An interface device, the cable modem, is used to bring the signal from the cable line to your Ethernet jack.

NOTE: *Some cable modem services offer a hybrid or "telco" service. This system uses an analog modem built into the cable modem that offers 33.6Kbps maximum uploads via a regular phone line. Although this may be the only way the service is available, other services offer the hybrid service as an intermediary step to sign up customers while they finish their rewiring of a neighborhood. Once the wiring is done (assuming it really is done), customers are moved to the higher-cost full service, and the preliminary service is discontinued.*

- *Wireless Internet*—Do you live in a city or small town where broadband seems years away, or may never come, because the work required is too great or the population density just isn't enough to support cable modems or DSL? There's yet a third choice: wireless. Whether by satellite disk or land-based transmitters, these services offer options that are otherwise unavailable.

20. Surfing the Net

They may cost more, and they may not give the same level of performance as a cable modem, but in some situations, they may be the only choice.

NOTE: *One wireless service, Sprint Broadband Direct, does promise (and usually delivers, as far as my experience with the service is concerned) speeds that are close to what a cable modem or the fastest DSL services provide. However, at press time, only a dozen cities offered the service. Visit the company's Web site, **www.sprintbroadband.com**, for a list of all cities currently supported.*

- *Future technologies*—Of course, determining the technologies of the future is a highly speculative matter, but many are betting that there will be even faster services, using all fiber-optic cabling or other new technologies. It may take billions upon billions of dollars to rewire a city, but if it all comes to pass, there will be speeds on the Internet that rival that of a standard high-performance Ethernet network. If this is realized, you'll be able to view full-screen, full-frame video presentations via the Internet as easily as you can via cable TV and satellite. What's more, you'll be able to transfer files across the Internet at the speed of a local network. The ultimate version of a wired generation may truly come far sooner than we expect. This is in keeping with the vision of a digital lifestyle espoused by Apple CEO Steve Jobs.

Mac OS X Web Browsers Profiled

The advent of Mac OS X has brought two kinds of software to surf the Net. The first is simply the Carbonized version of an existing Mac browser, as typified by Microsoft's Internet Explorer, which has been standard issue on Mac OS installations for quite some time. The second is unique to the new operating system, often from publishers with experience designing programs for the NeXTSTEP operating system, on which Mac OS X is based.

In the following pages, I'll describe three Web browsers that come from both environments. You'll learn the basic features, and then, in the "Immediate Solutions" section, you'll discover ways to maximize your online performance with these programs and others offering similar capabilities.

NOTE: *The client software for AOL and CompuServe 2000, both of which use browsers based on Internet Explorer, had not been optimized to run under Mac OS X at time of publication, but were expected to deliver updates before the summer of 2001. Check their Web sites to find out when such support will be available. In the meantime, you can probably expect to need to return to Mac OS 9.1, unless you run either service on an existing Net connection with another ISP.*

Microsoft Internet Explorer

Since becoming the default browser on the Mac as a result of Microsoft's $150 million investment in Apple in 1997, this application has taken over from rival Netscape as the number one Mac browser (see Figure 20.1).

Here are the basic features of the current version of Internet Explorer:

- *Tasman Browser Engine*—Beginning with Internet Explorer 5, Microsoft presented a new rendering engine that was designed for speedier display, particularly of graphics. The Tasman engine is designed to offer full support of the Internet standards in effect when the program was created.

- *Search Assistant*—This feature (see Figure 20.2) takes a task-based approach to locating information on the Internet. You click on the Search button, select the category of the search, and then enter the search request in the text field. You can easily switch among search engines if the first doesn't deliver the results you want.

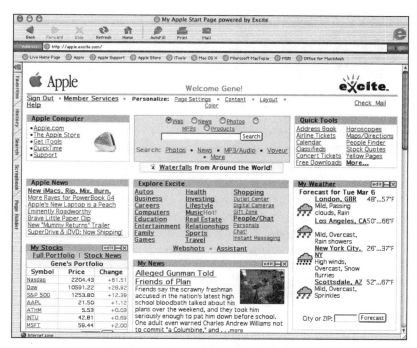

Figure 20.1   The Mac OS X version of Internet Explorer bears more than a striking resemblance to its Classic version.

20. Surfing the Net

Figure 20.2   Use the Internet Explorer Search Assistant to get information from the Net faster.

- *Improved Address Auto-Complete*—When you enter a site's address, a pop-up menu appears, when available, with additional choices that begin with the information you entered. Select the one you want, and you can revisit sites with the most complex addresses in minutes. Of course, adding a site to your Favorites list is best.

- *Auction Tracker*—If the online auctions from such services as eBay and Yahoo! interest you, this new feature (see Figure 20.3) lets you enter the information about the auctions in which you participate. If someone exceeds your bid for a particular item, you're notified via a browser display (or even by email), so you can decide whether to return and change yours.

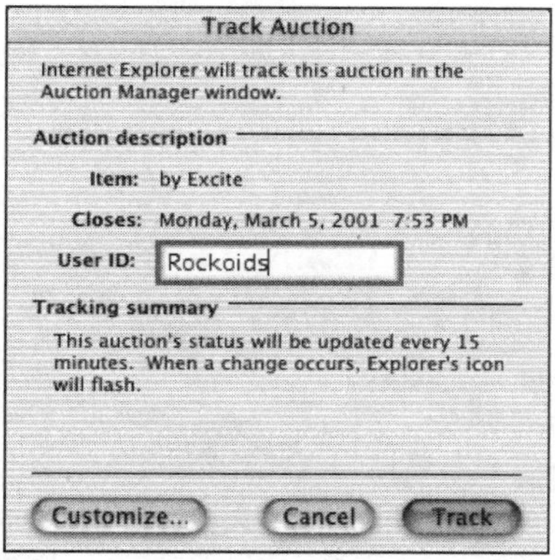

Figure 20.3   Don't let anyone outbid you. Internet Explorer's Auction Tracker makes it possible to know when you have to increase your bid.

- *Multiple Themes*—You can easily customize the browser's color scheme with your favorite Mac colors or move and replace items in the toolbar, as you prefer. This is a growing concession on the part of Microsoft to make their software more Maclike.

iCab

The subject of an extended public preview program, iCab (see Figure 20.4), the slim Web browser from a German-based software publisher, is designed to be competition for the big entrants in this product category.

NOTE: *You can download a copy of the latest version of this program from* ***www.icab.de****.*

Following is a list of major iCab features that are designed to differentiate this program from the pack:

- *Support for current Web standards*—The publisher of iCab promises support for current Web standards, including HTML 4.0 and eventual support for Cascading Style Sheets Level 2 (CSS2). In addition, there's extra support for specific Internet Explorer and Netscape extras, such as the **<BLINK>** command under the latter.

- *Support for older Macs*—In addition to the Mac OS X edition of iCab, there's another edition that runs with Mac OS 7.0.1 with 4MB free RAM; even Macs with a 68020 processor are supported. That may make it possible for you to deploy this browser on an entire system consisting of Macs with widely varying hardware and system setups.

Figure 20.4   iCab is a worthy alternative to the big guys.

- *Cookie filters*—Most Web-based cookies serve a useful purpose, such as the ability to track your visits to a Web site to ease navigation. However, if you want to selectively or completely disable the cookies, you can do so in this program.

OmniWeb

Another new contender in the Mac browser wars comes from a long-time NeXTSTEP developer, The Omni Group. OmniWeb is distinguished by being developed in Apple's Cocoa programming language and featuring a decidedly different interface (see Figure 20.5).

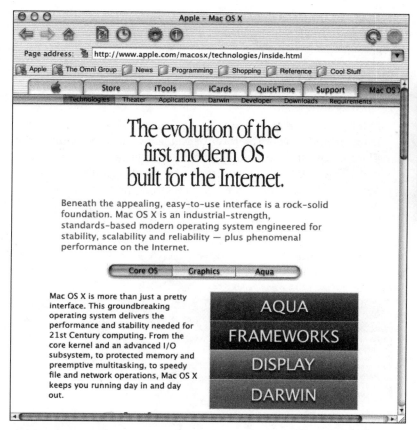

Figure 20.5 OmniWeb was created by the experienced developer of NeXTSTEP software.

TIP: You can easily get the latest versions of iCab or OmniWeb from a popular Web site that tracks and links to the latest software updates. Just point your browser to www.versiontracker.com. In addition to these programs, you'll find a healthy collection of software for both the Mac OS 9 and Mac OS X user environments.

Although most features simply match the other browsers, there are a few variations on the theme:

- *Full support of Web standards*—As with the other programs, and despite the fact that pages render differently from program to program, OmniWeb promises to deliver support for all or most current HTML standards and CSS2.

- *Slide-out drawers*—Rather than access menus, OmniWeb's bookmark and history lists are available as drawers that simply slide out from the main application window (see Figure 20.6). This is both an advantage and a disadvantage, as it can intrude on screen space.

- *Drag-and-drop bookmarks*—You can drag and drop pages to and from the bookmarks, and they'll be automatically checked for new material.

- *Easy importing of bookmarks*—Just copy the bookmarks file from either Internet Explorer or Netscape onto the bookmarks file used by OmniWeb and launch the program. The bookmarks will be automatically converted to the application's native format, so you can continue to use your existing repository of bookmarks.

NOTE: *I am not ignoring such browsers as Netscape and Opera. However, no Mac OS X versions of these programs were available for review when this book was written; in fact, the first public beta of Opera for the Mac had just appeared on the landscape. The watchword is to try all the browsers yourself and use the one that meets your needs.*

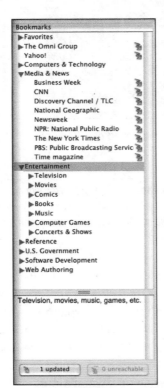

Figure 20.6   OmniWeb has a unique way to access your favorite Web sites.

Mac Internet access is a highly simplified process: You launch your browser and you connect. But behind those simple actions are many more considerations to get the maximum value from your online experience and steps you can take to get the maximum stability from your surfing experience. We'll look at these issues in the next section.

Immediate Solutions

Deleting Browser Caches

A Web browser uses a cache, consisting of a single file or several files, to store the artwork accessed from a Web site. Whenever you call up the site, the contents of the cache are compared with that at the site, and only the new artwork is downloaded. That can speed up Net performance, sometimes dramatically. But if performance bogs down or you find that your browser is crashing, the next step would be to delete the cache.

WARNING! *A separate set of cache files is stored in each user's Preferences folder, inside his or her Library folder. So if you remove the cache files while logged in under one user account, those files won't be removed for all others. However, the administrator can do a search of all user folders with Sherlock to find and remove all the caches.*

The following sections describe how to delete the caches in the three browsers described in this chapter.

TIP: *When you empty a Web cache, all the artwork is gone. That means it has to be retrieved again by the browser. You won't see a performance gain until the browser retrieves the site for a second time. And don't forget, the steps described here must be repeated for all users of your Mac unless done manually by the administrator via a file search.*

Killing the Cache in Internet Explorer

The user interface of the Carbon version of Internet Explorer is close enough to the Mac OS 9 version that the Preferences panels seem nearly identical. Here's how to clear the cache:

1. With Internet Explorer running, go to the Edit menu and choose Preferences.

2. In the Preferences panel, scroll to Browser, and click on the disclosure triangle to expose the settings under this category.

3. Click on the Advanced category, which produces the dialog box shown in Figure 20.7.

4. Click on Empty Now to delete the content of the cache file. Because Internet Explorer stores its entire cache in a single file, IE Cache.waf, this process should take only a second.

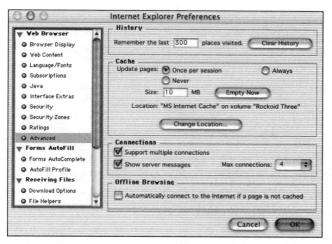

Figure 20.7 Empty the cache and perform some additional operations in this dialog box.

5. Now visit your favorite sites and see if the appearance or performance improves after the site is visited for the second time.

6. If performance doesn't improve, delete the actual file. You'll find it in the Preferences folder inside the Library folder, which is, in turn, located in the Users folder bearing your login name.

Killing the Cache in iCab

The process of emptying iCab's Web cache under Mac OS X is the same as in the Classic versions. Just follow these steps:

1. With iCab running, go to the Application menu and choose Preferences.

2. Locate the category labeled Caches, and click on the disclosure triangle to show all the subcategories.

3. Locate and click on Web Pages. You'll see iCab's various cache options, as shown in Figure 20.8.

4. To delete the cache, click on the Clear Cache Now button. Because the cache is stored in a number of separate files, it may take a little while to remove a large cache.

5. When the cache has been removed, click on OK. The Preferences dialog box closes.

6. Once the cache has been cleared, visit your favorite sites and see if the appearance or performance improves.

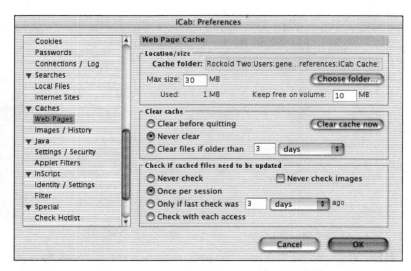

Figure 20.8   iCab's cache removal options are fairly straightforward.

Configuring the Cache in OmniWeb

It's not just the interface that's different. There is no actual preference for deleting the cache. The closest equivalent is a Cache Timeout
feature, which sets the time for when a cache is considered out-of-
date and when a new version of the site is available. Talk about different!

Here's how to use the feature:

1. With OmniWeb opened, choose Preferences from the Applications menu.

2. Click on the Advanced tab.

3. Scroll to Cache and click on it (see Figure 20.9); the listing isn't
   alphabetical, so you have to scroll almost to the bottom of the
   icon list.

4. Click on the Close button to store your settings.

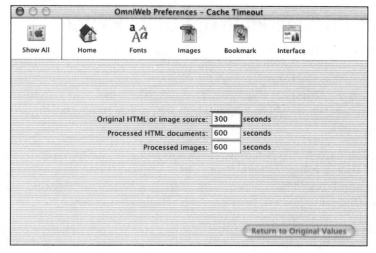

Figure 20.9   This setting adjusts cache timeout; it doesn't actually dump the cache.

Determining Whether a Larger Cache Is Necessary

The standard Web cache is usually 5MB to 10MB, but you can easily increase it to a higher figure if you prefer by accessing a browser's Preferences as described previously. Before you do so, however, consider that having a Web cache that's too large may be counterproductive. For one thing, if the browser spends additional time checking the contents of the cache before accessing an updated site from the Web, performance may actually be slower.

However, if you frequently access a large number of Web sites, with plenty of artwork, a setting of 15MB or even 20MB may be useful; iCab sets its cache at a maximum of 30MB and there doesn't appear to be an appreciable slowdown as a result. Your mileage may vary. If you choose to reduce the size of a cache, however, empty it first.

Using Bookmarks to Get There Faster

Over time, you'll come across Web sites you'd like to visit on a regular basis. The best way to keep track of these sites is to save them as bookmarks. Each browser has a different name for its bookmarks feature. For Internet Explorer, it's called Favorites, for iCab, it's the Hotlist, and OmniWeb uses the traditional name, Bookmarks (as does Netscape).

In each case, there is a menu with the name of the bookmarks feature. To add a page to your bookmarks, access that menu and use the command to add the current page. You may see a confirmation message that you must OK in order for it to appear on the list.

Removing a bookmark involves opening the list, selecting the bookmark, and then pressing the Delete key. Again, there will usually be a prompt you have to OK to delete the entry.

Solving Internet Connection Problems

On the surface, getting on the Net with Mac OS X should be no more complex than under Mac OS 9, but the new networking architecture may, from time to time, create problems, especially with programs that have only recently made the migration to the new operating system. Here's a list of some of the most frequent problems and what you can do to resolve them:

- *You cannot get online with a cable modem or DSL.* Some ISPs require special software to connect. You'll have to contact the service to see when a Mac OS X-compatible version is available, or whether other connection options can be found. In the meantime, check whether your service will give you a static set of IP access numbers, which, when entered via the Network pane of the System Preferences application, might get you connected.

TIP: Some cable providers require entering a dedicated modem ID number in your network settings to allow you to access their network. You will need to enter that information correctly in order for you to connect to that service.

- *Classic applications may not run with dial-up connections.* The watchword is to try it yourself and see. Aside from proprietary services, specifically AOL and CompuServe, this may not be something to be concerned about. There is enough Mac OS X–savvy software around to provide a satisfactory Internet experience until your favorite is updated.

- *The Mac OS 9 TCP/IP file is destroyed under Classic.* This happens from time to time. It occurs sometimes when you attempt to run a Classic Internet program with a dial-up connection. The symptom is a severe system crash early in the startup process when you return to Mac OS 9. Here's a possible solution to this dilemma:

    1. Quit all open Classic applications.

    2. Quit the Classic environment itself. It may take a minute or so for the Classic environment to close.

    3. Locate the TCP/IP Preferences file in your Mac OS 9.1's Preferences folder, within the System Folder.

    4. Drag the Preferences file to the Trash.

TIP: *It's a good idea to retain a backup of your TCP/IP Preferences file before installing Mac OS X to avoid problems in case you need to use your ISP when going back to Mac OS 9.1.*

---

    5. Launch the System Preferences application.

    6. Click on the Network pane, and then on the padlock icon (if it's closed). In the window that appears, enter the administrator's username and password.

    7. Click on the Configure pop-up menu and change it to Manually (see Figure 20.10). The DNS entries already present should stay there.

    8. Click on Save and restart your Mac to store the settings.

- *The artwork changes from browser to browser.* This is the fault of the inexact nature in the way a browser interprets a page and is a chronic problem (and the source of endless headaches) for Web authors. If you want to view a site in a particular way, you may want to stick with the browser that presents it the way you like. Another possibility is to report a display problem to the publisher of the browser application, so it can examine the situation and see if there's anything it can do to update the program for better display.

- *The site is not accessible.* This may be the fault of the site itself or of Internet congestion and not your browser or connection. The first possible solution is to click on the Refresh or Reload button on the browser, so that the site is retrieved again from

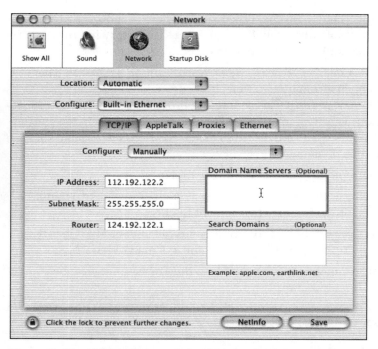

**Figure 20.10   This setting may help eliminate Classic environment woes
with the TCP/IP Preferences file.**

scratch. Another possible solution is to log off from your ISP and
then reconnect. If neither step resolves the problem, try to access
it again at a different time.

- *The site's artwork is distorted.* One possible solution is to just
  refresh or reload the page, which delivers the site from scratch. If
  that fails to resolve the problem, follow the steps in the earlier
  section, "Deleting Browser Caches," to empty the Web cache. If
  that doesn't resolve the issue, it may be the fault of the Web site
  itself, so there's nothing you can do other than complain to the
  Webmaster.

- *Download speeds vary.* It is quite normal for the speed of a file
  download to vary somewhat, no matter if you have a dial-up
  connection or broadband. This is a normal part of the process;
  sometimes it's a problem with your connection or with congestion on the part of the Web server hosting the site. However, if
  download speed bogs down, you may want to just stop it and try
  again. If you have a dial-up connection, you may also want to log
  off and then reconnect; however, if all other services run at
  normal speed, there may be nothing you can do to resolve the
  problem.

• *Internet Connect doesn't support your modem.* As with the Classic Mac OS, only a fixed number of popular modem makes and models are supported. Most Macs that can run Mac OS X already come with an Apple internal modem, so this may not be a serious issue for most of you. But, if you have a different modem, feel free to experiment with a similar make or model, or just use Hayes Compatible. Most modems that support standard setups will probably function in a satisfactory manner. If you still do not get satisfactory performance, contact the manufacturer of the modem directly for suggestions.

• *Dial-up connection fails.* You try to log in and don't succeed. Should this happen, verify the information you placed in the Internet Connect application. Review Chapter 8 for information on how to set up this program to work with your ISP. If the information is all right, try to connect once again. If it still fails, contact your ISP and see if it is doing system maintenance or can offer you alternate connection numbers.

• *The browser crashes.* With Mac OS X, you do not need to restart your Mac whenever a program freezes or suddenly quits. You can continue to work, and even run the application again to see if it runs all right. Because some of the applications for Mac OS X are beta versions, check with a publisher's Web site for newer versions. You should also read Chapter 19, which covers a number of ways to troubleshoot Mac OS X.

Related solution:	Found on page:
Using Internet Connect for Dial-up Networking	155

Chapter 21

Email Options Explored

If you need an immediate solution to:	See page:
Setting Up Your User Account	373
Importing Your Email Messages	376
Customizing Mails Toolbar	378
Composing a New Message	379
Responding to a Message	380
Quoting Messages	381
Spellchecking Your Messages	382
Sending Email Attachments	383
Forwarding Email	385
Adding Email Signatures	385
Formatting Email	386
Setting Mail Rules	386
Getting Your Email Automatically	388
Using the Address Book	389
Importing an Address Book	391
Finding a Message	392
Why Can't I Send My Email?	393
Why Are Messages Scrambled?	394
Why Doesn't Mail Check All My Accounts?	394

In Brief

Where would we be without email? Each day, hundreds of millions of messages cross the Internet on their way to folks across the world, and it has long since supplanted postal mail in the eyes of many people for sending messages to family and business contacts.

In addition, offices use email for exchanging messages within the company itself. This is becoming increasingly common, even if the recipient sits in an adjacent office or booth from you. In fact, email has sometimes replaced the practice of actually speaking with a nearby coworker.

NOTE: *Just as an example of what might be considered using email to the extreme, I have actually observed two coworkers seated next to each other exchanging lengthy messages rather than simply talking it over.*

All recent versions of the Mac OS have shipped with email software, usually Microsoft's Outlook Express and Netscape Communicator. With the arrival of Mac OS X, there's a new kid on the block named, simply enough, Mail (see Figure 21.1).

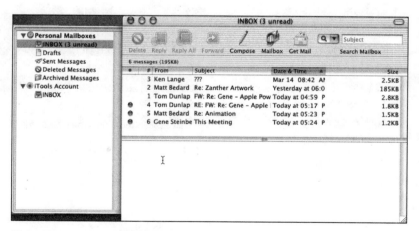

Figure 21.1   Apple's email client is clean, uncluttered, and lightning-quick.

Introducing Mail

Apple's new email program, based in part on the email software shipped with the NeXTSTEP operating system, the precursor to Mac OS X, isn't quite as full-featured as the other programs in this arena. However, Mail provides the essentials needed to manage one or more email accounts, and it is at least worth serious consideration.

Here's a brief list of its important features:

- *Multiple user accounts*—Do you have a home and office user account, or different email addresses for business and personal use? Mail lets you configure the program to handle all of them. You can set it to log in at specified time intervals so you're never out of touch. In addition, other users who work on your Mac can configure their own settings and store their own collections of email without having access to anyone else's mail.

- *Import Mailboxes*—No doubt, you have an email account set up with another program. With a reasonable degree of fidelity, you can import your mailboxes from Netscape 4 or later, Eudora, Outlook Express, and Claris Emailer.

- *HTML formatting supported*—You can send and receive messages with Web links and full text formatting, depending on the limits of the recipient's service.

- *Manage stored email*—With this feature, you can set up extra folders in your personal mailbox to store the messages you received in different categories. You can also use email rules to make sure that messages from specific sources are automatically placed in a particular folder. This is useful if you want to store mail for later retrieval, or if you receive lots of junk mail from a particular source for later disposal.

21. Email Options Explored

- *Automatic signatures*—You can create and store multiple signatures for personal and business messages. There's also a "rich text" option that lets you include automatic email and Web links in a signature.

- *Spell checker*—As you write a message, if you keep the option for interactive checking on, words with potential spelling problems are flagged in red. Otherwise, you can spellcheck manually before you send a message.

- *Message searching*—Messages can be searched by sender, recipient, subject, or content. This is a powerful tool that you can use to find information quickly in the messages you've stored.

NOTE: *Whenever email awaits you in the Mail application, the icon for the program in the Dock will include a number specifying how many messages are unread.*

How Does Mail Rate?

Considering that the Mac OS includes some pretty powerful email programs, just where does Mail stand when compared to Microsoft's Outlook Express and Entourage, Netscape Communicator, Qualcomm's Eudora, or even the defunct mail client, Claris Emailer? Here's a brief list of features that are lacking or only partly implemented in Mail:

- *Separate address book*—Apple has provided a different program, Address Book (see Figure 21.2), for managing your address list. This should suit most purposes. It is linked directly with Mail, and there are limited options to import the address lists from other programs.

- *Limited message filtering*—You can establish rules for messages, but you cannot have it flag possible spam email and have the messages automatically deleted, as you can with the options offered by the competing programs.

- *No newsgroup support*—Both Microsoft's Internet Explorer and Netscape Communicator can retrieve Usenet newsgroup messages. Mail doesn't support this feature. If you are interested in this option, look for a Mac OS X-savvy news-reading program to support your needs.

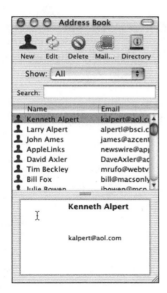

Figure 21.2   Use this program to configure an address book for messages.

TIP: *Two very useful options for reading newsgroup messages include NewsWatcher-X, the Carbon update to the popular free newsgroup application. Another useful candidate is Thoth, from Brian Clark, author of YA-NewsWatcher. The latter, however, is demoware, and the downloadable version is crippled in key functions, such as saving updates to subscribed newsgroups, unless you buy a user license. However, it is worth the modest fee and is my favorite.*

- *No automatic connections*—Microsoft's Outlook Express can be configured to check email at regular intervals, even if the program isn't opened, by launching and establishing your Net connection. Mail can only recheck for messages on a regular basis after it's actually launched.

- *No support for AOL email*—The only third-party program that can handle AOL's proprietary email system is Claris Emailer, discontinued but perhaps still available from Mac users groups or dealers handling older merchandise. If you wish to access your AOL messages otherwise, you have to log on to their Web site (**www.aol.com**) with your browser and access their NetMail feature.

NOTE: *As this book was written, there was no support for Microsoft's Hotmail service either. You can set that up courtesy of Microsoft's own email clients, or via your Web browser.*

If you've worked with other email programs, you'll find that setting up and using Mail is pretty straightforward, and the differences aren't all that great. The "Immediate Solutions" section covers the basics of using this application.

Immediate Solutions

Setting Up Your User Account

When I described how to work with the Mac OS X Setup Assistant in Chapter 3, I explained how to enter your email settings during the initial setup of the new operating system. However, if you need to change those settings or add an extra user account, just follow these steps:

> **NOTE:** If you have already given your email account information when you ran the Mac OS X Setup Assistant, it'll all be here, but you can edit as needed, or add whatever additional ISP accounts you want.

1. Launch the Mail application.
2. Go to Mail's Application menu and choose Preferences. The screen shown in Figure 21.3 appears.
3. Click on the Accounts icon, and then the Create Account, shown in Figure 21.4, to bring up the Account Information dialog box (see Figure 21.4).

> **NOTE:** If your Mac is set up for multiple users, each user will be able to configure Mail separately to handle his or her accounts and email from that individual's user account. That information isn't available to any other users, unless they log into the same account.

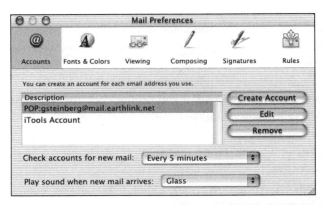

Figure 21.3   Set up and manage Mail's settings from this screen.

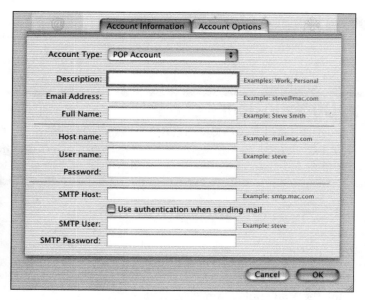

Figure 21.4   Enter your basic email user settings here.

4. Under the Account Type category, choose the type of email account you're establishing (usually it'll be a POP Account) and give a description, such as Work, Personal, or the name of the ISP (a default will be entered by the program otherwise).

5. Enter your Email Address and Full Name in the first section of the dialog box.

6. Under Host name, enter the name of your ISP's mail server, then insert your User name and Password, as needed, to connect to your ISPs.

7. In the final category, enter the name of the outgoing mail server of your ISP, and, if need be, authentication or password account information.

8. When your settings are complete, you can click on the OK button to store them. You can, if you prefer, click the Account Options tab (see Figure 21.5) to customize your settings still further.

9. Choose your optional account information under the various setup categories:

   • *Enable This Account*—Normally checked by default, you can disable a user account if you don't want to retrieve messages from it for a while.

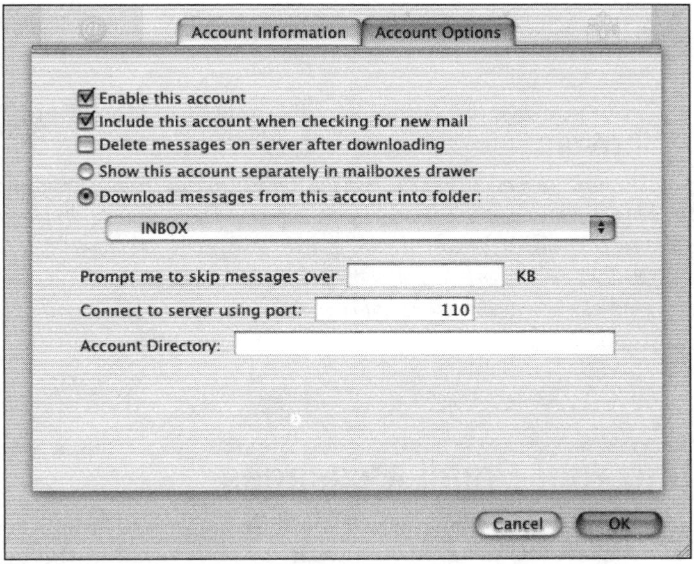

Figure 21.5 Customize your email sessions from here.

- *Include This Account When Checking For New Mail*—For whatever reason, you may choose not to check for a specific email account when new mail is automatically accessed, only when you want.

- *Delete Messages On Server After Downloading*—Normally they are left on your ISP's mail server, but if you get a lot of email you may find it convenient to check this option, so that they will be removed.

- *Show This Account Separately In Mailboxes Drawer*—Having a separate entry means separate mailboxes to check for different accounts. This may be a blessing or a curse, depending on your situation.

- *Download Messages From This Account Into Folder*—Normally it's the Inbox that applies to that account, but you can specify a separate folder if you want to organize the messages by account to check specific items more easily.

- *Prompt Me To Skip Messages Over*—Specify a size if you don't want to look at large messages or those with large attachments right away.

- *Connect To Server Using Port*—This setting is entirely based on the requirements of your ISP or network system. Normally it's best to just leave the default entry.

NOTE: *If you're not sure of the proper settings to enter, contact your ISP for the proper access information. This will vary considerably depending on an individual service's setup.*

---

10. When your settings are complete, click on OK to store them.

TIP: *Another useful email preference is available in the Viewing pane of the Mail Preferences dialog box. You can use that setting to determine when messages are automatically purged from your mailbox and whether to download email images, animations, or other HTML attachments. If you don't want to view lots of clutter in your messages, particularly if most such messages are really junk mail, you'll want to turn that option off.*

Importing Your Email Messages

Once you've given Mail a test run, perhaps you'll decide you'd really like to keep using the program. So what do you do about the messages already stored in your other software? Fortunately, Mail can import the contents of those mailboxes, with a reasonable degree of fidelity.

Here's how to use that option:

1. With Mail opened, choose Import Mailboxes from the File menu. This brings up import assistant shown in Figure 21.6. Click Next to proceed.

2. Choose the email client from which you want to import messages (see Figure 21.7). If the email client isn't listed, click the

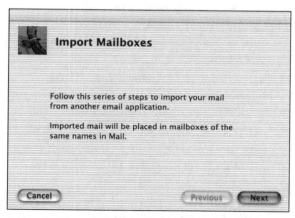

Figure 21.6   Begin the email import process here.

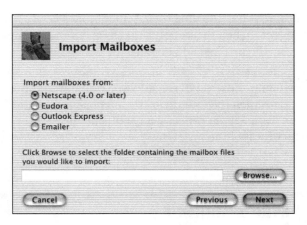

Figure 21.7   Select the name of the application that has your mailbox.

Browse button and locate the mailboxes (but don't expect miracles). Mail will clue you in on which folder to search for. When you're done, click Next to proceed.

NOTE: *This process has to be done separately for each email program you're using. In addition, the mailboxes will all be placed in separate message folders; there's no way to put them together except by manually dragging and dropping them into the proper locale.*

3. After you've selected the mailboxes that apply to the email application (see Figure 21.8), select the ones you want to convert and click Next to proceed.

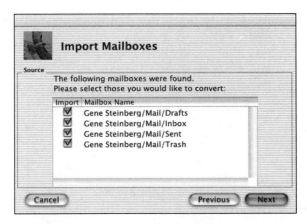

Figure 21.8   Once selected, a click of the Next button will begin the import process.

4. You'll see a progress bar showing the number of messages that are being retrieved. When the import process is complete, click Done to wrap up the process and dismiss the dialog box.

5. If the list of mailboxes isn't displayed, choose Show Mailboxes from the View menu. Now you'll see additional folders in your Mail drawer that match the ones in your email program. Click on any of them to finish the process, as Mail will update its database to incorporate the messages you've imported.

Customizing Mail's Toolbar

Extending the Finder-like display of Mail, you can easily customize the toolbar, in the same fashion as the Finder. To make these changes, follow these steps:

1. With mail open, choose Customize Toolbar from the View menu. The display shown in Figure 21.9 will appear.

2. To add icons to the toolbar, click and drag them to the desired location.

3. If you want to remove an icon, just drag it off the toolbar and it'll disappear.

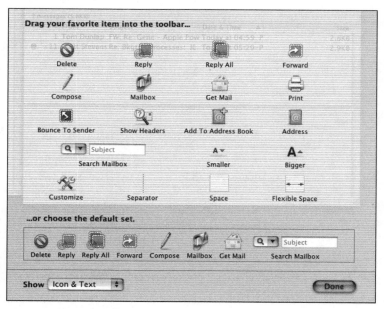

Figure 21.9   Click and drag the items you want to the toolbar.

4. To restore the default set, just click and drag the Default Set icons to the toolbar.

5. Click Done to store your settings.

Composing a New Message

To write a brand-new message in Mail, just follow these steps:

1. Click on the Compose button, which brings up a blank email screen, shown in Figure 21.10.

2. Type the recipient's email address in the To field (such as mine, **gene@macnightowl.com**). If you enter the name of more than one recipient, separate the names by a comma. If the email address you're looking for is in your Address Book, click on the Address button to bring up that program so you can add the names you want.

NOTE: *As you type the address, Mail will consult your Address Book and the messages you've sent and received, and attempt to auto-complete the address for you. If the right name is selected, click Tab or Enter to move to the next field.*

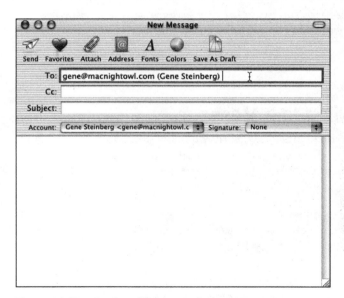

Figure 21.10   Begin writing your message here.

3. If you want to send courtesy or carbon copies to other recipients, place them in the CC field, each separated by a comma.

NOTE: *There is yet a third addressing option, BCC, which sends a blind carbon copy to recipients. None of the recipients will see the names of those in the BCC field. By default, this option is turned off, but you can activate it by going to the Message menu and choosing Add BCC Header.*

---

4. Enter a topic for your message in the Subject field. You can move through fields with a Tab key, or reverse the motion with a Shift-Tab. This is the same behavior you find in any email program.

5. Type the text of your message. If the spellcheck feature is turned on, you'll see spelling errors flagged in red.

6. When you've completed your message, click on the Send button to speed it on its way.

7. If you want to work on the message again at a later time, go to the File menu and choose Save As Draft. The message will be stored in your Drafts mailbox for later updating.

NOTE: *By default, the messages you send are saved in the Sent folder in your personal mailbox. This and other settings for the messages you write are saved under Mail Preferences, when you click on the Compose button. In this settings panel, you'll also be able to specify a different location for sent messages.*

Responding to a Message

When you receive messages, they'll show up in your Inbox, and just clicking on a title is sufficient to see the contents in the bottom pane of the Mail application window. New messages are signified by a blue button at the left of the message's title.

Once you've finished reading a message, you might want to write a reply. To do so, click on the Reply button. This brings up a response window, shown in Figure 21.11.

NOTE: *If the message went to more than one recipient, you have the option to reply to the original recipient, or by pressing the Reply All button, to everyone who got the message, including those listed in the CC field.*

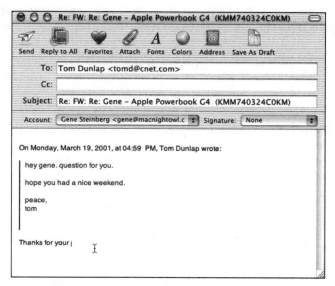

Figure 21.11   Write your response here.

When you've finished writing your message, click on the Send button to whisk it on its way (you have to be connected to your ISP for this to work, of course).

Quoting Messages

When you respond to a message, it's customary to quote relevant portions of the message to which you're responding. The normal way to do this is to first select the material that you wish to quote, then click on Reply. It'll show up in your response window.

WARNING! By default, if you don't select the portions of a message to be quoted, the entire message will appear in the response window. If you're responding to a long message, seeing so much material can be irritating for the recipient. It's better to just quote enough of the message so the recipient knows precisely what are your response concerns.

Spellchecking Your Messages

One way Mail excels is in its ability to automatically check your spelling as you type, marking the word with questionable spelling in red (see Figure 21.12).

Here's how you can handle Mail's powerful spellcheck features:

1. When mail flags a word where spelling is in question, you can either make your correction as you proceed, or Control+click the word to see a contextual menu with your spellcheck options (see Figure 21.13).

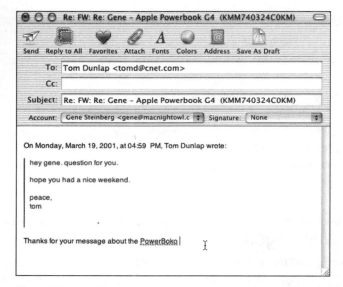

Figure 21.12   Where would your long-suffering author be without the ability to fix his spelling errors?

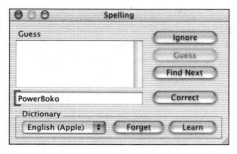

Figure 21.13   Correct the word or leave it as is.

2. From the contextual menu, you can choose a different spelling from the list of suggestions, or have the spell checker ignore or learn the word as it's spelled. When you specify a different spelling for the word, it'll be automatically replaced.

3. If you want to perform a batch spellcheck, simply choose Spelling from the Edit menu, and then Spelling from the submenu. Or type **Command+:**.

Sending Email Attachments

If you want to send one or more files with your email, you'll find the process is at once simple and complex. To attach a file to your email, follow these steps:

1. Open a Compose message window.

2. Click on the Attach button, which will produce an Open dialog box, shown in Figure 21.14.

3. Select one or more files to send, and click on the Open button.

4. Continue to prepare to send your message, then click on Send to speed it on its way. If the Activity Viewer window is displayed (it's a command in the Window menu), you'll see a progress indicator showing how much of your message has been sent. The time it takes to transfer depends on the size of the file you wish to send, and the speed of your Net connection.

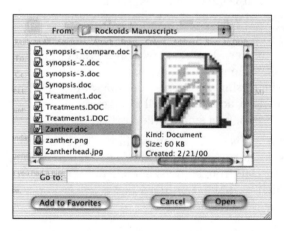

Figure 21.14   Select a file to accompany your email.

In sending attachments, you'll need to consider a few items to make sure that your files truly reach their destination intact:

- *Make sure your recipient can open it.* If your attachment was created in a particular application, you should check whether the recipient has the same program, or a program that can handle that type of document. For example, if you're using Microsoft Word, a Windows user with a recent version of the program can read the document. In addition, many other programs can read Word documents. However, more specialized software, such as QuarkXPress, requires that the recipient has the same program on hand.

- *Name windows files properly.* Whereas the Mac OS, both old and new, doesn't need a file extension to identify the type of file, Windows does. The names are entered as a three-letter extension. Common names include .doc for a Word document, .jpg for a JPEG file, and .gif for a GIF picture.

TIP: *Some programs, such as Word 2001 and recent versions of Adobe Photoshop, can be set to automatically append the proper extension for a file.*

- *Be careful about compressing files.* Whereas Mac users can handle files compressed in the industry-standard StuffIt format, users of Microsoft Windows generally use Zip files (although there is a StuffIt version for Windows as well). If you know your files are going to be read by both Mac and Windows users, consider the DropZip utility that comes with the latest versions of Aladdin Systems' StuffIt Deluxe. That's what I used to handle the cross-platform needs of my publisher while writing this book.

- *Don't send multiple attachments to AOL users.* AOL's email servers have problems decoding email with more than a single attachment. Just send one with each message. Instead, for convenience, consider using a compression program if you want to send more than one attachment. You'll also get the added benefit of being able to send a smaller file.

- *Watch out for file size limits.* You may run into problems with large attachments. As mentioned, some services, such as AOL, limit attachments to 2MB from sources outside the service. Others can be as high as 10MB (EarthLink and Excite@home, for example).

Forwarding Email

Have you ever received a message that you'd really like to send to a third party, whether a friend or business contact? If you want to send that message intact, or with some annotations of your own, just follow these steps:

1. With your new message opened, click on the Forward button.
2. Address the message in the appropriate field.
3. Add text before or after the message you're forwarding, if necessary.
4. Click on Send to speed it on its way.

WARNING! It's bad form to forward a message to a third party that the original sender might not want to disseminate. If you have any concerns about this, contact the original sender and ask if it's all right to send it elsewhere, and if need be, specify the names of the intended recipients.

Adding Email Signatures

Just as you put a signal on a regular letter, it's a good idea to use a signature on email as well. Although you can easily enter a signature manually, if you want to use it regularly, you can store it in Mail.

Here is how to set up a list of stored signatures:

1. With the Mail application opened, go to the application menu and choose Preferences.
2. Click on the Signatures button.
3. With the Signatures dialog box opened, click on Create Signature, and type the name for the signature you want to use.
4. Enter the signature's description in the Description box (see Figure 21.15).
5. Follow the preceding steps to add extra signatures as needed.
6. With all your new signatures set up, click on the OK button. Then, click the Active column next to the name of the signature to make it active. From here on, you can specify the signature to use from the Signature pop-up menu.

21. Email Options Explored

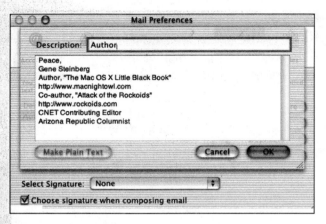

Figure 21.15   This is the author's standard signature.

TIP: *If you are sending a message to a recipient who might not be able to see email formatted with rich text, which will show Web links and formatted text, click the Composing icon and select Plain Text from the Default Message Format pop-up menu. The change will affect not just your signatures, but your entire message until changed.*

Formatting Email

Mail gives you a fairly decent set of formatting controls to handle the style of your messages. With a message window open, click on the Format menu to pick font style and size, and text orientation, such as left or centered. If you feel the recipient may not be able to see a styled message, click on Make Plain Text in the Format menu instead.

Setting Mail Rules

Within a limited range, you can specify custom rules to store and sort email messages. This will help you organize messages for later review or disposal. Although the feature isn't as powerful as the filtering options with other programs, it's nonetheless quite useful.

Here's how to establish a mail rule:

1. With the Mail application opened, choose Preferences from the Mail application menu.

2. Click on the Rules button, and in the setup pane that appears, click Create Rule, which brings up the setup dialog box shown in Figure 21.16.

NOTE: *By default, email rules are created for Apple's own information services. You can click the Remove buttons to dispose of them, or just uncheck the Active buttons to make them hibernate till you need them.*

3. Under Description, give your email sorting rule a name. By default, it'll be Rule #1, Rule #2, and so on.

4. In the first Criteria pop-up menu, select the field that applies to that specific rule, such as To, From, Subject, and so on.

5. In the second pop-up menu, choose the criteria that triggers the rule, such as whether the message Contains, Does Not Contain, Includes, etc.

6. Type the word or phrase that field must contain to trigger the rule. For example, if all messages from someone named **grayson@rockoids.com** are to be sorted, that's the information you'll enter for this particular rule.

7. Under Action, check the items that determine how your rule will be applied. The first two, Set The Color To and Play Sound, are simply appearance and notification options that don't actually change the message.

8. In the Transfer To Mailbox field in the pop-up menu, you can select the mailbox to which the message is to be moved. If an

21. Email Options Explored

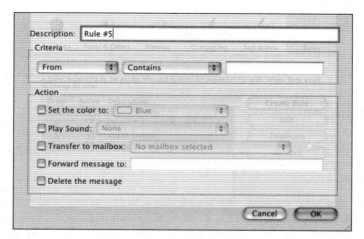

Figure 21.16   Create an email rule here.

appropriate mailbox isn't available, you can choose Create Mailbox from the application's Mail menu and produce a new one for your personal mailbox that does apply.

9. If you want to forward all messages that meet the criteria to another address, click the Forward Message To checkbox and specify the address.

10. You can also delete a message that meets the criteria, by clicking the Delete This Message checkbox. This option is a good way to dispose of known email offenders, although there are plenty of unknown ones that can keep you working over-time to create new rules.

11. When you're finished, click OK to close the Mail Preferences window. From here on, any email that matches the rule criteria will be stored as you've selected. You can create different rules for different messages to provide a full range of sorting options.

Getting Your Email Automatically

When you first use Mail, it automatically checks for your email on all active accounts at regular intervals. You can change this option if you want only to retrieve email manually.

Here's how to adjust the option:

1. With Mail opened, go to the Mail application menu and choose Preferences.

2. Click on the Accounts button and select the account for which you want to change the setting.

3. With the setup window opened, click on Show Advanced Options, then check or uncheck the Include This Account When Checking For New Mail option (it's checked by default).

4. Click on OK to store the settings. This returns you to the main Accounts setup window. From here you can choose the Check Accounts for New mail pop-up menu to look for new messages in your active accounts at a given interval (normal is five minutes) or manually.

5. The last setting allows you to select a sound that will notify you when a new message is received from the pop-up menu (you can select None if you don't want to be disturbed). Click on the close box after you've made your changes to complete the process.

Using the Address Book

No doubt you have regular contacts that you'd like to send messages to without having to enter the names manually in an email message window. Mac OS X includes an Address Book application (see Figure 21.17) that you can use to store your commonly used email addresses, or just to keep a record of your regular contacts. In addition, you can import your contacts from other email programs, though the range of information is not as extensive as, say, Microsoft's Outlook Express or Entourage.

To use this program, perform the following:

1. Choose Addresses from the Mail's Window menu. If Mail isn't opened, you'll find the Address Book application in the Applications folder.

2. Click on the category that describes your contact from the Show menu, All, Buddy, Home, Favorite, or Work.

3. To create a new contact, click New. Then enter the information in the appropriate contact field in the Address Card window (See Figure 21.18). Pop-up menus give you different categories for the information field.

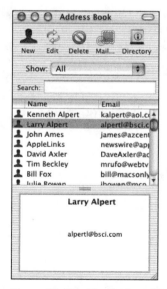

Figure 21.17   The Address Book application provides no-frills management of your regular contacts.

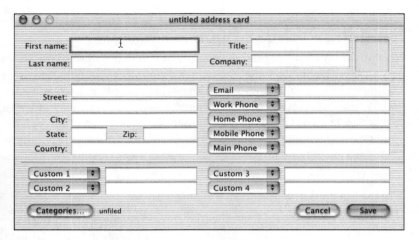

Figure 21.18   Fill in the blanks to set up a new contact.

NOTE: *The four Custom fields let you create custom labeled fields for different types of information, such as birthdays, anniversaries, or other information.*

---

4. When the address card is filled in, click the Categories button (see Figure 21.19) to produce the Choose Categories dialog box, and specify the appropriate ones.

NOTE: *You can attach one address card to multiple categories, or even create new ones, as needed.*

---

5. Click OK once a category or categories have been selected, and click Save to store the settings.

6. Repeat the preceding steps for each individual or group you wish to store.

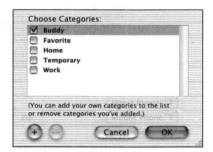

Figure 21.19   Select one or more categories here.

NOTE: *To delete an address book entry, just click on it and press Delete. Zap, it's gone. But be careful, as there's no way to restore it again without re-importing or typing it all over again.*

7. Once you've completed an address card for one of you contacts, you can click on its name and see the basic contents in the Preview window at the bottom of the Address Book window.

NOTE: *If you want to locate someone on the Internet whose email address or physical address is not known to you, click on the Directory button, then enter the information you do know in the text fields. Press Return or Enter to activate your search. If matches are found, they'll appear in the results window.*

Importing an Address Book

You do not have to redo your entire address book once you've moved on to Mail. There's a reasonably adept Import feature that will let you import basic information from other email programs. To use the feature, follow these steps:

1. Go to your email program and use the options available (if any) to export your address book as a separate file. Original email databases for the various programs are not likely to be recognized unless imported.

2. With Address Book opened, choose Import from the file menu, which brings up the Load Address Book dialog box shown in Figure 21.20.

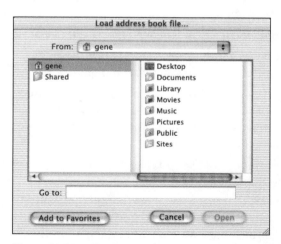

Figure 21.20   Choose the address book file from the Open dialog box.

3. Select the file you want and click Open. The list you selected will be added to your Address Book, using nearly the same fields as the original.

NOTE: *If the address book entries didn't come through accurately, you will need to select them in Address Book, click the Edit button and adjust them as needed.*

Finding a Message

Did you ever wonder what you said in that message you sent to a client a week earlier? Or perhaps you want to find out if you sent your aunt a birthday gift, or you just need to recheck the acknowledgement letter you got from a dealer so you can track the progress of an order. Mail provides a decent set of search options so you can easily locate the message you want.

Searching can be done by the message's header, such as the From and To information, or its subject, or by content. Here's how to run a search:

1. With Mail running, locate the mailbox you want to search, and click on its name in the Mailboxes drawer.

NOTE: *Mail indexes the contents of text messages, but you cannot search for text within an image or a file attachment of any kind.*

---

2. Enter the word or phrase that describes your search in the Search field of Mail's application menu.

3. If a match is found, you'll see it displayed in a results window.

4. If your search ends up with the wrong result or no result, consider these options to refine your search request:

   • *Include All Words*—With this option, a search request that reads "Cars and Ford", for example, will look for email that contains these words. Use the word "and" between each word in your search.

   • *Include One Word or the Other*—Here, if you enter "Cars and Ford", it will look for matches that contain either word.

   • *Use Either Or*—With this option, if you enter "Cars and (Ford or Cadillac)", material in the first category will be located, as well as either of the items entered within the parentheses.

Why Can't I Send My Email?

Although Mail is a fairly robust application, at times it simply won't work properly. If you encounter any difficulties getting your email to go out to its recipient, consider these remedies:

- *Are you connected?* Make sure that you are actually connected to your ISP. If you're using Internet Connect for a dial-up connection, open that application and look at the status screen to make sure a connection has been made. If your email still won't work, click on Disconnect to log off. Then, when the button changes to Connect, click on it again to log in. If you're using a broadband connection to the Internet, such as a cable modem or DSL, you may just want to try accessing a Web site to see if you have a connection. If you are connected via dial-up, or see no indication that your broadband connection is offline, contact the ISP directly for further help.

- *Message saved as a draft?* Maybe you pushed the wrong button when you wrote your message. To handle this problem, look at the folder where you put your draft email messages, and select the message you want to send. Then go to the File menu and choose Restore From Draft. Once this is done, you can try sending your message again.

- *POP server's port number is incorrect.* Open Mail's Preferences window, and click on the Account button. Then, click on the name of the account you're using, and click on the Edit Account button. With the account information displayed, click on the Show Advanced Options button. Then remove the entry at the bottom of the dialog box next to Connect To Server Using Port. Once you okay all the settings, Mail sets the proper number automatically when you again make your connection (assuming your ISP follows standard email protocols).

- *It's your ISP's fault.* Sometimes the fault lies with the service that provides your Internet connection. Check their Web site or call them for information about maintenance or system-related problems.

Why Are Messages Scrambled?

With your regular setup, Mail formats all of your messages in MIME (Multipurpose Internet Mail Extensions) or Rich Text Format. That way, you can use text styles, color, embedded graphics, and Web links in your messages. Keep in mind, however, that not all email programs can read these added frills.

To remove the formatting option, just open a new message window, then go to the Format menu and select Make Plain Text. That should take care of this problem.

NOTE: *Although Claris Emailer won't interpret Rich Text in messages, it usually provides the text along with the core HTML code, so the messages are, at least, readable.*

Why Doesn't Mail Check All My Accounts?

For Mail to automatically check for email from a specific email account, you must make sure the account is active and that it is accessed when you check for email. Here's how to confirm these settings:

1. Open Mail's Preferences window by choosing that option from the application menu.

2. Click on the Accounts icon, select the email account, and click the Edit button, and then click the Account Options tab.

3. Make sure that the Enable This Account option is checked. It is that way by default, but you might have unchecked it to test a preference, or to temporarily disable the account.

4. Click on OK to store the account changes, then close the Mail Preferences window.

With the settings configured properly, Mail should be able to retrieve your messages automatically from all active accounts.

Chapter 22

Apple's iTools Explored

If you need an immediate solution to:	See page:
Installing iTools	402
Configuring Email Software to Access Your Mac.com Email Address	404
Forwarding Mac.com Email	406
Telling Your Friends about Your New Address	408
Sending Vacation Notices	409
Configuring KidSafe	410
Using the iDisk Feature	411
Creating a Web Site with HomePage	413
Editing or Updating Your Web Page	416
Removing a Web Page	416
Solving HomePage Problems	417

In Brief

In his keynote address at the Macworld Expo in San Francisco in January 2000, Apple CEO Steve Jobs offered a visionary look at taking the company beyond the box. That means that instead of just selling computers, displays, peripherals, and the Mac OS, Apple wants to deliver additional user experiences that would make the platform more compelling.

The first new feature announced was iTools (see Figure 22.1), a collection of exclusive features that only Mac users with Mac OS 9 or later installed could set up (though some can be used by folks who have older versions of the Mac OS or computers with other operating systems installed).

Some of the features of iTools are fluff, such as a Mac.com email address and the ability to review Web sites and have the reviews appear online; the latter feature, in fact, was later dismantled. But some of the other tools are downright useful, particularly for parents with children learning to surf the Net or just to stay in touch with your online contacts. Both areas will be covered in this chapter.

NOTE: *During his keynote announcing iTools, Jobs said that additional features would be added periodically, so you may expect to see some that were not available when this book went to press.*

Reviewing iTools Features

iTools is designed to be a set of Internet-based services that, for the most part, are free and that help Mac users expand their surfing experience. Here's the list of the five features available to iTools members at the time this book went to press:

- *Email*—Create an email address with a Mac.com domain (see Figure 22.2). The feature can be set up with any email application, other than AOL and CompuServe 2000, and it gives you an email address that can be considered prestigious, or just a reflection of your commitment to your favorite computing platform.

NOTE: *Apple's iTools is not meant to replace your ISP. You need an Internet account to access these services. In addition, AOL's proprietary email system makes it impossible to send email via the Mac.com address.*

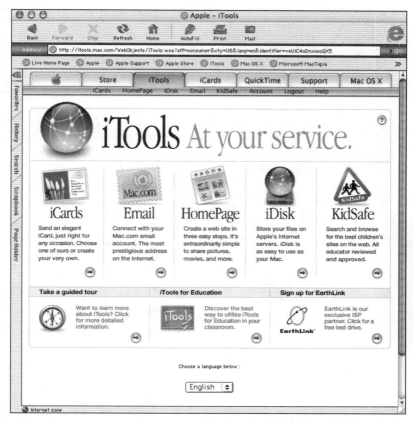

Figure 22.1   iTools is a collection of features that are only available to
Mac users.

- *KidSafe*—This is by far the most compelling reason to use iTools.
  KidSafe (see Figure 22.3) helps you provide a safer online environment. Using Mac OS X's Multiple User feature, you can restrict
  access to unapproved Web sites, Web-based email, chat rooms,
  and online gaming when your children use a Mac under the user
  account you set up for them. The advantage over a filtering
  system is that the site is restricted on the basis of content and not
  its name. This allows for a wider range of safe sites to be available.

- *iDisk*—Apple gives you 20MB of free storage space at their Web
  site, free of charge. You can use iDisk, shown in Figure 22.4, for
  backups, your personal Web sites, or to make files available to
  friends, family, and business contacts. Apple also lets you purchase extra storage space of up to 400MB for annual fees.

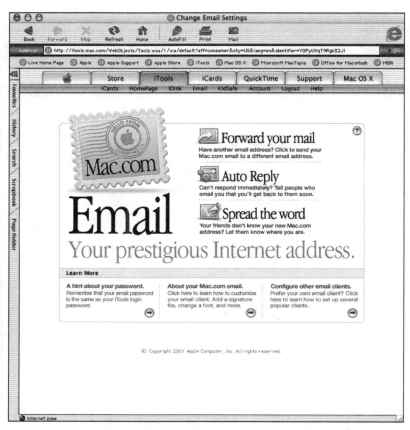

Figure 22.2   A Mac.com email address is one of the popular features of iTools.

- *HomePage*—Would you like to build a Web site, but you don't want to learn a new application or hassle with HTML coding? No problem. Apple's HomePage feature (see Figure 22.5) lets you put up your personal Web site with a photo album, iMovie home videos, résumés, and more in just three convenient steps, all in a matter of minutes. Once your site is set up, it is handled by Apple's Web site free. The feature is similar to those offered by such services as AOL and EarthLink. And, like the other free Web sites, the site can be accessed by anyone with Internet access; it's not restricted to iTools users or even to Mac users.

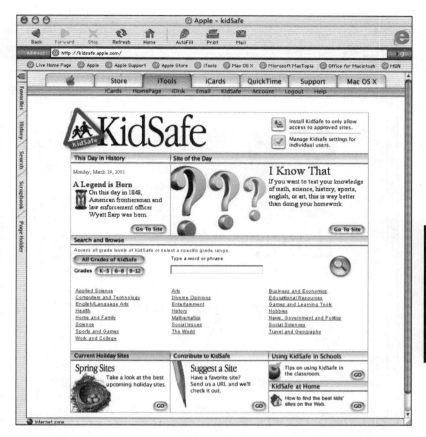

Figure 22.3 Allow your children to access only special educator-approved sites.

NOTE: *Such free no-hassle Web builders as HomePage aren't designed for a full-fledged business site. They are fine for a personal page or a family photo album or even for posting your own résumé. But if you wish to do business on the Web, the best way is to use a professional Web-authoring program for your site (such as Adobe's GoLive or Macromedia's Dreamweaver) and then get a regular "dot.com"-style custom domain name via a commercial Web hosting service.*

- *iCards*—Send personal greeting cards or business announcements using a convenient array of photos and artwork. iCards also features a fairly decent selection of fonts and color styles.

Figure 22.4   Use iDisk for online backups and other storage purposes.

Figure 22.5   Make a personal Web site with HomePage in minutes.

Immediate Solutions

To get started using iTools, you have to sign up at Apple's Web site. Once you're set up, accessing your user account requires just a simple login.

Installing iTools

The first stage of the setup process is to register your iTools account at Apple's Web site. This was actually part of the initial Setup Assistant process, so it may already be available on your Mac. However, if you didn't set up your account at that time, here's what to do:

1. Launch the System Preferences application from the Dock or its normal place in the Applications folder.

2. Click on the Internet pane and make sure the iTools tab is selected.

3. Click on the Free Sign Up button. This action will take you right to the iTools sign-up page, where you can enter your registration information (see Figure 22.6). Click on Continue to proceed.

4. As with a regular ISP, user names can't be duplicated. If the name you selected is already in use (don't even try steve@mac.com for obvious reasons), you'll see a Select Another Name prompt where a list of alternate names is shown. You can either select one, or enter another name in the information field and then click on Continue.

NOTE: *Don't be surprised if you have to continue to experiment with alternative names until one is accepted, in the event you don't pick the ones offered.*

---

5. After you've set up your account, you'll see a Save For Your Records page, which you can print out to have a hard copy record of your user name, password, and the required email settings (Apple's Mail application sorts most of this out for you in its setup box). A copy will also be emailed to you at your new mac.com address. Click on Continue to move on.

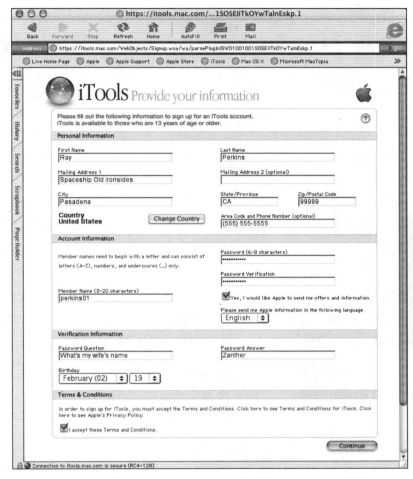

Figure 22.6   This is, of course, not a real registration.

6. Once your account is set up, you'll see a welcome screen, where a click of the Start Using iTools box (see Figure 22.7) will take you to a page where you can send an iCard to your online contacts, notifying them about your new address. You can, of course, click on the No Thanks button if you don't want to send the notice.

7. Once set up, you can continue to use iTools or return later to sample the features.

TIP: *If you plan on revisiting the iTools Web site frequently, you'll want to bookmark the site in your Web browser (it's called Favorites in Internet Explorer).*

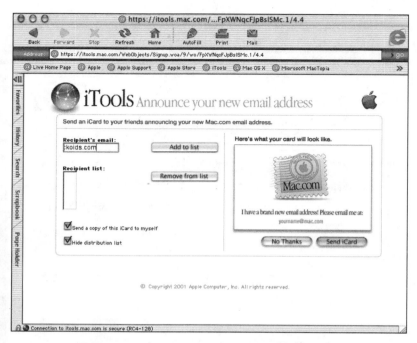

Figure 22.7   Send an email announcement about your new address.

Configuring Email Software to Access Your Mac.com Email Address

Once you've registered your new email address, you'll want to configure your email program to access the mail. For this chapter, I'll be using Apple's Mail application to show you the process, but you can also configure any other email client in pretty much the same way. Just follow these steps:

NOTE: For more information on using Mail, please read Chapter 21.

---

1. Go to the Dock and click on the Mail icon; if it's not in the Dock, go ahead and launch it directly from the Applications folder by double-clicking on its icon.

2. With the program running, go to Mail's Application menu and choose Preferences. The window shown in Figure 22.8 appears.

3. Locate and click on the Accounts icon, and click on the Create Account button to bring up the Account Information dialog box (see Figure 22.9).

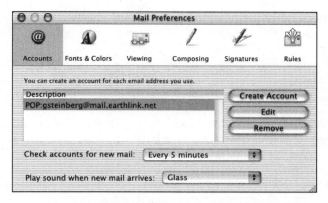

Figure 22.8   Switch to your Mac.com email account here.

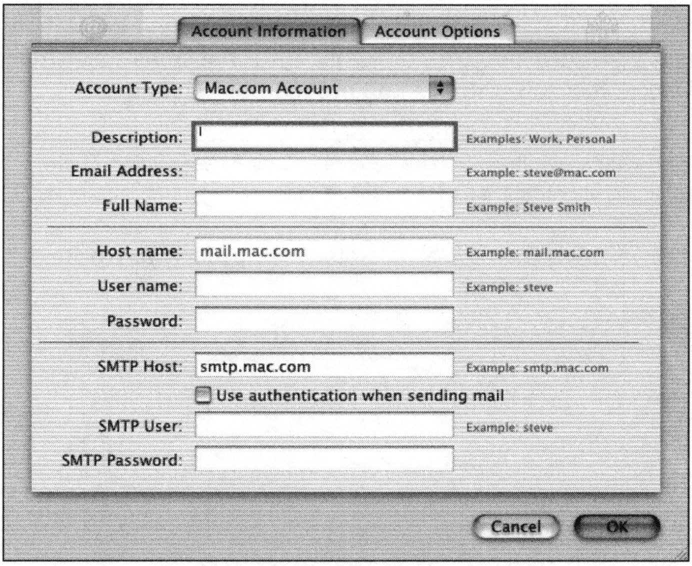

Figure 22.9   Place your new account information here.

22. Apple's iTools Explored

TIP: You can create separate Mac.com user accounts for each user of your Mac to give them maximum flexibility to use iTools on a single Mac; or, better, just set up individual user accounts for each, using Mac OS X's multiple users feature, as described in Chapter 6.

---

4. Choose Mac.com Account from the Account Type pop-up menu. This will automatically insert the default mail server settings needed.

5. Give your account a description (this is optional, but helpful if you want to recheck the settings later). I call mine iTools Account for obvious reasons.

6. Enter your Full Name, User name, and iTools password. You can't put in the Email Address (it'll be added automatically later on).

7. When your settings are complete (see Figure 22.10), click on OK to store them.

NOTE: *As soon as you establish your iTools user account, Apple's mail server will be checked and your mail database will be synchronized to make it up to date. This is also done to verify that your account settings are correct. If they're not, you'll see an error prompt indicating that the account couldn't be synchronized or located. If that happens, just recheck your account setup and make sure all information is correct.*

Forwarding Mac.com Email

If you prefer to keep using your existing email account to handle messages, you can arrange to have your Mac.com email forwarded to that address. Just follow this setup procedure:

NOTE: *In addition to being able to forward email, you can use your email software to create custom signatures, automatic message retrieval, and so on.*

---

1. Access Apple's iTools Web site at **www.apple.com/itools**.

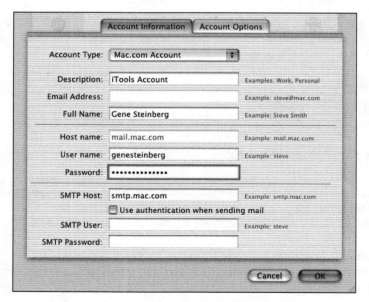

Figure 22.10   The author's account, already established.

2. Log on to iTools by typing your username and password at the Sign In prompt.

3. With the iTools page on your browser, click on the Email button at the iTools Web site (see Figure 22.11).

4. Click on the Forward Email button. The window shown in Figure 22.12 appears.

5. Change the radio button labeled Email Forwarding Is to On.

6. Enter the complete email address where you want your Mac.com email forwarded.

WARNING! When you opt to forward email, the messages are not stored on Apple's email server. The only way to retrieve those messages is from the address to which they were sent until the setting is changed.

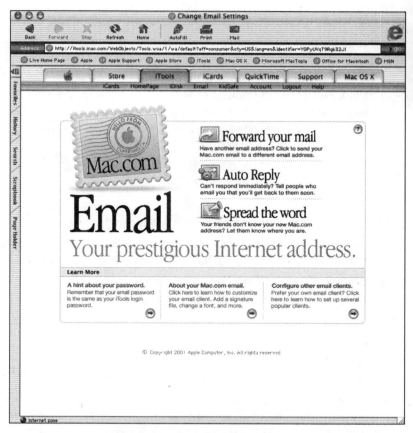

Figure 22.11   Configure Mac.com email features here.

Figure 22.12   Enter an address to forward your email to.

7. Click on the Submit button to store your changes. You'll be returned to the Mac.com setup page, and all your subsequent email will be forwarded to the email address you specify.

NOTE: *The address you specify isn't set in stone. You can change it to another address at any time, or just click on the Off button in the Email Forwarding page to deactivate the feature.*

Telling Your Friends about Your New Address

Now that you have a new email address, you'll want to let your friends know. Just follow these steps to have an iCard sent to your mailing list:

1. Bring up Apple's iTools Web site at **www.apple.com/itools**.

2. Log on to iTools by typing your username and password in the Sign In prompt.

3. On the main iTools screen, click on the Email button at the iTools Web site.

4. Click on the Send iCard button (see Figure 22.13).

5. In the Recipient's Email text field, enter the address of someone to whom you want to send the announcement.

6. Click on Add To List.

7. Repeat Steps 4 through 6 for each additional recipient. As they are added to the list, they'll appear in the Recipient List category.

Figure 22.13   Send iCards to your regular contacts.

8. If you want a copy for confirmation, click on the Send A Copy To Myself checkbox (it's set that way by default).

9. When you're finished, click on the Send button to speed announcements on their way.

Sending Vacation Notices

While you're away on vacation or on a business trip, wouldn't it be nice if folks who wrote to you knew that you were away and you were not being rude because you didn't respond to their messages? The iTools Email tool lets you send an automatic reply, so they'll know that you're just not around to give a personal response.

Here's how to use the feature:

1. Connect to Apple's iTools Web site at **www.apple.com/itools**.

2. Log on to iTools by typing your username and password at the Sign In prompt.

3. With the iTools page displayed, click on the Email button at the iTools Web site.

4. Click on the Set Auto Reply button. The window shown in Figure 22.14 appears.

5. Change the Auto Reply Setting radio button to On to activate the feature.

Figure 22.14   Tell your contacts you're not around to answer.

6. In the Auto Reply Message field, change the sample text if you want something with more details about when you'll be able to check and respond to messages. Or if you prefer to use the existing message, just leave it as it is.

7. Click on the Submit button to activate the feature.

8. Should you want to turn off the Auto Reply function, just return to the Email Auto Reply page and click on the Off button.

9. Click on Submit to store your changes.

Configuring KidSafe

One of the most important features that Apple Computer has made available to parents is KidSafe. It provides the ability to restrict a child's access strictly to Web sites and other online areas approved by a panel of educators.

Here's how to use the feature:

1. Access the Apple's iTools Web site at **www.apple.com/itools**.

2. Log on to iTools by typing your username and password at the Sign In prompt.

3. With the regular iTools member page displayed, locate Setting Up KidSafe at the bottom of the screen, and click on the Go button.

4. Follow the prompts to log in to KidSafe with your iTools username and password.

5. If you want to customize user access still further, you can log in to the KidSafe area at the iTools Web site, then locate the Edit Settings button on the KidSafe welcome page.

6. Once you've entered this area, you can add and remove Web sites and control access to online games, streaming video, and other features.

7. After you've changed the settings, your children will be able to work under the customized environment the next time they log in to your Mac.

NOTE: *For additional information on configuring your Mac for multiple user access, please read Chapter 6.*

Using the iDisk Feature

One of the more useful functions of iTools is iDisk, which, by default, gives you 20MB of free storage space to use as you wish. Here's how to use the feature:

1. Access the Apple's iTools Web site at **www.apple.com/itools**.

2. Log on to iTools by typing your username and password at the Sign In prompt.

3. On the main iTools page, click on the Go button in the iDisk category to bring up the setup page, shown in Figure 22.15.

4. If you want to open your iDisk, simply click on the Open Your iDisk button. Within a few seconds, the icon for your disk will show up on your Mac's desktop.

5. Among the features of iDisk is the ability to set aside a Public Folder, where other users of the feature can send and retrieve files. To open someone else's Public Folder, just enter his or her member name in the text field, then click on the Open Public Folder button. That folder will appear on your Mac's desktop.

Figure 22.15   Configure your iDisk options here.

6. Except for your iTools home page, the contents of your Public Folder are not available to the public unless you want to share it. To do so, click on the Publish Public Folder button. Once you do that, you can unpublish the folder by returning to the page and clicking on the option again, which reverses the action.

7. The remaining option costs extra: If you want to increase storage space beyond the standard 20MB, you can purchase up to 400MB of storage space, at an annual fee. Click on the Add Storage To Your iDisk button to access the information page where you'll see the latest price list and how to place your order.

NOTE: *You could, of course, create separate iTools accounts for yourself and get 20MB for each, but that might tend to be a rather convoluted way to manage the various free disk space features.*

Creating a Web Site with HomePage

Some of the popular ISPs offer a very convenient feature for budding Web authors: a free Web space where you can post a personal page. Depending on the service, you may even get a free setup program that uses templates and step-by-step wizards to set you up in minutes.

Here's how to set up your Web site on Apple's Web servers using Apple's HomePage Web authoring tool:

1. Connect to the Apple's iTools Web site at **www.apple.com/ itools**.

2. Log on to iTools by typing your username and password at the Sign In prompt.

3. When you see the main iTools page, click on the Go button under HomePage (see Figure 22.16).

4. At the left of the HomePage site are buttons that specify the type of page you can make. To get started, just click on a page category. As a sample, I'll use Personal, which produces the page shown in Figure 22.17.

5. On the next page, choose a theme for your page from those offered. I'm deliberately not showing you the choices here because they change on a regular basis.

6. To add your text, click on the Edit Text button, and make your entries in the text fields provided. You have several options with which to edit and style text to your taste.

7. Once your text is created or changed, click on Apply to store your text.

8. To add images to your site, click on the Choose button in the image area, then pick the image from those shown in the iTools Image Library. You can also choose any image that's stored on your personal iDisk.

NOTE: *When using your own pictures, stick with the tried-and-true Web picture formats, such as GIF, JPEG, or PNG. If you try to use pictures of other formats, at best, they just won't display and at worst, it'll result in downloads of unknown files for those accessing your site.*

---

9. If you want to add Web links pointing to your favorite sites, click again on the Edit Text button. Then enter the URLs of your favorite links.

Figure 22.16 Apple makes it super easy to build your personal page at their Web site.

10. When your links have been entered, click on Apply Text to store the settings.

11. At any time, you can look at your work in progress by clicking on the Preview button (see Figure 22.18). You can perform this step over and over again to double-check your work.

NOTE: *As explained in the next section, you can easily edit your pages even after they're published on the Web.*

---

12. All done? Just click on Publish to make your site available to anyone with Web access. You get an acknowledgment indicating the actual URL of your new Web site. Now you can send an iCard to your online contacts so they can pay a visit.

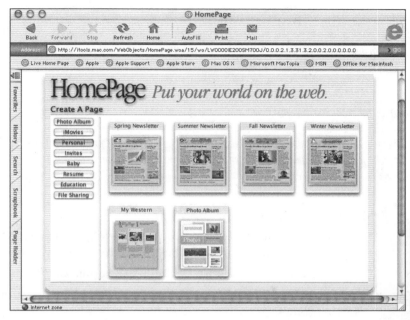

Figure 22.17   From here to a home page on the World Wide Web takes just a few minutes.

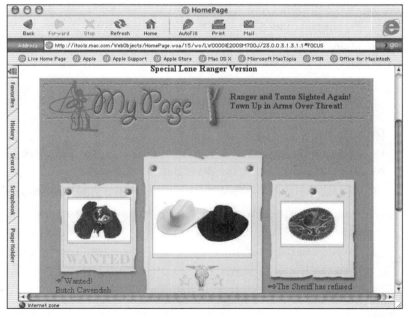

Figure 22.18   All right, it's not finished, but here's how the work I have done looks so far.

TIP: *You can follow the preceding steps to create additional pages at your Web site and then use links on a page to access the next one. This can greatly expand the features of your site. You can also keep them separate and give visitors the various URLs to access the pages you want them to see.*

NOTE: *The first page you create with HomePage is your site's home (or start) page as well. When you access the HomePage area, it'll be marked with an asterisk in the listing. If you want to change the home page that visitors access when they call up your set, just connect to the HomePage site, select the name of the page you want to make your site's home page, and click on Set Start Page.*

Editing or Updating Your Web Page

Once you've created and published your Web site, it's easy to change it any time to add text and pictures or adjust Web links. Here's what to do:

1. Access the Apple's iTools Web site at **www.apple.com/itools**.
2. Connect to iTools by typing your username and password at the Sign In prompt.
3. Go right to the main HomePage site, where you'll see a list of the pages you've created with HomePage.
4. Select the page you want to alter, and click on Edit Page.
5. On the next page, click on the Edit Text button.
6. Make your text changes and, as necessary, add or remove pictures from your page.
7. When you're through, just click on the Publish button to make the updated site available to visitors on the World Wide Web.

Removing a Web Page

Have you decided to take your site down, or you just want to remove some of the pages you've created? Here's what to do:

1. Access the Apple's iTools Web site at **www.apple.com/itools**.
2. Connect to iTools by typing your username and password at the Sign In prompt.
3. Go right to the main HomePage site, where you'll see a list of the pages you've created with HomePage.
4. Now select the page and click on Delete Page.

NOTE: *Even though you are deleting your Web page, the actual images that may be on that page will remain on your iDisk for storage or to use for another purpose.*

Solving HomePage Problems

When your site's URL is accessed, it should show the exact site that you created. However, there may be times when it doesn't look right. Here are some possible problems and solutions:

- *The site isn't available.* Are you sure you published your site in HomePage? Just to be sure, go back to HomePage, edit your Web page, and publish it again. If Apple's site itself can't be accessed, it may be due to maintenance at their Web servers. Of course, you should also double-check that you can access other sites. If not, you may need to log off your ISP and then reconnect.

- *The wrong version of the site appears.* First, click on the Refresh (or Reload) button on your browser to load the page from scratch. If that doesn't work, go back and edit and publish your site again. Perhaps you missed a step, but this way, you'll be sure that the correct version of the site is actually available.

NOTE: *AOL, CompuServe 2000, and some ISPs (such as Excite@home) may cache sites frequently accessed by their members. That means that the update may not be available immediately.*

- *It looks different on other browsers.* You probably can't do much about this problem. Different Web browsers interpret the HTML code that makes up a Web page differently. Text may be larger or smaller; tables, pictures, and other elements may appear somewhat different. You might want to examine your site in both Microsoft Internet Explorer and Netscape, and perhaps even OmniWeb, to be assured that the look is acceptable, even if different, from browser to browser.

- *The artwork looks fuzzy on AOL.* AOL has a program preference called Use Compressed Images, in their WWW settings. The purpose of this setting is primarily to increase the speed of retrieving a Web site, by compressing images on the fly at AOL using a proprietary format called .ART. But sometimes it will hurt the quality and may prevent Web animations from appearing. The best approach is usually just to turn it off. You can access it in current AOL versions from the My AOL toolbar button under Preferences.

Glossary

10BaseT—The designation for standard 10Mbs Ethernet run over twisted-pair network cable. 10BaseT is the most common form of Ethernet available today and has largely supplanted the other forms of Ethernet: ThickNet and ThinNet (which use coaxial cable). 10BaseT utilizes either Category 3 or Category 5 four-pair twisted-pair wire to send data up to 100 meters without the need for a repeater. The follow-up to 10BaseT is the newer 100BaseTX, which sends data at 100Mbps over Category 5 twisted-pair cable. As the cost of 100BaseT network adapters and the associated hubs and switches continues to drop, expect that 100BaseTX will replace 10BaseT. Other variations include 100BaseFx and 100BaseVG. The latest generation on the horizon is 1000BaseT, also known as Gigabit Ethernet.

active window—The Finder or document window that you are presently using. The Finder lets you work in single-window mode, where the nonactive Finder and document windows are collapsed and moved to the Dock.

alias—A pointer or reference to an original file that is accessed in the same fashion as the original. An alias allows you to more easily access a file, regardless of whether it is located on your Mac's drive, on a networked drive, or on the Internet.

America Online (AOL)—The largest Internet Service Provider (ISP) in the world, with more than 26 million members. Headquartered in Vienna, Virginia, AOL provides Internet access to users worldwide.

Apple menu—Sitting in its accustomed spot at the left side of the menu bar, Apple has revised the Apple menu to include system-wide commands formerly reserved for the Special menu. These include the ability to restart and shutdown the computer.

AppleScript—Apple's scripting language, a natural language programming feature that lets you automate repetitive or complex routines by running a small application (or applet).

AppleTalk—A network protocol developed by Apple Computer in the mid-1980s to provide networking services for Macintosh operating system (OS) computers. AppleTalk is available in two forms: AppleTalk Phase 1, which was developed in 1984, and AppleTalk Phase 2, which was released in 1988 to address many of the issues that plagued AppleTalk Phase 1. AppleTalk is available on all Macintosh-based computers and provides a quick and simple workgroup networking solution that can be set up in minutes.

AppleTalk Phase 1—Introduced in 1984, this protocol was a quick and easy way to network Macintosh computers together. Unfortunately, AppleTalk Phase 1 networks are limited to only 127 computers per network.

AppleTalk Phase 2—Introduced in 1988, AppleTalk Phase 2 was designed to address the limitations of AppleTalk Phase 1. Unlike AppleTalk Phase 1, AppleTalk Phase 2 networks can have up to 65,298 network segments, known as zones, and can have up to 254 AppleTalk devices per zone.

AppleTalk zones—Zones are the segments into which a network is divided. This method allows more AppleTalk devices on the same network segment than would normally be permitted by the limit of 254 AppleTalk devices per network. AppleTalk zones are also used in a manner somewhat like an office workgroup or department, in which all the computers in a specific AppleTalk zone have access to all the resources that are available on that zone.

application—The program that actually lets you do work on a Mac. An application may handle word processing or page layout chores, allow you to access the Internet, or perform preventive maintenance on your Mac, by checking your hard drive.

Application menu—Represented by the application icon or name at the left side of Mac OS X's menu bar, the Application menu lets you access additional features, such as quitting an application or accessing its preferences. In some programs, the File menu provides some of these features.

application programming interface (API)—This is the set of tools programmers use to develop software for a specific operating system. See also *Carbon*.

assistants—Special programs, such as the Setup Assistant, that are used to configure settings for your Mac operating system or to perform a complex function in software. Examples of the latter include the assistants provided with programs such as AppleWorks to set up a template for a specific type of document.

attachment—One or more files that are connected to your email message, in effect going along for the ride. You can attach a document, graphics, or program file, but your ISP may restrict the maximum size of the file.

back up—The process of making one or more extra copies of your files as a protection measure to guard against the possibility that your original file may become lost or damaged.

binary numbers—The ones and zeros that make up computer language.

bookmarks—See *Favorites.*

boot—Short for "bootstrap," the process of starting a computer. During the boot process, your Mac's hardware is checked, then the operating system components load.

browser—A program that's used to view files. The general use of this term is for a Web browser, a program that accesses and interprets documents on the World Wide Web and converts them to a form that reflects their original content.

byte—The basic object of data that a computer uses. In a modern computer, a byte consists of 8 bits—that is, 1s or 0s that represent a binary number. See also *binary numbers.*

cable modem—Device that works with a standard cable television connection to provide high-speed internet access.

cache—Usually a small amount of memory allocated for frequently used data. You'll find a cache in such places as a hard drive, a CPU, and a logic (or mother) board.

Carbon—A set of application programming interfaces that allow a software publisher to update its existing programs to support the Aqua interface and most of the other features of Mac OS X. See also *application programming interface.*

carbon copy (CC)—The process of sending one or more extra copies of email messages to other recipients.

CD-ROM—Stands for compact disc read-only memory; a variant of the music CD that stores computer data. CD-ROMs are also used for software installations. The departure of floppy drives from Macs, the lower cost of pressing CDs, and the larger space taken up by software have all contributed to the switchover.

Glossary

checkbox—A small, square box that's used to toggle a specific program function. You may, for example, click on a checkbox to insert a checkmark that activates a feature; then you click again to remove the checkmark and turn off the feature.

checksum—A number that is calculated based upon the data in a packet or file. Checksums are reviewed as the data is being examined after transmission to see if the checksum calculated before transmission and the checksum calculated after transmission are identical, indicating that the data did not get corrupted.

Chooser—In Mac operating systems prior to Mac OS X, a program that controls the Macintosh's networking and printer connections.

click—The process of taking your pointing device (mouse, trackball, and so on) over an item, then pressing the mouse button one time.

clipboard—A memory-resident area onto which you copy or cut data from a document. The present iteration of the Mac OS clipboard stores just one item, so when you copy a second, it replaces the first. However, some programs have their own clipboard-handling features, which give you additional storage areas.

Clock—An application that displays an analog or digital clock on the Dock or, optionally, as a floating window.

close box—The small red button at the top of a Finder or document window (it's gray when you access the optional Graphite interface). When you click on the box, it closes the window, but it may not necessarily result in actually quitting the application.

Cocoa—A programming environment for Mac OS X applications, Cocoa is descended from the NeXTSTEP programming interface, called Objective C, which is designed to make it easier to build complete applications using a set of predefined components called objects.

collapse button—The yellow Finder button that is used to minimize a window and move it to the Dock (under the optional Graphite interface, it's just gray).

ColorSync—A settings pane in the System Preferences application that allows you to configure color-matching options. ColorSync is a component of the Mac OS that allows input devices, computer monitors, and output devices, such as printers, to be more accurately calibrated.

command-line interface (CLI)—A way of interacting with a computer or router using commands that you type in via a keyboard. Mac OS X includes an application known as Terminal that allows you to interact with the operating system the same as you do with any Unix-based system.

commands—Commands are used to tell your computer how to perform a function. They may be entered by text or by selecting a menu item.

compression—Reducing the size of a file using mathematical algorithms that check for redundant data. Compression programs include such products as the StuffIt family from Aladdin Systems.

computer name—When you install Mac OS X, you assign your computer a name, allowing it to be properly located and identified on your network.

contextual menu—A pop-up menu accessed by a Control+click. It displays a set of commands that relate specifically to the selected item, such as file management functions. For example, Control+clicking on a folder or disk icon will bring up a contextual menu of file management functions.

cooperative multitasking—This is the inefficient multitasking scheme of the Classic version of the Mac operating system in which programs·are designed to work together to share CPU time. See also *preemptive multitasking.*

creator types—A 4-byte code assigned to a Macintosh file that tells the Finder the application program that created it. The Macintosh operating system (OS) uses creator codes to determine which application should be launched when a user attempts to open a specific file.

Darwin—The core of Mac OS X, incorporating a Unix microkernel that consists of Mac 3.0 and Free BSD 3.2. Making this element of the operating system open source (meaning the programming code is available for use by anyone signing Apple's legal document) allows third-party programmers to develop updates and improvements that can then be shared. These changes may be used by Apple for updates and improvements to Mac OS X.

Date & Time—A settings panel in the System Preferences application that lets you set the time and date and whether your Mac's clock is automatically synchronized to a network or Internet-based time server.

Glossary

423

DAVE—A tool from Thursby Software Systems, Inc., that allows the Macintosh to communicate using the Network Basic Input Output System (NetBIOS) protocol used on Windows-based networks. DAVE also provides Macintosh users with a variety of tools to access resources on the Windows-based network. See also *NetBIOS*.

desktop—The backdrop or background artwork that appears behind your Finder or file windows on your Mac. Icons representing files or disks may be placed upon the desktop for convenient access.

DHCP—Stands for Dynamic Host Configuration Protocol. A network protocol that automates the process of assigning an Internet Protocol (IP) address and other network-specific information to computers that request them on the network. A DHCP server on the network responds to requests from a computer on the network and then assigns an IP address to computers for a specified time. By only leasing the IP address to each computer, DHCP allows the IP addresses of computers that are no longer using them to be reclaimed and redistributed to other computers on the network. See also *IP*.

dialog box—A window that contains items you must click on or enter data into to activate a particular function.

directory—See *folder*.

Dock—Mac OS X's taskbar, consisting of a row of colorful icons at the bottom of the screen that are used for one-click access to applications, files, and folders. It's meant as a replacement for the application switcher and Control Strip features of previous versions of the Mac OS.

domain—The organization to which servers and computers belong. For example, **www.apple.com** is a computer in the **apple.com** domain. Like the Domain Name Service (DNS), which controls domain information on the Internet and your local network, Microsoft Active Directory is based upon the domain structure. See also *Domain Name Service* and *Microsoft Active Directory*.

Domain Name Service (DNS)—The service on the network that matches up a computer's host name with its Internet Protocol (IP) address. DNS servers receive requests from computers on the network that request the IP address of a server using a specific Internet domain name. For example, when you type in **http://www.apple. com** your computer contacts a DNS server to get the IP address assigned to the computer named www.microsoft.com. It then takes the IP address it receives from the DNS server and uses it to connect to the remote computer. See also *IP*.

double-click—An action whereby you point at an item, then press the mouse button twice in rapid succession to open or activate the item.

double-click speed—The rate or rhythm of a double-click required to activate a function. This setting is user-dependent and can be configured as a mouse setting in the Preferences application.

download—Receiving a file from another computer, whether on your network or via an ISP.

drag—Moving a selected item from one place to another. You can drag such things as picture objects, text, disk, and file icons.

drag-and-drop—Clicking on an item to select it, then dragging it to a new location and releasing the mouse button, thereby dropping it into its new locale.

driver—A program that allows your Mac to work with a peripheral device, such as a printer, removable hard drive, scanner, or digital camera.

DSL—Short for Digital Subscriber Line. A method designed to deliver high-speed Internet connections to a home or office using standard telephone lines.

duplex—The way that a computer transmits and receives traffic on the network. Half-duplex mode means that a computer must wait for all transmissions to it to cease before it starts sending data out. Full-duplex means that a computer can send and receive data at the same time. 10Mbps Ethernet is normally half-duplex (the full-duplex mode is not often implemented). 100Mbps Ethernet, also called Fast Ethernet, supports full-duplex mode. This allows a computer to send and receive data at 100Mbps each way, bringing the actual throughput up to 200Mbps. See also *Ethernet* and *Fast Ethernet*.

duplexing—A feature offered by some printers that allows you to automatically print on both sides of the page. If the option is available, you can configure it in Mac OS X's Print Center application and then the Print dialog box. Where the feature is offered, the printed page goes through a special paper path in which the paper is reversed so that the back side is printed after the front side.

DVD drive—A device using an updated version of CD technology that allows it to store a much greater amount of data. DVD-ROM drives can read regular CDs, plus those based on DVD technology (including videos). DVD stands for Digital Versatile Disc (not Video as commonly believed) because of the variety of formats it supports.

Glossary

Edit menu—This menu is used for text and picture editing functions, such as copying and pasting.

Eject—This Finder command has two functions, depending on the kind of drive selected when it's accessed. The first is to dismount a drive from your Mac. The second, if the drive is removable, is also to eject the disk media from the drive.

email—Short for electronic mail. One of the most popular forms of online communication. It's the process of sending messages across a network within an online service or across the Internet. See also *attachments*.

email address—The identity of the person you're contacting. The email address consists of two parts. The first is the username; the second, followed by an @ symbol, is the location or domain that hosts the user's account. AOL and CompuServe members, on the other hand, use just their username (called a screen name) without a domain to communicate to other members of the service.

Empty Trash—A Finder command that removes any items placed in the Trash.

Energy Saver—A settings pane in the System Preferences application that lets you set an idle time interval for Mac system shut down or sleep.

Erase Disk—A Finder command that is used to delete the contents of a selected disk and create a new directory (the same as the Initialize function in a disk formatting program). This function is disabled on the startup disk.

Ethernet—A network standard developed in the 1970s by Bob Metcalfe at Xerox PARC as a way to provide a high-speed connection between computers and printers. Over the years, Ethernet has become the principal network technology that links computers and other network-based devices on a local area network (LAN). Ethernet is most commonly seen in two varieties these days: standard Ethernet, which moves data at 10Mbps, and Fast Ethernet, which moves data at 100Mbps. Gigabit Ethernet, which moves data at 1 billion bits of data a second, is starting to become more widespread since its introduction in the desktop Power Macintosh line in the Summer of 2000 See also *Fast Ethernet*.

Fast Ethernet—The version of Ethernet that transfers data at 100Mbps in half-duplex mode. Fast Ethernet can operate in full-duplex mode as well, so actual throughput using Fast Ethernet can reach 200Mbps.

Favorites—A feature of Mac OS X, where you can store aliases to items you wish to revisit on a regular basis. A similar feature is provided with a Web browser, where links are stored in a menu for quick access to the sites to which you want to return. However, the names of this feature vary. While it's "Favorites" with Internet Explorer, Netscape calls it "Bookmarks" instead. See also *history*.

file extensions—The three-character suffixes on MS-DOS, Unix, and Windows files that tell the operating system what type of data the file contains. For example, a .doc file extension tells Windows that the file in question is a Microsoft Word document.

File menu—The menu that accesses file-related functions, such as opening and saving documents.

File Sharing—A feature of the Mac OS that allows you to easily share your Mac's files with other computers on a network or over the Internet.

file system—The fashion in which files are stored on your Mac.

file types—The 4-byte code that tells the Macintosh operating system (OS) what type of data is contained in the file. For example, a file type of TEXT indicates that the file contains text.

Finder—An application that manages the file viewing and transfer process for the items available to your Mac, either locally or via a network. The Finder displays the list of available files, allowing you to open or transfer them to another location (such as a different drive volume or a networked volume).

firewalls—Computers or routers that are configured to act as a gateway between your local area network (LAN) and the Internet. Firewalls can be anything from a Cisco router with some access lists applied to the interface that is connected to the Internet, to special software you set up on your Mac. By limiting the access that computers on the Internet have to your LAN, the firewall protects you from attack and intrusion by hackers and other unfriendly elements.

Glossary

FireWire—A high-speed peripheral bus that is now featured on all Macs but the entry-level iMac. It provides plug-and-play capability, a potential throughput of 400Mbps, and support for up to 63 daisy-chained devices for each FireWire port. See also *USB*.

floppy disk—An older magnetic storage medium consisting of a small square object, inside of which is a flexible sheet of magnetic material. Because of the limitations of this storage medium, newer Macs have dispensed with such drives. However, a newer generation of storage devices called SuperDisk uses floppy-based media with 120MB of storage capacity. The Iomega Zip drive, with 100MB and 250MB capacities, also uses some floppy disk-based technology.

folder—A container-like item on your Mac identified by a folder-like icon that holds other folders and files.

formatting—(1) The process of erasing the contents of a drive and preparing it for reuse. (2) The characteristics of the text in your document, which include font, size, style, and color, along with the layout of the document.

fragmentation—In terms of disk storage, fragmentation occurs when the various segments of files are separated and placed on different parts of a drive. It happens when larger files are frequently copied and removed from a drive. Computer memory may also become fragmented, but Mac OS X is designed to control the situation by allocating memory dynamically as needed by an application.

FTP—Stands for File Transfer Protocol. A protocol used to move files across the Internet, usually from a remote server to your desktop computer. FTP is commonly used to move files larger than 1MB because it is a more efficient protocol for moving data than Hypertext Transfer Protocol (HTTP). FTP uses Transmission Control Protocol (TCP) port 21 to send FTP commands between the sending and receiving computers, and a randomly assigned TCP port above 1024 to actually transfer the data. The most common FTP application on the Macintosh is known as Fetch. See also HTTP and TCP.

gateway—A computer or router that directs traffic off the current network segment and out to the rest of the network.

General—A settings pane in the System Preferences application. It's a throwback to the General Control Panel of Mac System 6 and earlier, where appearance options for titles and highlighting are set. By default, you can choose the Blue "Aqua" interface or a more subtle Graphite ("Gray") option.

Glossary

gigabyte (GB)—A term that refers to 1,024 megabytes.

Go menu—A menu, new for Mac OS X, that offers access to frequently used document folders, networked computers, and the Finder's toolbar buttons.

Grab—This application is used to perform screen captures, such as those you see in this book. It replaces the standard Mac OS keyboard shortcut, Command+Shift+3, plus some others.

hard disk—A storage mechanism that consists of an assembly of rapidly spinning disks placed inside a sealed, rectangular enclosure. Data is read and written by one or more heads that access the data stored on the spinning disks. Also known as a fixed hard drive or just as a hard drive or fixed disk.

Help menu—This menu, when accessed from the Finder or desktop, provides immediate access to the Mac OS Help menu. Most other applications also offer a Help menu of one sort or another.

hexadecimal numbers—Another method of describing the numeric value of a byte. Hexadecimal values are based upon base 16 math, where numbers range from 0 through F. To display the full value of a byte, you use two hexadecimal numbers. For example, to represent a byte with the value of 255, type FF. See also *binary numbers*.

HFS+—A version of the Macintosh file system that increases the number of files that can be supported on a Mac drive, thus reducing the minimum file size on larger devices. Similar to FAT32 under Windows. Sometimes known as Mac OS Extended.

Hierarchical File System (HFS)—The standard system for organizing files on the Macintosh operating system (OS). Similar to FAT16 on the Windows platform. Sometimes known as Mac OS Standard.

history—A feature of a Web browser that displays a list of recently visited sites. In contrast to a Bookmarks or Favorites feature (which includes the links you actually store), the history constantly updates as newer sites are accessed. The history list is normally cleared when you quit the application. See also *Favorites*.

home page—The introductory or index page of a Web site. A home page usually contains information about the site's purpose, along with links to its popular features. You can specify a default home page in your Web browser so that you always visit that site upon launching the browser.

Glossary

HTML—Stands for Hypertext Markup Language. A text-based formatting language used to describe the elements of a Web page.

HTTP—Stands for Hypertext Transfer Protocol. The Internet Protocol (IP) network protocol that is used to move data from Web servers to your Web browser. HTTP utilizes Transmission Control Protocol (TCP) port 80 to send and receive information from a Web server and then to send back information to the Web server, allowing you to interact with it. It is a connectionless protocol, meaning that it sends or receives one piece of information and then closes down the connection. Although this made sense with small amounts of data like that present on the early Web pages, as Web pages grew, performance was apt to suffer. To improve HTTP's performance, HTTP version 1.1, which allows whole Web pages to be downloaded without breaking the connection, was developed. See also *HTTPS, IP,* and *TCP.*

HTTPS—The version of Hypertext Transfer Protocol (HTTP) that uses Secure Sockets Layer (SSL) encryption when you are sending and receiving data from secure Web servers. HTTPS normally uses Transmission Control Protocol (TCP) port 443 to send and receive information. HTTPS can use either 40- or 128-bit encryption, depending on where the browser or the server is located. See also *HTTP* and *TCP.*

hub—A connection device that forms the center of an Ethernet network; also used to extend the ports available via FireWire or USB.

hyperlink—An item in a document or on a Web page that, when you click on it once, takes you to another page or site.

icons—One of the key features of a graphical computer operating system, such as Mac OS X. Icons are pictures used as metaphors for real-world items, such as folders, files, documents, or disks.

ICQ—An instant-message protocol that sends instant messages across the Internet. A related protocol, ICQW, also allows users to see when others are connected to the Internet and to set up multiperson conversations across the Internet.

insertion point—A thin vertical bar in a text box that indicates where text is being entered.

Instant Messenger—A program from America Online (AOL) that sends instant messages across the Internet. This program also allows users to see when others are connected to the Internet and to set up one-on-one conversations with them. Special "branded" versions of

Instant Messenger are provided by such companies as EarthLink and Netscape (a subsidiary of AOL). Microsoft's variation on the instant messaging theme is called MSN Messenger. See also *MSN Messenger*.

International—A settings pane in the System Preferences application where you can specify system languages and currency conversion options, in addition to date and time formats unique to a specific part of the world.

Internet—A worldwide computer network consisting of hundreds of millions of computers that's used to spread data from computer to computer. The Internet has become the focal point for such enterprises as email, shopping, and mass communication.

Internet—A settings pane in the System Preferences application that lets you enter settings for hooking up to your ISP.

Internet Relay Chat (IRC)—A set of client software and servers that allows groups of users from all across the world to have interactive conversations in realtime. Users who want to join an IRC chat use an IRC client to connect to server networks on the Internet. Once connected to one of the many IRC networks, users can create or join conversations on just about every subject known to humans.

Internet Service Provider (ISP)—A company that provides users with a connection to the Internet. From huge ISPs such as America Online (AOL) and EarthLink to small local operations such as FastQ and Teleport.com, an ISP allows users to dial up and connect to the Internet from their home or office.

IP—Stands for Internet Protocol. The network protocol that is used to send information over the Internet. IP was developed in the 1970s by Vincent Cerf and others to provide a reliable method of transferring data over the Internet. IP can send network traffic over many network media, from low-speed serial connections to multigigabit fiber connections.

Jaz drive—Removable storage product from Iomega that users standard hard drive technology and supports storage of 1GB or 2GB depending on the drive and media used.

Java—The brainchild of Sun Microsystems, Java is a cross-platform programming language that allows applications (or mini applications called applets) to execute or run on computers running a variety of operating systems. Mac OS X's Cocoa component includes native support for Java.

Glossary

JetDirect—The trade name of a series of network interface cards and their associated software created by Hewlett-Packard for use with its DeskJet and LaserJet printers. JetDirect cards provide the printer with an Ethernet port and allow it to send and receive data from a server or workstation that is configured to host the printer.

Keyboard—A settings pane in the System Preferences application that's used for keyboard speed and repeat rates.

kilobyte (KB)—The equivalent of 1,024 bytes of data.

link—See *hyperlink.*

local area networks (LANs)—High-speed networks, either in a single building or multiple buildings at a single site. LANs are almost always connected by some sort of high-speed networking infrastructure such as Ethernet.

LocalTalk—This is the name of the Mac's original networking method, a slow but usable way to transfer data. Over time, Ethernet support was added, and native LocalTalk was removed from new Macs beginning in 1998k, with the introduction of the iMac. See also *network adapter.*

Login—A settings pane in the System Preferences application where you can also specify whether or not a login prompt appears at startup, and which applications are turned on with your system. In that way, it provides a function similar to the Startup Items folder in previous versions of the Mac OS.

log in—The process of entering your username and password to access a specific computer or network service.

log off—The process of ending your access to a computer or network service.

Macintosh HD—The common name Apple gives to the hard drive on your new computer. This name can be easily changed, so long as the drive itself is not being shared over a network.

Mail—The email application that Apple provides with Mac OS X. It provides simple management of user accounts and also offers timed retrieval of messages.

mailbox—In email programs, a folder that contains the email messages you've stored or received.

maximize—The act of expanding a Finder or application window to its largest-possible size. The maximize function under Mac OS X is controlled by a green button at the left side of a window's title bar (it stays gray in the optional Graphite view).

Mbps—Short for megabits (millions of bits) per second; typically a measurement of data transfer rate.

megabyte (MB)—The name for 1,024 kilobytes of computer data.

menu—A small window without title or control bars or buttons that contains a list of commands that you can access to perform a function on your computer.

menu bar—A horizontal bar that extends across the top of your Mac's display, displaying a list of labels of functions relevant to the Mac OS or the program you're using. Clicking on any of those labels produces a menu with commands that relate to that label.

minimize—The act of reducing a Finder or application window to an icon that appears on the Dock. The minimize function under Mac OS X is activated by a yellow button at the left of a window's title bar. See also *Dock*.

modem—A device that is used to transfer digital computer data across analog telephone lines.

Monitors—Similar to the Control Panel under Mac OS 9, the settings pane, available from the System Preferences application, that lets you change screen depth and resolutions. For some Apple brand displays, there will also be geometry adjustments present.

Mouse—Part of the System Preferences application, the settings pane used to set mouse clicking and tracking rates.

MSN Messenger—Microsoft's version of an instant messaging program. See also *Instant Messenger*.

multitasking—The act of a computer performing more than a single function or running more than a single program at the same time.

Music Player—A program descended from the AppleCD Audio Player in older versions of the Mac OS. In addition to the spiffy new interface, it adds playlists and MP3 capabilities.

NetBIOS—A networking scheme that allows applications and network services to communicate in a more or less transparent way. It is

Glossary

used by such programs as Thursby Software's DAVE and Connectix's DoubleTalk to provide networking between Mac and Windows-based personal computers.

network—A system consisting of two or more computers or a computer with shared printers. A network may be connected by wires or by such wireless features as Apple Computer's AirPort products.

Network—A settings pane in the System Preferences application used for your network options.

network adapter—The piece of electronics that connects a computer to the local area network (LAN). One example of a network adapter is the Ethernet port that is included on all current Apple computers (such as the iBook, iMac, PowerBook, and Power Macintosh) and many modern Windows-based PCs. Other types of network adapters include Token Ring, an older IBM network system, and LocalTalk, the original network solution that Apple developed for inclusion with the Macintosh. See also *LocalTalk*.

network hubs—Small electrical devices that connect several network connections together. To prevent signal loss, Ethernet hubs, for example, amplify the network signal so that it does not become degraded as it goes through the hub to its destination. The downside to hubs is that they connect all the computers on the network together and thus frequently cause performance degradation because of packet collisions. See also *network switches* and *packet*.

network segment—The portion of the network that is connected to a router. Network segments can range from a small two- or three-host network connected to an interface on a router to a large switched network with hundreds of computers all connected to a series of switches and then a router.

network switches—Small network devices that connect several network connections together. To prevent signal loss, network switches amplify the network signal so that it does not become degraded as it goes through the switch to its destination. Switches, unlike hubs, do not connect all the computers on the network together except as a virtual circuit and thus avoid performance degradation caused by packet collisions because they create a connection directly between the source and the destination. See also *network hubs*.

newsgroups—Internet-based bulletin boards where users from all over the world can converse and share information regarding a variety of topics. If, for instance, you are looking for technical information about a problem that you are having with a computer or your network, checking the appropriate newsgroups or posting a message may well get you an answer. Also called Usenet. You can use such programs as the Messenger component of Netscape Communicator or NewsWatcher to access newsgroup messages.

online service—The outgrowth of the original bulletin board systems (BBS) in the early days of personal computing. An online service consists of such features as message boards, email service, information centers, files for download, and chat rooms. The popular online services of the present day, including AOL, CompuServe, and Prodigy Internet, also include Internet access.

Open GL—An industry standard 3D technology commonly used for games, such as Quake 3 Arena from id Software. It is also used for 3D rendering programs, such as Maya, an animation program from Alias/ Wavefront widely used in the motion picture industry.

Open dialog box—The dialog box used to select a document to open from within an open application.

packet—Simply stated, it means dividing data transferred over a network into little pieces for efficient transfer.

password—A set of characters (consisting of letters and/or numbers) that is used to gain access to a protected feature. You use a password for such functions as logging in to your Mac, to a network, or to your ISP.

Password—A settings pane in the System Preferences application where you can login as administrator or a user with master privileges can create a new password.

point—The act of directing the mouse cursor above a specific item.

pop-up window—A menu listing various commands that is accessed by a Control+click (Apple's contextual menus feature) or from a dialog box.

port—A connection jack used to attach peripherals to your Mac. These include such staples as your keyboard and mouse, as well as printers, removable drives, digital cameras, and other items. Current-model Macs include Ethernet and USB ports and, for some, FireWire.

Post Office Protocol (POP)—The primary network protocol that mail servers use to distribute email to users across the network. Programs such as Eudora, Microsoft Outlook Express, Microsoft

Glossary

Entourage, and Apple's Mail connect to the central email server using POP, and once they have logged on to the mail server, they can receive email that has been stored on the server waiting for the user to retrieve it.

PostScript—A page-description language developed by Adobe Systems in the early 1980s to improve the print quality of documents. In PostScript, the contents of a page are reduced to mathematical calculations, and as such, PostScript is commonly regarded as being "device-independent." This means that the quality of the printed document depends on the capabilities of the output device. Over the last 15 years, PostScript has evolved into the primary printer description language. PDF, or Portable Document Format, which is the basis of Mac OS X's imaging technology, is based on PostScript. See also *TrueType*.

PostScript Printer Description (PPD) file—Files that are used to tell your computer how to communicate with a specific PostScript printer to support its special features. For example, a PPD may tell your computer that the printer has multiple paper trays and allow you to select among them. You normally encounter PPDs only on the Macintosh, and they must be installed on the Macintosh in order to work.

PPP Connect—An application used to make dial-up connections to your ISP. It combines functions from both the Remote Access and TCP/IP control panels of previous versions of the Mac OS.

preemptive multitasking—A feature of Mac OS X and other operating systems in which the operating system serves as the task manager or traffic cop, parceling out CPU time to the various programs you are running. Compare with *cooperative multitasking*, a feature of older versions of the Mac OS in which the programs themselves shared CPU time.

preferences—A Mac OS X application or dialog box in which you make a set of configuration settings.

PrintCenter—An application used to select printers, manage printer options, and track and control printer job queues.

printer drivers—Programs that tell your computer how to communicate with the printers on your network. A LaserWriter printer drive ships with Mac OS X. Some laser printers require special, custom drivers to deliver specific features. Other kinds of printers, such as ink jet models, come with their own software that must be installed for them to work with your Mac.

Glossary

print queue—The service on the computer or server hosting the printer that stores print jobs as they are getting ready for the printer. Setting access rights on the print queue is very important so that you do not allow inappropriate users to delete another user's print jobs.

Process Viewer—An application that lets you see how much RAM and processor power the system and opened applications are viewing. It can also be accessed via the Terminal when you do an ADMIN login and type the command **TOP**.

protected memory—A feature of Mac OS X and other operating systems in which the programs you run each get a separate memory space. If the program crashes for any reason, it will be shut down and the memory address space closed. This prevents that program from affecting other functions on your Mac and helps prevent a system-wide crash.

pull-down menu—A list of commands that appears when you click on an item in the menu bar.

Quartz—The new imaging technology that is used for Mac OS X. It combines several standards, such as Open GL, PDF, and QuickTime, to provide the stunning visual effects that are part of the Aqua user interface.

QuickTime—Apple Computer's multimedia protocol, which supports a variety of audio and video compression methods to create and play back such productions. QuickTime is available in both Macintosh operating system (OS) and Windows versions. Preferences for Apple's QuickTime software can be set with the panel available from the System Preferences application.

QuickTime TV—A service of QuickTime, similar to RealAudio and its competitor, in which streaming audio and video presentations can be viewed from the Internet.

radio button—A small button usually in a dialog box that functions similarly to a checkbox. However, whereas more than one checkbox may sometimes be selected, when clicked, a radio button toggles a function.

RAM—Stands for Random Access Memory. A computer chip designed to hold temporary memory, such as your Mac OS software and the application software you are using.

RAM Disk—A portion of RAM allocated to simulate a hard drive.

Glossary

RealAudio—A popular Internet-based multimedia streaming protocol that allows users with a RealAudio or RealVideo player to hear audio and video productions direct from a Web site. It competes with QuickTime TV, which offers a similar capability.

reset switch—A small button (sometimes recessed) with a triangular-shaped icon above it or inside it. This button is used to force your Mac to restart in the event of a system crash. Mac OS X is designed to minimize the prospects of such problems.

router—A specialized computer whose sole purpose is to move network traffic from one network segment to another.

Save As—A dialog box that drops down as a sheet in the appropriate document window. It's used to name your file and to specify such items as file format and the location where the file is to be stored.

Save—The command you access to continue saving the contents of a document that has already been named and stored via the Save As dialog box.

scalable font—A font that can be viewed or printed in any available point size. Both PostScript and TrueType fonts are scalable font formats.

Screen Saver—A pane available via the System Preferences application. It lets you activate Apple's new screen saver and set the idle time interval. This is a feature that more or less mimics the one previously available under Windows.

scrollbar—A vertical or horizontal bar that you drag to navigate a Finder or document window.

seed routing—The seeding of an AppleTalk network with a network number, also known as a cable range. By seeding the AppleTalk network's cable range, you can create zones on AppleTalk Phase 2 networks.

serial port—A connection jack used for such devices as modems, some printers, and digital cameras. Serial ports send data 1 bit at a time to the printer. Until Apple switched to USB for low-speed serial devices, all Macs had separate modem and printer ports for these functions (though it was combined in some PowerBooks).

Services—A feature of the application menu that displays links to programs that work with the one you have open to provide additional features.

Glossary

Sharing—A pane under the System Preferences application where you can activate file sharing. The Mac OS X version also accesses Telnet and FTP features.

Sherlock—Apple's search program, which is used to locate items on your Mac's drive, on a networked volume, and on the Internet.

SMTP—Stands for Simple Mail Transfer Protocol. The network protocol that transfers mail between mail servers over the Internet. SMTP is a text-based protocol that runs over Transmission Control Protocol/Internet Protocol (TCP/IP) on port 25.

Sound—The settings pane in the System Preferences application that lets you set system and alert volumes, and choose from the repository of alert sounds.

Special menu—No longer included with Mac OS X. The functions have been moved to the Apple menu.

Speech—The settings pane in the System Preferences application that is used to select alert voices and speech rates for applications that support text-to-speech translation.

spooler—A program on a printer or on a server controlling the printer that stores up print jobs until the printer is ready to print them. A printer spooler allows multiple people to print to the printer at the same time and then have each printer job stored and printed in the order that it came in. Some spooler programs prioritize the order in which print jobs are actually printed, based upon who has sent them and the priority that was assigned to them. The Mac OSX print spooler is the Print Center application.

Startup Disk—The settings pane in the System Preferences application used to choose the disk from which your Mac starts. This can also be used to select between Mac OS X and older Mac OS environments.

StuffIt—A data-compression program from Aladdin Systems commonly used on Macintosh-based computers. Stuffed files are compressed using mathematical algorithms to reduce the space that the files take up on the computer. Stuffed files are commonly sent over the Internet because they can check themselves for consistency when the file is being unstuffed. Similar to the ZIP protocol on the DOS and Windows platforms. See also *ZIP*.

SuperDisk—A removable device format that reads both regular HD (1.4MB) floppy disks and special 120MB floppy-disk media.

Glossary

surf—The act of browsing through Web sites in search of the ones that interest you.

System Preferences—An application that, in part, replaces the Control Panels folder. It offers direct access to Mac OS X system preferences, such as for date and time, monitor resolution, and network configuration.

TCP—Stands for Transmission Control Protocol. A connection-oriented network protocol that moves data over the local area network (LAN) or the Internet safely and reliably using Internet Protocol (IP). TCP relies upon a built-in error-correction system to identify problems in the transmission of data and then correct them, ensuring that the data is transferred properly. TCP can also dynamically alter the speed of transmission to reflect changing network conditions or the load on either the sending or receiving computer. See also *IP*.

Telnet—A text-based network protocol that operates on Transmission Control Protocol (TCP) port 23. Telnet is frequently used when you want to communicate with a computer or router on the network that uses a command-line interface (CLI). Telnet is the preferred tool to use when you are connecting to routers on the network because it allows you to connect to any router on the network from one workstation. You can also use Telnet programs to connect to other TCP ports, such as port 25—Simple Mail Transfer Protocol (SMTP)—to probe them, and see if the programs that use these ports are functioning as expected. See also *command-line interface, SMTP,* and *TCP.*

Terminal—A Mac OS X application used to access the Unix command-line interface.

title bar—A rectangular area at the top of a Finder or document window that contains its name and navigation buttons.

toolbar—A row of icons or buttons that when clicked once activate a specific command in a program.

TrueType—A printer technology that was developed in the 1980s and 1990s by Apple Computer as an alternative to Adobe's PostScript fonts. Like PostScript, TrueType describes fonts as mathematical expressions so that they can be scaled or manipulated without destroying the original font's proportions. Although originally designed for the Macintosh operating system (OS), it has actually become more popular on the Windows platform. See also *PostScript.*

Glossary

typeface—A specific design for a set of printed letters and other characters. An example of a typeface is Helvetica Bold.

type size—The size of letters and numbers, measured in points (approximately 1/72 of an inch). The point size is measured from the top of a capital letter to the bottom of a "descender," such as appears in the letter *y*, plus a little space for "air."

type style—Altering the look of a typeface in various forms, such as italic, bold, bold italic, and underlined.

Unix—A popular industrial-strength multitasking operating system that was developed at AT&T Bell Laboratories. Originally intended for minicomputers, it has been modified for use on personal computers. There are various flavors of Unix available. Popular variations include Linux and Mac OS X.

upload—The process of transferring a file from your Mac to another computer on a network or via the Internet.

URL—Stands for Uniform Resource Locator. The information used to locate and access a site on the Internet.

USB—Stands for universal serial bus. A low- to moderate-speed plug-and-play peripheral standard developed by Intel that is used on Macs for the keyboard, mouse, digital cameras, drives, and printers. A high-speed variation, USB 2.0, debuted early in 2001 but had not been supported by Apple at the time this book was written. Compare with *FireWire*, which handles high-speed peripheral devices.

View menu—Available from desktop or Finder, this menu sets Finder viewing options, such as icon or column view, and whether the toolbar buttons should appear.

virtual memory—A method used to extend the memory available to your Mac by allocating a portion of your hard drive as a swap file. When built-in memory is not sufficient to meet operating system or program needs, Mac OS X uses the file to swap unneeded data. Beginning with Mac OS X, the memory needs of an application are established dynamically as needed.

virus—Computer code that attaches itself to a program or document and causes an unsavory side effect (a silly message or, at worst, damage to the file or drive) or that just replicates itself and passes itself on to another program or document. All personal computers are vulnerable to viruses, and it's a good idea to purchase up-to-date software to protect your Mac.

Glossary

Web (World Wide Web)—The preeminent Internet feature that provides animation, graphical and text displays of information. The Web is read by using a program called a browser. See also *Web browser*.

Web browser—A program designed to view documents created for display on the Web. The most popular Web browsers are Microsoft Internet Explorer and Netscape Navigator (or Communicator). A third Web program, OmniWeb, strictly supports Mac OS X.

Web page—A single document designed for display on the Web.

Web site—A location on the Web that contains one or more Web pages and is designed for business or personal use (or both).

window—A rectangular (or square) object that displays the contents of a document or directory.

Window menu—The window used to select from open document or folder windows.

Wireless Internet—Technologies that use either satellite transmissions or fixed wireless transmission systems to deliver high-speed Internet to a home or Office without the need for a wired connection. An example of such a service is Sprint Broadband Direct.

ZIP—A compression tool from PKWARE that works on PCs, Macintoshes, and Unix-based computers. The ZIP file format employs mathematical algorithms to reduce the space that the files take up on the computer. Zipped files are also frequently sent over the Internet because they can check themselves for consistency when the file is being expanded. See also *StuffIt*.

Zip drive—A removable storage device from Iomega Corporation. This drive uses media that looks like a thick floppy disk and stores either 100MB or 250MB of data (depending on the kind of drive and media type you use).

Index

A

ADB, 210–211
ADB-to-USB adapter, 213
Address Book application, 389–391
Administrator accounts, 105,164
Adobe, 8, 247
   InDesign, 280
   PageMaker, 274
   Photoshop, 167, 247
Adobe Type Manager. *See* ATM.
AirPort, 37, 216, 232
   Location Manager setup, 160–161
   Mac OS X support, 26
   networking, 147
   signal strength icon, 94
Aladdin
   iClean, 164
   StuffIt Expander, 242
Alerts
   sounds, 63
   volume, 62
Alsoft
   DiskWarrior, 24, 231
   MasterJuggler, 276
AOL, 36, 117, 249, 271, 350, 371
Apache Web server, 6
Apple channel, 122
Apple Desktop Bus. *See* ADB.
Apple menu, 75–76, 90–92
Apple Pro Keyboard, 340
Apple Remote Access, 155
Apple Type Solution. *See* ATS.
AppleCare warranty, 204, 207

AppleScript, 101
   applets, 169
   application support for, 167
   Basics scripts, 171
   batch files compared to, 166
   compatibility of, 169
   Dock Scripts, 169, 172
   Finder scripts, 171
   functionality of, 168–170
   future of, 170
   Info scripts, 171
   Mail Scripts, 172
   Navigation Scripts, 172
   Quit the Dock script, 172
   sample scripts, 171–172
   script creation, 174–176
   Script Editor Scripts, 172
   script text files, 169
   Sherlock Scripts, 172
   SoundJam scripts, 172
   Unix support, 170
   URLs Scripts, 172
   Web site, 101
AppleTalk, 58, 143
Applets, 169
AppleWorks, 251–254
   Assistants tab, 252
   Basic tab, 252
   Plus (+) tab, 252
   Recent Items tab, 252
   Starting Points, 251
   Table tool, 252–254
   Templates tab, 252
   Web tab, 252
AppleWorks 6, 169, 226, 247
Application icon, 74

Application menu, 33, 75, 77, 92
Applications
    Font panel, 181
    installing, 178
    launch failure, 332
    Open dialog box, 179–180, 185–186
    Packages, 178, 182
    performance in Classic
        environment, 266–268
    Quit command, 33, 77, 181, 331
    removing, 178
    Save dialog box, 180, 187–189
    Services command, 179
    Services menu, 189–190
    startup applications, 184–185
Aqua interface, 5, 9–12, 70, 196,
    203, 247
Asante, 163, 322
ASD Software, 107, 293–294
Asymmetric Digital Subscriber Line.
    See ADSL.
AtEase, 104
ATI Technologies, 197, 261
ATM, 8, 275–276
ATM Deluxe, 276
ATS, 277
Audio. *See* Sound.
Automatic Repeat keyboard mode, 55
AutoStart virus, 310

B

BackJack, 297–298
Backups, 290
    automatic, 305–306
    BackJack, 297–298
    CD-RW, 300
    CopyAgent, 295
    daily backups, 302–303
    DVD-RAM, 300
    file recovery software, 306
    floppy drives, 298
    iDisk, 298
    incremental backup features, 306–
        307
    Internet backups, 296–297
    iTools, 296–297
    Jaz drives, 299
    network, 307
    network volumes, 301
    offsite disk storage, 305
    ORB drive, 299–300
    Personal Backup, 293–294
    portable hard drives, 300
    QuickSync 3, 295
    Retrospect, 291–293
    scheduling, 304–305
    software, 303–306
    Software Restore CD, 291
    Software Rewind, 295–296
    SuperDisk drives, 299
    tape drives, 300–301, 307
    testing, 305
    for work-in-progress, 306
    Zip drives, 299
Basics Scripts, 171
Batch files, 166
Battery Life icon, 94
Battery Monitor application, 227–228
BeOS, 4
Bitmap fonts, 274
Bookmarks, 356, 362
BOOTP network setting, 27
Broadband Internet access, 348
Browsers
    artwork alteration
        troubleshooting, 363
    artwork distortion
        troubleshooting, 364
    bookmarks, 362
    cache deletion, 358–359
    cache sizing, 361
    crash troubleshooting, 365
    download speed
        troubleshooting, 364
BSD networking stack, 142
Button colors, 33

C

Cable modems, 37, 310, 312, 349, 362
Cached sites, 417
Calculator application, 242
Carbon, 9, 170, 179, 203, 240, 247
CarbonLib extension, 9, 240

Casady & Greene
Conflict Catcher, 268
SoundJam MP, 169, 172
Castlewood ORB drives, 299–300
CDs
burners, 216, 339
CD-Rs, 216
CD-RWs, 216, 300
CE Software QuicKeys, 168
Channels, 121–123
Children
KidSafe, 397, 410–411
Multiple Users and, 116–117
passwords and, 116
Chooser, 34, 142
Classic Compatibility environment,
9–10, 258–259
application installation
troubleshooting, 340
application performance in,
266–268
CPU-intensive applications
and, 260
dial-up connections and, 362–363
disappearing cursor problem, 340
Force Quit, 42
games and, 262
hard drive formatters and, 261
Internet software
compatibility, 262
launching applications in, 263–264
limitations of, 259–262
locating downloaded files in, 340
Mac OS 9.1 and, 20–21
peripherals and, 260–261
preferences, 41–42
printers and, 261
Restart command, 42
as startup application, 264–265
system extensions, 260
system folder protection, 269
troubleshooting, 270–271, 333
Windows emulators and, 261–262
Clean installations, 336–338
Clock application, 44, 242
Cocoa, 8, 170, 179, 241
Color balance adjustment, 45
Color calibration adjustments, 45
Color depth settings, 45

ColorSync, 45
preferences, 42
profiles, 46
Communicator, 368
CompuServe 2000, 36, 117, 271, 350
Computer icon, 12, 73
Conflict Catcher, 172, 268, 272
Connect To Server dialog box,
143, 146
Connectix Copy Agent, 295
Console application, 243
ContentBarrier, 322
Contextual menus, 87
Control Strip, 14, 92
Cookies, 354
Copland, 4
CopyAgent, 295
CPR networked printer setting, 67
CPU Monitor application, 243
Create illustration suite, 8, 249,
254–256
Inspector window, 254
Web page creation with, 255–256

D

Dantz Development Retrospect,
291–293
Darwin, 142
Date & Time preferences, 43–44
Desktop, 15, 101–102
Finder Preferences, 97–99
folder content
troubleshooting, 335
icon arrangement, 98
icon size, 98
picture, 98
Show Disks, 99
Desktop icon, 93
Desktop Pictures, 98
DeskZap, 336
Dial-up networking, 155–158
connectivity verification, 159–160
failure troubleshooting, 365
DiamondSoft Font Reserve, 276
Digital cameras, 215, 244
installing, 220
troubleshooting, 339

Digital Subscriber Line. *See* DSL.
Disk First Aid, 21, 231, 329, 340
Disks
    ejecting, 87
    imaging, 182–184
    swapping, 7
Disk Warrior, 24
DiskUtility application, 242, 340–341
DiskWarrior, 231
Display Calibrator Assistant
    application, 46
Displays preferences, 44–50
Dock, 14–15, 90
    accessing items on, 14
    adding items to, 15
    AppleScript applets in, 169
    application animations, 97
    application switching, 100
    Battery Life icon, 94
    Desktop icon, 93
    Document icon, 93
    "Genie Effect," 14
    hiding, 51, 97
    icon additions to, 100
    icon rearrangement, 100
    icon removal from, 101
    left side, 92
    magnification, 51, 97
    Mail icon, 93
    Minimized Window icon, 94
    pop-up menus, 95
    preferences, 50–51, 96–97
    print icon, 67
    program launch animations, 51
    resizing, 50
    right side, 92
    scripts for, 101
    single-click access, 100
    sizing, 96–97
    System Preferences icon, 93
    Trash icon, 15, 90, 94
    Web Sites and Servers icon, 94
Document icon, 93
DoorStop Personal Firewall, 321
Double-Click Delay settings, 56
Dreamweaver, 249
Drive indexing, 126
Drive Setup, 261, 340
Drive X, 231, 314, 315

Driver updates, 17
DriveUtility, 200
Drop Box folder, 106, 144, 161
DSL, 310, 312, 349
    connection troubleshooting, 362
    modems, 37
Duo system, 227
DVD drives, 224, 230
    DVD-RAM, 216, 300
    support for, 235

E

EarthLink, 117
EarthLink Mobile Broadband
    service, 234
eBook readers, 217, 220
Edit menu, 78
Email, 368. *See also* Mail application.
    file backups with, 234–235
    filtering, 117
    Mac.com addresses, 396, 404–408
    preferences, 54
    vacation notices, 409–410
Empty Trash command, 77
Emulators, 258
Energy Saver preferences, 51–52, 228
Energy Star compliancy, 52
Entourage, 242
Ethernet, 57, 145, 211, 213, 227
Expansion cards, for
    PowerBooks, 214
Extensions folder, 179
Extensions Manager, 267, 272
Extensis Suitcase, 276–277

F

Farallon, 163, 216, 322
Favorites icon, 74, 283–284
Fax machines, as printers, 235
Fiber-optic cables, 350
File aliasing, 87
File Buddy utility, 336–337
File channel, 121
File menu, 78
File names, 187
File recovery software, 306

File sharing, 61, 88, 147–152. *See also*
  Networking.
  AirPort networking, 147
  neighborhoods, 143
  peer-to-peer file transfers, 142
  preferences, 61
  Sharing settings pane, 146
  TCP/IP sharing, 147
File Sharing Control Panel, 143
FileMaker, 247
Find File application, 121
Finder, 12–14, 70
  Apple menu, 75–76
  Applications menu, 75–77
  Applications icon, 74
  category list resizing, 84
  category order alteration, 84
  Column View, 72–73
  Computer icon, 12, 73–74
  contextual menus, 87
  copying files in, 86–87
  Customize Toolbar screen, 86
  desktop settings, 97–99
  Edit menu, 78
  Favorites folder, 87
  Favorites icon, 74
  file aliasing, 87
  File menu, 78
  folder view preferences, 81–83
  Go menu, 79
  Help menu, 80
  hiding toolbar in, 75
  Home button, 12
  Home icon, 74
  icon additions to, 85
  icon arrangement, 83
  icon removal from, 86
  icon sizing, 83
  Icon View, 70–71
  List View, 71, 84–85
  navigating, 73
  relocating files in, 86
  resizing, 33
  Separator icon, 85
  Show Info window, 88
  toolbar, 73–75, 85–86
  View menu, 79
  view preferences, 82–84
  Window menu, 79–80

Finder Scripts, 171
Firewalls, 164, 312, 320–323
  hardware firewalls, 322–323
  NAT firewall protection, 323
FireWire, 212, 216
  drives, 25–26
  storage devices, 219
  USB combination cards, 213
Firmware, 25, 329
Flash, 249
Floppy drives, 298
Font formats, 8
Font Panel, 181, 278–279, 281–282
  Collections feature, 284–285
  font display sizes, 285
Font Reserve, 276
Fonts
  Adobe Type Manager, 275–276
  Apple Type Solution, 277
  bitmap fonts, 274
  collections, 284–285
  custom sizes, 285–286
  extra characters, 286
  Font Reserve, 276
  formatting, 279–280
  installing, 281–286
  kerning, 279
  ligature, 279–280
  MasterJuggler, 276
  OpenType, 181, 275
  PostScript, 181, 274
  range kerning, 279
  Scalabale fonts, 274–275
  storing as Favorites, 283–284
  Suitcase, 276–277
  system-wide, 277
  tracking, 279
  troubleshooting, 288
  TrueType, 181, 275
  user-specific, 277
Force Quit command, 77, 331–332
FreeBSD 3.2, 6
FreeHand, 249
FTP access, 149
FWB SoftWindows, 262

G

Gamma calibration, 48
Gassée, Jean-Louis, 4
General preferences, 52–53
"Genie Effect," 14
Gibson Research, 323
Go menu, 79
Grab application, 243
Graphics cards, 26
Graphics management, 196
Graphite interface, 33, 52–53
Greg's Browser, 13, 70
Gross, Evan, 270

H

Handheld computers, 217, 220
Handspring handheld computers, 217
Hard Disk Toolkit, 329
Hard drives, 215–216
    portable, 300
    troubleshooting, 205
Hardware
    drive defragmentation, 201
    drive diagnostics, 200
    drive updates, 201
    dust and, 201
    firewalls, 322–323
    installations, 199–200, 202
    maintenance, 200
    new Mac purchases, 202–204
    power failures, 202
    routers, 163–164
    software installation for, 218
    software updates, 201
    troubleshooting, 205–207
    warranties, 204
Harman Kardon
    iSub speakers, 217
    SoundSticks, 217
Headphones, 230
Help menu, 80
Home button, 12
Home icon, 74
HomePage, 398–399. *See also* WWW.
    troubleshooting, 417
    Web page editing with, 416

Web page removal with, 416
Web page updates with, 416
Web site creation with, 413–416
.hqx file extension, 183
Hybrid cable modem services, 349

I

iBooks, 57, 77, 160, 227, 229, 348
    airport security and, 233
    AV output ports, 226
    Batter Monitor application,
        227–228
    climate protection, 230–231
    DVD drive, 224, 230
    email file backups, 234–235
    Energy Saver preferences, 228
    Ethernet, 227
    extending battery life for, 228–230
    file backups, 231
    FireWire capability, 225–226
    games, 233
    headphones, 230
    iMovie software, 225–226
    input devices, 232
    insurance for, 233
    international connection cables,
        232–233
    ISP access abroad, 234
    modems, 227
    on-the-road printing, 235
    operating temperature, 231
    patch cables, 232
    PC cards, 229
    power requirements, 224
    screen brightness, 229
    sleep mode, 225, 228
    software diagnostic
        applications, 231
    storage devices, 231
    trackpad settings, 224
    travel bag for, 230
    wireless connections, 232
iCab, 353–354
    cache deletion, 359
    HotList, 362
iCards, 399, 408–409
iClean, 164

iDisk, 298, 397, 411–412
iMacs, 25, 210, 348
ImageCapture application, 244
iMovie software, 225–226
Incremental backup features,
  306–307
InDesign, 280
Info Scripts, 171
Input devices, troubleshooting,
  339–340
Installations, 16–17, 28–30
  application removal, 178
  Classic applications, 340
  clean installations, 336–338
  data backups, 25
  digital cameras, 220
  disk imaging, 182–184
  drive partitions, 25
  driver updates, 17
  Easy Install screen, 30
  eBook readers, 220
  fonts, 281–286
  hardware, 25, 199–200, 202
  installer applications, 182
  Installer CD bootup, 338
  iTools, 402–403
  language kit selection, 28
  Mac OS 9.1, 27
  Packages, 178
  Palm OS handheld computers, 220
  paritions and, 21
  peripheral compatibility, 16
  preparation for, 20–21, 27
  printer compatibility, 17
  processor upgrade cards and,
    17, 26
  scanners, 218–219
  Select a Destination screen, 29
  serial device compatibility, 17
  software compatibility, 16–17
  software for hardware, 218
  Software License Agreement, 29
  storage devices, 219–220
  system requirements, 16
  troubleshooting, 191, 329–331
  upgraded CPU support, 17, 26
Insurance, 290

Intego, 326
  ContentBarrier, 322
  NetBarrier, 321–322
  VirusBarrier, 315–317
International connection cables, 232
International preferences, 53–54
Internet
  access configuration, 36
  backups, 296
  bookmarks, 356
  broadband access, 348
  network security, 163–164
  people searches, 131–135
  searching with Sherlock, 128–135
  wireless access, 349
Internet channel, 121
Internet Connect application,
  244–245
  dial-up networking, 155–158
  modem support
    troubleshooting, 365
Internet control panel, 27
Internet Explorer, 241, 350–353
  address auto-complete, 352
  Auction Tracker, 352
  cache deletion, 358–359
  custom color schemes, 353
  Favorites, 362
  Search Assistant, 351
  Tasman Browser Engine, 351
Internet preferences, 54–55
Iomega
  Jaz drives, 219
  QuickSync 3, 295
  Zip drives, 219
iSub speakers, 217
iTools, 37, 396
  backups with, 296–297
  email, 396
  HomePage, 398–399, 413–416
  iCards, 399
  iDisk, 397, 411–412
  installing, 402–403
  KidSafe, 397, 410–411
  Mac.com email address
    configuration, 404–406
  preferences, 54
  vacation notices, 409–410
IX Micro, 261

J

Jaz drives, 219, 299
Jobs, Steve, 9, 247, 350, 396

K

Kensington, 57
Kernel troubleshooting, 338
Kerning, 279
Key Caps utility, 242, 286
Keyboard preferences, 55
Keychain Access application, 105,
   111–113
   launching, 113
   mobile keychains, 114–115
   settings alterations, 113–114
   troubleshooting, 115–116
KidSafe, 397, 410–411

L

LaCie Silverlining, 330
LANs, 36
Language kits, 28
Ligature, 279–280
LinkSys, 163
List View, 84–85
LiveUpdate utility, 328
Local Area Networks. *See* LANs.
LocalTalk-to-Ethernet bridges, 213
Location Manager, 160–161
Log Out command, 77
Login preferences, 56
Loudspeakers, 217

M

Mac OS 7, 142, 166
Mac OS 8, 4
Mac OS 8.1, 247
Mac OS 8.5, 121, 143, 151
Mac OS 9.1, 20–21, 27, 41, 150, 267,
   269, 271–272
Mac OS X Server, 5

Mac.com email addresses, 396
   configuring email software for,
      404–406
   distributing, 408–409
   forwarding mail to, 406–408
Mach 3 microkernel, 6
Macro viruses, 310
Macromedia, 249
   Dreamweaver, 249
   Flash, 249
   FreeHand, 249
MacSense, 163, 323
Mail application, 37, 54, 242, 245,
   368–372. *See also* Email.
   address books, 370
   AOL email support, 371
   attachment troubleshooting, 384
   attachments, 383–384
   automatic connections, 371
   automatic message retrieval,
      388, 394
   composing new messages in,
      379–380
   formatting messages in, 386
   forwarding messages in, 385
   HTML formatting support, 369
   importing address books to,
      391–392
   importing mailboxes to, 369,
      376–378
   locating messages in, 392
   message filtering, 370
   messages quotation, 381
   messages responses, 380–381
   message searches, 370
   MIME format, 394
   multiple user accounts, 369
   newsgroup support, 370
   rules, 386–388
   setup categories, 374–375
   signatures, 370, 385–386
   spell checking, 370, 382–383
   stored message management, 369
   toolbar customization, 378–379
   troubleshooting, 393–394
   user account setup, 373–376
Mail icon, 93
MasterJuggler, 276
Maya animation application, 248

Memory management, 327
Menu Bar Clock, 44
MicroMat
  Drive X, 231
  TechTool Deluxe, 24, 207
  TechTool Pro, 23–24, 207, 231,
    314–315
Microsoft, 57, 179
  Entourage, 242
  Office 2001, 226, 241–242
  Outlook Express, 241, 368
Microsoft Internet Explorer, 241,
  350–353
  address auto-complete, 352
  Auction Tracker, 352
  cache deletion, 358–359
  custom color schemes, 353
  Favorites, 362
  Search Assistant, 351
  Tasman Browser Engine, 351
MIME, 394
Minimized Window icon, 94
Mobile keychains, 114–115
Modem control panel, 27
Modems, 36–37, 145, 227
Mouse preferences, 56–57
Multiple Users feature, 32, 104
  access restrictions, 104
  account creation, 108–110
  administrator accounts, 105
  and children, 116–117
  Drop Box folder, 106
  passwords, 105, 107
  security and, 106–107
  shared folders, 106
  system logins, 106
  troubleshooting, 115–116
  Unix and, 104
  user account editing, 110–111
  user account removal, 110–111
Multiprocessing, 197
Multipurpose Internet Mail
  Extension. *See* MIME.
My Channel, 123

N

NAT firewall protection, 323
Neighborhoods, 143, 153
NetBarrier, 321–322
Netscape
  Communicator, 368
  Navigator, 362
Network address translation.
  See NAT.
Network Associates, 317–318, 326
Network backups, 307
Network preferences, 57–58
Network settings pane, 145
Network Time, 43–44
Network Utility application,
  162–163, 245
Networking, 142. *See also*
  File sharing.
  access failure, 333
  access privileges, 149–150
  accessing shared computers,
    152–154
  AirPort, 216
  backups, 296
  dial-up networking, 159–160
  Drop Box folder, 144
  Location Manager, 160–161
  with Mac OS 9.1, 150
  Mac name alterations, 148
  neighborhoods, 153
  network backups, 301
  Public folder, 144
  security, 163–164
  troubleshooting, 162–163
  viruses and, 312
  with Mac OS 8.5, 151
Newer Technology, 206
News channel, 122
News preferences, 55
NeXT Inc., 5, 70, 249
NeXTSTEP, 5, 12, 72, 350, 354
Norton
  AntiVirus, 164, 318–320, 328
  Integrated Security, 164
  Personal Firewall, 164, 321
  System Works, 328
  Utilities, 21–22, 231, 328
NVIDIA graphics chip, 197, 205, 261

O

Office 2001, 241–242
Omni Group, 354
OmniWeb, 189–190, 354–357
   Bookmarks, 362
   cache deletion, 360
Open dialog box, 179–180, 185–186
Open Door Networks DoorStop
   Personal Firewall, 321
OpenType fonts, 8, 181, 275
OS 7, 142, 166
OS 8, 4
OS 8.1, 247
OS 8.5, 121, 143, 151
OS 9.1, 20–21, 27, 41, 150, 267, 269,
   271–272
OS X Server, 5
Outlook Express, 241, 368
Owner access privileges, 149–150

P

Packages, 178, 182
Padlock icon, 40, 105
Page Setup dialog box, 34
PageMaker, 274
Palm handheld computers, 217, 220
Passwords, 36, 105, 107, 111–113, 334
   children and, 116
   Password Reset utility, 107, 331
Paulson, Peter, 34
PC cards, 229
PDF, 8, 277
Peer-to-peer file sharing, 61, 142
People channel, 122
Peripherals, 214–215
   adapter cards, 212
   Classic environment and, 260–261
   support for third-party
      products, 235
   troubleshooting, 206, 221–222
Personal Backup, 293–294
Point to Point Protocol over
   Ethernet. *See* PPPoE.
Portable Document Format. *See* PDF.
Portable hard drives, 300
Portable printers, 233

PostScript fonts, 8, 181, 274
Power On Software Rewind, 295–296
PowerBooks, 25, 57, 77, 160, 227
   airport security and, 233
   Batter Monitor application,
      227–228
   climate protection, 230–231
   DVD drive, 224, 230
   email file backups, 234–235
   Energy Saver preferences, 228
   Ethernet, 227
   expansion bay devices, 229
   expansion cards, 214
   extending battery life for, 228–230
   file backups, 231
   FireWire capability, 225–226
   games, 233
   headphones, 230
   iMovie software, 225–226
   input devices, 232
   insurance for, 233
   international connection cables,
      232–233
   ISP access abroad, 234
   modems, 227
   on-the-road printing, 235
   operating temperature, 231
   patch cables, 232
   PC cards, 229
   power requirements, 224
   S-video output, 226
   screen brightness, 229
   sleep mode, 225, 228
   software diagnostic
      applications, 231
   storage devices, 231
   Titanium PowerBook G4, 227, 229
   trackpad settings, 224
   travel bag for, 230
   wireless connections, 232
PowerMac G3 (Beige), 25
PowerOn Software, 107
PowerPC processors, 258
PPPoE, 57–58
Preemptive multitasking, 7, 9, 126,
   197, 259–260, 327
Print Center application, 34, 101, 261
Print dialog box, 34
Print drivers, 210

Printers, 34
  configuring, 65–67
  Dock icon, 67
  driver updates, 17
  fax machines as, 235
  portable, 233
  recognition troubleshooting, 339
Processor upgrade cards, 26
Protected memory, 7, 9, 259–260,
  326–327
Proxies settings, 58
Public folder, 144

Q

QuarkXPress, 167, 249, 274, 280
Quartz imaging layer, 8, 70, 196, 249
QuickDraw, 8
QuicKeys, 168
QuickSync 3, 295
QuickTime Player, 242
  AppleScript and, 169
  preferences, 59–60
Quit command, 33, 77, 181, 331
Quit the Dock script, 172

R

Range kerning, 279
Reference channel, 122
Registration, 32, 35
Remote Access, 27, 155
Removable drives, 215–216
Resolution settings, 44
Restart command, 77
Retrospect, 291–293
  Desktop Backup, 292–293
  Express Backup, 291–292
  multiple snapshots, 292
  security, 293
  Workgroup Backup, 293
Rewind, 295–296
Rhapsody, 5, 240
Rich Text Format. *See* RTF.
Robbin, Jeffrey, 172
Rocket eBook, 217
Root access, 342–343
RTF, 394

S

Safeware, 233
Save As dialog box, 11–12
Save dialog box, 11–12, 180, 187–189
Scalabale fonts, 274–275
Scanners, 215
  drivers, 219
  installation, 218–219
  troubleshooting, 339
Screen Saver, 60
Screenshots, 27, 243
Script Editor application, 168, 242
Script Runner application, 169, 173
Scripts, 167, 169
  creating, 174–176
  running from Unix command
  line, 176
SCSI, 216
  cards, 26, 213
  peripherals, 219
  ports, 211
  SCSI-to-FireWire converters, 213
  SCSI-to-USB converters, 213
Search utilities. *See* Sherlock.
Security. *See also* Viruses.
  administrator passwords, 164
  ASD Software, 107
  firewalls, 164
  hardware routers, 163–164
  Multiple Users and, 106–107
  networking, 163–164
  PowerOn Software, 107
  Retrospect, 293
  root access and, 343
Separator icon, 85
Serial ports, 211
Serial-to-USB converters, 213
Services command, 179
Services menu, 189–190
SetupAssistant, 30, 32, 35–39
  AirPort setup, 37
  AOL support, 36
  Compuserve support, 36
  dial-up networking settings, 155
  Internet access configuration, 36
  iTools setup, 37
  Mail setup, 37

modem setup, 36–37
registration information, 35
time zone selection, 38
Sharing. *See* File sharing.
Sherlock, 120–121, 242
    Apple channel, 122
    channel creation, 137–138
    channel customization, 137
    channels, 121
    drive indexing, 126
    excluding words from
        searches, 132
    File channel, 121
    file content searches, 125–128
    file text searches, 125–126
    group searches, 132
    indexing settings, 127
    Internet channel, 121
    Internet searches, 128–130
    module installations, 138–139
    More Search Options window,
        133–135
    multiple folder plug-in
        installation, 139
    My Channel, 123
    News channel, 122
    People channel, 122
    people searches, 131–135
    plug-in modules, 138
    plus (+) character, 132
    Reference channel, 122
    removing modules from, 139
    saving search patterns in, 135
    searching for files with, 124–125
    searching specific folders
        with, 136
    Shopping channel, 122
    vertical bar (|) character, 132
Shields Up, 323
Shopping channel, 122
Show Info window, 88
Show Modes Recommended By
    Display checkbox, 45
Shut Down command, 77
Silverlining, 330
Single-window mode, 11, 14–15
.sit file extension, 183
Sketch, AppleScript and, 169
SkyLINE, 216

Skytag, 336
Sleep command, 52, 77
Software License Agreement, 29
Software Restore CD, 291
Software Update, 328
    Control Panel, 62
    preferences, 61–62
SoftWindows, 262
Sound Jam MP, 172
Sound preferences, 62–63
SoundJam MP , 169, 172
SoundSticks, 217
Spaminator, 117
Speakable Items folder, 64
Speakers, 217
Speech Manager, 63–64
Spell Catcher, 270
Sprint Broadband Direct, 312, 350
Startup applications, 184–185,
    264–265
Startup Disk, 64–65, 271–272
Stickies, 242
Stone Design, 249, 254
Stone Software, 8
Storage devices
    installing, 219–220
    troubleshooting, 339
StuffIt Deluxe, 183
StuffIt Expander, 183, 242
Suitcase, 276–277
SuperDisk drives, 219, 299
Symantec, 326
    Norton AntiVirus, 164,
        318–320, 328
    Norton Integrated Security, 164
    Norton Personal Firewall, 164, 321
    Norton System Works, 328
    Norton Utilities, 21–22, 231, 328
Symmetric multiprocessing, 197
System crashes, 331
System Preferences application,
    32–33, 39–65, 92, 160–161
    Classic, 41–42
    ColorSync, 42
    Date & Time, 43–44
    Displays, 44–50
    Dock, 50–51
    Energy Saver, 51–52
    General, 52–53
    International, 53–54

Internet, 54–55
Keyboard, 55
Login, 56
Mouse, 56–57
Network, 57–58
Screen Saver, 60
Sharing, 61
Software Updates, 61–62
Sound, 62–63
Speech, 63–64
Startup Disk, 64–65
time zone selection, 43
Users, 65
System Preferences icon, 93
System Update control panel, 326
System-wide fonts, 277

T

Table tool, 252–254
Tape media backups, 300–301, 307
Target Gamma settings, 48
Target White Point settings, 48
Tasman Browser Engine, 351
TCP/IP, 142–143
    control panel, 27
    file sharing with, 147
TechTool Deluxe, 24, 207
TechTool Pro, 23–24, 207, 231, 314–315
"telco" cable modem services, 349
Telnet, 149
Terminal application, 7, 245–247
    root access, 342–343
    running scripts from, 176
Text-to-Speech, 64
TextEdit, 189, 287
    AppleScript and, 169
    avoiding small fonts in, 287
Time zone selection, 38, 43
Titanium PowerBook G4, 227, 229
Tracking, 279
Trackpad preferences, 57, 224
Transfer Control Protocol/Internet Protocol. *See* TCP/IP.
Trash icon, 87, 90, 94
Trashcan, 15
Trojan horses, 311

Troubleshooting
    Apple Pro Keyboard, 340
    application launch failure, 332
    boot failure, 206
    browser artwork changes, 363
    browser artwork distortion, 364
    browser crashes, 365
    cable modem connections, 362
    CD burning, 339
    Classic application
        installations, 340
    Classic dial-up connections,
        362–363
    Classic environment, 270–271, 333
    crashes, 206
    desktop folder contents, 335
    dial-up connection failure, 365
    digital cameras, 339
    disappearing cursor under
        Classic, 340
    Disk First Aid, 340
    DiskUtility, 340
    Drive Setup, 340
    DSL connections, 362
    file deletion errors, 335–336
    fonts, 288
    hard drives, 205
    hardware problems, 205–207
    HomePage, 417
    input devices, 339, 340
    installation failures, 329–331
    installer CD bootup, 338
    Internet Connection modem
        support, 365
    kernel, 338
    keychains, 115–116
    login failure, 115, 330–331, 334
    Mac OS 9 TCP/IP destruction, 363
    Mail application, 393–394
    Mail attachments, 384
    modem support, 365
    Multiple Users, 115–116
    network access failure,
        162–163, 333
    password recognition, 115, 334
    peripherals, 206, 221–222
    printer recognition, 339
    root access, 342–343
    scanners, 339

shaking login window, 334
small fonts in TextEdit, 287
smoke, 207
software installations, 191
software problems, 205–207
sparks, 207
storage drives, 339
"sufficient write privileges" error, 161
system crashes, 331
system usage monitoring, 343–344
upgrade cards, 206
Web site inaccessibility, 363–364
TrueType fonts, 8, 181, 275

U

Universal Serial Bus. *See* USB.
Unix, 6–7
AppleScript support for, 170
command line, 341
multiple users and, 104
running scripts from, 176
Terminal application, 245–247
viruses and, 311–312
USB, 212, 216
drives, 25–26, 226
FireWire combination cards, 213
User accounts. *See* Multiple Users.
User profiles, 32, 40
User-specific fonts, 277
Users preferences, 65

V

VersionTracker, 201
View menu, 79
Virex, 317–318
Virtual memory, 7, 9, 30, 327
VirusBarrier, 315–317
Viruses. *See also* Security.
AntiVirus, 318–320
AutoStart, 310
ContentBarrier, 322
firewalls and, 312, 320–323
macro viruses, 310
NetBarrier, 321–322
networking and, 312
Personal Firewall, 321

Shields Up, 323
TechTool Pro, 314–315
Unix and, 311–312
Virex, 317–318
VirusBarrier, 315–317
WDEF, 310
Voodoo graphics cards, 205

W

WDEF virus, 310
Web browsers
artwork alteration
troubleshooting, 363
artwork distortion
troubleshooting, 364
bookmarks, 362
cache deletion, 358–359
cache sizing, 361
crash troubleshooting, 365
download speed troubleshooting, 364
Web Sites and Servers icon, 94
Window menu, 79–80
Windows 2000 Mac Support Little
Black Book, 34
Windows emulators, 261–262
Wireless computing. *See also* AirPort.
connections, 312
Internet access, 349–350
World Wide Web. *See* WWW.
Wozniak, Steve, 5
WWW. *See also* HomePage.
AppleScript site, 101
BackJack site, 297
distorted artwork, 364
download speed troubleshooting, 364
OmniGroup site, 189
preferences, 55
Safeware site, 233
Sherlock plug-in modules site, 138
site inaccessibility
troubleshooting, 363–364
Skytag site, 336
VersionTracker site, 201

Z

Zip drives, 219, 299